CANADA IN THE CONTEMPORARY WORLD

JOHN RUYPERS
London District Catholic School Board

JOHN RYALL
Toronto Catholic District School Board

LINDA CONNOR
Gray Academy of Jewish Education, Winnipeg

WILLIAM NORTON
University of Manitoba

2007
EMOND MONTGOMERY PUBLICATIONS LIMITED
TORONTO, CANADA

Copyright © 2007 Emond Montgomery Publications Limited. All rights reserved. No part of this publication may be reproduced, stored in a retrieval system, or transmitted, in any form or by any means, photocopying, electronic, mechanical, recording, or otherwise, without the prior written permission of the copyright holder.

Printed in Canada.

We acknowledge the financial support of the Government of Canada through the Book Publishing Industry Development Program (BPIDP) for our publishing activities.

Library and Archives Canada Cataloguing in Publication

Canada in the contemporary world / John Ruypers ... [et al.].

Includes index.
ISBN-13: 978-1-55239-224-9
ISBN-10: 1-55239-224-4

1. Civics, Canadian—Textbooks. I. Ruypers, John

JL15.C33 2007   320.471   C2006-905290-5

Publisher
Tim Johnston

Product concept and instructional design
Dayne Ogilvie   Jessica Pegis

Senior developmental editor
Dayne Ogilvie

Editorial assistant
Eunice Hamilton

Developmental editor, production editor, copy editor, & image researcher
Francine Geraci

Image researcher & permissions editor
Lisa Brant

Cover designer, interior designer, & compositor
Tara Wells, WordsWorth Communications

Proofreader
David Handelsman, WordsWorth Communications

Indexer
Paula Pike, WordsWorth Communications

Production coordinator
Jim Lyons, WordsWorth Communications

Reviewers
Meera Bhalla (and students)
Louis Riel School Division

A. Grant Caldwell
Prairie Spirit School Division

Kathleen Elgar
Lord Selkirk School Division

Doug Fast
University of Manitoba

Yvonne Inniss
Lord Selkirk School Division

Betty Mateychuk
Prairie Spirit School Division

Barb Murphy
Southwest Horizon School Division

Wendy Murray
Frontier School Division

Arlin Scharfenberg
Red River Valley School Division

Lindsay D. Storie
Pembina Trails School Division

Sandi Wagner (and students)
Louis Riel School Division

Donna Willson
Turtle Mountain School Division

Tracy Wilson
Park West School Division

Connie Wyatt Anderson
Joe A. Ross School, Opaskwayak Educational Authority

Aboriginal content reviewers
Jacquie Mignot
Winnipeg No. 1 School Division

Maryann Simpson
Frontier School Division

Francophone content reviewer
Caterina M. (Bueti) Sotiriadis
Independent consultant

Table of Contents

Features of This Text ... viii

Unit 1 Diversity and Pluralism in Canada

CHAPTER 1 Welcome to Canada! ... 2
Becoming a Citizen of Canada ... 3
    Immigration: Who Gets in and How? ... 4
    From Permanent Resident to Citizen ... 5
    The Broad New World of Citizenship ... 6
Human Rights and Canadian Citizenship ... 9
    The United Nations and Human Rights ... 9
    The *Universal Declaration of Human Rights* and Canada ... 9
CivicStar John Diefenbaker ... 11
Introducing the Geography of Canada ... 12
Canada: Physical Geography ... 13
    Landforms and Soils ... 13
    Surface Waters ... 15
    Climate and Natural Vegetation ... 16
Canada: Human Geography ... 18
Skills Toolkit How to Construct Maps ... 19
    Canada's Population Increase Since 1867 ... 20
    The Canadian Population Today ... 21
    The Economic Geography of Canada ... 22
    The Political Geography of Canada ... 22
Geography as Destiny ... 23
Skills Toolkit How to Select, Use, and Interpret Maps ... 25
Study Hall ... 26

CHAPTER 2 How Do You Define Citizenship? ... 27
Citizenship and the Aboriginal Peoples of Canada ... 28
    Who Are the Aboriginal Peoples? ... 28
    From Injustice to Recognized Rights ... 28
CivicStar Dr. Lillian Eva Dyck ... 32
Two European Founders ... 33
    Citizenship and French Canadians ... 33
    Citizenship and British Canadians ... 36
Canadian Immigration ... 38
    History of Immigration ... 38
    The Creation of Canadian Citizenship ... 40
    A Colour-Blind Policy ... 41
Face Off Immigration: Open Borders or Lockdown? ... 42
Citizenship and Multiculturalism ... 43
    Celebrating Diversity ... 44
    Canadians Reaching Out ... 46
Skills Toolkit How to Form Inquiry Questions ... 48
Study Hall ... 50

CHAPTER 3 What Are Rights and Responsibilities? ... 51
Where Do Rights and Responsibilities Originate? ... 52
What Are Rights? ... 52
    What Are Responsibilities? ... 52
    Rights in Conflict ... 53
    The *Canadian Charter of Rights and Freedoms* ... 54
    "Reasonable Limits" on Rights and Freedoms ... 54
    Appealing to Courts to Protect Rights and Freedoms ... 54
What Are Charter Freedoms? ... 55
    Freedom of Religion ... 55
    Freedom of Thought and Expression ... 56
Face Off Freedom of Religion versus Right to Security ... 57
    School Powers and Freedom of Expression ... 58
What Are Our Charter Rights? ... 58
    Democratic Rights ... 59
    Legal Rights ... 59
    Equality Rights ... 60
CivicStar Steven Fletcher ... 62
    Minority Language Education Rights ... 63
    Aboriginal Rights ... 64
Face Off The Manitoba Schools Question: Should Francophones and Catholics Have Their Own Publicly Funded Schools? ... 65
CivicStar Mother of Red Nations Women's Council of Manitoba (MORN) ... 66
Skills Toolkit How Can I Break This Down? ... 68
Study Hall ... 69

TABLE OF CONTENTS

CHAPTER 4 What Shapes Our Identities and Cultures? 70

What Is Identity? 71
   Factors That Shape Identity 71
CivicStar Cindy Klassen 72
   Manitoba Identities 73
Mass Media and Identity 74
   Shaping Opinions and Attitudes 74
   Emergence of New Media 75
   Questions to Consider 76
What Is Pop Culture? 76
   The Selling of Pop Culture 76
   Fads and Trends 77
   Popular Culture as Global Culture? 78
   The Influence of the United States 79
   Other Influences on Popular Culture 79
Maintaining an Identity in the Face of Popular Culture 79
   Keeping and Making a Culture:
     The Aboriginal Peoples 80
   Keeping a Language Alive:
     Francophones in Canada 81
   How Is Canadian Identity Reflected
     in the Mass Media? 82
Protecting and Promoting Canadian Identity and Culture 83
   Canadian Broadcasting Corporation 83
   Canadian Content Rules 84
   Charter Protection of Identity and Culture 84
Face Off Should Government Protect Canadian Culture? 85
   Canadian Sporting Events 86
   National Celebrations 86
Skills Toolkit Media Literacy: How to Identify Advertising Techniques 87
Study Hall 89

Unit 2 Democracy and Governance in Canada

CHAPTER 5 Ideals and Institutions of Democracy 92

Government: Why Is It Necessary? 93
   The Shipwreck Scenario 93
   How Are Decisions Made? 94
   Politics: What Is It? 95
Types of Government 96
   Authoritarian Governments 96
   Democratic Governments 97
   Government by Consensus 97
   Subjects versus Citizens 98
Face Off Humans Are Selfish! No, Humans Are Good! 99
Power and Politics 100
   How Do Governments Use Power? 100
   People Power, Civil Society, and a Healthy Democracy 101
   Civil Conflict and the Rule of Law 101
Democracy: Yesterday and Today 102
Becoming Democratic 105
   The Elements of Democracy 105
   Obstacles to Democracy 106
   The Spread of Democracy 107
   Democracy in Canada 109
CivicStar Elijah Harper 109
Skills Toolkit How to Identify Bias 111
Study Hall 112

CHAPTER 6 What Is Government? 113

Why Does Canada Have Different Levels of Government? 114
   Aboriginal Self-Government 114
   Responsibilities of Different Levels of Government 115
Face Off Should Governments Sponsor Gambling? 118
Branches of Government in Canada 119
The Executive Branch 121
   The Governor General 121
   The Lieutenant Governor 122
   The Prime Minister and Cabinet 123
   The Premier and Cabinet 124
CivicStar Eric Robinson 124
The Legislative Branch 125
   The House of Commons 125
   The Senate 128
CivicStar Emily Murphy and the Famous Five 129
   The Legislative Assembly 130
   Territorial Legislative Assemblies 131
   Local Government Councils 132
The Judicial Branch: Federal and Provincial/Territorial Levels 133
   The Supreme Court of Canada 133
   Provincial and Territorial Courts 133
Skills Toolkit How to Locate Information 136
Study Hall 137

TABLE OF CONTENTS   v

CHAPTER 7   How Do Laws and Regulations Affect You?   138

Where Do You Encounter Laws and Regulations?   139
    Welcome to Your Life   139
    Rules at Home and at School   140
City and Town Bylaws   141
    Safety-Conscious Bylaws   141
    Pet Smart   141
    Environment Friendly   142
Provincial and Territorial Laws and Regulations   142
    The Manitoba *Human Rights Code*   143
Federal Laws and Regulations   145
    Criminal Law   145
    The *Canadian Charter of Rights and Freedoms*   147
CivicStar Justine Blainey   148
    The Canadian *Copyright Act*   149
Face Off Downloading Music from the Internet   149
The Political Spectrum   151
    Right, Left, What?   151
    When Philosophies Clash   152
Skills Toolkit How to Identify the Main Idea and Supporting Evidence   154
Study Hall   155

CHAPTER 8   How Do Governments Make Policy?   156

Platforms and Policies   157
    Do Citizens Really Want to Hear About Policies?   157
How Are Policies Developed?   159
    Major Influences on Policy   159
    Consequences of a Policy   161
Interest Groups and Policy Makers   163
    Competing Interests   163
Face Off Homelessness and Public Spaces   164
    A Spectrum of Influence   165
CivicStar Hannah Taylor: Ladybug Ladybug   166
How Policy Becomes Law   167
    The Stages in Passing a Federal Bill into Law   167
    The Passage of Municipal Bylaws   169
Where Do I Come In?   170
    Contact Your Representative   170
    Get Involved at the Grassroots Level   171
    The Role of Public Opinion Polls   171
CivicStar Lester Pearson: Superman in a Bow Tie?   173

Skills Toolkit How to Look for and Detect Different Points of View   175
Study Hall   176

CHAPTER 9   How Do Citizens Elect Governments?   177

Voting   178
    Checks on Representatives' Powers   178
    The Election Process   178
Elections in Canada   181
    Canada's Recent Voting Record   183
    Who Can Run for Office?   184
    What Do Political Parties Stand For?   184
Political Parties in Canada   186
    Majority and Minority Governments   187
    Two-Party and Multiparty Systems   188
CivicStar Lac du Bonnet Senior School   189
Electoral Reform   190
    Western Initiatives   191
Face Off A New Electoral System for Canada?   192
    Referenda   193
Skills Toolkit How to Avoid Petition Pitfalls   195
Study Hall   196

CHAPTER 10   How Does the Judicial System Work?   197

Canada's Judicial System   198
    Fundamental Legal Rights   198
    The Changing Justice System   199
    Attitudes Toward the Law   199
    Wrongful Convictions   201
CivicStar Dianne Martin   202
    Youth Criminal Justice   203
The Criminal Justice Process   204
    The Criminal Investigation   204
    The Courts   204
    The Trial   205
    Verdict and Sentencing   205
Face Off Young Offender or Young Adult?   208
Civil Law   209
    Procedure in Civil Cases   209
    Decisions in Civil Cases   210
Aboriginal Justice   211
    The Manitoba Experience   211
Skills Toolkit How to Organize Information   217
Study Hall   218

TABLE OF CONTENTS

CHAPTER 11 Citizenship in Action — 219
Canadian Issues and Conflicts — 220
    Negotiation and Compromise:
        The Canadian Way — 220
    Subjugation, Confrontation, Negotiation:
        Aboriginal Perseverance — 222
What Beliefs Should Guide Elected
  Representatives? — 224
    Moral Issues and Controversies — 224
Face Off Church? Conscience? Constitution?
  The Same-Sex Marriage Debate — 225
How Can Citizens Act on Their Beliefs
  and Values? — 227
    Civil Liberties Organizations — 227
    Peace, Order, Good Government—
        And Protest? — 228
    Other Ways to Stand Up for Your Rights — 229
Finding Positive Ways to Effect Change — 230
    People Taking Action Together — 230
CivicStar Joe Opatowski — 231
    Service Clubs, Youth Groups, and
        Community Organizations — 232
    Communicating, Celebrating, and
        Commemorating — 233
CivicStar Jean Vanier and L'Arche — 234
Labour Negotiations, Strikes, and Lockouts — 235
    Methods of Labour Negotiation — 236
Skills Toolkit How to Be Heard: Preparing
  an Effective Speech — 239
Study Hall — 240

Unit 3 Canada in the Global Context

CHAPTER 12 Canada and the Global Economy — 242
Canada: An Industrialized Nation — 243
    Canada within the World Economy — 243
    Stages of Economic Development — 243
Economic Divisions within Canada — 246
    The Growing Significance of Cities — 246
    Why Heartland and Hinterland? — 247
How Does Canada's Economy Work? — 248
    Demand Economy versus Mixed Economy — 250
    Measuring Standard of Living and the
        Quality of Life — 250
CivicStar Tommy Douglas — 251
    Influences in a Consumer-Based Society — 252
    How Well Do Private Profit and the
        Public Good Work Together? — 252
Face Off Do Taxes Benefit or Harm
  the Economy? — 253
Globalization — 255
    Positive and Negative Effects of
        Globalization for Canadians — 255
    Foreign Investment in Canada — 257
    Free Trade Between Canada and the
        United States — 258
    Numbers Tell a Story — 259
How Can Consumers Influence the Economy? — 261
    Non-Profit Organizations and Charities — 261
    Social Awareness and Corporate Social
        Responsibility — 262
    Back to the Future: Some Basic Questions — 262
Skills Toolkit How to Select, Use, and Interpret
  Graphs — 265
Study Hall — 266

CHAPTER 13 Canada in the Global Community — 268
What Is Global Citizenship? — 269
    Protecting Human Rights Internationally — 269
    Tyrannical Regimes in Europe — 270
    Fascism in Germany and Italy — 270
    Other Nations Respond — 272
    Putting War Criminals on Trial — 273
Skills Toolkit How to Respond to a
  Racist Remark — 273
Human Rights Since the Universal Declaration — 274
    Rwanda: A UN Failure — 275
    The International Criminal Court — 277
Face Off The International Criminal Court:
  Giant Step or Stumble? — 278
Canada: Facing the Human Rights Challenge — 279
    Not a Perfect Record — 279
    The International Centre for Human
        Rights and Democratic Development — 281
Canada's Foreign Policy — 282
    Foreign Affairs and International Trade — 282
    The Canadian International
        Development Agency — 283
    World Poverty and Foreign Policy — 283
NGOs and International Relations — 285
    Doctors Without Borders — 285
    Different Crises, Different Responses — 286

CivicStar Stephen Lewis	287
Canada on the World Stage	288
Skills Toolkit How to Use Multimedia Technology	290
Study Hall	291

CHAPTER 14 Global Conflicts and Global Interdependence — 292

A World of Inequalities and Interconnections	293
CivicStar Ryan Hreljac	294
Global Poverty and Human Development	295
Human Activities and Global Environments	296
Face Off Famine and Misery? Or Future Abundance?	297
The Globe within Our Borders: Canadian Demographics	298
Canada's Population Challenges	299
Canada's Population Growth in Historical Perspective	300
Source Areas of Immigration	302
When and How Does a Good Citizen Intervene?	303
Peacekeeping: 50 Years and Changing	303
Peacekeeping: At the Breaking Point?	303
The Changing Face of Global Conflict: Terrorism After 9/11	306
Modern Responses to Terrorism	307
Canada's Dilemma: Good Global Citizen or Good Neighbour?	307
Environmental Interdependence	309
Face Off The *Kyoto Protocol*: Is It Worth the Price?	311
Hope through Global Citizenship	312
Measuring Progress	313
The Global Citizen Takes Time to Think	313
CivicStar Lloyd Axworthy	314
Skills Toolkit How to Assess Yourself and Your Work	316
Study Hall	317

Unit 4 Canada: Opportunities and Challenges

CHAPTER 15 Challenge 1: Identity and Citizenship	320
CHAPTER 16 Challenge 2: Technology, Society, and Change	324
Alternative Challenge 2: Technology, Society, and Change	326
CHAPTER 17 Challenge 3: Pioneers of Tomorrow	328
CULMINATING ACTIVITY	331
GLOSSARY	333
INDEX	341
CREDITS	349

Features of This Text

Social studies is a way for you to explore what connects you to your family, your friends, your neighbourhood, your country, and the world. It will also challenge you to consider a number of questions. What are your beliefs and values? How do your views compare with those of other people? How are conflicts resolved? How are you involved in decision making? What does citizenship mean to you?

Canada in the Contemporary World asks you to investigate these and other questions. In this way, you will better understand the roles you can play in the world, locally and globally. Social studies is a science—a social science. The Chapter Challenges in Unit 4 are like a social studies lab. Here, in a variety of tasks, you can apply the big ideas you are exploring—and the communication, information, and thinking skills you are learning—to the real world, right now. Consider these Chapter Challenges a guide to this course. You might want to start by looking at them now and revisit them throughout the year. This approach will enrich your learning and help keep you on track, as will the many other features that run throughout the text.

What You Need to Know
- What are some of the criteria for becoming a citizen of Canada?

What You Need to Know lists clear guiding questions about what you will need to learn and understand from the chapter.

Key Terms
citizenship   politics
government   power

Key Terms are the most important terms and concepts in the chapter. Key and other glossary terms are **bold-faced** the first time they're used and are also defined within the text.

Key Question
Are Canadians over-regulated?

Key Question is an overarching inquiry question that helps you to focus on the content of the chapter and on chapter sections.

CivicStar

CINDY KLASSEN
Cindy Klassen became Canada's most decorated Olympic athlete when she captured five medals at the 2006 Turin Games.

CivicStar profiles people or groups—Aboriginal people, francophones, men, women, young, old, differently abled, famous, infamous, and ordinary—who have challenged the system, created change, and made other contributions to society.

Skills Toolkit develops the critical thinking skills that you are expected to learn throughout your education.

▶ DID YOU KNOW ◀
The levy on CD-Rs in 2004 was 21 cents each.

Did You Know presents interesting facts that highlight and complement the main text.

☐ DISCUSSION POINT
Should Canadians be given the right to vote at age 16?

Discussion Point presents questions to spark class or small-group discussion.

FACE OFF

Face Off examines situations where people's ideas, values, and philosophies come into conflict. Its scope ranges from local to global and from past to present to future.

LITERACY COACH
Whenever you read poll results, check the questions asked, the sample size, and the margin of error.

Literacy Coach offers reading and literacy tips on topics such as previewing and predicting, activating prior knowledge, reading headings, reading captions, summarizing, and note taking.

PAUSE, REFLECT, APPLY
1. How does the Aboriginal concept of justice differ from the European idea? In what way does it reflect the traditional way of life of Aboriginal peoples?

Pause, Reflect, Apply lets you check your understanding and progress at the end of each major section. Activities include summarizing, explaining ideas, organizing information into different formats, and expressing opinions with supporting evidence.

Replay summarizes the chapter's major concepts in list form.

SOURCES

Sources offers a direct connection to important primary and original sources such as newspaper reports, legislation, editorials, cartoons, and historical photos.

STUDY HALL

Study Hall provides an extensive end-of-chapter assessment of your progress.

THE WEB ▶▶▶
Learn more about levies introduced because of Internet downloading at www.emp.ca/civics

The Web points you to Web sites that offer supplementary material.

UNIT 1
Diversity and Pluralism in Canada

Chapter 1
Welcome to Canada!

Chapter 2
How Do You Define Citizenship?

Chapter 3
What Are Rights and Responsibilities?

Chapter 4
What Shapes Our Identities and Cultures?

CHAPTER 1
Welcome to Canada!

Between 1928 and 1971, more than 1 million people landed at Pier 21 seeking a new life in Canada. One in five Canadians can trace roots to this very spot. Can you?

What You Need to Know
- What are the criteria for becoming a citizen of Canada?
- How do human rights shape citizenship and identity?
- How can we understand the vast physical and human geographies of Canada?
- How have Canada's population patterns changed over the last century, and what trends are emerging?
- How do mapmakers construct maps?
- How can we select, use, and interpret maps?

Key Terms
stateless	pluralism
immigration	human rights
permanent resident	constitution
push–pull factors	topography
refugees	demography
naturalization	sovereignty

Key Question
What does Canada mean to you?

World War II (1939–1945) was over and Linda Hiie's entire family was presumed dead. She was all alone in a "displaced persons" camp organized by the United Nations. Linda was afraid to return to her home country, Estonia. It had been occupied by Russia. Like millions of "DPs," she was **stateless**.

Linda applied and got a one-year contract to work as a housekeeper in Winnipeg. Clutching her single suitcase, she sailed away from a shattered life. Later, with 300 others, Linda stepped onto Pier 21 in Halifax, Nova Scotia, the "gateway to Canada." Frightened, speaking little English, she waited in line to have her **immigration** *papers processed and to have a medical examination. She passed.*

The train to Winnipeg took a week. When Linda arrived, an immigrant couple was greeting newcomers at the station—in Estonian! They befriended Linda. Later, these kind strangers became my godparents. Linda Hiie was my mother. She told me, Linda Connor, her story over the years.

Like so many, my mother came to Canada with so little and contributed so much. One of her proudest moments was the day she acquired her Canadian citizenship. Never again could she be labelled a "DP." Linda Hiie was a new Canadian!

Becoming a Citizen of Canada

If someone found your wallet, how much of your **identity** would it reveal? Check it out. How many cards do you have? Student? Library? Consumer loyalty? Gym? Certificate of Indian status? Bank? **Permanent resident** card?

As you get older, you will acquire many more cards. To work in Canada you will need a Social Insurance Number. That card will come from the federal government. When you turn 18, you will get your own health card from your province.

In some ways, these are all membership cards. They have criteria: standards you must meet in order to belong to a group or organization. Is there a birth certificate among your cards? Most of us had one issued at birth. It may signify the most important membership of all: your citizenship.

Are you a citizen of Canada because you were born here? This is true for most Canadians. Anyone born in Canada is "naturally" a Canadian citizen (except for children born to foreign diplomats).

Maybe you immigrated to Canada and then became a citizen? One in six Canadians did just that.

Then there are the first peoples, the first "citizens." Long before "Canada" existed, the **First Nations** and **Inuit** had ancient cultures and traditions around citizenship. European contact and immigration drastically changed these cultures and systems. Still, the **Aboriginal peoples** have survived and maintained their cultures. Today, citizenship for Aboriginal peoples reflects a unique and hard-won status within Canada. You will explore this history in the next and following chapters. This First Nations person's story reveals how inclusive the concept of citizenship can be:

> "The real benefit of Canadian citizenship ... is the shared core values that allow citizens to claim other circles of participation as part of their Canadian identity. The ability to maintain a diverse society is what makes Canada unique. I am a Canadian ... but my residency in the Treaty Six area and in Saskatchewan's Waterhen Lake Cree First Nation is what defines me most strongly. Participation in these territories is not subordinate to [less important than] my Canadian citizenship but an integral part of it."
>
> —Gordon Martell, "A First Nations Perspective," from Stories of Citizenship, www.cea-ace.ca/foo.cfm?subsection=edu&page=sto&subpage=mar

---

THE WEB

Find hundreds of stories about citizenship and immigration at www.emp.ca/ccw

---

LITERACY COACH

Flip through this book and examine the headings. The largest headings (with a yellow line above them) break the chapter into its main sections. By examining these you get a sense of the chapter's scope. Locate and write down all the largest headings in this chapter. At any given time, this list will help you understand the chapter's focus and what is coming up next.

IMMIGRATION: WHO GETS IN AND HOW?

☐ **DISCUSSION POINT**
Do you know people who have moved to your area from other communities? What about people who have moved away from your community? What factors pushed and pulled them?

Many factors influence people to migrate from one country to another. These can be described as **push–pull factors**. For example, World War II and Russian occupation *pushed* Linda Hiie out of Estonia. Opportunities *pulled* her to Canada (see Figure 1.1).

FIGURE 1.1 Push–pull factors. What factors would you add to each side?

You will explore the immigration system further in Chapter 2. But it is important here to realize that in Canada, a federal department—Citizenship and Immigration Canada (CIC)—decides who gets in.

To get into Canada, immigrants apply for permanent residence under the *Immigration and Refugee Protection Act* (2002). This Act establishes Canada's refugee system and immigration guidelines and classes: Skilled Worker, Business, Family, International Adoption, and Quebec-Selected Immigration.

Immigrants must pay a fee for the right to become a permanent resident. Citizenship and Immigration Canada requires immigrants to have a medical examination, funds to cover living expenses for a period of six months, and educational and employment documentation. It may also require a police certificate from the country of origin.

THE WEB
For federal and Manitoba immigration services and advice to newcomers, go to www.emp.ca/ccw. Do you feel this is enough information? If not, what would you add?

Each province sets immigration criteria and quotas. Manitoba prefers immigrants who have legal status in the birth country, specific work experience, the ability to communicate in English or French, and settlement supports—for example, housing and employment.

Refugees are people who have fled persecution, and sometimes the threat of death, in their home countries because of their race, religion, or political beliefs. Because of persecution, anyone claiming refugee status in Canada applies to CIC for protection. A CIC officer decides whether the person is eligible to make a claim to the Immigration and Refugee Board. If accepted, refugees are granted **asylum** in Canada and can attain their permanent resident cards.

FROM PERMANENT RESIDENT TO CITIZEN

In the opening story, you learned how proud Linda Hiie felt the day she became a Canadian citizen. Citizenship can bring a strong sense of belonging, and much more. It is not surprising that many immigrants to Canada wish to become citizens. Their desire has to be strong. The process they go through, known as **naturalization**, takes time and effort.

Criteria for Canadian Citizenship

Citizenship and Immigration Canada sets the criteria for citizenship. To apply, a person must

- be 18 years of age or older (parents may apply for those who are under 18)
- be a permanent resident of Canada
- have lived in Canada for three of the previous four years
- be able to communicate in English or French
- know about Canada's history, geography, and political systems
- know about the rights and responsibilities of citizenship.

A person cannot apply for citizenship if he or she

- is considered to be a risk to Canada's security
- is under a **deportation** order to leave Canada
- has been convicted of an indictable (serious) criminal offence in the past three years
- is in prison, on parole, or on probation
- is being investigated for or has been convicted of **war crimes**
- has had his or her citizenship revoked in the last five years.

FIGURE 1.2 These refugees are protesting police treatment in Macedonia in 2001. More than 200,000 refugees from the former country of Yugoslavia were living in overcrowded camps in Macedonia. They fled their home country during a bloody civil war.

▶ **DID YOU KNOW** ◀
Eighty-five percent of immigrants to Canada become citizens.

Could You Pass the Citizenship Test?

Citizenship applicants must complete a form and pay a fee, which is less for children under 18. Successful applicants then take an oral or written test of their knowledge of Canada. This includes how to vote and run for political office; Canadian history and geography; the rights and responsibilities of citizenship; and how the Canadian government works.

Those who pass the test receive a Notice to Appear to Take an Oath of Citizenship. Family and friends are invited to attend the ceremony. The ceremony can be very emotional. It can be held anywhere from a government office to the local mall or school gym. However, a citizenship judge must preside, and an RCMP officer must attend.

In front of witnesses, the applicant takes the Oath of Citizenship (see the Sources feature) and signs the Oath of Citizenship form before receiving the official Certification of Canadian Citizenship.

FIGURE 1.3 Three-year-old Nectarios Chroniaris waves the flag during ceremonies at Edmonton's Heritage Amphitheatre in 2003. Fifty-three people took the citizenship oath that day.

Check out citizenship and immigration fee schedules at www.emp.ca/ccw

SOURCES

The Canadian Oath of Citizenship (as of 2006):

I swear (or affirm) that I will be faithful and bear true allegiance to Her Majesty Queen Elizabeth the Second, Queen of Canada, Her Heirs and Successors, according to the law and that I will faithfully observe the laws of Canada and fulfill my duties as a Canadian citizen.

Bill C-63 (1998) proposed changing the Oath (but was not passed into law):

From this day forward, I pledge my loyalty and allegiance to Canada and Her Majesty Elizabeth the Second, Queen of Canada. I promise to respect our country's rights and freedoms, to defend our democratic values, to faithfully observe our laws and fulfill my duties and obligations as a Canadian citizen.

THE BROAD NEW WORLD OF CITIZENSHIP

All people in Canada have **rights** and **responsibilities** and must respect Canada's laws (see Figure 3.1 on page 53). But unlike native-born Canadians, new citizens take an oath or affirm their commitment to

Canada. They agree to respect the equality rights of all; to work to eliminate discrimination and injustice; to protect the environment; and to work together to support these and other Canadian beliefs and **values** (principles), such as **pluralism** (a belief in mutual acceptance and respect of diverse ethnic, racial, religious, and social groups within society).

Citizens have democratic rights—to vote and run for office in Canadian elections. Citizens can apply for a Canadian passport, making international travel possible. Citizens are not restricted from working in different provinces. As citizens, former immigrants may qualify for membership in professional associations that require Canadian citizenship (for example, certain medical and law associations).

Canadian citizens also enjoy certain rights and privileges within the **Commonwealth** countries. For example, Canadian citizens who are permanent residents of the United Kingdom can vote in UK elections. Citizens of the Commonwealth also have special status in Canada. Want to play soccer in Britain or, as a British citizen, play hockey in Canada? Commonwealth citizenship makes it possible. Canada is also a member of **La Francophonie**, an international organization of francophone governments.

THE WEB
Play the Canadian Immigration Process game at www.emp.ca/ccw

Citizenship and Honour

Is Canadian citizenship a right or a privilege? For immigrants, the answer is obvious: they have to apply. Citizenship acquired through lies can be revoked (cancelled). The same is true if a person is considered a threat to national security or to the **human rights** of others. This is called **denaturalization**. Denaturalized people can be deported back to their home country.

Ernst Zundel, a permanent resident of Canada for many years, was jailed for publishing hate literature. In 2005, he was deported back to Germany, where he was placed on trial for denying the Holocaust and inciting racial hatred.

Citizenship can also be awarded as an honour. In 1985, the Canadian government made Raoul Wallenberg (1912–1947?) of Sweden the first honorary citizen of Canada, posthumously (after his death). Wallenberg risked his life saving tens of thousands of Hungarian Jews from being killed during the **Holocaust**.

In 2001, the former President of South Africa, Nelson Mandela, became the first living foreigner to be made an honorary citizen of Canada (see Figure 1.4). Mandela spent 27 years in prison for taking

8 CANADA IN THE CONTEMPORARY WORLD

FIGURE 1.4 Nelson Mandela greets a cheering crowd in Ottawa after being made an honorary citizen in 2001. What does this image say to you about Canadian values and citizenship?

action against South Africa's racist system of **apartheid** (a government system that denied rights to non-white citizens). When he became president, Mandela promoted peace and reconciliation.

Multiple "Memberships"

Some countries require anyone applying for citizenship to give up their original citizenship. Before 1977, it was necessary to renounce Canadian citizenship to become a citizen of another country. Today, the *Canadian Citizenship Act* is inclusive, not exclusive. A Canadian citizen can now also be a citizen of another country, or countries. Not surprisingly, as global connections increase, so do the number of people with dual, or multiple, citizenship.

> **THE WEB** ▶▶▶
> Learn more about Wallenberg and Mandela at www.emp.ca/ccw

PAUSE, REFLECT, APPLY

1. Why did the "DP" in the opening story prize her Canadian citizenship?
2. Create a two-column chart. In the left column, list criteria for Canadian citizenship; in the right, note why you agree or disagree with each criterion.
3. How important is Canadian citizenship to you? How do you show this?
4. What reasons would you give to new immigrants to become citizens?
5. Take Citizenship and Immigration Canada's citizenship test at www.emp.ca/ccw. Take it again after you have completed your study of this chapter.
6. Analyze the two oaths of citizenship in the Sources feature on page 6. Which do you think better reflects Canadian values? Explain your response.
7. Create a diagram showing the steps to becoming a citizen of Canada.
8. List some of the restrictions that non-citizens experience in Canada. Do you think the restrictions are too strict or not strict enough? What restrictions would you add or remove?
9. Use a web diagram or comparison chart to show what the terms "stateless," "immigration," "refugee," and "push–pull factors" might mean for (a) an immigrant, (b) an eighth-generation francophone Canadian, (c) an Aboriginal person, and (d) a refugee seeking asylum in Canada.

Human Rights and Canadian Citizenship

One of the great benefits of citizenship is the right to have rights. One of the greatest injustices a person or group can suffer is to have those rights denied. Thus, rights are at the very centre of what we explore in social studies.

> **KEY QUESTION**
> How basic are human rights to our lives in Canada?

THE UNITED NATIONS AND HUMAN RIGHTS

At the end of World War II, Canadian diplomats joined efforts to create an organization to promote peace. In 1945, Canada became one of 51 founding member countries of the organization that resulted: the United Nations (UN). Today, the UN has 191 member countries.

The UN is not a government. It cannot enforce its decisions. It relies on cooperation to do its work in international law, security, economic development, and social **equity**.

The founding diplomats soon realized that to succeed, the United Nations would have to promote human rights. One key person who helped achieve this goal was a Canadian, John Humphrey (1905–1995). In 1946, as director of the UN's new Human Rights Division, Humphrey wrote the first draft of the *Universal Declaration of Human Rights*.

THE *UNIVERSAL DECLARATION OF HUMAN RIGHTS* AND CANADA

Rights are created to correct wrongs.

In the past, Canada's laws have discriminated against Aboriginal peoples. For Aboriginal peoples, Canada's growth through immigration came at their expense. Until recently, government plans for economic growth overlooked the rights and needs of Aboriginal peoples, who have not shared in Canada's prosperity.

By today's standards, Canada's early immigration laws were also discriminatory. For decades, Chinese, Jews, Japanese, Ukrainians, Germans, Southern Asians, people of colour, and others were barred from immigrating or were treated unfairly. The consequences of these and other social injustices are still being addressed.

When the UN proclaimed the *Universal Declaration of Human Rights* (UDHR) in 1948, it was the first agreement among nations to state and outline certain absolute rights for all people everywhere. These include the right to

- life, liberty, and security of person
- an education
- full participation in cultural life.

The UDHR also states that all human beings are entitled to certain freedoms:

- freedom from torture or cruel, inhumane treatment or punishment
- freedom of thought, conscience, and religion
- freedom of expression and opinion.

The UDHR had no legal force. Instead, it had to inspire nations to incorporate human, civil, economic, and social rights into their own legislation. This would give human rights the force of law.

The United Nations and the *Universal Declaration of Human Rights* did inspire people in Canada. Canada had helped create an organization and a document that could make the world a fairer place. In turn, Canada was changed. (You will explore the UDHR in more detail in Chapter 13.)

The UDHR also inspired **indigenous peoples** (the original inhabitants of a region) around the world to take action. Many years later, in 1994, the UN's draft of the Declaration on the Rights of Indigenous Peoples was adopted by the United Nations High Commissioner for Human Rights. By 2006, however, this declaration had yet to be proclaimed by the United Nations.

From the *Canadian Bill of Rights* to the *Canadian Charter of Rights and Freedoms*

A Canadian drafted the UDHR, but in 1948 Canada itself had no bill of rights. After 1948, many Canadians demanded one. However, that required a change to Canada's **constitution** (the central law of a country). The provinces could not agree about how this might be done.

In 1960, the federal government under Prime Minister John Diefenbaker passed the *Canadian Bill of Rights* without involving the provinces. Because it was not part of the constitution, the Bill of Rights had limited power. It did not apply to provincial laws. It could not overrule existing laws. Nonetheless, it was a human rights milestone in Canada (see Figure 1.5).

> **DISCUSSION POINT**
> The Charter protects all people in Canada, including non-citizens and people who may be here illegally. Do you agree with this policy? Explain.

In 1982, Canada's constitution was changed. Under the leadership of Prime Minister Pierre Elliott Trudeau (1919–2000), the *Constitution Act, 1982*, became Canada's new constitution. The *Canadian Charter of Rights and Freedoms* is the first part of that Act. It, too, was inspired by the UDHR. Both Diefenbaker and Trudeau championed human rights.

As part of the constitution, the Charter has more power than the Bill of Rights. It legally guarantees democratic rights, language rights, and the rights of minorities. It establishes the principle of "equality before the law and under the law." This means that all laws must be written and enforced to respect the equality of all people. Any law, provincial or federal, that defies the Charter can be cancelled in court. You will explore Canada's constitution and the Charter in greater detail in chapters 2 and 3.

- **1944** Ontario *Racial Discrimination Act*
- **1947** *Saskatchewan Bill of Rights*
- **1948** *Universal Declaration of Human Rights*
- **1960** *Canadian Bill of Rights*
- **1982** *Canadian Charter of Rights and Freedoms*

FIGURE 1.5 A rights timeline. Each document marks a step forward for rights in Canada. You have just read about the last three. Learn more about the first two by viewing a timeline and rights map at www.emp.ca/ccw.

THE WEB ▶▶▶

Pierre Trudeau inspired strong feelings in Canadians, positive and negative. Yet in 2004, he was voted number three in CBC Television's Greatest Canadian contest. Check out why at www.emp.ca/ccw

CivicStar

JOHN DIEFENBAKER

John Diefenbaker (1895–1979) was born in Ontario and was raised and educated in Saskatchewan. As a boy, he experienced discrimination because of his German last name. He became a tireless campaigner for human rights.

In an interview with CBC television in 1977, Diefenbaker described how, as a child, he saw discrimination against Métis, francophones, First Nations people, and European immigrants: "I saw them ill-treated, regarded by the people as a whole as intruders, not invaders, who could never hope to become Canadians. They were second-class citizens."

Diefenbaker became a lawyer. In 1936, he began drafting a bill of rights. Four years later, he was elected to Parliament in Ottawa. He soon became the first member of Parliament ever to introduce a motion for a bill of rights.

In 1957, Diefenbaker became the first person without a French or British background to become prime minister of Canada. His quest continued. By 1960, his dream of a bill of rights became a reality when his government passed the *Canadian Bill of Rights*.

Your Turn

1. Have you ever experienced discrimination? If so, how has this experience affected your attitude toward human rights?
2. The photograph above shows Diefenbaker wearing a headdress from the Sioux First Nation of South Saskatchewan. He was made a full chief in 1959. Using the library or the Internet, research rights "firsts" that Diefenbaker achieved as prime minister in terms of status Indians and women. Prepare a poster or brief report on your discoveries.

PAUSE, REFLECT, APPLY

1. Create a collage of people, places, and symbols that reflect what it means to be Canadian.
2. Design a Charter of Rights and Responsibilities for your classroom.
3. Merhan Karimi Nasseri's refugee claims were rejected throughout Europe, and he refused to return to his native Iran. In 1988, he became a stateless person living in the departures area of Charles De Gaulle International Airport in France. What role do you think the UN should play in helping stateless people such as Nasseri? (Nasseri's plight inspired the 1993 French film *Tombés du cie* (*Lost in Transit*) and the 2004 US film *The Terminal*. Learn more about Nasseri at www.emp.ca/ccw.
4. a) Should the international role of the UN increase or decrease?
   b) What are the pros and cons of having the UN "supersized" or "undersized"?
5. Nominate a Canadian to become the next head of the UN. Hold a class vote after all the nominations are presented.

Introducing the Geography of Canada

▶ **KEY QUESTION**
Why are the three basic facts of Canadian geography so important?

Canada is immense. Only one country, Russia, is larger. Canada is only slightly smaller than all of Europe, a region of about 45 countries. Canada stretches about 4,800 kilometres north to south, from the Arctic Ocean to Lake Erie, and about 5,000 kilometres west to east, from Pacific to Atlantic.

Canada is a northern country, like Russia. So much of Canada (about 90 percent) is so far north that the **growing season** is too short for agriculture.

Canada is separated by great distances from other countries, with the exception of the United States.

These three facts—size, northern location, and isolation—help us understand Canada and Canadians. They provide a context for Canada's history:

- the migration from northern Asia of Aboriginal peoples into and through Canada (a theory held to be true by most scientists today)
- the interest shown much later by European peoples, both French and English
- large-scale immigration of the 20th century
- Canada's involvement in the two world wars without great danger of attack.

▶ **DID YOU KNOW** ◀
One theory of origin states that Aboriginal peoples of the Americas originated here and then migrated to Asia. This is known as the theory of American Genesis. Few scientists support it.

These three facts also provide a context in which to describe the physical and human geographies of Canada.

PAUSE, REFLECT, APPLY

1. List and rank the four facts you know about the size of Canada.
2. Create a diagram to show how Canada's size, northernness, and isolation affect four circumstances of Canadian history.
3. It has been joked that "Canada has too much geography." Explain what this statement means to you.
4. Imagine what it would be like if your school were a one-room schoolhouse. Now picture your school being housed in the MTS Centre. How would each of these locations affect your ability to connect with (a) your friends and (b) your teachers? Create a chart listing the positive and negative effects that these locations would have on your school community.

Canada: Physical Geography

The physical geography of an area can be broken into landforms, soils, surface waters, climate, and vegetation. In Canada, these five components vary considerably from place to place.

> **KEY QUESTION**
> How does the physical geography of Canada vary from place to place?

LANDFORMS AND SOILS

Physically, Canada is the product of three primary **geologic** developments.

First, the Canadian Shield was formed about 2,000 million years ago when seven ancient micro-continents collided and merged together. Much of the Shield consists of rocks, mostly granite, that are 2,500 million years old.

Second, as sediment accumulated in long, narrow basins, three regions around the Shield margins developed mountains. These are (1) the Cordilleran mountain system, in Western Canada, with a history that includes volcanic and earthquake activity; (2) the Appalachian system in Eastern Canada, which is older than the Cordilleran and lowered by erosion; and (3) the Innuitian system across the high Arctic, from Alaska to Greenland.

The third geologic development was the depositing of sediments in shallow seas in the intervening areas, about 500 million years ago.

Landscape was also affected by **glaciation**. Almost all of Canada was under ice at some time during the last 1.5 million years. Only 1 percent is under ice today. The largest ice sheet in the northern hemisphere covered Canada during the last glacial period, which ended about 10,000 years ago.

Physiographic Regions of Canada

This sketch of Canada's geological history helps us to understand the physiographic regions of Canada. These regions, mapped in Figure 1.6, are defined by underlying geologic structures and **topography** (surface landforms). They are as follows.

- *Canadian Shield.* This, the largest physiographic region, includes most of Quebec and Ontario, northern Manitoba and Saskatchewan, Nunavut, and more than half of the Northwest Territories. The rugged landscape comprises rock outcrops, bogs, **muskeg**, **drumlins**, **eskers**, and lake basins. Soils are poor, thin, acidic, or non-existent. Natural resources include forest and mineral deposits, including gold, uranium, copper, and nickel.
- *Western Cordillera.* Oriented northwest to southeast, this region includes a Pacific mountain system and the interior Rocky Mountains. The landscape is deeply dissected and eroded, with

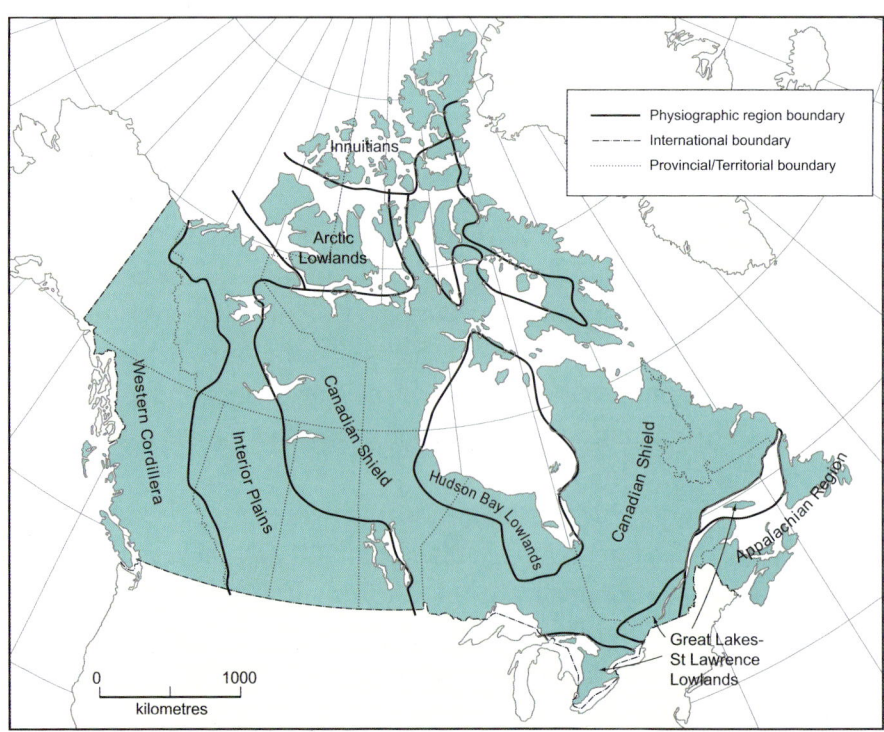

FIGURE 1.6 Physiographic regions of Canada

many peaks over 3,000 metres, and there are large valleys and other intermontane (between mountains) regions. Soils are limited to valley and intermontane regions. Natural resources include forest, minerals such as gold, and opportunities for hydroelectric power.
- *Appalachians.* These older mountains are eroded to an undulating upland about 150–1,200 metres high. Glacial landforms, such as drumlins and eskers, are common. Soils are mostly poor and sometimes swampy. There are a few areas of good soil in the lowlands, including throughout Prince Edward Island. Other natural resources include coal.
- *Innuitians.* Located in the far north, this rugged and isolated mountain area comprises glaciers and ice fields.
- *Great Lakes–St. Lawrence Lowlands.* This relatively small region rests on **sedimentary** rocks. Natural resources include fertile soils, construction materials, and opportunities for hydroelectric power.
- *Interior Plains.* Sedimentary rocks also underlie this region, extending from the Mackenzie River delta to the border with the United States. Landforms are diverse, with flat areas, rolling areas, and valleys created by glacial meltwater. In the southern area there are thick glacial lake soils. From east to west, the prairies increase in elevation. Natural resources include several minerals and oil and gas.
- *Hudson Bay Lowlands.* A level area, this region comprises muskeg and other poorly drained areas. There are few natural resources.
- *Arctic Lowlands.* This region is a series of low islands. Natural resources include fossil fuels.

SURFACE WATERS

The geological history of Canada also helps us understand **hydrography**, the study of surface waters. The map in Figure 1.7 shows Canada's five **drainage basins**: Hudson Bay (3,681,279 km^2), Arctic (3,576,501 km^2), Atlantic (1,502,444 km^2), Pacific (1,037,885 km^2), and Gulf of Mexico (26,213 km^2).

The location and size of drainage basins is important for many reasons. In particular, rivers can be main transportation routes. Both rivers and lakes also offer opportunities for power, fishing, and recreation, and provide water for domestic, agricultural, and industrial use.

> **THE WEB**
> Explore Canada's physiographic regions and natural resources through photos, maps, satellite images, key glossary words, and more at www.emp.ca/ccw

> **DID YOU KNOW**
> Glacial Lake Agassiz was formed by the melting ice sheet about 12,000 years ago. Today, many lakes, including lakes Winnipeg, Manitoba, and Winnipegosis, are remnants of Agassiz. The rich soils of the Red River Valley formed at the bottom of the lake.

CLIMATE AND NATURAL VEGETATION

Four main factors help explain why different parts of Canada have different climates:

- *Latitude.* Because the sun's rays have to travel farther through the Earth's atmosphere to reach northern parts of Canada, less solar radiation reaches these northern areas. As a result, temperatures decrease from south to north in the northern hemisphere.
- *Distance from oceans.* Close to oceans, climates are temperate, with warm summers and cool winters and high levels of precipitation. Away from oceans, climates are more continental, with hot summers, cold winters, and less precipitation.
- *Prevailing air movement.* Because air moves from west to east at Canada's latitudes, weather patterns move in an easterly direction.
- *Landforms.* The Western Cordillera prevents warm, moist Pacific air from moving east across Canada. The Interior Plains sometimes let moving air spread easily; at other times, they act like a saucer, holding bodies of cold air in winter and hot air in summer.

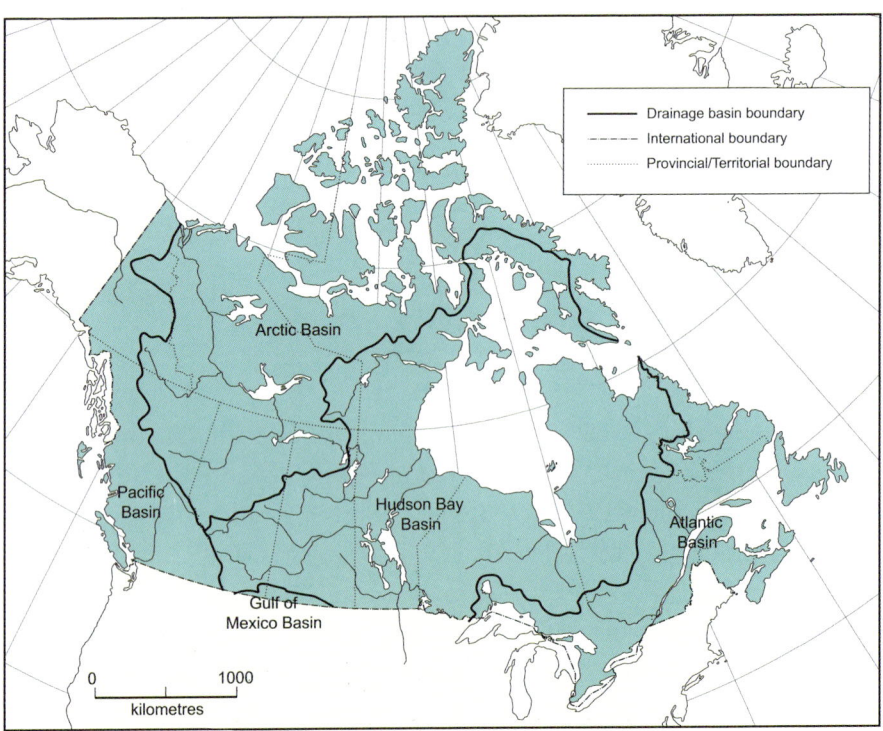

FIGURE 1.7 Drainage basins of Canada

Climate Regions of Canada

Geographers recognize climate regions. These are defined by long-term averages of temperature and precipitation. Because climate affects vegetation, each region also has characteristic natural vegetation.

The map in Figure 1.8 is divided into seven climate regions:

- The *Arctic* is characterized by light snowfall, high winds, and long periods of very low temperatures. Vegetation is limited to **tundra**.
- The *Subarctic* has very cold winters, with about six months of snow, and warm summers. Vegetation is **boreal** forest with open areas and some stunted growth. The transition zone between tundra and boreal forest is called the **tree line**.
- The *Pacific* has high rainfall, with mild winters and cool summers. Vegetation is mostly coastal rainforest.
- The *Cordillera* has temperatures that vary widely with elevation, with most precipitation in the south. It is a varied montane (mountain) and boreal forest region.

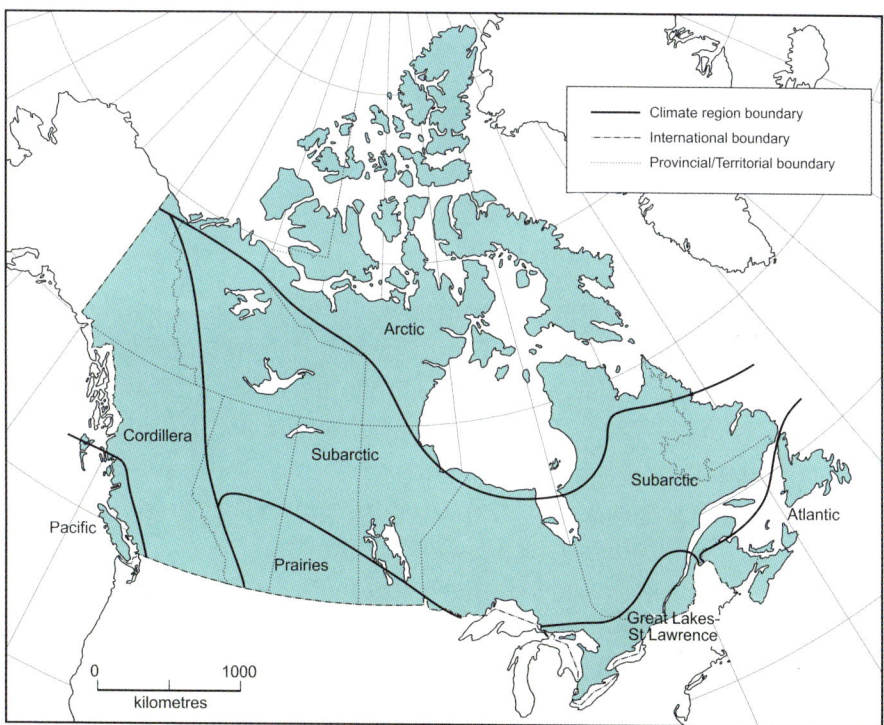

FIGURE 1.8 Climate regions of Canada

18 CANADA IN THE CONTEMPORARY WORLD

▶ **DID YOU KNOW** ◀

Much of the ground in northern Canada is permanently frozen to a great depth, as much as 400 metres at Resolute, Nunavut. Even with this **permafrost**, in some areas a surface layer thaws in summer, allowing tundra vegetation to grow.

- The *Prairies* region has light precipitation, with very cold winters and hot summers. This is a grassland and parkland zone.
- The *Great Lakes–St. Lawrence* region has high humidity, with warm summers and cold winters. The natural vegetation is broadleaf and mixed forest. Most Canadians live in this climate region.
- The *Atlantic* has high precipitation, with cool winters and warm summers. This is a region of mixed and boreal forest.

PAUSE, REFLECT, APPLY

1. List the three primary geologic developments that have affected Canada's physiography.
2. List the eight physiographic regions of Canada. Which are upland regions, and which are lowland regions?
3. a) Why is the hydrography of Canada important?
   b) Why is it significant that most of Canada's rivers drain into the Arctic Ocean or into Hudson Bay?
4. List four factors that help explain why different parts of Canada have different climates.
5. List the seven climate regions of Canada.
6. How might physiography and climate relate to economic activity and settlement patterns across Canada?

▶ **KEY QUESTION**

How does the human geography of Canada vary from place to place?

Canada: Human Geography

The physical and human geographies of Canada are closely related. In particular, Canada is a northern country with little land suitable for agriculture. As a result, the area of Canada inhabited by significant numbers of people is small. The map in Figure 1.9 shows how unevenly population is distributed. Where does the map show that the vast majority of people live? This figure, and the preceding figures that map aspects of physical geography, divide Canada into regions.

Canada can also be divided into five regions based on political boundaries: Atlantic (Newfoundland and Labrador, Prince Edward Island, Nova Scotia, and New Brunswick); Central (Quebec and Ontario); Prairie (Manitoba, Saskatchewan, and Alberta); West Coast (British Columbia); and North (Nunavut, Northwest Territories, and Yukon Territory).

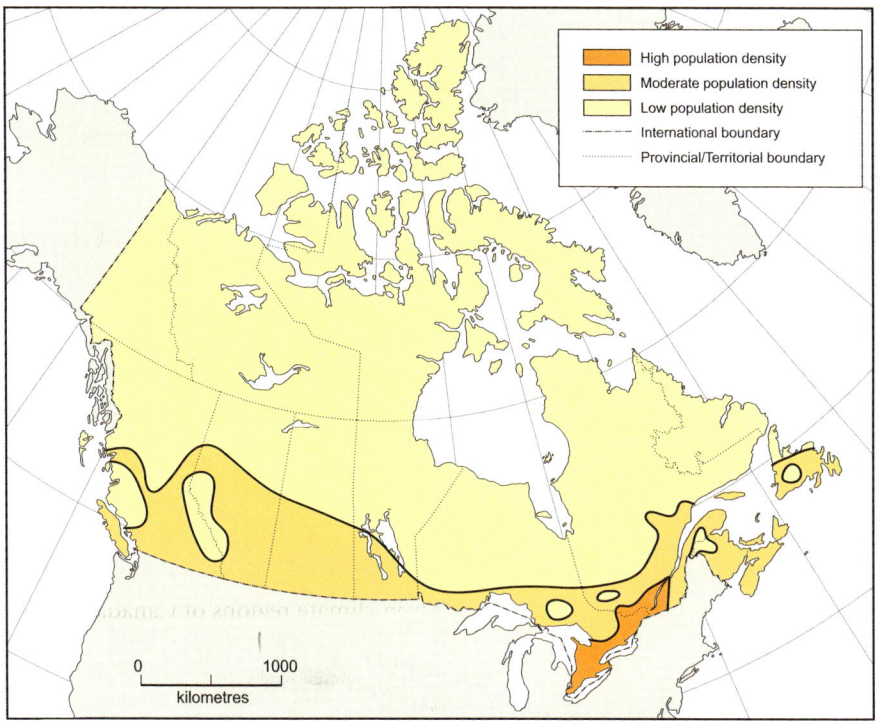

FIGURE 1.9 Population density in Canada. *Data source: Statistics Canada, Canadian Population Census*

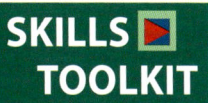

How to Construct Maps

Figure 1.9 can be used to analyze map construction. First, it shows the required components of a map. Second, it indicates where the **cartographers** acquired the information that they put on the map.

All maps need

- an explanatory title
- a scale: Cartographers must "shrink" the area that they map. Scales can be expressed as a line scale (as in all the maps in this chapter), a ratio scale, or as a statement. Line scales are generally preferred.
- an indication of direction: Maps of small areas usually include an arrow or compass rose indicating north. Maps of very large areas, such as Canada, more often have lines of latitude and longitude. These indicate direction very effectively. World maps often will not include an indication of direction because it is understood that north is at the top.

Maps generally need

- a key: Because Figures 1.6 (physiographic regions) and 1.7 (drainage basins) have simple content, the key is simple. In contrast, Figure 1.9 must distinguish three different population densities. Cartographers use colours or shadings to reflect categories.
- a **map projection**: Because maps represent a curved surface (the Earth) on a flat surface, they must use a projection. There are

hundreds of systems of projection. (In this chapter, for example, the Canada maps use a Lambert Conformal Conic projection.) Projection is essential for large areas, such as the world, or all of Canada. For maps of local areas, such as the city of Winnipeg, projection is usually ignored.
- a neat line: This is drawn around the map to make it attractive and effective.

What about the information? What data are used to construct a map, and where do they come from?

- Some maps are based on traditional knowledge. For example, Aboriginal peoples gathered information about local and regional geographies and created maps. These were shared with the Europeans who first travelled into the interior of Canada.
- Many maps are based on observation. For example, French and English colonial officials drew maps that reflected the observations of settlers and fur traders. If you draw a map of your school grounds or neighbourhood, you will probably rely on observation.
- Maps constructed following observation of geography are "directly sensed." Other maps may include information from "remote sensing," for example, from aerial photographs or satellite images.
- Some maps use data collected from published sources. Figure 1.9, for example, uses data from Statistics Canada.
- Increasingly, cartographers use a **geographic information system** (GIS) to construct maps from various data sources, including global positioning system (GPS) receivers. A GIS is a computer-based tool that enables geographic data to be stored, displayed, analyzed, and mapped.

Skill Practice

1. You must redo the population map, Figure 1.9, without colour. Instead, you must use shading. What shadings will you use, and why?
2. Using an atlas, find a political world map. Does it include a key? If not, why not? How is scale indicated? What projection has been used?
3. Draw a map of your school's grounds or neighbourhood. Include a title, scale, direction arrow, key, and neat line. How will you acquire the information to be included on the map?

▶ **DID YOU KNOW** ◀
At about three people per square kilometre, Canada has one of the world's lowest population densities. With 7 percent of the Earth's surface, Canada has less than 0.5 percent of the world's population.

CANADA'S POPULATION INCREASE SINCE 1867

A very helpful tool in exploring human geography is **demography**, the scientific study of population. Demographic terms can be very technical. Sometimes they refer to actual numbers. Sometimes they refer to rates of change. Always note the difference. For example, a key demographic term is **natural increase**. This is the numerical difference between the number of births and the number of deaths in a population in a given period. The **rate of natural increase** refers to the overall rate at which a population increases.

At Confederation, in 1867, what is now Canada had a population of about 3.4 million people. Since then, the population has increased through natural increase and immigration. Between 1867 and 1901, the population increased to about 5.4 million. The table in Figure 1.10 shows population change after 1901.

From 1901 until 1921 (excluding World War I, 1914–1918), immigration to Canada was substantial. Many people emigrated from Eastern Europe to the prairies. Between 1921 and 1951, terrible economic conditions in the 1930s and World War II contributed to low immigration. Government regulations also restricted immigration (see Chapter 2). Greater immigration resumed in 1951. It continued, largely because Canada's economy needed immigrants to develop and grow.

The table in Figure 1.10 shows that natural increase (births minus deaths) was fairly steady between 1901 and 1951. What happened between 1951 and 1971? In this period, Canada's **birth rate** (the number of people born per thousand) skyrocketed during the "baby boom." Since 1971, Canada's birth rate has steadily fallen.

> ☐ **DISCUSSION POINT**
> Different groups have different birth rates. The average birth rate in Canada for the Aboriginal population, for example, is almost double the birth rate for the non-Aboriginal population. How might this fact shape Canada's future?

THE CANADIAN POPULATION TODAY

In 2006, Canada had about 32 million people. Birth and death rates were fairly typical for a **more developed country** (see Chapter 12). The annual rate of natural increase is 0.3 percent. Predicting future population is uncertain, but it is estimated that Canada might have 36 million people by 2025 and 37 million by 2050.

Slow population growth reflects a demographic fact: Canadian women are having fewer children. Today, the **fertility rate** is 1.5 children per woman—too low to maintain current population levels.

> ▶ **DID YOU KNOW** ◀
> **Life expectancy** in Canada is among the highest in the world. The average age to which women can expect to live is 83 years. For men, it is 78 years. In Afghanistan, it is 42 years, for men and women; in Zimbabwe, 37 years for men and 34 years for women.

Time Period	Immigration Minus Emigration (thousands)	Births Minus Deaths (thousands)	Total Population Growth (thousands)	Population at End of Period (thousands)
1901–1911	810	1,025	1,835	7,207
1911–1921	311	1,270	1,581	8,788
1921–1931	230	1,360	1,590	10,377
1931–1941	–92	1,222	1,130	11,507
1941–1951	169	1,972	2,141	13,648
1951–1961	1,080	3,148	3,228	18,238
1961–1971	722	2,608	3,330	21,568
1971–1981	1,188	1,913	3,101	24,820
1981–1991	1,351	1,974	3,325	28,031
1991–2001	1,621	1,528	3,149	31,021

FIGURE 1.10 Population change in Canada by 10-year intervals, 1901–2001. Changes are expressed in absolute numbers, not rates of change. *Source: Statistics Canada*

22 CANADA IN THE CONTEMPORARY WORLD

▶ **DID YOU KNOW** ◀
About 80 percent of Canada's population lives in urban centres. In 1871, the figure was about 18 percent.

THE WEB ▶▶▶
See Canada's population density in a satellite image of the Earth at night at www.emp.ca/ccw

THE ECONOMIC GEOGRAPHY OF CANADA

Canada is highly urbanized and industrial, with a rapidly changing economic geography. Increasingly, Canadians work in service industries, such as retail, finance, and consultancy. Increasing numbers of women are in the labour force.

International trade agreements—including the **North American Free Trade Agreement** between Canada, the United States, and Mexico—are also reshaping Canada's economy.

One economic fact remains unchanged: Canada is intimately linked to the United States. This link applies both to ownership of economic activities and trade. About 80 percent of Canada's exports go to the United States; 65 to 70 percent of Canada's imports come from the United States.

THE POLITICAL GEOGRAPHY OF CANADA

We belong to something called Canadian society. But how uniform is it? Clearly, there are divisions. These are important to explore because they help us understand the dynamics of Canada. They reveal Canada's political strengths, weaknesses, and potential.

First is the division between the Aboriginal peoples of Canada and other Canadians. One of the most dramatic implications of this is geographic—Aboriginal land claims are changing Canada's political geography.

Second is the division between francophone and other Canadians. This reality could transform Canada if Quebec, for example, or a part of Quebec, were to secede (break away) from Canada.

Third, as a federal state, Canada has two levels of government: central (national) and provincial/territorial. There is often debate about which level should have more power and how well federalism (the division of power between the national government and the provinces/territories) works.

Some Canadians favour a stronger central government. Others favour **decentralization**, with stronger provinces or regions. Canada's

FIGURE 1.11 The tag on the dog riding the "Power & Influence, Ottawa" pickup says "West." What **stereotypes** (usually negative generalizations) is the cartoonist playing with?

immense size only intensifies this conflict. Many people in the West, for example, feel the central government neglects them. This "Western alienation" has become a major political force.

Fourth, the ethnic identity of the Canadian population has changed. Governments have adopted policies based on pluralism. Cultural traditions of immigrants from diverse ethnic, religious, and linguistic groups are respected within Canadian society. They are not forced to conform. The "face" of Canada keeps changing.

All four divisions affect our identity—who we think we are. With which social group do you identify? Is your primary loyalty to Canada? Your First Nation? Your province? Your region? Is ethnic background the most important facet of your identity?

In summary, all four of these divisions could weaken Canada. They could also be components of a Canadian identity that is resilient, strong, and ever-changing.

PAUSE, REFLECT, APPLY

1. Why do most people live in a few small clusters located in the southern part of Canada?
2. List two components of Canadian population change through time.
3. Identify the 10-year time periods when immigration into Canada was relatively high, and suggest why these periods occurred.
4. Start a demography dictionary by listing the terms described in the section above in your social studies notebook. Add to it as you come upon new terms in this book and elsewhere.
5. a) Why is the natural increase of the Canadian population quite low today?
   b) If a lower rate of natural increase continues as a trend, what actions might governments have to take?
6. List three ongoing changes in Canada's economic geography. How would you rank them in importance, and why?
7. Canadians hold different views about our future.
   a) List four divisions evident in Canada.
   b) Which of the four divisions poses the greatest challenge to Canada, and why?
   c) With which group or groups do you identify?

Geography as Destiny

KEY QUESTION
Why does geography matter?

Does geography really matter? Recall that Canada is an immense and mostly northern country. It is located a great distance from much of the rest of the world, except, of course, the United States.

Today, many people talk about an increasing interconnectedness of peoples and places of the world. It is important to appreciate that

FIGURE 1.12 *Nanuq* (Inuit for polar bear) is part of Inuit tradition. Global warming could make it extinct. What impact would this have on Inuit and Canadian identity?

Canada is just one part of that world. Yet, Canada is also independent. It is different from and often competes with other countries.

Competition can be seen in disputes over Canada's **sovereignty** (absolute authority and ownership) in the Arctic region. As **global warming** raises temperatures, the northern ice melts. Resulting physical changes could open up a sea passage—the fabled Northwest Passage—as a trade route. Oil and gas exploration could also increase. How will these changes affect Canada's northern identity?

Great size, northernness, isolation—these characteristics have shaped Canada's physical and human geographies. In turn, these geographies provide a valuable context to help us understand Canada.

PAUSE, REFLECT, APPLY

1. Why is it appropriate to think of Canada as both part of an increasingly interconnected world and also separate from it?
2. Why might Canada become involved in political conflict with other countries in the foreseeable future?

REPLAY

In this chapter, you have explored these concepts:

1. Identity and citizenship are closely interrelated.
2. Canadian citizenship may be acquired through birth or through naturalization.
3. Canada's commitment to human rights has evolved over the years.
4. Being aware of Canada's geography—its size, northernness, and isolation—helps us understand Canada's past, present, and future.
5. Canada's physical and human geographies are interconnected.
6. Demographic patterns in Canada continue to change, creating tensions and opportunities.

SKILLS TOOLKIT

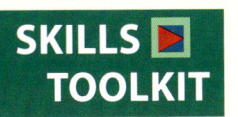

How to Select, Use, and Interpret Maps

If a picture is worth a thousand words, then so is a map. All peoples in all places at all times have created and used maps. Maps are a fundamental way to record and communicate about where things are located in relation to other things, spatially. Maps are also much more than this. They are representations of the world.

Most maps are created for a specific purpose and readership. The maps in this chapter are intended for this course and grade level. Maps designed for grade 1 would be much simpler. Maps can also be much more complex, integrating different types of information on a single map.

But maps cannot show everything. By definition, a map records only the information the cartographer judges to be significant. Map users may also need to know something about what is not on the map.

Being able to select, use, and interpret maps is a form of visual literacy. This can be as important as being able to read and write. Look at the maps in this chapter. What do you see? To "read" them, you must be able to make sense of symbols, images, and colours. These, not words, are the maps' contents.

In Figures 1.6, 1.7, and 1.8,

- scale allows us to estimate the dimensions of the several regions or areas
- longitude and latitude let us determine direction (north, south, east, or west) at any point.

In Figure 1.9, the key allows us to

- locate areas of Canada of different population densities, from relatively high, to moderate, to low. We also see these different areas in relation to one another.
- distinguish political boundaries between countries from political boundaries within countries.

Skill Practice

1. Referring to Figure 1.6, estimate the west-to-east extent of the Interior Plains region close to the US border.
2. Judging from Figure 1.9, where would you say most of Canada's population lives?
3. Statistics Canada creates population maps. Compare its "Total Aboriginal Identity Population by 2001 Census Subdivision" map to Figure 1.9. Using information you gather, give at least three reasons why you think Aboriginal people live where they do in Canada. Or, compare the Statistics Canada map "Proportion of Francophones, 2001 by Census Division" to Figure 1.9. Go to www.emp.ca/ccw or locate an atlas with similar maps.

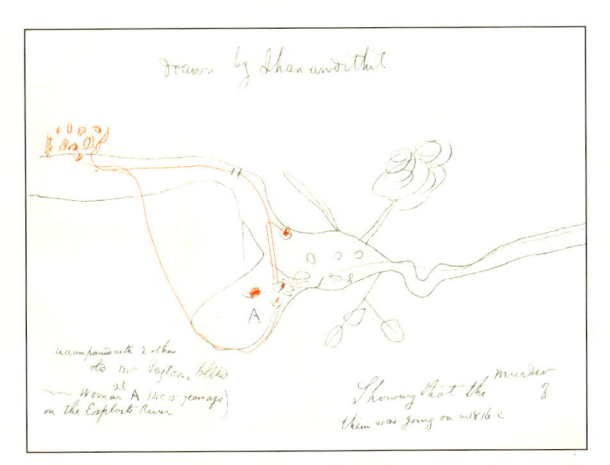

FIGURE 1.13 In 1828, Shanawdithit (1801–1829) created this map illustrating the murder of one of her tribeswomen by European settlers several years earlier. Shanawdithit was the last of the Beothuk, a First Nation on the island of Newfoundland that is now extinct.

STUDY HALL

Be Informed

1. What level(s) of government must you contact if you would like to become a Canadian citizen: municipal, provincial, or federal?
2. What are the advantages of citizenship?
3. What are some basic human rights and freedoms?
4. Create a political map of Canada, using all the components of a map (see Skills Toolkit, page 19). Identify all provinces and territories, capital cities (including the national capital), major urban centres, surrounding oceans, foreign areas (United States, Alaska, Greenland), and provincial/territorial and international boundaries. Keep your map and add to it throughout the year. If you wish to use GIS software, speak to your teacher for guidance.

Be Purposeful

5. In *The Journals of Susanna Moodie*, Canadian writer Margaret Atwood wrote, "We are all immigrants to this place, even if we were born here." How do you interpret this quotation? Explain what it means to you.
6. Should government make it easier or harder to acquire citizenship?
7. "The more money you have, the easier it should be to come into Canada." Support or refute this statement.
8. Describe how knowledge about the physical geography of Canada—especially physiography and climate—can be useful to (a) average Canadians in everyday life and (b) an understanding of Canadian history.
9. Should more Canadians be encouraged to live in the north, perhaps through housing **subsidies** and other financial incentives? Explain your response.
10. Canada's birth rate is declining. What are some of the specific implications? On balance, is this a good, bad, or neutral fact? Explain your response.

Be Active

11. The deep historic connections that Aboriginal peoples have to the land are different from those of mainstream Canada. Use either direct contact or research to find one or more quotations from an Aboriginal elder or leader that expresses this worldview.
12. Role-play a situation in which one student plays an immigration officer and the other plays a person applying for refugee status. Pick a specific time in Canada's history. Remember, Canada's immigration doors have been "open" or "closed" at different times. Be prepared to role-play refugees of different ages, educational background, and work experience. The immigration officer should state the political, social, and economic realities at the beginning of the role-play. The refugee must describe personal and political circumstances pushing him or her out of the home country. The refugee must also explain how he or she will be an asset to Canada. At the end of each interview, the class must vote on whether the immigration officer should accept or reject the refugee. Students must clearly and respectfully state their reasons for accepting or rejecting this person.
13. Create a Charter of Rights and Responsibilities for your school.
14. Research changes that are occurring as a result of human-caused global warming in the Arctic. Research the community of Churchill, Manitoba. Describe what it will be like 50 years from now if the climate continues to change.
15. On page 18, you read about the five regions of Canada based on political boundaries. Do these regions make sense to you? If not, why not? Draw a map with an alternative regionalization of Canada and then justify your set of regions.

CHAPTER 2
How Do You Define Citizenship?

"Our differences make us strong."

"Well, as the saying goes: 'I am Canadian.' What does that mean to me? Lots of different things. For one thing, my family speaks French; we moved here from Morocco in the mid-1990s. We are Muslim, and we are happy to see other Muslims moving here. Being Canadian might be different for you, though, because there's no cookie-cutter shape. You can be many things and still share this idea—of Canada, and of being Canadian. Our differences make us strong. I like that."

—Samira, a grade 9 student in Manitoba

In many ways, Canada contains the globe within its borders. Built by three founding peoples—the Aboriginal peoples, the English, and the French—Canada has offered citizenship to people from all corners of the world. What does being Canadian mean to you? Do you think our differences make us strong? Why or why not?

What You Need to Know

- What are the unique characteristics of Aboriginal citizenship?
- What are the historical roots of bilingualism in Canada?
- What forms does bilingualism take in Canada today?
- How has Canada changed its immigration and Aboriginal policies?
- What is multiculturalism, and what forms does it take?
- What is the meaning of Canadian citizenship?
- How can you create effective inquiry questions?

Key Terms

Anishnaabe
First Nations
Inuit
Métis
residential schools
assimilation
Official Languages Act
United Empire Loyalists
republicanism
Holocaust
points system
multiculturalism

Key Question

How has the past influenced Canadian citizenship?

Citizenship and the Aboriginal Peoples of Canada

The Aboriginal peoples were the first inhabitants of the land that is now Canada. Before the arrival of the Europeans, they had established a variety of governmental systems.

On the West Coast, some hierarchical societies evolved with top-down decision makers. In the East, the **Iroquois Confederacy** emphasized decision making by consensus and diplomatic relations with neighbouring nations. The Confederacy also had its own constitution, which was based on many democratic ideals. In Manitoba and elsewhere, the **Anishnaabe**-Ojibwe have had a clan system of governance from earliest times. **Clans** (groups connected by kinship or blood) help to unite all Anishnaabe-Ojibwe as one nation. This also creates a sense of identity and responsibility among clan members.

WHO ARE THE ABORIGINAL PEOPLES?

> ▶ **DID YOU KNOW** ◀
> Soon after contact, Europeans began to approach First Nations to enter into agreements. These early **treaties** were made to establish peace, trade, alliance, neutrality, and military support.

Section 35 of the *Constitution Act, 1982* defines the term "**Aboriginal peoples of Canada**" as including the **First Nations**, **Inuit**, and **Métis** peoples of Canada. "First Nations" refers to the original inhabitants of the Americas; it does not include the Inuit of the North or the Métis, who are of mixed European and First Nations origin.

FROM INJUSTICE TO RECOGNIZED RIGHTS

Today, Aboriginal peoples have the same rights as other Canadians. Most importantly, existing "treaty or other rights" are protected under section 25 of the *Canadian Charter of Rights and Freedoms*. First among these is the right to self-government. This includes control over areas such as health, education, housing, and economic development. Federal and provincial governments must respect that the right to self-determination is basic to "citizenship" for Aboriginal peoples in Canada.

Historically, Aboriginal peoples in Canada were excluded from decision making. They were not invited to the Confederation conferences. After Confederation (1867), they were moved onto reserves as European immigrants claimed western lands to farm. The federal government created a Department of Indian Affairs to "oversee" the Aboriginal peoples.

The *Indian Act*, first enacted in 1876, banned ancient cultural practices, such as the western potlatch. This ceremony involved the exchange of gifts and was a kind of economic system. The Blackfoot sun dance and the Cree and Saulteaux thirst dance—both ritual dances—were also banned. A 1927 amendment to the *Indian Act* also stripped Aboriginal peoples of the right to form political organizations.

Assimilation and Residential Schools

At the end of the 19th century, Aboriginal children were taken from their homes and sent to **residential schools**. Federal authorities wanted them **assimilated** (absorbed) into mainstream Canadian culture. Approximately 100,000 children attended residential schools over the decades.

The Catholic, Anglican, United, and Presbyterian churches ran the residential schools for the federal government. Aboriginal children were not allowed to speak their own language, even though most could not speak English or French. Children were cut off from their families—and from their culture, history, and identity. Government planned for Aboriginal cultures to simply vanish within two generations. This was "progress."

Years later, survivors of residential schools told stories of terrible abuse and neglect. Life in residential schools was harsh. Students worked in kitchens, barns, or fields, without pay. At Duck Lake School in Saskatchewan, for example, half the students died from disease or malnutrition.

In 1988, after years of demands from survivors, the Canadian government created the Aboriginal Healing Foundation. In the following years, many more survivors shared their stories. They and their communities demanded compensation for their pain and suffering and loss of culture. Nothing, of course, could compensate them for separation from family and community.

In 2006, the federal government agreed to compensate all former students of residential schools. The deal committed a total of $1.9 billion. This includes cash settlements for survivors and the establishment of an education fund.

> ▶ **DID YOU KNOW** ◀
> The trauma caused by the residential school system is passed on from generation to generation. The cycle is called the "intergenerational" impact of abuse. You can read about some of these intergenerational effects at the Web site below.

> **THE WEB** ▶▶▶
> Take an interactive tour of the residential schools and their legacy at www.emp.ca/ccw

Organizing Politically

Even though it was illegal, Aboriginal peoples organized politically. By the 1960s, resistance to government policies was growing. Aboriginal **activists** spoke out against assimilation. They opposed the government's

> **DID YOU KNOW**
>
> Land claims are based on continuing Aboriginal rights and title to land and natural resources that have not been dealt with by treaty or other legal means. They are settled through negotiation with federal and provincial or territorial governments. Compensation can include land, protection of language and culture, cash, and local self-government.

1968 "White Paper," which outlined plans to eliminate the special legal status of Aboriginal peoples in Canada. First Nations increased pressure on the federal government to settle disputed land claims based on their traditional occupancy and treaty rights.

In 1969, Harold Cardinal (1945–2005), a Cree writer and lawyer in Alberta, published *The Unjust Society*. It became a bestseller across Canada. In it, Cardinal attacked Prime Minister Pierre Trudeau's "White Paper" and vision of a "Just Society." Cardinal accused Trudeau of simply giving assimilation a nicer name. A "buckskin curtain," said Cardinal, separated Aboriginal peoples and mainstream society in Canada. Cardinal demanded change. He and other Aboriginal leaders did something about it.

Cardinal helped create the National Indian Brotherhood in 1968. Its goal was to give Aboriginal peoples a voice in Ottawa. The group's successor was the Assembly of First Nations. Today, the AFN brings together representatives from over 600 bands across Canada. One of the AFN's top priorities is to improve the state of First Nations education.

In December 1994, Manitoba Grand Chief Phil Fontaine and Indian Affairs Minister Ron Irwin agreed to reduce the influence of the Department of Indian Affairs in Manitoba. This agreement marked the start of developing and recognizing self-determination for Manitoba's 62 Indian bands.

In 1981, the northern Manitoba First Nations also established the Manitoba Keewatinook Ininew Okimowin (MKO). The organization represents 53,000 citizens and 30 northern Manitoba First Nations. The group addresses northern issues and is working toward a self-governing legislature for Manitoba's northern territory.

Continuing to Meet the Challenges

As you read in Chapter 1, Aboriginal peoples have not shared equally in Canada's general prosperity. This injustice is considered by many to be a result of mistreatment.

The United Nations Human Development Index (HDI) measures economic status, literacy, education, life expectancy, and other indicators of human well-being yearly. Since 1990, Canada has ranked first in the world many times. Compared with mainstream Canada, Aboriginal people live shorter lives, receive less education, make less money, more often live in inadequate housing conditions, experience more health problems, and face much higher rates of imprisonment.

FIGURE 2.1 Nunavut resident Jordin Tootoo (left) was the first Inuit athlete to play in the National Hockey League. The Nunavut territorial government featured Tootoo and four local teenagers on an inspirational poster encouraging young people to stay in school and set goals.

SOURCES

A Declaration of First Nations

This declaration is posted on the Assembly of First Nations' Web site.

We the Original Peoples of this land know the Creator put us here.

The Creator gave us laws that govern all our relationships to live in harmony with nature and mankind.

The Laws of the Creator defined our rights and responsibilities.

The Creator gave us our spiritual beliefs, our languages, our culture, and a place on Mother Earth which provided us with all our needs.

We have maintained our Freedom, our Languages, and our Traditions from time immemorial.

We continue to exercise the rights and fulfill the responsibilities and obligations given to us by the Creator for the land upon which we were placed.

The Creator has given us the right to govern ourselves and the right to self-determination.

The rights and responsibilities given to us by the Creator cannot be altered or taken away by any other Nation.

Source: www.afn.ca/article.asp?id=52

CivicStar

DR. LILLIAN EVA DYCK

She was born Lillian Quan in 1945. Her father was Chinese and her mother was Cree. As children living in small towns in Saskatchewan and Alberta, she and her brother struggled for acceptance. In grade 9 she was placed in a class for slow learners, despite her high intelligence.

Later, Lillian considered becoming a high school science teacher. But she withdrew from teacher's college. She didn't enjoy speaking in public. Then she realized she wanted to pursue a career as a scientist.

Inspired by her mother, Eva, Lillian obtained a master's degree and a doctorate from the University of Saskatchewan. She overcame her fear of public speaking through constant practice. After becoming a professor of biological psychiatry, she went on to research treatments for conditions such as Parkinson's disease, schizophrenia, and Alzheimer's.

Until she received her doctorate in 1981, Lillian kept her Aboriginal origins hidden. "The 1950s were a time when there was actually a hierarchy of racism, when being Chinese was difficult enough," she has said.

Today, Lillian Dyck exults in her heritage: "I am my mother's daughter. Like her, I am part of the circle of women warriors, each of us in our own way fighting for a better world for our children and our children's children." In 2005, she was appointed to the Canadian Senate.

Your Play

1. Describe three obstacles in life that Lillian Dyck had to overcome.
2. Have you ever hidden a part of who you are? Do you think such secrecy is justifiable? Why or why not?
3. What does "hierarchy of racism" mean to you?
4. Use the Internet or library to find **primary sources** (first-hand documents, such as speeches, diaries, interviews, government legislation, broadcasts, etc.) from the 1950s that reveal what we now consider racist attitudes. Create a presentation to show how and why these attitudes are no longer tolerated.

PAUSE, REFLECT, APPLY

1. What does the idea of "citizenship" include for the Aboriginal peoples in Canada?
2. How are the rights of Aboriginal peoples guaranteed?
3. a) What impact did residential schools have on Aboriginal cultures?
   b) What impact do you think these schools have had on the communities in which they were based?
4. a) What has the Assembly of First Nations identified as a top priority for Canada and the Aboriginal peoples?
   b) Why is this issue a priority?
5. Describe the rights and responsibilities of Aboriginal citizens in Canada and the world as expressed in the Declaration of First Nations (see Sources, page 31).

Two European Founders

The first Europeans to settle in Canada were the French, followed by the British. The two nations have contributed a great deal to Canada's collective past, especially to its bilingual identity.

CITIZENSHIP AND FRENCH CANADIANS

The first French settlement dates back to 1534, when explorer Jacques Cartier claimed areas around the St. Lawrence River. France established settlements in Acadia (now Nova Scotia and New Brunswick) and Quebec. In Quebec, individuals such as Jean Talon, a chief administrator, and Marguerite d'Youville, the founder of the Sisters of Charity, made important contributions to society.

The Origins of French-Language Rights

In 1759, New France was defeated by the British in the Battle of the Plains of Abraham. To maintain the loyalty of French-speaking colonists, the British granted Quebec language, religious, and legal rights.

When Canada was created in 1867, the *British North America Act*, its constitution, recognized French-language rights in Parliament and in Quebec. In the 20th century, recognition of Canada's French–English linguistic heritage was extended with the issuing of

- dual-language postage stamps (1927)
- dual-language currency (1937)
- simultaneous translations of House of Commons debates (1959)
- dual-language labels for consumer products (1974).

Canada adopted federal bilingual policies under Prime Minister Lester Pearson in 1963. At the same time, several groups in Quebec were working for separation from Canada. Two roads to independence emerged. The Front de Libération du Québec (FLQ) advocated terrorism. The Parti Québécois (PQ) used legal democratic methods.

In 1969, Prime Minister Pierre Trudeau oversaw passage of the **Official Languages Act**. This Act proclaimed French and English Canada's two official languages—and made the federal public service and judicial systems bilingual.

> **KEY QUESTION**
> Why is Canada a bilingual nation?

> **DID YOU KNOW**
> In 1666, Jean Talon conducted the first census (official analysis of the population) in North America. He found 3,215 citizens in New France.

In the same year, New Brunswick became Canada's only officially bilingual province. One out of three New Brunswickers is francophone.

In 1982, the *Canadian Charter of Rights and Freedoms* further guaranteed pre-existing language and education rights for official-language minorities. Section 23 of the Charter guarantees that parents for whom English or French is an original language, or the language they were schooled in, have the right to have their children educated in that language even if they are a minority within their community.

Bilingualism and the Founding of Manitoba

When Manitoba joined Canada in 1870, 50 percent of its population was francophone. Most of the people in the Red River Settlement (located near present-day Winnipeg) were francophone Métis.

The Métis considered the Red River community to be their homeland. Many saw the Canadian government's plans for their homeland as a grave threat to their way of life. Under the leadership of a determined young Métis lawyer named Louis Riel, the Métis demanded that their rights be recognized. Because of this, Manitoba joined Confederation with guarantees in place for francophones and for the Métis:

- guaranteed language rights for speakers of French and English (official bilingualism)
- two systems of education—Protestant and English-speaking, and Catholic and French-speaking
- Métis land rights.

FIGURE 2.2 Louis Riel fought for provincial status and the rights of the people who lived at Red River. In *Louis Riel: A Comic-Strip Biography*, by Chester Brown, Riel tells a representative of the new Ottawa-appointed lieutenant governor that the Métis are willing to join Canada on their own terms. What does the second panel of the cartoon say about Riel's vision of Canada?

FIGURE 2.3 The federal government operates Web sites for francophone communities across Canada. These provide information in French and English about community histories, population statistics, and cultural events.

> **THE WEB** ▶▶▶
> Visit the official Web site of Manitoba's francophones at www.emp/ccw and examine the map of francophone Manitoba. What do you notice about many of the place names?

These protections, however, were not upheld. Twenty years after the *Manitoba Act*, which created the province of Manitoba, English-speaking immigration—mostly from Ontario—had reduced the francophone population in the province to only 10 percent. Official bilingualism was abolished. French Catholics lost the right to run their own French-speaking schools (see the Face Off feature in Chapter 3, page 65).

Today, Manitoba's 50,000 francophones account for 5 percent of the population. In the 1990s, the Manitoba government handed back the management of francophone schools to francophones. It was one way to "enhance the vitality of Canada's official-languages communities." Francophones also have the right to communicate with the federal government, and to access other government services, in French. However, Manitoba is not officially bilingual.

> ▶ **DID YOU KNOW** ◀
> In only three provinces—Manitoba, New Brunswick, and Quebec—new laws must be written in both English and French. Manitoba also places bilingual road signs along certain routes.

LITERACY COACH

Prior Knowledge/New Knowledge

You may have picked up some knowledge of Quebec language laws in the media or by hearing talk about bilingualism. Before reading the paragraphs on the next page, make a table with two columns. Label the left column Prior Knowledge and the right column New Knowledge. In the left-hand column, write down what you currently know about language laws in Quebec (or the use of French in Quebec). In the right-hand column, summarize the new information you learned after reading these paragraphs.

Bill 101 and Quebec Language Rights

The province of Quebec took a different approach to language. In 1976, the Parti Québécois, led by founder René Lévesque, came to power. In order to make Quebec "as French as Ontario is English," the PQ passed Bill 101.

Bill 101 made French the official language of Quebec. The use of any other language in the workplace and on outdoor signs was strictly regulated. Today, only children with at least one parent educated in an English school in Quebec can be educated in English. Immigrants must send their children to French-language schools. Although this law may sound rigid, its intention is to protect a minority language—French—in an English-dominated country.

French Canadian Citizens

French Canadians have been an integral part of Canadian culture and society. They have contributed to politics, arts, education, sports, entertainment, and philosophy. Canada's first French-speaking prime minister was Wilfrid Laurier. He was succeeded by leaders such as Louis St. Laurent, Pierre Trudeau (architect of the *Canadian Charter of Rights and Freedoms*), and Jean Chrétien. French Canadian artists—painters, novelists, filmmakers, hockey legends, and performers—have thrilled millions of fans around the world and created interest in Canada.

CITIZENSHIP AND BRITISH CANADIANS

The **United Empire Loyalists** were the first large-scale wave of English-speaking immigrants to arrive in Canada. They came to Nova Scotia and Upper Canada (Ontario) in the years following the American Revolution (1775–1783). The Loyalists, 40,000 strong, voted with their feet. That means they rejected revolution and **republicanism** (government without a king or queen). In doing so, they became refugees. These men and women formed the backbone of early English Canada. They believed in "peace, order, and good government." This phrase describes Canada's governing philosophy in the 1867 constitution.

Canada's Parliament, judicial system, and many street and place names have English roots. The May 24 holiday, for example, celebrates Queen Victoria's birthday. The English monarchy has been a part of

FIGURE 2.4 Poking fun at Canada and its neighbour to the south is also part of the Canadian identity. Television programs like the *Royal Canadian Air Farce*, *This Hour Has 22 Minutes*, and the *Rick Mercer Report* often lampoon (make fun of) the differences—and similarities—between Canadians and Americans. Here, Rick Mercer (right) enjoys a bike ride with federal NDP leader Jack Layton.

Canada since Confederation. It still adorns Canadian money and is commemorated in the royal anthem, "God Save the Queen."

Canadians are also familiar with the Royal Canadian Mail, the Royal Canadian Mounted Police, the Royal Canadian Air Force, the Royal Canadian Mint, and royal commissions. Some movement away from the British influence has occurred. The Canadian flag was adopted in 1965, Canada Post was created in 1969, and "O Canada" was proclaimed the national anthem in 1980.

Scottish Canadians

Tens of thousands of Scots (Scotland is now part of the United Kingdom) immigrated to Canada to escape hardship and unemployment at home. Some took their place in Canadian history. Rebel leader William Lyon Mackenzie, clergyman John Strachan, inventors Sandford Fleming and Alexander Graham Bell, and prime ministers John A. Macdonald and Alexander Mackenzie were all Scottish immigrants.

In 1812, Thomas Douglas, Earl of Selkirk, brought some of the earliest Scottish settlers to Manitoba. The settlement evolved into the present-day cities of Winnipeg and Selkirk, just north of Winnipeg. The influence of Scots culture is still evident in Winnipeg. Many streets are named after Scots Canadian families, for example, Bannatyne, McDermot, and McPhillips. Every year, Selkirk hosts a Highland Gathering, one of the largest Scottish festivals in the world.

▶ **DID YOU KNOW** ◀
Some Métis were of Scottish descent. The Scottish–Cree language, Bungi, combines Cree and a Scottish dialect from the Orkneys (70 islands about 10 km north of Scotland's mainland).

▶ **DID YOU KNOW** ◀
Scottish immigrant Sandford Fleming (1827–1915), a railway engineer, designed the first Canadian postage stamp, issued in 1851. He also invented the worldwide system of 24 standard time zones.

> **DID YOU KNOW**
> At the quarantine station of Grosse-Île in the St. Lawrence River, near Quebec City, 5,294 Irish immigrants died of typhus or dysentery. They were buried in mass graves in the summer of 1847.

Irish Canadians

Traditionally, the people of Ireland depended on the potato as their staple food. In the 1840s, faced with mass starvation when the potato crops failed, hundreds of thousands sailed for Canada. The crowded ships were called "coffin ships" because many immigrants died on board or shortly after arriving in Canada. Most of those who survived the Atlantic crossing settled in Ontario and Quebec.

PAUSE, REFLECT, APPLY

1. Create a timeline to outline the development of French language rights in Canada.
2. By the 1970s, Quebec's birth rate, traditionally the highest in Canada, had become the lowest. Using this information, explain what you think are some of the reasons for the passage of Bill 101 by the Parti Québécois government in 1977.
3. List six examples of the English presence in Canada.
4. Create a list of push–pull factors for these immigrant groups: (a) United Empire Loyalists, (b) Scottish, and (c) Irish.
5. Scottish Canadian writer Hugh MacLennan (1907–1990) observed that four immigrant groups that helped found Canada—the French, Loyalists, Scots, and Irish—had all suffered defeats at home or in their adopted land. He wrote that this tradition of being on the "losing side" has had a psychological impact on the Canadian character, or identity: Canadians try not to offend, they are humble, they seek approval, they do what they are told. Do Canadians act like "losers"? Support or reject MacLennan's argument by using evidence from your experiences, this text, or both.

> **KEY QUESTION**
> Why has the concept of Canadian citizenship changed?

Canadian Immigration

In 2005, immigration accounted for more than 50 percent of Canada's population growth. Canada's immigrants continue to come mainly from Asia and the Middle East. One in six Canadians is a member of a visible minority.

HISTORY OF IMMIGRATION

Immigration has played a huge role in Canada's history. At the beginning of the 20th century, hundreds of thousands of Ukrainians, Scandinavians, Americans, and Eastern Europeans came to claim and work the lands of the vast prairies. Only white Europeans were recruited by the

FIGURE 2.5 *The Iron Road* is a modern Canadian opera that memorializes the work of thousands of Chinese Canadians on the Canadian Pacific Railway.

▶ **DID YOU KNOW** ◀
In June 2006, Prime Minister Stephen Harper apologized to Chinese Canadians for the head tax and expressed his "deepest sorrow" for the exclusion of Chinese immigrants from 1923 until 1947.

▶ **DID YOU KNOW** ◀
Three hundred seventy-five Sikh emigrants on board the *Komagata Maru* in May 1914 were barred from entry into Canada at Vancouver despite the fact that they all had valid British passports. The ship was sent back to India.

▶ **DID YOU KNOW** ◀
In 1939, 907 Jewish passengers who fled Nazi persecution on the ocean liner *St. Louis* were not granted promised entry at their destination of Cuba. Canada and the United States did not respond to their appeals for help. About half of the passengers died in the **Holocaust** after the ship returned to Europe.

government and considered desirable. Non-whites were often turned away, unless cheap labour was needed.

Fifteen thousand Chinese men came to Canada in the 1880s to build the Canadian Pacific Railway. All were denied citizenship. Other immigrants from Asia had a difficult time entering the country. Regulations were devised to keep numbers low—even if they were British subjects living in Commonwealth countries:

- Only 400 Japanese immigrants a year were allowed until 1920.
- Chinese immigrants faced a "head tax" of $50 a person in 1885, an amount that was increased to $500 per person by 1904.
- Would-be immigrants from India were required to arrive on ships that followed a "continuous" or direct route to Canada. No shipping companies followed such a route.
- Thousands of free black people were among Loyalists who settled in Nova Scotia. Before the American Civil War (1861–1865), runaway slaves found refuge in Upper Canada. However, during massive waves of immigration in the first half of the 20th century, people of colour were deliberately excluded. So too were many Jewish people, including those fleeing persecution in Europe in the 1930s.

> **DID YOU KNOW**
>
> The father of hockey star Paul Kariya was born in a British Columbia internment camp for Japanese Canadians during World War II.

- Full citizenship was not granted to certain ethnic groups. In British Columbia, where most Asian Canadians lived, immigrants from China, Japan, and India did not win the right to vote until the late 1940s. Once groups were excluded from the voting list, they could also be excluded from certain professions, since the right to vote was a precondition for employment in areas such as law, medicine, and pharmacy.
- Twenty-three thousand Japanese Canadians were placed in internment camps in the interior of British Columbia during World War II. They were legally defined as "enemy aliens." After the war, almost 4,000 were forcibly repatriated to Japan. Of these, more than half were Canadian born and two-thirds were Canadian citizens.

THE CREATION OF CANADIAN CITIZENSHIP

In 1947, the Liberal government of Prime Minister Mackenzie King created the legal concept of Canadian citizenship. Until then, Canadians had been defined as British subjects living in Canada or as immigrants. Some immigrants could now qualify for full citizenship after they had resided in the country for five years.

SOURCES

Speech by Prime Minister W.L.M. King

The policy of the government is to foster the growth of the population of Canada by the encouragement of immigration. ...

[A]s respects immigration from Europe, the emphasis for the present should be on the admission of the relatives of persons who are already in Canada, and on assisting in the resettlement of displaced persons and refugees. ...

Selection officers will ... consider applicants for entry into Canada, examine them on a basis of suitability and physical fitness, and make arrangements for their orderly movement and placement. ... In taking these steps, the government is seeking to ensure that the displaced persons admitted to Canada are of a type likely to make good citizens. ...

[M]uch has been said about discrimination. I wish to make it quite clear that Canada is perfectly within her rights in selecting the persons whom we regard as desirable future citizens. It is not a "fundamental human right" of any alien to enter Canada. It is a privilege. It is a matter of domestic policy. ...

There will, I am sure, be general agreement with the view that the people of Canada do not wish, as a result of mass immigration, to make a fundamental alteration in the character of our population. Large-scale immigration from the orient [Asia] would change the fundamental composition of the Canadian population. ...

Source: House of Commons Debates, May 1, 1947, pp. 2644–2646; www.abheritage.ca/albertans/speeches/king_1.html

A COLOUR-BLIND POLICY

By the 1960s, some of the old prejudices that had shaped Canadian immigration and citizenship were fading. In 1962, Conservative Minister of Immigration Ellen Fairclough—Canada's first female Cabinet minister—eliminated most of the entrance regulations that discriminated on the basis of race and country of origin. Most immigrants to Canada, however, continued to be Europeans (see Figure 2.6).

In 1976, Canada created different admission categories. It streamlined the process for sponsoring (supporting) family members and created a **points system** for independent applicants. The system awarded applicants points for knowing English or French and for level of education and job skills. The separate category for refugees was also created.

Removing racial regulations and introducing the new points system led for the first time to major immigration from Africa, Asia, the Caribbean, and Latin America. Newcomers settled mainly in Vancouver, Toronto, and Montreal, making those cities vibrant centres of **multiculturalism**. By the end of the 20th century, Canada had also become a major refugee-receiving country, admitting thousands of refugees from Bosnia, Kosovo, Rwanda, and other places.

> ▶ **DID YOU KNOW** ◀
> Canada accepted 60,000 Vietnamese refugees in 1979–1980, in the aftermath of the Vietnam War (1965–1973). It also accepted some 30,000 young Americans who fled to Canada to avoid being forced to fight during the war, which Canada did not support.

	Before 1961 Number	Before 1961 %	1961–1970 Number	1961–1970 %	1971–1980 Number	1971–1980 %	1981–1990 Number	1981–1990 %	1991–2001* Number	1991–2001* %
Total immigrants	894,465	100.0	745,565	100.0	936,275	100.0	1,041,495	100.0	1,830,680	100.0
United States	34,805	3.9	46,880	6.3	62,835	6.7	41,965	4.0	51,440	2.8
Europe	809,330	90.5	515,675	69.2	338,520	36.2	266,185	25.6	357,845	19.5
Asia	28,850	3.2	90,420	12.1	311,960	33.3	491,720	47.2	1,066,230	58.2
Africa	4,635	0.5	23,830	3.2	54,655	5.8	59,715	5.7	139,770	7.6
Caribbean, Central and South America	12,895	1.4	59,895	8.0	154,395	16.5	171,495	16.5	200,010	10.9
Oceania and other countries	3,950	0.4	8,865	1.2	13,910	1.5	10,415	1.0	15,385	0.8

* Includes data up to May 15, 2001

FIGURE 2.6 Place of birth by period of immigration, Canada, 2001. *Source: Statistics Canada, www12.statcan.ca/english/census01/products/analytic/companion/etoimm/tables/canada/period.cfm*

FACE OFF: Immigration: Open Borders or Lockdown?

Should Canada welcome as many immigrants as it does—about 200,000 annually? Many people say yes. Immigrants are eager to contribute to the well-being of the country. They often bring with them valuable skills in medicine, law, research, engineering, and the humanities. They enrich Canada culturally and economically.

Those who support immigration also applaud Canada's acceptance of refugees. Canada abides by the 1951 United Nations *Convention Relating to the Status of Refugees*. This document states that nations have a duty to accept those from the world community who have a "well-founded fear of being persecuted for reasons of race, religion, nationality, membership of a particular social group or political opinion" (article 1A).

In 2005, immigration accounted for more than 50 percent of Canada's population growth. Because of a declining birth rate in many parts of Canada, immigrants are seen by many as contributing vitally to the country's labour, industrial, and consumer markets.

> Canada still needs the skills, talents and enthusiasm of newcomers to build our country, together with those who have come before them.
>
> — Government of Canada, "A Newcomer's Introduction to Canada," www.cic.gc.ca/english/newcomer/guide/section-07.html#6

Others argue that Canada should not accept so many immigrants when some Canadians are still without jobs. They say that even those immigrants with a professional background still have to retrain in Canada, a costly proposition. It is also expensive for Canada to fund all the support services associated with immigration, such as welfare payments and EAL (English as an additional language) classes.

> An immigration tsunami is heading for North America.
>
> — Paul Fromm, white supremacist, speaking in Texas, USA, March 12, 2005

Another argument against widespread immigration is that it might also result in problems such as terrorism. This argument says that countries have a right and a duty to control their borders, and that dangerous people should be kept out. If that means accepting fewer immigrants, that is a reasonable compromise.

What Do You Think?

1. In your opinion, is immigration good or bad for Canada? Explain why.
2. How would you go about evaluating the argument that the threat of terrorism means that fewer immigrants should be accepted into Canada? What information would you need?
3. Are there any measures that the Canadian government could undertake to increase the country's birth rate? Propose some, and explain how they might work.

▶ DID YOU KNOW ◀

In 2004, Canadians adopted 1,955 children from abroad. Adoptions from China accounted for 51 percent of all international adoptions.

FIGURE 2.7 Students at a Winnipeg elementary school laugh as a Lion Dancer performs on Chinese New Year, February 8, 2005. The traditional Lion Dance is said to bring good fortune in the New Year.

PAUSE, REFLECT, APPLY

1. Explain three ways in which the entry of certain groups of immigrants to Canada was limited in the late 19th and early 20th centuries. How might these limitations have reflected the values of the times?
2. a) Summarize Prime Minister King's view of Canadian citizenship in the Sources feature on page 40.
   b) Do you agree or disagree with this view?
   c) In what ways is the policy a political mixture of generosity and racism?
3. Examine Figure 2.6 on page 41. What area of the world provided the largest number of immigrants to Canada in the period before 1961? In the period 1991–2001? What is the percentage in each case?
4. Describe Canada's current immigration policy.
5. Why has the concept of Canadian citizenship undergone changes since the beginning of the 20th century?

Citizenship and Multiculturalism

> **KEY QUESTION**
> What are the benefits of multiculturalism?

In 1971, Canada became the first country in the world to adopt multiculturalism as an official policy. Multiculturalism ensures that all citizens can keep their identity, heritage, and language once in Canada. Immigrants can take pride in their ancestry and also feel a sense of belonging.

Through multiculturalism, programs and services are provided to many different groups that preserve heritage, and individuals are helped to participate fully in Canadian society.

CELEBRATING DIVERSITY

As citizens of the world, Canadians celebrate diversity in a number of ways. Some of these are described below.

Human Rights Day

On December 10, 1948, the United Nations General Assembly adopted the *Universal Declaration of Human Rights*. This document has become a standard for defending and promoting human rights. Every year on December 10, people around the world are reminded that "all human beings are born free and equal in dignity and rights" (article 1 of the Declaration). By marking this day, Canadians are also reminded of their guaranteed rights and freedoms, and of the way of life that Canadians value.

National Aboriginal Day

The Canadian government has declared June 21 National Aboriginal Day. This day celebrates the cultures and contributions of First Nations, Inuit, and Métis in Canada. Celebrating National Aboriginal Day is a way to learn more about the heritage of the Aboriginal peoples, and a way to foster understanding and acceptance of different perspectives. National Aboriginal Day was first proclaimed in 1996. (See the CivicStar feature in Chapter 5, pages 109–110.)

Black History Month

In 1995, Canada's Parliament recognized February as Black History Month. Today, approximately 2 percent of Canada's population identify themselves as black Canadians. Their contributions, past and present, are recognized and celebrated.

American immigrant and anti-slavery advocate Mary Ann Shadd was Canada's first female newspaper editor in the mid-1800s.

Baseball pitcher Ferguson Jenkins—the only Canadian in the Cooperstown, New York, Baseball Hall of Fame—is the descendant of

FIGURE 2.8 Canadian gold medal wrestler Daniel Igali hits the road to build a school in his home village in Nigeria, accompanied by two Canadian teenagers.

pre–Civil War refugees who settled in the same Chatham, Ontario, area where Mary Ann Shadd lived.

At the 1996 Olympics, Donovan Bailey became "the world's fastest man" when he won the gold medal in the 100 metre race. Bailey, who came to Canada at age 13 from Jamaica, took up business and charity work at the end of his running career. He has been a spokesperson for Big Brothers Big Sisters of Canada.

In 2005, award-winning journalist and broadcaster Michaëlle Jean became Canada's 27th governor general, the first black person to hold this title. Jean fled Haiti with her family in 1968, when that country was ruled by a dictator. She grew up in the province of Quebec.

Athletes Jarome Iginla, a hockey star, and Olympic wrestling champion Daniel Igali are proud of their Nigerian heritage. After his Olympic victory, Igali went on to raise $200,000 to replace the one-room school in his impoverished Nigerian hometown of Eniwari. The Canadian International Development Agency (CIDA) matched the funds. In 2005, Igali entered provincial politics as a Liberal candidate.

Asian Heritage Month

To acknowledge the rich history of Asian Canadians and their contributions to Canada, Parliament in 2001 designated May as Asian Heritage Month. Some famous Asian Canadians:

- Adrienne Poy was born to Chinese parents in Hong Kong in 1939. At age three, she and her family came to Canada as refugees. In 1999, after a long career as one of Canada's first female television broadcasters, Adrienne Poy Clarkson was appointed governor general of Canada. She was only the second woman and the first person of colour to hold the position.
- Ujjal Dosanjh, who arrived in Canada at age 21, was born in a small village in Punjab, India. In Canada, Dosanjh established himself as a civil rights activist and lawyer. He became Canada's first Indo-Canadian provincial premier (British Columbia, 2000) and first Indo-Canadian federal cabinet minister (minister of health, 2004).
- Canadian actor Sandra Oh, who appeared in the 2004 Academy Award–nominated film *Sideways*, was born in Ottawa to Korean immigrants. She also appears in the television series *Grey's Anatomy*.
- The grandparents of David Suzuki and Vicky Sunohara came from different parts of Japan to Canada early in the 20th century. Today, broadcaster and author Dr. David Suzuki is recognized as a world leader in the study of sustainable ecology; Vicky Sunohara has been a star player on Canada's women's hockey team.

FIGURE 2.9 Award-winning Canadian film and television star Sandra Oh

DISCUSSION POINT

According to the Ethnic Diversity Survey, released in September 2003, almost half of black Canadians surveyed said they had experienced some form of discrimination or unfair treatment in the past five years. Why might a country that has tried to eliminate racism still experience it to this degree?

International Day for the Elimination of Racial Discrimination

The International Day for the Elimination of Racial Discrimination is observed on March 21. On that day, in 1960, South African police killed 69 men and women who were demonstrating against apartheid, the government policy that enforced discrimination against non-whites. Proclaiming the day in 1966, the United Nations called on the international community to increase its efforts to eliminate all forms of racial discrimination. Canada was one of the first countries to support the proclamation.

CANADIANS REACHING OUT

Canadians have a tradition of reaching out to the global community that dates back more than 60 years. In Chapter 1, you learned about Canada's role in founding the UN as World War II was ending. In 1952, future Canadian Prime Minister Lester Pearson became president of the UN

General Assembly. Four years later, as Canada's minister of external affairs, Pearson proposed the creation of the UN's first peacekeeping force. Since that time, many Canadians have reached out to the global community by working for human rights and peace, and by assisting with aid and development.

Tommy Douglas

Tommy Douglas worked tirelessly to introduce universal health care to Saskatchewan. As premier of that province from 1944 to 1961, Douglas faced down powerful doctors' organizations. He was condemned as a dangerous "communist" and "socialist," both in Canada and in the United States. Despite this, Douglas achieved his goal, and not only in Saskatchewan. In the 1960s, Prime Minister Lester Pearson adapted Douglas's health care plan for all of Canada. Today, it has become part of the Canadian identity. (See also the CivicStar feature on Tommy Douglas in Chapter 12, page 251.)

Rosalie Silberman Abella

Rosalie Silberman's parents survived four years in Nazi concentration camps, but they lost their two-year-old son and most of their relatives in the Holocaust. Rosalie was born after World War II, in a displaced persons' camp in Germany. She arrived in Canada in 1950, at age four, as a Jewish refugee. As a lawyer, she became a leading spokesperson for human rights in Canada and around the world. In 1984, she created the term "employment equity" as the commisioner for the federal Royal Commission on Equality in Employment. In 2004, Rosalie Silberman Abella became the first Jewish woman ever to be appointed a justice of the Supreme Court of Canada.

Roméo Dallaire

Retired General Roméo Dallaire was born in Holland and arrived in Montreal at age one. He later joined the Canadian military and was active in many peacekeeping missions. Dallaire accepted the leadership of the United Nations mission in Rwanda in 1994. This mission was a turning point for him. To stop the ongoing **genocide**, combat soldiers as well as peacekeepers were needed, yet the UN would not supply them. Following this gruelling mission, Dallaire became a strong international spokesperson for equal treatment of all peoples.

► **DID YOU KNOW** ◄
You, too, can reach out by taking part in volunteer work that relates to the local or global community. Every act of positive involvement makes you a better citizen of Canada and the world. Consider the ideas presented in this chapter's Study Hall under the heading Be Active.

PAUSE, REFLECT, APPLY

1. Describe the accomplishments of one representative for each of the following groups: black Canadians, Japanese Canadians, Korean Canadians, Chinese Canadians, Indo-Canadians, and Jewish Canadians.
2. a) In what sense does Canada contain "the globe within its borders"?
   b) How does Canada reach out to the globe?

REPLAY

In this chapter, you have explored these concepts:

1. Canada has three founding peoples—the Aboriginal peoples, the French, and the British.
2. The concept of Canadian citizenship has evolved since Confederation.
3. In the past, full citizenship was denied to some groups because of ethnic origin or religion.
4. Canada's pluralistic identity has been shaped through extensive immigration during the 20th century.
5. Multicultural policies ensure that all citizens can keep their identity, heritage, and language once in Canada.
6. Canadian citizenship involves certain fixed rights, but may be viewed differently by different groups of people.

SKILLS TOOLKIT: How to Form Inquiry Questions

What are you curious about? What do you ask questions about? From early childhood, this is how we learn naturally. Listen to a two-year-old's endless questions. The child asks one question and gets an answer, which leads to another question, and another. This is the inquiry method at work, and it is fuelled by questions.

An inquiry question must meet several criteria. In order to be effective, it should

- matter to you
- be specific and focused
- be answerable
- be reasonable
- lead to other questions.

Inquiring can have monumental results. In the 16th century, the Polish monk Nicolaus Copernicus questioned the relationship among the Earth, the other planets in our solar system, and the sun. Eventually, his investigations proved that the Earth and planets revolve around the sun. Because powerful, educated people believed the universe revolved around the Earth, Copernicus's inquiry got him into trouble. It also opened up the science of cosmology (the study of the universe).

Some successful businesses also use an inquiry method. Using company resources, employee groups formulate inquiry questions, for example, "Are we operating as efficiently as possible?" The employees follow a process like that in Figure 2.10. They gather information, share ideas, and ask new questions that help refine the original question. "How can we serve our customers more efficiently?" Employees in these kinds of businesses go beyond following orders. They define and solve problems, work as a group, and influence the company. They become agents of change.

You can use inquiry questions to achieve similar results. In this course, for example, you are examining ways to be an active citizen—someone who works to bring about positive change in the community. To do that, you need to be able to identify and explore issues that concern you, and ask questions about them. The inquiry method is ideal for this purpose—and it may also lead you to act in ways that benefit your community.

Skill Practice

1. a) Develop inquiry questions on the following topics: (i) your school's rules, (ii) school video surveillance, (iii) your student council.
   b) Compare your questions with those of other students. Does short discussion lead you to change your questions?
   c) Decide what information sources to use to answer one of your questions.
2. Use the inquiry method to determine three issues that matter to you. Record your questions and responses and return to them during your study of *Canada in the Contemporary World*.

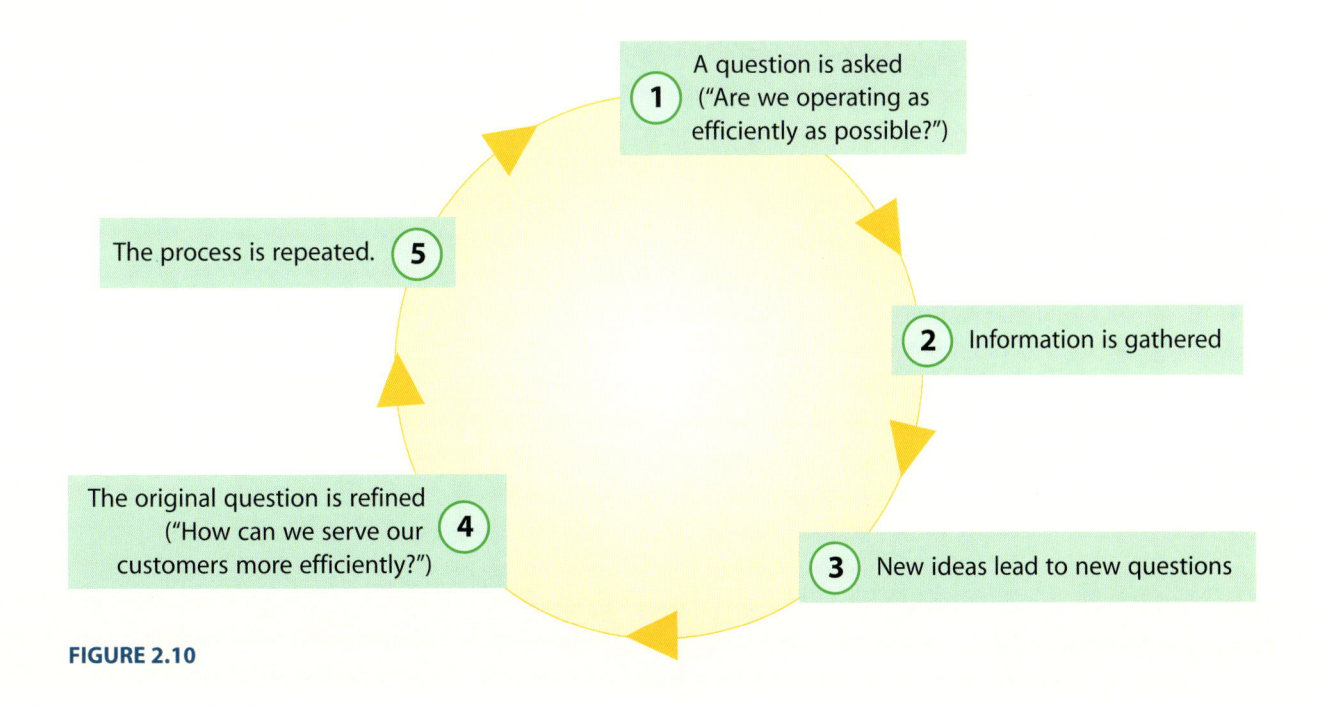

FIGURE 2.10

1. A question is asked ("Are we operating as efficiently as possible?")
2. Information is gathered
3. New ideas lead to new questions
4. The original question is refined ("How can we serve our customers more efficiently?")
5. The process is repeated.

STUDY HALL

Be Informed

1. a) Find out more about Canadian citizenship by inviting one or more of the following people to your class to speak about their views of citizenship:
   - representative of First Nations
   - World War II veteran
   - survivor of the Holocaust
   - representative from Greenpeace
   - immigration lawyer assisting refugees.

   b) Once a selection has been finalized, develop questions to ask your visitor.

2. Read about the United Nations *Convention on the Rights of the Child* (1989) at www.emp.ca/ccw. In a written report, argue whether or not Canada is meeting its obligations toward its non-adult citizens.

3. To review your knowledge of Canadian citizenship, take the test found at www.emp.ca/ccw.

Be Purposeful

4. In 2001, the Aboriginal Justice Implementation Commission recommended an affirmative action program that would allow Aboriginal people to be employed in the justice system at a rate equal to their representation in the Manitoba population (12 percent).

   a) Present reasons for this type of program.

   b) Explain how such a program might work.

   c) Find out what other groups in Canada have been targeted for affirmative action in the past. How did they benefit?

   d) In your opinion, is affirmative action a good way to achieve greater equality in Canadian citizenship? Explain.

Be Active

5. Create a national day for some group that you think has not been given sufficient attention. Write a brief history of this group, outline its contributions to Canada, and suggest some events for the day. Present your idea to the class, using a combination of posters, speakers, displays, music, announcements, or videos.

6. In this chapter you read about citizens who have made contributions to the global community by undertaking specific projects. Read about Dr. Chandrasekhar Sankurathri, a Canadian who lost his entire family in the terrorist bombing of Air India Flight 182 in 1985. Learn how he transformed grief into social action. Then explore a list of other projects described at www.emp.ca/ccw. Select one project to research and possibly support. As a follow-up activity, write a brief report on how the project expanded your own view of global citizenship.

7. Exercise some aspect of citizenship by becoming involved in an activity such as one of the following:
   - Volunteer to teach EAL students.
   - Volunteer to work at a food bank.
   - Join a human rights and anti-discrimination organization such as Amnesty International.
   - Join an anti-poverty organization such as Oxfam or Habitat for Humanity International.

CHAPTER 3
What Are Rights and Responsibilities?

A land of freedom? You're kidding, right?

What You Need to Know
- What are the origins of rights and responsibilities?
- What are Canadians' rights and responsibilities?
- What happens when the rights of two or more people conflict?
- Why are rights and freedoms limited?
- What are Canadians' Charter freedoms?
- What are Canadians' Charter rights?
- How can you break down information from books, newspapers, and reports?

Key Terms
freedoms
privacy rights
right
responsibilities
mobility rights
reasonable limits
common good
democratic rights
equality rights
disability rights
minority language education rights
Aboriginal rights

"A land of freedom? You're kidding, right? I'm pierced, my hair's blue, and I get hassled all the time about my jeans hanging too low on my backside. My friend Dave got suspended for getting a tattoo. That's unfair—you can cover them up! Another friend, Karla, got a fine for supposedly smoking on school property. Last month, police dogs did a sniff search of our lockers. On our way into the school dance last Friday, we were actually searched by a teacher! I do my school work and I get good marks, but I don't get much respect. We live in a dictatorship."

—Deborah, a grade 9 student in a Manitoba high school

Are Deborah's complaints about lack of freedom valid? Why or why not? Why do you think there are restrictions on her **freedoms**?

Key Question
How should government be involved with people's rights and freedoms?

Where Do Rights and Responsibilities Originate?

> **THE WEB**
> To learn about the history of human rights in Canada, visit the Canadian Human Rights Commission's "time portal" at www.emp.ca/ccw

Canada, like other democracies, has developed a framework for the rights and responsibilities of citizens. All democracies have a tradition of respecting citizens' rights and encouraging responsibility through civic participation.

In Canada, citizens' rights are written down in the *Canadian Human Rights Act* (1977), provincial human rights codes, and, most importantly, the federal **Canadian Charter of Rights and Freedoms** (1982).

Canadians' **privacy rights** are covered under the federal *Privacy Act* and the 2001 *Personal Information Protection and Electronic Documents Act*. Privacy rights limit the ability of others to enter your private spaces, take your property, or collect personal information about you. Privacy is not explicitly addressed in Canada's constitution. However, it is considered a fundamental human right and an important part of a democratic society.

The responsibilities of Canadians are less well defined. However, they exist through a common appreciation of what it means to be Canadian and belong to Canadian society.

The government of Canada outlines Canadians' rights and responsibilities as shown in Figure 3.1.

What Are Rights?

A **right** is something to which a person is morally or legally entitled. At home, young people should have the right to safety, the right to food, and the right to be treated with dignity. In Canada, the government protects these rights. In extreme cases, the government removes a child from a parent's home in order to protect the child's rights.

In school, you have the right to an education and the right to be treated with respect. In the larger community, you have the right to express an opinion, the right to drive a car, the right of mobility, and the right to privacy.

WHAT ARE RESPONSIBILITIES?

In the democratic tradition, rights always carry **responsibilities** (something you are accountable for). For example, along with the right to be

CHAPTER 3 WHAT ARE RIGHTS AND RESPONSIBILITIES?

RIGHTS AND RESPONSIBILITIES

RIGHTS AND FREEDOMS

Some rights and freedoms are:

- freedom of thought
- freedom of speech
- freedom of religion
- right to peaceful assembly
- legal rights
- equality rights
- Aboriginal peoples' rights

RESPONSIBILITIES

Some responsibilities are:

- obey Canada's laws
- express opinions freely while respecting the rights and freedoms of others
- help others in the community
- care for and protect our heritage and environment
- eliminate discrimination and injustice

RIGHTS AND RESPONSIBILITIES OF CITIZENSHIP

RIGHTS AND FREEDOMS

Citizens have all the rights listed above and the right to

- apply for a passport
- run in elections
- vote in elections

RESPONSIBILITIES

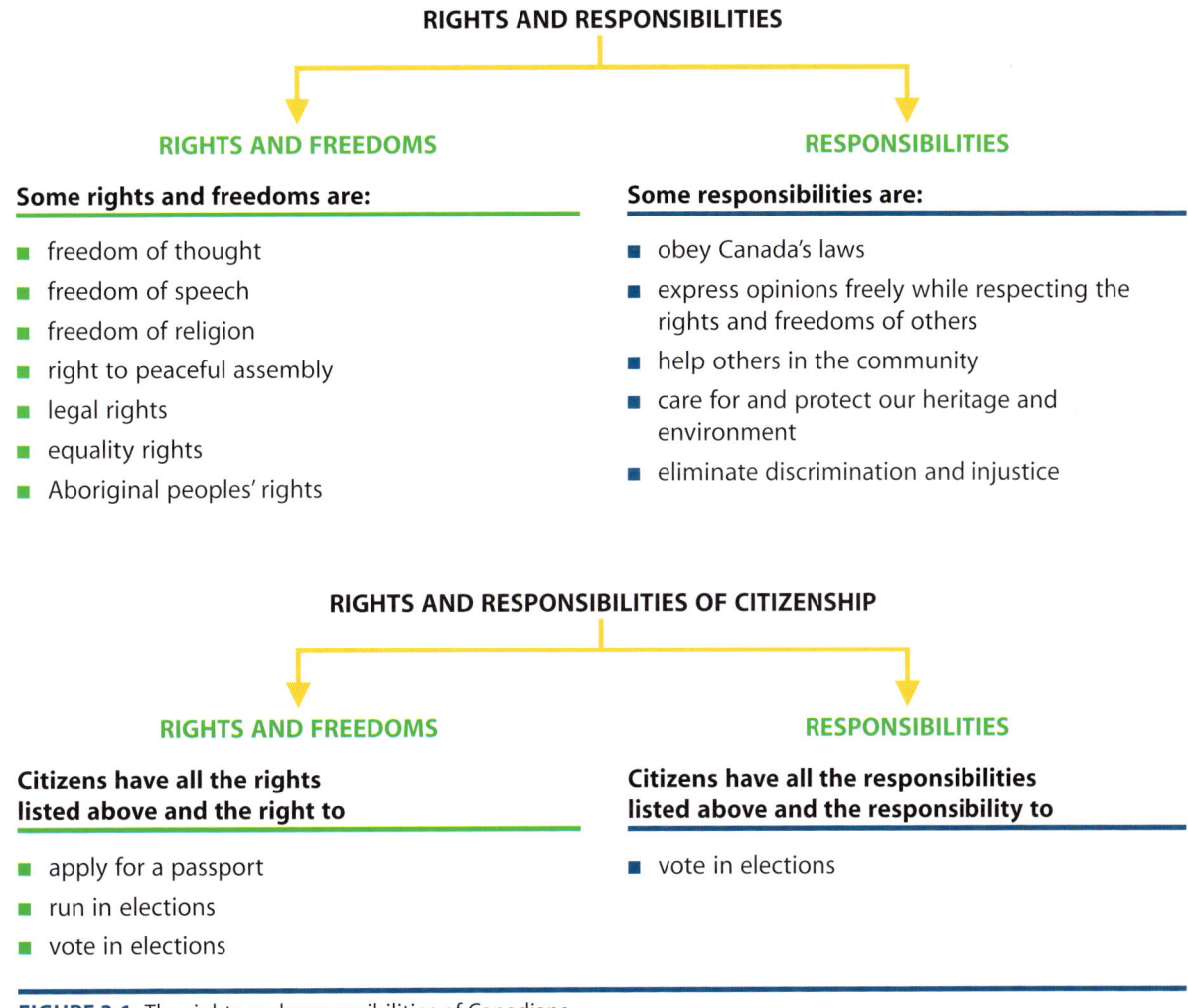

Citizens have all the responsibilities listed above and the responsibility to

- vote in elections

FIGURE 3.1 The rights and responsibilities of Canadians

treated with dignity in your home and school comes the responsibility to treat others respectfully. The right to drive a car carries with it the responsibility to pass a test and follow the rules in the driver's handbook. **Mobility rights** (to move about as you wish) come with the responsibility to obtain a passport for certain travels. A parent's right to choose a child's education includes the responsibility to oversee the education in a school or home setting.

RIGHTS IN CONFLICT

At different times, rights conflict. For example, a child's right to security may clash with a parent's right to exercise authority. Your right to freedom

FIGURE 3.2 Do you think people should be allowed to express sentiments like this in public? Why or why not?

THE WEB
To read the Charter, visit www.emp.ca/ccw

of expression may clash with someone else's right not to be exposed to certain words and sentiments.

THE CANADIAN CHARTER OF RIGHTS AND FREEDOMS

At the federal level, your rights are protected by the *Canadian Charter of Rights and Freedoms*, which forms Part I of Canada's constitution. The Charter deals with a citizen's relationship with the government. It lists many rights and freedoms, some of which are discussed in this chapter. (Chapter 2 examined Aboriginal rights, and legal rights are addressed in more detail in Chapter 10.)

When you deal with other people in areas such as housing, employment, and services (non-governmental areas), you do not need to invoke (call upon) your Charter rights. In these situations, you are protected by either the Manitoba *Human Rights Code* or the *Canadian Human Rights Act*.

"REASONABLE LIMITS" ON RIGHTS AND FREEDOMS

In a democratic society, individual rights and freedoms need to be balanced with the needs of society. In other words, rights and freedoms are not absolute; they have **reasonable limits** (as stated in section 1 of the Charter). Your freedom of expression, for example, does not allow you to yell "fire" in a crowded movie theatre. Your right to privacy ends when you enter the customs zone of an airport.

APPEALING TO COURTS TO PROTECT RIGHTS AND FREEDOMS

If you feel that you have been unfairly treated, you have the right to take your complaint to a court or human rights commission. (See Chapter 7, CivicStar: Justine Blainey, page 148.) If you lose your case in a lower court, you may seek to have a higher court hear your case. A higher court can overrule a lower court, just as a store manager can overrule the decision of a sales clerk. The highest court of appeal is the Supreme Court of Canada.

PAUSE, REFLECT, APPLY

1. a) Why are there limitations on our rights?
   b) Give three examples of authorities limiting rights. In each case, explain why you agree or disagree with the limitation.
2. List three rights and the responsibilities attached to those rights.
3. Nelson Mandela has said, "[O]vercoming poverty is not a gesture of charity. It is an act of justice." In many major Canadian cities, there are numerous homeless people. Should everyone have the right to a basic standard of living? Explain. What responsibility do working Canadians have to those who cannot work and thus cannot afford housing?

What Are Charter Freedoms?

As you just read, rights impose duties on the government. The government has a duty to set up voting stations so that you can vote. It also has a duty to protect you against unlawful searches. Freedoms may be viewed as rights that do not impose this kind of duty on the government. For example, you have freedom of religion and freedom of expression.

The Charter also describes freedom of the press, of peaceful assembly, and of association. You are free to live without persecution, and you are free to criticize and oppose government policies. You are free to do anything not prohibited by law. Moreover, you can ask the government to come to your aid if your freedoms are threatened.

> **KEY QUESTION**
> Do Canadians have too few or too many freedoms?

FREEDOM OF RELIGION

Freedom of religion means the freedom to practise the faith of your choice. It also means that society cannot impose any one religious faith on citizens.

Until 1985, retail stores in Canada were closed on Sunday, the Christian day of rest. Until 1992, public schools in Manitoba started the day with Christian prayers. Court decisions ended these practices. Citing section 2(a) of the Charter, the courts ruled that non-Christians' "freedom of conscience and religion" was disturbed by Sunday closing laws and school religious exercises. Today, Manitoba allows communities to regulate Sunday shopping on non-religious principles.

In 1994, the Quebec Human Rights Commission ruled that public schools cannot forbid Muslim students to wear the *hijab*, or Islamic

> **DID YOU KNOW**
>
> In 1986, Chris Tait, a Manitoba student, was suspended from school for a week for refusing to stand during the Lord's Prayer, which was mandatory in the province. By 1988, three provincial governments—Manitoba, Ontario, and British Columbia—faced court challenges for compulsory prayers, prompted in part by Tait's protest.

> **DID YOU KNOW**
>
> Quebec bans all advertising aimed at children under the age of 12. It is the strictest such provincial law in Canada. Manitoba bans tobacco at checkout counters to protect children. These laws have been judged a reasonable limit on manufacturers' freedom of expression.

veil. In this case, individual freedom was protected from government interference.

However, if a religious practice threatens the well-being of citizens, religious freedom may be limited. For example, seriously ill children have been removed from the custody of Jehovah's Witnesses parents who refused permission for life-saving medical treatments on religious grounds. Once in the care of the state, the children receive the treatments. In this situation, courts have decided that to limit religious freedom is "reasonable."

FREEDOM OF THOUGHT AND EXPRESSION

You are free to think whatever you like. You are also free to express your thoughts and beliefs. However, our laws and courts place "reasonable limits" on freedom of expression. For example, cigarette companies cannot advertise their products in Canada. Liquor companies are limited in the kind of advertising they can use. Producers of pornography cannot sell their products everywhere. They can also be prosecuted for producing certain types of pornography.

Parliament and the courts impose limitations on expression in order to protect the **common good** of society. Because cigarette smoking and alcohol consumption can be hazardous, their advertising is restricted. The depiction of sexuality in a violent or degrading manner is also limited because it is thought to create a harmful environment.

Teachers are limited in what they may say in the classroom. Jim Keegstra was an Alberta high school teacher who consistently made anti-Semitic (anti-Jewish) remarks to his history students. When he was charged with promoting hatred, Keegstra claimed he had a Charter right to freedom of expression. In a 1990 decision, the Supreme Court declared that he and others do not have the right to say absolutely anything they desire. For the greater good of society, there is a reasonable limit to what anyone can say.

> ☐ **DISCUSSION POINT**
>
> A 16-year-old Ontario youth was arrested and spent 34 days in jail after writing a fictional short story about a teen who tries to blow up his school in revenge for bullying. He read the story, "Twisted," to his grade 11 drama class in November 2000. Police said the story included death threats. Do you think the boy should have been arrested? Was his right to freedom of speech infringed?

CHAPTER 3 WHAT ARE RIGHTS AND RESPONSIBILITIES?

FACE OFF — Freedom of Religion versus Right to Security

What happens when religious beliefs clash with other people's right to security?

Khalsa Sikhs pray every morning and evening and forgo alcohol and tobacco. They observe the five Ks: *kesh* (uncut hair), *kanga* (comb), *kara* (bracelet), *kachha* (undergarment), and *kirpan* (dagger). Each "K" has spiritual meaning for believers. The sheathed kirpan stands for justice and inner strength. It has been compared to the Christian cross in significance.

In 2001, 12-year-old Gurbaj Singh was banned from his Montreal school for wearing a *kirpan*. A year later, the Quebec Superior Court ruled that Singh could wear the *kirpan*—as long as it was wrapped and checked by school officials. Under police escort, the boy returned to school. His arrival prompted dozens of parents to remove their children from the school.

The school appealed to a higher court, arguing that the blade posed a danger to other students. Quebec's highest court, the Court of Appeal, agreed with the school and ruled that the ban was a reasonable limit on religious freedom. In 2005, the case moved to the Supreme Court of Canada for a final decision. In March 2006, the Supreme Court of Canada ruled in favour of Singh.

Some commentators saw Singh as a victim of racism. The *kirpan* is sewn into a sheath and would make a poor weapon. Singh's lawyer argued that it is no more dangerous than a geometry compass.

Others argued that zero tolerance of weapons in schools means all knives, including ceremonial daggers. They argued that a *kirpan* could be seized by another student and used as a weapon. The steel *kirpan* should be replaced by a plastic version. The safety of all children is more important than the religious beliefs of a minority. *Kirpans* have been banned on airlines, and should also be banned in schools.

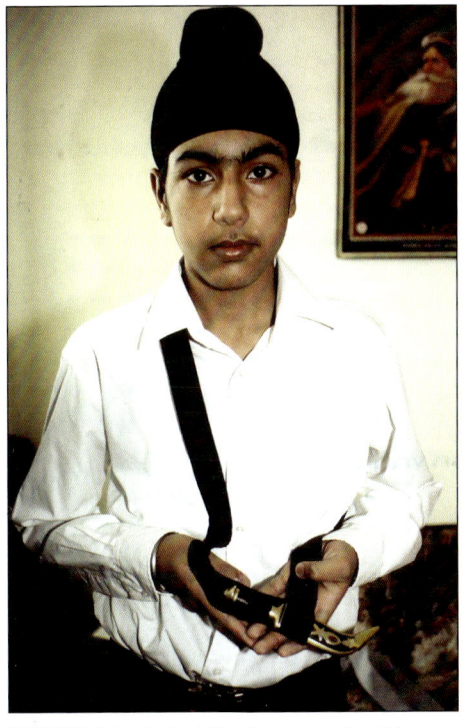

FIGURE 3.3 Gurbaj Singh returned to his school in Montreal in April 2002.

What Do You Think?

1. In their ruling, the Supreme Court judges wrote: "A total prohibition against wearing a kirpan to school undermines the value of this religious symbol and sends students the message that some religious practices do not merit the same protection as others."
    a) What Canadian value does the court's ruling uphold?
    b) Do you agree or disagree with the Supreme Court's ruling in favour of Singh? Explain.
2. In 2004, France banned the wearing of religious symbols such as headscarves, skullcaps, and large crosses in public schools. The government stated that it wanted to promote equality and prevent religious conflict. Many of France's 5 million Muslims saw this as an attack on their beliefs. Do you think Canada should adopt a similar law?

▶ DID YOU KNOW ◀

There has been no incident of *kirpan*-related violence in a Canadian school in 100 years.

SCHOOL POWERS AND FREEDOM OF EXPRESSION

Most schools allow students as much self-expression as possible, especially in student publications. However, in certain cases, censorship occurs. If the school administration thinks that a story or editorial poses a threat to the safety of students or to the positive climate in the school, it can cut the articles.

Dress is a form of self-expression. The courts have confirmed that schools have the power to create dress codes. Schools can set reasonable limits on certain freedoms. For example, your school most likely has a policy prohibiting you from downloading violent, racist, or sexual images on a school computer.

School boards have a say about the types of books taught as part of the curriculum. However, their power is not absolute. In 2002, the Supreme Court of Canada ruled that a British Columbia school board should not have banned kindergarten and grade 1 books that depicted same-sex parents.

PAUSE, REFLECT, APPLY

1. Why do governments and courts limit our freedom of expression? Give three examples of limits on freedom of expression. In each case, explain why you agree or disagree with the limitation.
2. Why do you think the Supreme Court in 1985 declared the Sunday store closing law unconstitutional (not in keeping with the Charter)?
3. In Canada, do we have too much or too little freedom? Give specific examples.

> **KEY QUESTION**
> How much power should courts have in interpreting Charter rights?

What Are Our Charter Rights?

Among the rights addressed by the Charter are democratic rights, mobility rights, legal rights, equality rights, minority language education rights, and Aboriginal rights. Many of these rights are discussed in other sections of this text.

While the Charter outlines your basic rights, Canadian courts, especially the Supreme Court, clarify those rights. The courts interpret the Charter to determine exactly what those rights mean. For example, what is meant by the right to "security of the person," the right "not to be subjected to any cruel and unusual treatment or punishment," or the right to "the equal protection and equal benefit of the law"? By responding to the cases brought before them, Canadian courts have been answering these questions since the Charter was created in 1982.

DEMOCRATIC RIGHTS

The **democratic rights** of Canadians are outlined in sections 3, 4, and 5 of the Charter. These rules guarantee Canadians a democratic government and the right to elect their representatives. The rules apply to federal, provincial, and territorial elections.

The voting age in Canada used to be 21. Based on a decision of the Supreme Court of Canada, the right to vote (known as "the franchise") has been extended to every Canadian citizen over the age of 18. Most recently, the franchise was extended to all inmates in Canada's prison system, including those serving life sentences.

LEGAL RIGHTS

Your **legal rights** (sections 7 to 14 of the Charter) ensure that you are treated fairly when dealing with the justice system. Section 8, for example, guarantees you "the right to be secure against unreasonable search." Section 9 says you have "the right not to be arbitrarily detained."

In most cases, searches are conducted because someone in authority suspects that a law or rule has been broken. When the person searching you is a police officer, the search is legal if there is

- a search warrant,
- an arrest, or
- reasonable cause.

In a school, your teachers, the vice-principal, and the principal are considered to be acting in place of your parents. This gives them the authority to search you, your bag, or your locker if they have a good reason for doing so. School officials have this authority (backed by court decisions) so that they can maintain order and safety in schools.

If there is no good reason for the search, school authorities can be punished for invading students' privacy. In

FIGURE 3.4 Would it be legal for a school official to search your locker just because it's messy and he or she wants to check to see what's inside?

1998, in a high school in Kingsville, Ontario, 19 grade 9 boys were strip-searched after a classmate reported $90 missing from a gym bag. The incident grabbed media attention. Eventually, the vice-principal and the gym teacher who ordered the students to remove their clothes were suspended without pay for 10 days and reprimanded by the school board. The $90 was never recovered.

In some circumstances, it is legal to detain people, even if they are not suspected of committing a crime. For example, during highway spot checks, any driver can be detained to determine if he or she has consumed alcohol. Because alcohol-related traffic accidents are frequent and deadly, the Supreme Court has decided that spot checks are a reasonable limit on the right not to be detained.

EQUALITY RIGHTS

The rights of all Canadians to be treated equally before the law (when facing a charge in the justice system) and under the law (meaning that laws apply equally to everyone) are guaranteed by the Charter. Governments are prohibited from discriminating against anyone on specific grounds, as listed in section 15(1) of the Charter:

> Every individual is equal before and under the law and has the right to the equal protection and equal benefit of the law without discrimination and, in particular, without discrimination based on race, national or ethnic origin, colour, religion, sex, age or mental or physical disability.

Equality rights are meant also to ensure that everyone has equal access to opportunity. How? Supreme Court Justice Rosalie Abella has said, "equality is not a concept that produces the same results for everyone. It is a concept that seeks to identify and remove, barrier by barrier, discriminatory disadvantage."

▶ **DID YOU KNOW** ◀
Canada is a leader in protecting and promoting the rights of minority groups. Lawmakers in many countries, including Serbia, Croatia, Latvia, and Sri Lanka, are attempting to apply the principles of Canada's Charter as possible solutions to ethnic and religious divisions in their own countries.

Equality Rights and Sexual Orientation

Some rights protected by the Charter are not explicitly stated. However, the Supreme Court of Canada has identified similar grounds for protection in addition to those listed in section 15(1). Among these grounds is sexual orientation.

FIGURE 3.5 In 2002, in Ontario, 17-year-old Marc Hall (left) took the Durham Catholic District School Board to court. It had ruled that he could not take his boyfriend to the high school prom. The board stated that Hall's action would violate Catholic teachings on homosexuality. Hall's lawyer argued, successfully, that the board's decision violated Hall's Charter rights to equality, freedom of expression, and freedom of association.

The basic goal of section 15 is to protect human dignity. It does this by ensuring that the law treats all Canadians as equal in value and worth. In a series of court decisions, gay and lesbian Canadians have been guaranteed equal treatment under the Charter. This means that lesbian and gay Canadians are protected from discrimination in accommodation and employment. Same-sex couples are also entitled to the same benefits (such as pensions and support payments) as heterosexual couples. By June 2005, courts in eight provinces and one territory had recognized same-sex marriage. In July 2005, the *Civil Marriage Act* became law, recognizing same-sex marriage across Canada (see the Face Off feature on same-sex marriage in Chapter 11, pages 225–226).

Disability Rights

Disability activists fought hard to have **disability rights** included in the Charter. Their victory was considered a significant achievement for the disability movement. Since then, many legal challenges have ensured that people with physical or mental disabilities have access to a full range of services. Access to buildings and facilities has also improved. In one landmark case, a person in British Columbia who was deaf won the right to communicate with health care providers using a sign language interpreter provided by the government.

CivicStar

STEVEN FLETCHER

He clicks his mouse by means of an infrared remote attached to his forehead. He moves about in a high-tech wheelchair. He is Steven Fletcher, a Conservative MP who cannot move his body below the neck.

At age 23, Fletcher was a mining engineer. Driving home one day, he had an accident. A moose crashed through his windshield. Fletcher's life changed in a second. As a result of a spinal cord injury, he cannot feel hunger, pain, or physical pleasure. Yet his head works just fine.

Fletcher adapted to his condition. He returned to university, earned a business degree, and was elected student president. Several years later, he became leader of the Manitoba Progressive Conservative Party. In the 2004 federal election, Fletcher ran as a Conservative candidate in a Winnipeg riding, won the seat, and was appointed his party's health critic.

The Parliament buildings had to be adapted to accommodate Fletcher, Canada's first quadriplegic MP. In Ottawa, Fletcher has continued to advocate for *community living*—the integration of physically or mentally challenged individuals into society. He has said, "Community living is better for the individual for sure, better for their families, and in most cases—not all—it's better on the taxpayer too."

Fletcher's words express his optimism: "I'd rather be paralyzed from the neck down than the neck up." In his determination and accomplishments, he tests and strengthens Canada's commitment to equal opportunity and equal treatment for all members of society.

Following the Conservatives' victory in the 2006 federal election, Prime Minister Stephen Harper appointed Fletcher Parliamentary Secretary to the Minister of Health.

Your Play

1. How would your home or school have to be adapted in order to be accessible to Steven Fletcher?
2. Fletcher has observed that politicians in Parliament had no real grasp of what it means to be seriously physically disabled before he arrived. He says there's a difference between dealing with "issues" and dealing with people. Describe what you think that difference involves.

Tracy Latimer: Equality Rights or the Right to Die?

Tracy Latimer was a 12-year-old girl living with severe cerebral palsy in rural Saskatchewan. She could not move her limbs and communicated only by means of facial expressions, laughter, and crying. Tracy enjoyed music from a radio, which she controlled with a special button. However, she was in constant pain.

When Tracy faced further painful surgery in 1993, her father, Robert, made a decision. He placed her in his pickup truck while her mother and siblings were at church. He then inserted a hose from the exhaust pipe into the cab. Tracy died from carbon monoxide poisoning.

The legal case pitted Tracy's equality rights against her father's claim that he was releasing her from a life that was too painful. At trial, he was convicted and sentenced to one year in jail and one year of house arrest. A higher court, however, ruled that he was guilty of second-degree murder. He would have to serve the same sentence as anyone else: life, without parole for 10 years. Latimer defended his action as euthanasia, or "mercy killing." He argued that it would be "cruel and unusual treatment or punishment" (section 12 of the Charter) to incarcerate him for an act of compassion.

Disability activists disagreed, passionately. The Charter, they said, gives no one the freedom or right to kill anybody. Instead, section 15 guarantees equal protection of the law "without discrimination based on … mental or physical disability." Canada's Supreme Court agreed. In 2001, it ruled that Latimer had other options. For example, he could have explored further ways to manage Tracy's pain, or put her in a long-term care facility where staff have experience in pain management.

> **► DID YOU KNOW ◄**
>
> Assisted suicide and euthanasia are illegal in Canada. Under section 241(b) of the *Criminal Code*, anyone who aids a person in committing suicide can be jailed for up to 14 years. Suicide itself, by contrast, is legal.

MINORITY LANGUAGE EDUCATION RIGHTS

Section 23 of the Charter deals with **minority language education rights**. It ensures that French- and English-speaking minorities in every province and territory can receive publicly funded primary and secondary education in their own language. (These rights apply only when there are enough minority-language children in the region to justify providing separate public schooling.) For example, although French is the official language of Quebec, children there may be educated in English if their parents are anglophones or if their parents were educated in English.

In 1993, the Supreme Court of Canada ruled that Manitoba's education laws violated the Charter. That ruling was made because the province

CANADA IN THE CONTEMPORARY WORLD

LITERACY COACH

On page 65, you'll find a timeline showing the key events of the Manitoba Schools Question. You may find it easier to read the timeline by starting from the last date and reading back. The last date usually shows you how the events turned out. Once you have that information, it's easier to understand what happened along the way.

THE WEB

Read about Mary Two-Axe Earley's life and achievements at www.emp.ca/ccw

did not provide French-language schools for its many francophone students. Soon after, new legislation established the public French-language school system that exists today (see Face Off, page 65).

ABORIGINAL RIGHTS

Section 25 of the Charter describes **Aboriginal rights**. It recognizes the historic treaty rights of the first peoples of Canada to land and self-determination. The *Indian Act* of 1876 had abolished many of these rights. Through it, the federal government claimed exclusive power over First Nations people and lands, and deprived many Aboriginal people of their "treaty Indian" status, through which they had derived certain rights and benefits under the law.

Part II, section 35 of Canada's 1982 constitution further affirms Aboriginal rights by defining "Aboriginal peoples of Canada" to include the Métis, as well as Indians and Inuit. It also extends these rights equally to women and men.

In 1985, sections of the *Indian Act* that deprived Aboriginal people of their status were declared in violation of the Charter. The Act was amended with Bill C-31, which restored status to some 118,000 Aboriginal people who had previously lost it for a variety of reasons, most usually marriage to a non-Native man. Bill C-31 also returned some legal powers to Indian bands that the federal government had claimed under the *Indian Act*.

DID YOU KNOW

Under the *Indian Act*, those who lost their "treaty Indian" status included Aboriginal women who married non-Aboriginal men, and Aboriginal people who wished to vote, own property, become a lawyer or minister, serve in the armed forces, live in another country, or drink alcohol. The Act also required status Indians to obtain a special pass if they wished to leave their reserve for a period of time.

FIGURE 3.6 Mary Two-Axe Earley fought to re-establish the rights of Aboriginal women who had lost treaty status after marrying non-Aboriginal men. In 1967, she founded the group Equal Rights for Indian Women. Over the next three decades she gave speeches, made presentations to government officials, and wrote letters to influential politicians. In 1996, shortly before she died, the 84-year-old activist received a National Aboriginal Achievement Award "for her drive to establish Bill C-31 and her commitment to the rights of women."

FACE OFF

The Manitoba Schools Question: Should Francophones and Catholics Have Their Own Publicly Funded Schools?

The Manitoba Schools Question was a conflict that lasted 80 years. It divided Manitobans and Canadians, pitting many anglophones against francophones, Protestants against Catholics, and provinces against the federal government.

- **1870** The *Manitoba Act* creates the province of Manitoba. It gives English and French equal status in law (based on the *British North America Act*) and establishes a dual system of Protestant and Catholic public schools.

- **1871** The *Constitution Act, 1867* is amended to incorporate the terms of the *Manitoba Act* into Canada's constitution.

- **1880s** Manitoba's population grows more slowly than expected. As many settlers arrive from Ontario, the proportion of francophone Catholics falls in relation to the anglophone Protestant population.

- **1888** A federal bill to compensate the Catholic Church for properties confiscated in 1763 (when the British defeated the French) stirs controversy. It incites anti-Catholic and anti-French feeling throughout Canada.

- **1889** The Equal Rights Association, an Ontario citizen's group, campaigns to abolish public funds for bilingual schools and Catholic separate schools. Its slogan? "Equality to all; privileges to none."

- **1890** Defying Canada's constitution, Manitoba's government abolishes public funding of Catholic schools and establishes English as the province's only official language.

- **1890s** Franco-Manitobans challenge the province's new legislation in court. Protestant groups criticize francophones and Catholics for failing to assimilate into the majority, British-based culture.

- **1894** The federal government advises Manitoba to consider the minority in the "most earnest hope" of "establishing perfect freedom and equality" for all.

- **1894** Manitoba defends its education legislation, claiming that it "gives to every citizen equal rights and equal privileges, and makes no distinction respecting nationality and religion."

- **1897** Federal government pressure continues. Manitoba finally allows some French-language and Catholic religious instruction in public schools. This weak compromise satisfies neither side.

- **1916** Manitoba abolishes the terms of the 1897 compromise protecting French education.

- **1969** The federal *Official Languages Act* guarantees equal status of English and French throughout Canada.

- **1970** Manitoba legalizes 100 percent French-language education from kindergarten to grade 3. Franco-Manitobans establish Français, a French-only school program, for children of francophones and anglophones wanting French immersion.

- **1994** Manitoba establishes a public Francophone School Division.

What Do You Think?

1. Summarize the positions of the federal and Manitoba governments. What does each mean by "equality"?
2. The Manitoba Schools Question has been described as "Canada's most significant loss of French and Catholic [minority] rights." How does the Charter ensure that such a conflict will not arise again?
3. How might French immersion programs affect the attitude of non-francophones to minority language rights? Give specific examples.

THE WEB
To learn more about the Manitoba Schools Question and other issues in Manitoba's history, visit www.emp.ca/ccw

CivicStar

MOTHER OF RED NATIONS WOMEN'S COUNCIL OF MANITOBA (MORN)

Before European contact, Aboriginal women contributed greatly to the health, welfare, and economies of their tribal communities. They looked after children and elders and made major decisions about planting, shelter, food gathering and food preservation, clothing, and other day-to-day matters. Since that time, the quality of life and status of Aboriginal women in Canada has sharply declined.

In recent decades, Aboriginal women have begun to reclaim their voices and status in society by establishing **interest groups** to advance their causes. The Mother of Red Nations Women's Council of Manitoba (MORN) is an example of an advocacy (support) group.

Based in Winnipeg, MORN was established in 1999. It is a non-profit organization that aims to protect and maintain the well-being of Aboriginal women and children in Manitoba. The group gives Aboriginal women a voice by providing information, encouragement, and intervention.

MORN operates a Transition Resource Centre that helps Aboriginal women in such areas as housing, child welfare, transportation, addiction, income assistance, health, education, and traditional Aboriginal counselling. It also offers an Aboriginal Human Resource Development Program. This program offers Aboriginal women who live off-reserve an opportunity to find employment, valuable work experience, and skills necessary to succeed in the mainstream workforce.

Another issue that MORN focuses on is Bill C-31, which was passed in 1985 and enabled non-status Aboriginal women and their children to regain their "treaty Indian" status. MORN is concerned that Bill C-31 did not create equality for Aboriginal women and their families, and also that the federal government claims sole power to define who is and is not a status Indian. The organization has created pamphlets, held consultations, and published reports recommending that the bill be amended.

A 16-member council consisting of four Manitoba regions—North, South, East, and West—governs MORN. Council positions are elected at an annual General Assembly, with two elected adult positions, one youth, and an appointed elder for each region. MORN is one of several Aboriginal women's groups in Canada whose aim is to better the life of Aboriginal women.

Your Play

1. What role do organizations like MORN (and other non-profit advocacy groups such as clubs, societies, churches, charities, and committees) play in Canada?
2. Find out more about Bill C-31. What negative effects do critics believe it has on Aboriginal women and children?

FIGURE 3.7 Aboriginal women who live off-reserve can benefit from programs that provide assistance with housing, health, and employment.

PAUSE, REFLECT, APPLY

1. Rights are clustered under different categories within the Charter. What are those categories, and how do they differ?
2. Justice Rosalie Abella said, "equality is not a concept that produces the same results for everyone. It is a concept that seeks to identify and remove, barrier by barrier, discriminatory disadvantage." Write a two-paragraph opinion piece on the meaning of these comments. Use examples from real life to illustrate your point of view.

REPLAY

In this chapter, you have explored these concepts:

1. Democracies have a tradition of rights and responsibilities.
2. Canadians' rights are protected in human rights codes, in the *Canadian Charter of Rights and Freedoms*, and in privacy law.
3. Rights always imply responsibilities.
4. There are reasonable limits on individual rights in order to protect the needs of society.
5. If you feel you have been treated unfairly, you may take your case before a human rights commission or the courts.
6. When individual and societal rights clash, courts interpret which rights will prevail.
7. Aboriginal rights to land and self-determination are enshrined in Canada's constitution.

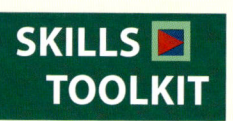

SKILLS TOOLKIT — How Can I Break This Down?

To analyze means to break something down into its parts. Keep this in mind when analyzing information from books, newspapers, reports, and so on. It's a good idea to read the whole item first. Then approach the item as you would a puzzle.

Start by doing the following:

- Take your time.
- Look up unfamiliar words in a dictionary.
- Use an Internet search engine to learn more about unfamiliar phrases, concepts, or people.
- Examine all the parts. For example, with a statistical table, make sure you know exactly what is being measured. Look at all the labels. Check the legend, if there is one. If you are reading a report, scan the headings to get a sense of the main structure. Use the headings to zero in on the information that is pertinent to your research. Examine photographs and captions.

Next, go a little deeper:

- Try to grasp the purpose of the piece. Why did the author write it? The answer to that question is usually the "big idea" of the piece.
- Examine the first and last sentence of each paragraph for clues about the main idea.
- Look for chronology (time order) as an organizing principle. That way, you can sometimes jump to particular events that interest you or relate to your research.
- Look for the arguments the author makes, as well as evidence to support those arguments. What cause-and-effect claims does the author make?
- Remember that words and images may have a symbolic meaning. In political cartoons, the artist often uses symbolism or exaggeration to make a point.
- Remember that words in italics can be the names of published works, the names of ships, or phrases from a language other than English.

Skill Practice

1. Read Face Off: Freedom of Religion versus Right to Security on page 57. Identify points of comparison between different views. Identify cause-and-effect sequences (one thing happens because of something else).
2. Read the CivicStar feature on MORN on page 66. What is the main message of the feature? Identify and explain key words and phrases.
3. Find a political cartoon in this book or in a magazine or newspaper that you think is effective. Analyze the techniques that the cartoonist has used to give the political message humour or impact.

STUDY HALL

Be Informed

1. Distinguish between a freedom and a right. Use an example for each.
2. Obtain a copy of the *Canadian Charter of Rights and Freedoms* (for example, at http://laws.justice.gc.ca/en/charter/index.html). After reading the following sections of the Charter, find an example in this chapter of how each of the sections has been applied by Canadian courts: 1, 2(a), 2(b), 3, 7, 8, 12, and 15(1).

Be Purposeful

3. With a partner and using the library or the Internet, research changes in the status of women in Canadian society from the early 20th century on. Consider issues such as pay equity, reproductive choice, and representation in government. Organize your findings in a timeline (for an example of a timeline, see the Face Off feature on page 65) and present the timeline to your class.

4. In small groups, decide whether a right has been violated in each of the cases described below. If a right has been violated, explain the right and its relationship to the *Canadian Charter of Rights and Freedoms*.

    - Seventeen-year-old Timothy is a suspect in a murder. In an effort to locate Timothy, police publish his photograph in a local newspaper.
    - With her parents out of town, Ella is having a party at home. Police knock on the door. Upon learning that the parents are absent, police enter the home and charge five teens with underage drinking.
    - Sheema is suspended for a day because she refused to remove her *hijab* (headscarf worn by many Muslim women) in her physical education class.
    - Although Aron's high school grades are good, he doesn't get into the college of his choice. Later, Aron discovers that several Aboriginal students with lower averages were admitted to the same college.
    - A police dog is brought into Dave's school. As a result of the dog's sniffing, Dave's locker is searched by the school administration.

5. Paula refuses to stand for the playing of "O Canada" during her school's opening exercises. She says she disagrees with the values in the song. It is male-oriented ("True patriot love in all thy sons command"), has a militaristic flavour ("we stand on guard for thee"), and is religious ("God keep our land glorious and free!"). Paula believes in feminism, pacifism, and atheism. She has been told that according to Manitoba law, the national anthem must be played each morning, and she must respect the song by standing. If she does not comply with school rules, she will be suspended for three days.

    In small groups, decide what rights and responsibilities are present in Paula's protest. Attempt to resolve the apparent conflict of rights and responsibilities in this scenario.

Be Active

6. Posters at your school encourage students to visit a certain Web site. The site preaches hatred against Muslim Canadians, black Canadians, and Jewish Canadians. What steps could you take to make certain that Canadian rights and freedoms are protected in this situation?

7. Organize a classroom debate on the topics listed below. Before the debate, research your position and your opponent's position. After the debate, summarize your position on each debate topic in a well-written paragraph.

    - All spanking of children should be made illegal.
    - Doctor-assisted suicide under certain circumstances should be legalized in Canada.

8. Interview a person with a disability in your school or community. Find out how the disability has affected his or her rights and freedoms.

CHAPTER 4
What Shapes Our Identities and Cultures?

What You Need to Know
- What factors shape personal, regional, and national identities?
- How do mass media influence you and other individuals?
- How do mass media influence groups and communities?
- How do mass media and popular culture influence Aboriginal and francophone identities? Is this influence positive, negative, or both?
- How are identity, culture, and diversity protected in Canada? Should they be?

Key Terms

identity
culture
regional identity
mass media
stereotype
consumerism
trend
pop culture
advertising
fad
diversity
Canadian content

Key Question

What is identity, and what influences contribute to shaping an identity?

Tamara: Hey, Bob, do you think Canada has an identity?

Bob: Nope.

Tamara: Oh, come on. I just learned in Social Studies that we invented peacekeeping.

Bob: That's because we don't think enough of ourselves to start a war.

Tamara: Very funny. Canadians do have a reputation for being polite.

Bob: Well, there's your identity, then. I'd rather be original.

Tamara: Oh, but we are! We invented medicare, and we promote multiculturalism. Those are pretty special.

Bob: OK, then—Canadian: Polite and Special.

Tamara: All right, Bob. I can see this isn't going anywhere.

Bob: Hey, Tamara?

Tamara: Yes?

Bob: Make me up a T-shirt, OK? As slogans go, it's growing on me.

What are Bob and Tamara discussing? Which perspectives do you agree with? How would you define Canadian identity?

What Is Identity?

Everybody has an **identity**. Your identity is defined as how you see yourself, your sense of who you are. Many factors contribute to identity. Do you see yourself as a Manitoban? As a young Canadian? Bilingual? A trendsetter? A teenager? How do you define yourself?

FACTORS THAT SHAPE IDENTITY

Have you ever met someone who describes himself or herself as "just Canadian"? Maybe that person doesn't think about his or her ancestors or consider them significant. Other people sometimes call themselves "hyphenated Canadians," for example, "Italian Canadian" or "Ukrainian Canadian." Their **culture** (traditions, values, and behaviours of a group) is important to their identity. These are two different ways of having a Canadian identity.

Some people view themselves as part of a borderless community. Francophones, for example, consider themselves part of a worldwide community that speaks French. Many Aboriginal peoples have their own identity as a nation, but also feel part of the large network of indigenous

> ▶ **DID YOU KNOW** ◀
> La Francophonie is an international organization of francophone and observer governments that provides a forum for discussion of worldwide cultural and linguistic diversity. In 2006, it had 53 member governments and 10 observer states, representing 175 million francophones on five continents.

> **THE WEB** ▶▶▶
> Learn more about La Francophonie at www.emp.ca/ccw

FIGURE 4.1 Fans cheer the Canadian men's basketball team at the 2000 Olympic Games in Sydney, Australia. Showing which sports team you support is another way to communicate identity.

> **DID YOU KNOW**
>
> The St. Boniface *Riels* are a Manitoba Junior Hockey League team from Winnipeg. In 1869, in Manitoba, Louis Riel tried to defend Métis rights and identity against a new culture—English Protestant culture, which arrived with settlers from Ontario.

peoples worldwide. Some individuals feel as though they are global citizens—citizens of the whole planet, not just one nation.

Identity is also made up of other personal characteristics, including physical appearance; personal qualities, such as friendliness; and interests, skills, and habits. Some young people, for example, create a powerful personal identity through their clothing or jewellery, their music, or the teams they follow.

Personal identity can also be shaped by family, peers, religion, media, and community. Some Canadians have a strong identity based on their family history. Other people identify strongly with their chosen faith. Sometimes, a shared history and shared values can shape a whole community, as is the case with the Hutterites of Manitoba.

CivicStar

CINDY KLASSEN

Cindy Klassen became Canada's most decorated Olympic athlete when she captured five medals at the 2006 Turin Games. Klassen, a speed-skater, set a Canadian record by winning a gold, two silver, and two bronze at the 2006 Games to add to a bronze she won in 2002.

Klassen was born in Winnipeg and is a descendant of Mennonite immigrants. She attended Mennonite Brethren Collegiate Institute and McIvor Mennonite Brethren Church in Winnipeg, and played elite AAA boys' hockey in that city.

With the urging of her parents, Klassen decided to take up speed-skating. "I didn't even want to do it because I thought it looked ridiculous with the long blades and wearing a tight skin-suit," she once said.

Klassen recovered from a 2003 skating accident in which a razor-sharp skate blade caused a 10-cm gash that tore through 12 tendons, a nerve, and an artery in her right forearm. But she saw the recovery period in a positive light—an opportunity to become better acquainted with her faith and family.

One of Klassen's former teachers, Ken Opalko, says that she is a great role model because her faith is important to her. He credits Klassen's faith with helping her skating because it has kept her focused and grounded. "She comes across as being a shy, compassionate, kind person, and that's totally how she is. But underneath that, she is a fierce competitor."

Your Play

When someone from your region makes his or her mark on the world stage, does that have an impact on you? Explain your answer.

MANITOBA IDENTITIES

Calling yourself a Manitoban (as opposed to a Quebecker, for example) is one way to express a **regional identity**—the way you belong to a place. For example, Manitobans are familiar with the isolation and cold of a prairie climate. Some Manitobans would say that an important aspect of their identity is living in a rural community. However, they might also poke fun at the landscape and joke about the province's four seasons—almost winter, winter, still winter, and road construction.

Do Manitobans have an identity that is distinct from the rest of the country? Manitoba is similar to the other two prairie provinces—Saskatchewan and Alberta. In this region of Canada, people's identities are not only linked to the land, but also to a tradition of multiculturalism that includes Aboriginal peoples (First Nations and Métis), francophones, and descendants of European settlers.

▶ **DID YOU KNOW** ◀
Manitoba comes from the Cree word for "place of the Great Spirit."

▶ **DID YOU KNOW** ◀
Winnipeg has strong francophone roots. St. Boniface, which merged to form greater Winnipeg, is still largely francophone, as are some of the smaller towns surrounding the city—Ste. Agathe, Ste. Rose du Lac, St. Jean Baptiste, Beausejour, and St. Norbert.

FIGURE 4.2 Billy Jack Grieves, of Oxford House Cree Nation, carried the flame during the opening ceremonies of the 1999 Pan-American Games in Winnipeg. How might such an event communicate aspects of Canadian culture to the rest of the world?

PAUSE, REFLECT, APPLY

1. What is meant by identity? What factors shape identity? List as many as you can.
2. Create a series of concentric circles (circles around each other) in which you list all the factors that shape your identity, from the most personal (inner circle) to the global (outer circles).
3. In your opinion, is there such a thing as a Manitoban identity or a Canadian identity? Explain your answer in a short paragraph.

> **KEY QUESTION**
> How do the mass media influence identity?

Mass Media and Identity

Individual and collective (group) identity are also influenced by the **mass media**. The term "mass media" refers to the various means of communication used to reach a large, or mass, audience. These include newspapers, magazines, films, books, television, radio, and the Internet. All segments of the mass media have the power to create images of individuals and groups that can affect individuals and all of society.

For example, by presenting scenes of different ethnic groups in Canada working together and cooperating, the media make Canadians more accepting of multiculturalism. By presenting profiles of minority groups, the media make Canadians more supportive of equal rights and encourage minorities to feel included in the broader culture.

At times, mass media may reinforce a **stereotype**—a group image held by one social group about another. Stereotypes are often used in a negative way. Many minorities say that they are not well presented in the media because writers and producers don't know much about their culture. They argue that media accounts could be less stereotypical if Canadian minorities told their own stories.

SHAPING OPINIONS AND ATTITUDES

Do you think the mass media influence your opinions and attitudes? Consider the following examples:

- On television, you witness scenes of human suffering as a result of a recent war.
- On radio, you listen to messages about not drinking and driving.
- You see posters promoting safer sex.
- You read magazine stories about attractive and affluent celebrities.
- You view popular film actors smoking cigarettes onscreen.
- You see signs and hear jingles encouraging you to eat fast food.
- You view a commercial asking you to support orphaned children in a developing country.

Have you been influenced? Most media production is a business, and the main reason for influencing you is profit in somebody's pocket. It is important to ask questions about who is paying for a media message and why the message is being sent. Occasionally, the motivation might not be profit. Government departments and volunteer agencies often sponsor messages aimed at keeping you healthy and well, or raising money to help other people. Can you spot such messages in the list above?

Some media messages have assumptions and attitudes already built into them. For example, the media may present many messages about the nature of the "good life," the value of **consumerism** (buying products and services), the role of women, and the acceptance of authority.

However, not everyone receives these messages in the same way. Your personal taste—and, perhaps, your identity—plays a role in how you will receive or interpret media messages. Factors such as heritage, faith, financial status, family life, or sexual orientation can determine a response to media messages, whether positive or negative. For example, people who have traditional values might not watch a program featuring same-sex couples and might prefer seeing traditional families featured in advertisements.

FIGURE 4.3 How does this poster from Oxfam Canada's Make Trade Fair campaign seek to shape public opinion? Visit the campaign's Web site to find out more.

EMERGENCE OF NEW MEDIA

Do you use a cellphone, text messenger, an iPod, a compact disc (CD), a digital versatile disc (DVD), or the Internet on your computer? If you do, you are a player in the new media.

Have you responded to an online survey? Have you used a chat room? Do you use e-mail? Have you downloaded music from the Internet? Have you performed research on Internet sites? If you answered yes, you are also part of the new media.

Blogging is a major **trend** (a general direction of people's preferences) in the new media. A *blog* is an online journal that is regularly updated—sometimes more than once a day. The term "blog" is a shortened form of "Web log." The individual entries on a blog are usually called *posts*. Blogging is powerful because it is so fast and can easily be accessed by many people. Sometimes bloggers are ahead of the regular media in reporting important stories. They can also be opinionated and, therefore, influence their readership.

▶ **DID YOU KNOW** ◀

Most media and other institutions maintain Web sites that offer information and news electronically. Each year, advertising on the Internet increases. In 2006, more than two-thirds of Canadians used the Internet regularly, more than half of them from home.

QUESTIONS TO CONSIDER

In viewing media, always consider the following:

- Why is the story being told?
- What is left out of the message?
- What values, beliefs, and lifestyles are presented?
- Who created the message, and what was his or her purpose in creating it?
- How might another person or group see the message differently or from a different perspective?

PAUSE, REFLECT, APPLY

1. Explain how the mass media may influence you in a positive manner and in a negative manner.
2. Advertisers pay attention to demographic patterns (the characteristics of human populations). Suggest a product that might be advertised during each of the following television programs and explain your reasoning:
   a) reality show
   b) home improvement show
   c) documentary
   d) MuchMusic program
   e) afternoon "soap opera"
3. Identify some ways in which the new media could further influence your identity.

> **KEY QUESTION**
> Does pop culture make us all the same?

What Is Pop Culture?

Popular culture, or **pop culture**, is the culture of ordinary people. The content of pop culture is determined by people's daily interactions, needs, and desires. It can include trends in fashion, decorating, entertainment, music, food, sports, literature, and mass media.

Mass media are the vehicles for pop culture. In other words, mass media transmit pop culture messages through images, stories, and **advertising** (the paid promotion of goods or services by a sponsor). Mass media are also part of pop culture trends, for example, following a certain television series, text messaging, and so on.

THE SELLING OF POP CULTURE

Although popular culture is often viewed as the things people follow or admire, it is also about things to buy. Mass media exert a great influence through the trends they cover and the advertising they carry.

Advertisers pay attention to demographic patterns. One target of advertisers is the demographic group aged 14 to 24. This group has growing access to money and is open to trying new products. Products pitched to this group are mostly advertised on television programs watched by this segment of the population.

Advertisers are also selling an image: something you might like to be. Do you want to look like the Gap models? Do you want to dance like the guy with the PLD (portable listening device)? Do you want to join that group in the fast-food commercial? Advertisers are only too happy to sell you those dreams in the form of their products.

FADS AND TRENDS

Popular culture often rides on the wave of a trend or a **fad** (something in style for a very short time). Novelty (newness) is an important aspect of pop culture. What is important one day may soon fade.

Because popular culture is built upon people's needs and desires, it changes as people change. Convenience food, for example, became hugely popular after many more women started entering the workforce in the 1970s. In the early years of the 21st century, the popularity of computers spawned a "geek" revolution. Once seen as social outcasts, "computer

▶ **DID YOU KNOW** ◀
Many phrases have been injected into the language over the years from popular culture. You might recognize the expressions "voted off the island" or "extreme," both made popular by successful US television shows. What phrase is current right now? Where did it come from?

FIGURE 4.4 MuchMusic VJ Jenn Howlett poses on the set of the MuchMusic Video Awards. MuchMusic is Canada's national music station. Its young hosts, combined with its youth-oriented advertising, ensure that it attracts and keeps the attention of a younger audience.

nerds" were suddenly revered as the smart people who could fix your problem.

POPULAR CULTURE AS GLOBAL CULTURE?

Popular culture often emphasizes "sameness," and with good reason. Brand-name advertising, for example, must be instantly recognizable in order to succeed.

Have you travelled away from your local area to another city in Manitoba or outside the province? Some things in the new area may appear different. But you recognize the McDonalds, Pizza Hut, Tim Hortons, Wal-Mart, and Canadian Tire signs quite easily. The same is true all over the world. Famous brand names are instantly recognizable, whether you are in Winnipeg or Tel Aviv.

Another aspect of the sameness of popular culture is more controversial. When people around the world start to watch the same television programs, recognize the same brands, and are exposed to some of the values of popular culture, they may be encouraged to become "Westernized."

This process is sometimes called the "branding" of society. What happens to local culture when a McDonalds restaurant opens in Beijing, China, or when Disneyland theme parks attract families in Hong Kong or Paris? Are these developments good or bad? What do you think?

▶ **DID YOU KNOW** ◀
Disney Corporation also makes movies and owns the television networks ABC and ESPN and a variety of print media and Internet sites.

FIGURE 4.5 José Bové is a French farmer who vandalized a partially completed McDonalds restaurant in France. His supporters (shown here wearing mustaches like Bové's) demonstrated outside a Paris McDonalds, handing out French salami sandwiches on French bread. What was their message?

THE INFLUENCE OF THE UNITED STATES

Because the United States has more products to sell than any other country, it exerts a powerful influence on the rest of the world. US media also "sell" an American lifestyle and culture. What you define as your own popular culture has often been created in the United States.

The United States is also home to some of the most recognized celebrities in the world. Famous people contribute to popular culture by their choice of fashions, products, and actions. Because they are highly recognizable, US celebrities influence popular culture in many ways. Some people argue that Canadian personalities make it "big" only when they are recognized as celebrities in the United States.

OTHER INFLUENCES ON POPULAR CULTURE

The development of popular culture does not spring solely from US roots, although it often seems that way. Television reality shows started in Britain. India's film industry—Bollywood—produces more movies per year than Hollywood does. Fashion forecasters are saying that Paris and Milan, the centres of high fashion, must soon "make room for China on the catwalk." Asian cars and technological inventions are some of the most sought-after brand names around the world. In an increasingly global world, there are more and more influences to consider.

▶ **DID YOU KNOW** ◀
The internationally acclaimed 2005 film *Capote* was shot in Manitoba, though the setting was actually rural Kansas.

PAUSE, REFLECT, APPLY

1. Describe the presence of popular culture in your life.
2. Why is the United States so influential when it comes to popular culture?
3. Give three examples of the global nature of popular culture.
4. Create a Venn diagram comparing Canadian perspectives on global popular culture with American and French perspectives. Use examples from this book, and research if necessary.

Maintaining an Identity in the Face of Popular Culture

Popular culture is largely English-language culture. Yet, Canada has three founding peoples: the Aboriginal peoples, the French, and the British. Only one of these groups uses English as its heritage (original)

▶ **KEY QUESTION**
How can a unique identity be maintained in the face of popular culture?

language. Aboriginal peoples and francophone Canadians are minorities in this country. Within Aboriginal culture, there is a huge **diversity** of languages and heritage. Many different Aboriginal groups strive to maintain a unique identity in the face of an overwhelming popular culture.

KEEPING AND MAKING A CULTURE: THE ABORIGINAL PEOPLES

Mass media and popular culture exert both positive and negative influences. First Nations, Inuit, and Métis peoples have used new media to create a sense of community and identity. Internet Web sites such as Windspeaker and the Turtle Island Native Network provide news and information. They open up discussion about Canadian and Aboriginal cultures. They broadcast perspectives and stories that cannot be found in the mainstream media. The Turtle Island Native Network alone receives about 2 million hits a month!

Yet, the mass media have also undercut Aboriginal culture. About 53 Aboriginal languages are spoken in Canada today. But each year, the number of people speaking most of these languages gets smaller and smaller. (One notable exception is Inuktitut, the language of the Inuit, which showed a 7.5 percent increase in use as a primary language between

> **THE WEB**
> Visit Windspeaker, Turtle Island Native Network, and Aboriginal Peoples Television Network Web sites at www.emp.ca/ccw

> **DID YOU KNOW**
> The annual Aboriginal Music Awards recognize talented artists. In 2005, Manitoba's Ryan D'Aoust received the best fiddle album honour for *Southside of the Strings*.

FIGURE 4.6 Aboriginal artists from Manitoba also break into the mainstream. (Left) Adam Beach, of the Lake Manitoba (Ojibwe) First Nation, was recently signed by Disney. (Right) Inuit singer and songwriter Susan Aglukark was born in Churchill, Manitoba. Aglukark often refers to her people in her songs and is considered a spokesperson for northern issues.

1996 and 2001.) Why are Aboriginal languages disappearing? According to the report *Aboriginal Language Broadcasting in Canada*:

- Most Aboriginal people have access to television.
- Mainstream media have been a factor in the loss of Aboriginal culture.
- Mainstream media still tend to stereotype Aboriginal peoples.
- Aboriginal artists, including writers, actors, and producers, are largely excluded from mainstream productions.

Today, many people in Aboriginal communities use broadcasting as a way to address some of these issues. The Aboriginal Peoples Television Network (APTN) is the first national Aboriginal television network in the world. Its programming is by, for, and about Aboriginal peoples. It is shared with all Canadians and viewers around the world. APTN's programming is 60 percent in English, 15 percent in French, and 25 percent in Aboriginal languages.

KEEPING A LANGUAGE ALIVE: FRANCOPHONES IN CANADA

Francophone Canadians live in every province and territory of Canada. The largest number live in Quebec. Support for francophone culture has led to vibrant radio, television, music, film, and other cultural industries inside Quebec.

Radio-Canada is the CBC's French-language network. Télé-Québec is the television network operated by that province. Two-thirds of the programming on these networks is Canadian, not American. Although Quebeckers have access to US television, they seem to prefer locally made French-language programs over US shows.

Outside Quebec, francophones have more difficulty maintaining their culture and identity. In Alberta and Manitoba, francophone parents have fought for the right to run French-language schools (see Chapter 3). When

THE WEB

Visit *Say Magazine*, a Winnipeg-based magazine for Aboriginal youth, at www.emp.ca/ccw

LITERACY COACH

The first time you visit a Web site, examine how the menus operate. Some sites have separate menus for fixed content—categories that do not change from month to month. Other sites have one menu for all their content categories. Another strategy is to take down the names of the menu items you know you'll go back to, along with a brief description of what's in them. This can save time on your next visit, especially when you are doing research.

FIGURE 4.7 Hoop dancer Buffy Handel performs with Eagle and Hawk at the 2005 Festival du Voyageur in Winnipeg. The festival is the largest winter cultural celebration held in Western Canada. It always features a great line-up of francophone and Aboriginal talent.

> **THE WEB**
> For more on Canadian culture, link to the Government of Canada site at www.emp.ccw

children of francophones go to school in English, watch television in English, and play with their friends in English, they may forget how to speak French. They may lose touch with the rest of the francophone community. French-language education is seen as one way to combat this trend.

In Western Canada, francophones work hard to counteract English-language and US mass media. Local festivals, conferences, and awards celebrate many aspects of francophone culture: the visual arts, dance, film, choral singing, and folklore. Some festivals, such as the Festival du Voyageur, attract people from all over the world.

HOW IS CANADIAN IDENTITY REFLECTED IN THE MASS MEDIA?

Canadian artists and Canadian films, television shows, books, and songs are known around the world. Award-winning TV shows such as *Corner Gas*, *Degrassi Junior High*, *Cold Squad*, and *The Nature of Things* are syndicated and shown in other countries, including the United States, Britain, and Australia. People who have never been to Canada get to see some of our communities up close through television.

Canadian producers also make documentaries and films about key figures in Canadian history. The CBC television series *Canada: A People's History* tells the story of Canada from 15,000 BCE (Before the Common Era) to the present day. "Heritage Minutes" are 60-second films that focus on interesting events in Canada's history.

Through the mass media, Canadians explore what it means to "be Canadian." Television advertising has associated the word Canadian with Tim Hortons coffee. In the early 2000s, a Molson advertising campaign featured an "I am Canadian" rant that connected strongly with Canadians. Among its pronouncements: "I believe in peacekeeping, not policing; diversity, not assimilation"—pop culture references to Canadian values and government policies.

> ▶ **DID YOU KNOW** ◀
> *Anne of Green Gables*, set in Prince Edward Island in the early 1900s, is popular in Japan, China, and Taiwan. Residents of these countries have made Prince Edward Island a major tourist destination.

PAUSE, REFLECT, APPLY

1. Describe some ways in which Aboriginal peoples use the mass media to maintain their identity.
2. What is the specific challenge that francophones face when it comes to loss of culture?
3. What is your favourite reflection of Canadian identity in the mass media? Explain your choice.

Protecting and Promoting Canadian Identity and Culture

In a world where popular culture is dominated by the United States, can Canada stay Canadian? Politicians and citizens have struggled with this question since Canada was formed.

Government has often tried to promote and protect Canadian culture. Not everyone has agreed that this is a good thing (see Face Off, page 85). Many Canadians, however, have benefited from policies and court decisions that have safeguarded Canada's culture and heritage. Without government support, this might not have been possible.

> **KEY QUESTION**
> What role should the government play in protecting Canadian culture?

CANADIAN BROADCASTING CORPORATION

The Canadian Broadcasting Corporation (CBC) is Canada's public (government-funded) radio and television broadcaster. The French-language network is called La Société Radio-Canada (Radio-Canada, or SRC). Together, they are called CBC/Radio-Canada.

CBC/Radio-Canada's *Hockey Night in Canada* has long been one of its most popular broadcasts. Its public affairs programs and national news programs also connect Canadians—and create an identity—from coast to coast.

In 2005, the CBC began experimenting in podcasting—distributing audio or video files over the Internet. Consumers listen to the files, often songs or videos, on portable devices. With podcasting, new content can be created all the time. The difference is that people can listen when, where, and how they want.

FIGURE 4.8 With traditional broadcasting, you listen to a few sources of information on your radio or television through a single service provider. With podcasts, you subscribe to different programs from various sources and download them whenever you wish.

> **DID YOU KNOW**
> *Podcasting* is a word made up from "broadcasting" and "iPod" (a portable player with a computer hard drive in it).

CANADIAN CONTENT RULES

The Canadian Radio-television and Telecommunications Commission (CRTC) is a government agency. By law, it requires radio and television stations to air **Canadian content** on a regular basis. "Canadian content" is defined as content that is at least partly written, produced, presented, or otherwise contributed by Canadians.

For music on radio, the criteria are defined using the "MAPL" system. To qualify as Canadian content, a musical selection must have a Canadian presence in at least two of the following: music composition (M), artist performing (A), production (P), and lyrics (L).

The CRTC requires that 60 percent of television programming aired between 6:00 a.m. and midnight, and 50 percent of programming aired between 6:00 p.m. and midnight, be of Canadian origin. News, sports, weather, talk shows, and current affairs programs can be included.

CHARTER PROTECTION OF IDENTITY AND CULTURE

In previous chapters, you learned that the *Canadian Charter of Rights and Freedoms* is part of Canada's written constitution. The Charter might not be the first thing that comes to mind when you think of popular culture, but it does protect identity. It has been used to give equal protection to many minority groups in Canada.

Under Charter rulings,

- a Sikh student is allowed to wear his *kirpan* (traditional dagger) to school (see Face Off, page 57)
- disabled Canadians can insist upon better access to their place of employment (for example, having ramps or elevators installed)
- same-sex couples can attend their high school prom with their straight friends (see Figure 3.5, page 61)
- francophone students can receive an education in French, even if they are a minority in their community (see Face Off, page 65).

These are just a few examples of decisions that affect the culture Canadians live and work in. As a result of Charter court rulings, Canadian society has become more visibly diverse. This means that Canadian society and law are committed to **pluralism**—to recognizing and respecting cultural diversity. The law strives to create social conditions where no one has to be invisible.

FACE OFF: Should Government Protect Canadian Culture?

Should government protect Canadian culture? Is there a Canadian culture worth protecting?

Defenders of Canadian culture argue that Canada is at a disadvantage. With its smaller population, Canada cannot compete against US-made television, music, film, sports, and magazines. Without government support, Canadian arts and media might soon cease to exist.

This group argues that Canadians need to tell their stories, sing their songs, play their music, and create their art—as Canadians. Canadians need to hear the news reported by Canadian journalists on a Canadian channel, not a US one.

> Canadian content does have a place on our television dial. We're bombarded by US television. It comes across the border on US stations carried by our cable and direct satellite companies … . Unfortunately, US television shows, no matter how good, miss some basic truths about life in Canada.
>
> —Elisabeth Hurst, blogger
>
> Source: http://bad.eserver.org/issues/2001/57/hurst.html

Others argue that if Canadian culture cannot stand on its own merits, then it is not worth protecting. Canadians choose music, television programs, and magazines based on quality. If Canadian material is good, why wouldn't people select it? Canadian culture can best be protected by striving for excellence, not by protection by a government watchdog.

This group says that Canadian content rules can make a mockery of reality. For example, if you were a Canadian artist with a chart-topping album, but you co-produced it with a non-Canadian living in Los Angeles, that might make you ineligible for a Canadian music award.

A third position argues that Canadian culture will eventually be swallowed by US culture, and that Canada might even join the United States one day. This group says there is not much sense in attempting to stop the march of time.

> There is nothing stopping Canadians from supporting Canadian art. If they want to, they will. If not, I don't see any point in forcing them. … Protecting Canadian art has been a failure. There is something faintly ludicrous in the idea that art is the only thing that stands between us and annexation [by the United States].
>
> —Andrew Coyne, writer
>
> Source: www.yorku.ca/ycom/gazette/past/archive/021297.htm

What Do You Think?

1. Elisabeth Hurst says that "US television shows, no matter how good, miss some basic truths about life in Canada." What truths do you think she means? List some that you know about.
2. Do you follow any Canadian or Manitoba artists? Do you like them because they are distinctively Canadian or because you just like them? How does your answer express your own ideas about protecting Canadian content?
3. Visit the timeline, "A Chronology of Canadian Film and Television" at www.emp.ca/ccw. Select one event and describe in a short paragraph how it contributed to a growing or changing sense of Canadian identity.

Source: "A Chronology of Canadian Film and Television." *Take One's Essential Guide to Canadian Film*. Edited by Wyndham Wise. Toronto: University of Toronto Press, 2001, pp. 229–258.

FIGURE 4.9 George Stroumboulopoulos hosts CBC Newsworld's *The Hour*, a prime-time news and current affairs program. The show is wide-ranging and irreverent. Look at the host: What age group do you think the show is targeting?

CANADIAN SPORTING EVENTS

Canada has achieved national and international recognition through sports. Your parents or grandparents probably watched the 1972 hockey Summit Series between Canada and the Soviet Union. Paul Henderson became a national hero when he scored the winning goal in the last minute of the last period. Canada has nurtured a hockey culture, and hockey has become part of Canada's identity.

In recent years, Canada has raised its international profile at the Olympic Games. At the 2006 Winter Olympics, Canada placed third in the medals rankings, with a total of 24—our best showing ever.

NATIONAL CELEBRATIONS

Canadians celebrate national identity on many occasions, such as Canada Day (July 1), National Flag Day (February 15), and Remembrance Day (November 11). The last two days are probably celebrated in your school. Other celebrations you may take part in include Saint-Jean-Baptiste Day (June 24), Black History Month (February), and Asian Heritage Month (May).

PAUSE, REFLECT, APPLY

1. Explain how the Canadian Radio-television and Telecommunications Commission tries to protect Canadian culture.
2. Describe how your favourite personality in sports or the arts helps to shape Canada's identity, (a) nationally and (b) internationally.
3. Explain how Canada's official policy of multiculturalism helps to form Canada's identity. Give two specific examples.
4. What is the difference between protecting and promoting culture? Do you agree that Canada should do both? Explain your answer.

REPLAY

In this chapter, you have explored these concepts:

1. Identity is influenced by many factors, including interests, family, peers, religion, media, community, heritage, and language.
2. Mass media are various means of communication used to reach a large, or mass, audience, such as print, television and radio, and new media.
3. Pop (popular) culture is the culture of ordinary people. It is transmitted and influenced by mass media.
4. Many Aboriginal peoples and francophones strive to maintain their cultures, and their unique identities, in the face of an overwhelmingly English-language popular culture.
5. Canadian culture is protected by the Canadian government through content regulations.

SKILLS TOOLKIT
Media Literacy: How to Identify Advertising Techniques

Media literacy means being able to understand the techniques used in different kinds of media messages. Advertising is one kind of message. It uses persuasive techniques to get you to purchase a certain product or service.

Advertising is encountered in traditional places: in print, on television and radio, through the mail, outdoors, and on the Internet. You also find it in less obvious places. For example, many films and television programs display brand-name products during the story. Many people are completely unaware that these products have been "placed." The goods are being advertised—and businesses have paid to have their products shown.

Advertisers spend millions to persuade you to buy their products, even if there is a good chance the purchase will not benefit you or humanity. Responsible citizenship requires you to think critically about what you hear, see, and read.

ONLINE AD WOES

Online ads can be annoying. Here are some popular online ad techniques. The ad

- pops up in front of your window
- tries to trick you into clicking on it
- covers what you are trying to see
- has no "close" button, or has an unresponsive one
- does not say what it is for
- blinks on and off
- announces that you have won a prize.

You can block many of these ads by activating your "pop-up blocker." This is usually located in the Tools menu of your Web browser.

The following advertising techniques are used in all media:

- *Appeal to vanity*. If you buy this product, you will be more desirable.
- *Endorsement by celebrity or authority*. If X uses the product, it must be good.
- *Surveys or statistical evidence*. For example, "Ford LTD—700 percent quieter." When forced to substantiate the claim, Ford revealed that they meant the inside of the Ford was 700 percent quieter than the outside.
- *Appeal to innovation*. The product is "new" or "improved."
- *Fear factor*. Do you have bad breath? Do you carry too much weight?
- *Good feelings*. In subtle ways, the use of the product is associated with human happiness, satisfaction, good health, or well-being.
- *Herd effect*. Everyone is using this product; why aren't you?
- *Vague claim*. "Helps control dandruff symptoms with regular use."
- *Leading question*. "Shouldn't you be using ———?"

Skill Practice

1. Identify three ads on television, three in print, and three online, and determine which technique is being used in each case. Refer to the list above.
2. Determine whether each ad presents fact or opinion. Remember that a fact is a statement that can be proven to be true; for example, Winnipeg is the capital of Manitoba. An opinion expresses a belief, feeling, or judgment; for example, "My high school is the best in the district."
3. In each case, determine what you do not know about the product. In other words, what important questions would you want answered about the product that are not answered by this ad?

FIGURE 4.10 In 2005, Andrew Fischer of Omaha, Nebraska made close to $50,000 by selling ad space on his forehead in the form of temporary tattoos. People have also offered their bald heads for advertising space on eBay.

STUDY HALL

Be Informed

1. After reflection, create a brochure in which you take a tour of your own identity. Focus on these three ideas:
   - your own personal identity
   - the identity of Manitoba
   - the identity of Canada.

2. Write a paragraph in which you describe how your attitudes and opinions have been influenced by the mass media. Use as many specific examples as possible.

3. Interview a francophone Canadian and someone who is First Nations or Métis. Determine how each maintains her or his identity in the face of mass media and popular culture. Write a summary of your interviews.

4. Find an article, feature, or quiz at Windspeaker at www.emp.ca/ccw. Windspeaker is Canada's national Aboriginal news source. Explain how your selected article, feature, or quiz from Windspeaker reflects Aboriginal identity as presented in the mainstream media.

5. Identify your favourite television program, celebrity, musical artist or group, movie, magazine, and Web site. Determine how many of your favourites are Canadian and how many are American. What conclusions can you make based on your informal survey?

6. Find three pieces of popular Canadian music that contain lyrics (words) that directly refer to Canadian people, places, or events.

Be Purposeful

7. a) Some of the cultural values that are promoted by the mass media through advertising are competition, consumerism, individualism, and technological advancement. In small groups, brainstorm to find examples of each of these values in print or television advertising.

   b) In the same small groups, identify groups of people in Canada who might not share these values. What values do these groups promote? Do you think their voices are heard by other Canadians? How? (The groups you identify can be cultural groups or groups bound by a common activity, such as interest or advocacy groups.)

8. In this activity, you will examine one story from several different perspectives. This is a good way to learn how different groups of Canadians hold different points of view about the same issue or event.

   a) As a class, pick a news story that deals with an important issue or event. Your teacher will give you some leads.

   b) In a small group or with a partner, tape four newscasts that deal with the issue or event you have selected:
   - one from the Aboriginal Peoples Television Network
   - one from a francophone television station
   - one from a US television network
   - one from the Canadian Broadcasting Corporation.

STUDY HALL (cont.)

c) In class, view the four newscasts and prepare a written news log (this could be in the form of a chart) comparing how the issue or event you selected was represented in the different broadcasts. As you do this, keep the following questions in mind:

- What pictures or images did each newscast use to illustrate the story?
- How did the news reader describe the event? (Consider tone of voice; whether the report was mainly factual or whether it expressed an opinion or a conclusion.)
- What kind of coverage did the story get? (Was it a short item or a longer piece?)
- What information was missing in each newscast?

Be Active

9. Invite one of the following people to your class to speak about identity in the face of popular culture:

    - a representative from the francophone community or
    - a representative from a First Nations or Métis community.

    Develop questions to ask your visitor. Your questions should focus on the issues of identity and culture.

10. Organize a classroom debate on the topic, "Is Canadian culture worth protecting?" Before the debate, research your position and the position of your opponent. After the debate, summarize your position on each debate topic in a well-written paragraph.

UNIT 2

Democracy and Governance in Canada

Chapter 5
Ideals and Institutions of Democracy

Chapter 6
What Is Government?

Chapter 7
How Do Laws and Regulations Affect You?

Chapter 8
How Do Governments Make Policy?

Chapter 9
How Do Citizens Elect Governments?

Chapter 10
How Does the Judicial System Work?

Chapter 11
Citizenship in Action

CHAPTER 5
Ideals and Institutions of Democracy

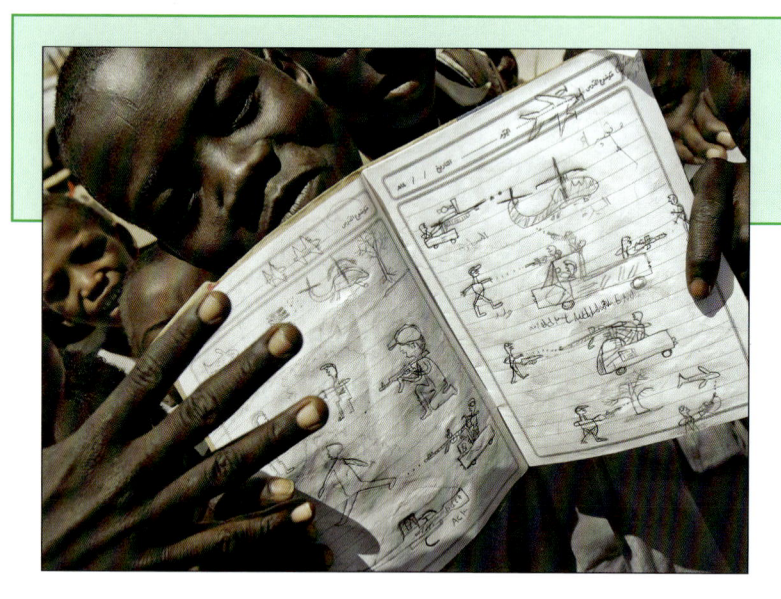

September 2004: A refugee shows his drawings of fighting that he witnessed in Darfur, Sudan. Since 2003, tens of thousands of people have fled civil unrest in Darfur province.

Imagine that a militant group in Quebec demands that Canada grant their province independence. The federal government fears the group will resort to terrorism. It promises rewards to Quebeckers who report suspected terrorists. Some anglophone media reports use hateful language, implying that all francophone Quebeckers are separatists and potential terrorists. Some anglophone Quebeckers attack francophone neighbours, and police do not intervene. Chaos follows and spreads to other provinces, as francophones are hunted down. Canada is engulfed in violence. Hundreds of thousands of people are killed before it ends. Nobody knows if law and order can be restored. The countries of the world do nothing.

This scenario is extremely unlikely in a **democracy** like Canada, where disputes are settled by legislatures and the courts. But similar events in 2003 devastated Darfur province in Sudan, a country in north-central Africa.

In the past, differences, sometimes bitter ones, have divided Canadians. Our history has also seen violence. What do you know about Canadian citizenship and government systems today that help to prevent civil conflicts from spreading out of control?

What You Need to Know
- What are some of the causes of civil conflicts?
- How do different forms of government resolve conflicts?
- What are some fundamental democratic values and beliefs?
- What is the difference between being a citizen and being a subject?
- What are the advantages and disadvantages of democratic processes in Canada?
- How have democratic ideals shaped contemporary Canadian society?
- How can you identify bias?

Key Terms
democracy
government
society
authoritarian
consensus
politics
power

common good
rule of law
restitution
direct democracy
representative democracy

Key Question
How does a democracy resolve conflicts among people?

Government: Why Is It Necessary?

During this course, you will explore and discuss many interrelated concepts. One of the most important of these concepts is **civics**. Civics can be defined as the study of the **rights** (things you are morally or legally entitled to) and duties of citizenship. The rights and responsibilities of citizenship were introduced in chapters 1 and 3.

Let's look at citizenship again. You are a member, or citizen, of your classroom and your school. You are a member, or citizen, of your family, neighbourhood, and so on. More formally, **citizenship** is defined as the condition of receiving rights, duties, and responsibilities as a member of a state or nation.

Discussions of citizenship can raise some difficult questions. For example:

- Who defines rights, duties, and responsibilities?
- How do we balance rights with duties and responsibilities?
- Who gets to be a citizen?

As you learned in Chapter 1, anyone born outside Canada must follow government procedures to become a citizen. This brings in another key civics concept: government. What, exactly, is it? Why is it necessary?

Government is a system by which a group of people makes the **laws** (principles and regulations) that are enforced to guide the affairs of a community. This chapter explores citizenship and its relationship to government and public decision making.

THE SHIPWRECK SCENARIO

We still haven't answered the question, "Why is government necessary?" The "shipwreck scenario" is a good way to explore what government is and why we need it.

A group of people are shipwrecked on a remote island. To survive, they must find food and water and create shelter and protection. Because these people form a community that shares these **basic needs and wants**, the group can be seen as a **society**.

How will the basic necessities be shared in this society? Who will perform essential tasks?

> ▶ **DID YOU KNOW** ◀
> The *Front de libération du Québec* was a separatist group founded in Quebec in the 1960s that used violence to advance its goal of independence from Canada. In October 1970, FLQ members kidnapped a British diplomat and the Quebec minister of labour. In response, the federal government declared a state of emergency and used the *War Measures Act* to arrest and hold over 450 Quebeckers without laying charges against them. Most of those arrested during the "October Crisis" were later released. (See Chapter 11.)

FIGURE 5.1 Earth: a society in which we are all citizens? This satellite image, taken by the US space agency NASA in 1972, was unlike any other photograph ever taken. Humans had never gotten far enough off Earth to photograph the whole planet. This first image of Earth from space allowed humanity to experience a deep and emotional new awareness of our world.

▶ **DID YOU KNOW** ◀
April 22 is Earth Day, when people around the world celebrate the Earth and acknowledge our environmental responsibility to the planet and one another.

The group might choose a leader. Possibly the captain is chosen to make major decisions. Perhaps a smaller group is chosen to make less important decisions. Perhaps the strongest individual or group imposes its decisions. Whatever method is used, it creates a simple government: a way of making decisions.

If the group is not soon rescued, disputes will break out. The government will face the challenge of resolving problems. It will have to devise rules (laws and regulations) of conduct that it can enforce. In this way, conflict will be reduced. This will ensure the safety and survival of the whole group. Government, then, is an activity or method of making and enforcing decisions that are binding upon a society.

HOW ARE DECISIONS MADE?

Suppose a new school sports team is considering different names and logos for its uniform. Different methods could be used to make a decision:

- One person could decide for the whole team. This person might be a school authority, such as the principal or coach. Team members would have little or no input. This is an example of **authoritarian** decision making.
- The team could reach a decision by giving each member a vote. This is **democratic** decision making.
- The team could discuss names and logos and make a decision only when all members agree. This is decision making through **consensus**.

Each decision-making method has advantages and disadvantages.

Authoritarian decision making is speedy, yes. But it doesn't take account of how decisions may affect different people. Because individual members have little input, they may not support decisions.

The democratic method gives each individual equal input into decisions through a vote. The choice that gets the most votes, wins. This seems fair, but it has a downside: the other choices lose! If the issue is important or emotional, the "losers" may be resentful.

Consensus decision making respects and listens to each individual to reach a collective decision. This is a decision that each member of the group agrees on and supports. Reaching consensus can take a great deal of time and discussion—and may not always be possible. Group members must understand the issues and be willing to share opinions openly. Another disadvantage is that sometimes only a watered-down decision can be reached.

POLITICS: WHAT IS IT?

Back on the island, the captain is chosen to be leader by a majority vote. Some of the people, however, become upset with her. They say they have been assigned too many tasks and not enough food. They try to persuade her to make changes. She says no. They devise plans to replace her and try to win support from others. This is called **politics**: a human activity in which one individual or group opposed to another mobilizes support to obtain **power** to govern. (Power is the ability of a group or individual to get what it wants.)

The term "politics" is formally associated with governments. Informally, politics occurs whenever individuals or groups struggle for advantage. Politics can be done openly and honestly. It can also be done secretly and through manipulation, threats, and bribes.

☐ DISCUSSION POINT
Why do you think consensus decision making has sometimes been called the highest form of democracy?

LITERACY COACH
When you read, must you start with the first word on the left-hand page? No! On these two pages, you could first look at the photo, the cartoon, the Did You Know and Discussion Point features, and the first sentence in each paragraph. Looking at these elements first will help you figure out what this material is about so that when you do read these pages, they will probably make more sense to you.

▶ DID YOU KNOW ◀
Question Period is held every day that Parliament is in session. During these 45 minutes, opposition parties can question the government on any of its policies. You can view Question Period on CPAC, the Cable Public Affairs Channel.

FIGURE 5.2 This cartoon shows Canadian students "learning" about democracy by visiting Question Period in Parliament. What message do you think the cartoonist wanted to convey?

PAUSE, REFLECT, APPLY

1. Which methods of decision making would work best in the following situations?
   - a group of friends is choosing a movie
   - a basketball team must declare its starting players
   - a class must decide on a fundraising program
   - a principal must work out a program to prevent violence on school property
   - parents are trying to work out a reasonable curfew with their children
2. What type of decision making would be best for the shipwrecked passengers
   a) immediately after the shipwreck?
   b) later, if they are not rescued?
3. Why might the captain be chosen as leader?
4. Why do you think Canada's provincial and federal governments use democratic rather than consensus decision making?
5. Describe politics, government, and citizenship in your own words. How are these terms interrelated?
6. What is the difference between formal and informal politics? Give an example for each.
7. In what sense does politics occur within a) a family, b) a school, and c) a workplace?

Types of Government

> **KEY QUESTION**
> What is the relationship between you and your governments?

Governments are usually classified according to how they make decisions and come to power. This broadly creates three types of government: authoritarian, democratic, and consensual (by consensus).

AUTHORITARIAN GOVERNMENTS

As you learned earlier, authoritarian decision making allows little or no input from "the people" (those being governed). Often, an authoritarian government is dominated by one person in what is called a **dictatorship**.

If dictators try to carry out the will of the people (what people want), they may enjoy wide public support. However, authoritarian dictatorships do

FIGURE 5.3 Comic genius Charlie Chaplin played Adenoid Hynkel, of Tomania, in his 1940 film, *The Great Dictator*. What historical figure is he ridiculing?

Democratic governments	Authoritarian governments
Two or more political parties	Only one political party
Free press	Government-controlled press
Free media	Censored media
Free, fair, frequent elections	Fake elections or no elections
Equal legal rights	Unequal legal rights
Courts free of political control	Courts under political control
Minorities respected	Minorities often under attack

FIGURE 5.4 Comparison of the usual features of democratic and authoritarian governments

not tolerate opposition. They may rely upon a large military, informers, and secret police to eliminate opposition and to stay in power. They may also use and control the media, schools, and public events to build support for their policies.

DEMOCRATIC GOVERNMENTS

Democratic governments make decisions based on the will of the people. Usually, citizens choose individuals in elections to represent them in government. In contrast to authoritarian governments, democracies tolerate opposition. This can be expressed by individual citizens, groups, and the media. Opposition can also be expressed by other **political parties** (organizations of people who share similar political beliefs and who work to have their candidates win votes during elections).

Opposition and criticism are part of the democratic system. A true democracy, therefore, cannot rely on secret police and informers to ensure support for its decisions.

> **THE WEB**
> Visit www.emp.ca/ccw for a link to Democracy Watch, a Canadian citizens' group that focuses on government and corporate accountability.

GOVERNMENT BY CONSENSUS

Before their contact with Europeans, Aboriginal peoples in what is today Canada had a variety of decision-making structures. Each culture had its own system of government and law that reflected its values, practices, and traditions. In many cultures, decisions were reached by consensus. The people—men and women, elders and youths—discussed an issue until everyone agreed to accept a resolution.

The traditional Aboriginal attitude toward governance was **egalitarian** (based on the equality of all people). This attitude is reflected in the Cree word *weyasowewin*, or "setting the standard" for individual and group behaviour. Another word associated with Cree governance was *nakayatotamowin* ("what is usually done").

SUBJECTS VERSUS CITIZENS

How do authoritarian, democratic, and consensus-based governments view and treat their people?

It may be tempting to believe that all authoritarian governments treat people badly, and that all democracies and consensus-based societies treat people well. But it would not be accurate. In rare cases, authoritarian governments, especially prosperous ones, provide education, health care, subsidized housing, and other social benefits. The **communist** government of the Soviet Union (which owned all land and property) provided these and other benefits to its people (from 1917 to 1989). Soviet leaders criticized many democracies—especially the United States—for ignoring the wants and needs of the poor.

In authoritarian governments, individuals are seen as **subjects**. As such, they are under the absolute control of the government and subject to its commands. In contrast, individuals in a democracy or a consensus-based society are citizens. They are free to participate in community affairs and to act to bring about change.

Citizens in a democracy can vote and hold office. In most democracies, citizens have other rights as well—to education, for example. Many democratic governments today also provide social benefits such as pensions, employment insurance, and health care.

In traditional Aboriginal societies, the community's resources, such as land and food, were freely shared. This custom helped create social stability by redistributing community wealth. For example, one important custom among the First Nations of the West Coast was the potlatch. This was a formal ceremony during which gifts, such as food, clothing, jewellery, and crafts, were given to the guests. When the Canadian government banned the potlatch in the 19th century, it weakened the civic structure of these First Nations.

THE WEB
Learn more about the tradition of the potlatch at www.emp.ca/ccw

FACE OFF: Humans Are Selfish! No, Humans Are Good!

Philosopher Thomas Hobbes (1588–1679) lived during a long period of civil war in England. He wrote that without government, human life is "nasty, brutish, and short." Because of scarcity (insufficient resources), Hobbes believed, people must be willing to surrender their freedom to a ruler. That ruler must have absolute power, backed by force. Otherwise, human selfishness would always lead to civil conflict and war.

According to Hobbes, as long as the ruler protects the people, revolt or resistance is not justified. Only if the ruler/government fails to do so is revolution justified. The people then have to find another ruler who can protect them.

French philosopher Jean-Jacques Rousseau (1712–1778) disagreed. He believed that humans' state of nature—before societies and governments came into being—was free and friendly. "Man was born free, but everywhere he is in chains," Rousseau wrote in *The Social Contract*, in 1762.

Rousseau believed that the only way people can improve morally and mentally is to come together in societies. The challenge is to preserve humankind's natural state of freedom. For Rousseau, the solution was for people to form a "social contract" with the "general will," or the **common good**, and place themselves under its direction. Majority opinion was not always the way to achieve this. One person, or a few, might realize the common good (the interests of all people in a community or society; for example, peace, justice, economic stability) more clearly than others. Government deserved to be obeyed only as long as it followed the common good in its actions.

What Do You Think?

1. a) How do Hobbes's and Rousseau's views of human nature differ?
   b) Do you agree with Hobbes or with Rousseau? Explain.
2. Which philosophy would more likely lead to democratic government and which to authoritarian government? Briefly explain your answer.
3. Compare Hobbes's and Rousseau's ideas under these headings: a) human nature, b) the purpose of government, c) the right to revolt.

DID YOU KNOW
The stuffed tiger "Hobbes" in the comic strip "Calvin and Hobbes" was named after Thomas Hobbes for his negative view of human nature.

PAUSE, REFLECT, APPLY

1. How is the method of decision making different in authoritarian, democratic, and consensus-based governments?
2. How is opposition dealt with in
   a) authoritarian decision making,
   b) democratic decision making, and
   c) consensual decision making?
3. How do opposition, power, and politics connect in a democracy?
4. Is it accurate to say that authoritarian governments never enjoy public support? Explain.
5. Is it accurate to say that democratic governments, by definition, always treat people well? Explain your answer, with reference to Canada.
6. What is the difference between a citizen and a subject?

Power and Politics

> **KEY QUESTION**
> What is required of a society and its citizens for government to function democratically?

Let's go back to the people shipwrecked on the island. As primary decision maker, the captain has been exercising her power. She must be able to do so for government to function. The group members have gone along with her decisions because they have seen that unity is vital to their survival.

As you can see, government, politics, and power work together. The captain's **authority** (the right to give orders or make decisions) will last only as long as she can persuade others that she is the best decision maker. If political opponents can turn the group against her, she will lose power, the ability to govern.

> **DID YOU KNOW**
> In 1789, there was a mutiny on the ship *The Bounty*. In this real-life shipwreck scenario, 18 mutineers set up a "civilization" on Pitcairn Island. By 1808, only one crewman remained alive.

HOW DO GOVERNMENTS USE POWER?

The first and foremost task of any government is to preserve order within society. This means that it must find a way or ways to enforce its decisions. In other words, governments must also use power so that people obey laws.

As mentioned earlier, authoritarian governments rely heavily on the threat or use of military or police force to ensure orderly behaviour. This form of power—which uses threats and force to intimidate citizens—is called **coercion**. Democratic governments rely far more on other kinds of power to enforce decisions.

> **DISCUSSION POINT**
> If a democracy relies on coercion to maintain order, can it still be considered a true democracy?

One kind of power that democracies rely on is **influence**: the ability to persuade people to do something. For example, rather than pass harsh laws, governments may use advertising and public service announcements to try to influence people to stop smoking, speed less, and reduce family violence.

Democratic governments also rely on their authority. This form of power is based on the respect people have for the person or institution and the orders or laws they issue. Most Canadians obey laws because they respect their government and fellow citizens, not because they fear the police.

Of course, democracies do maintain police and military forces. Usually, this is done to arrest lawbreakers and to preserve public order if it is threatened.

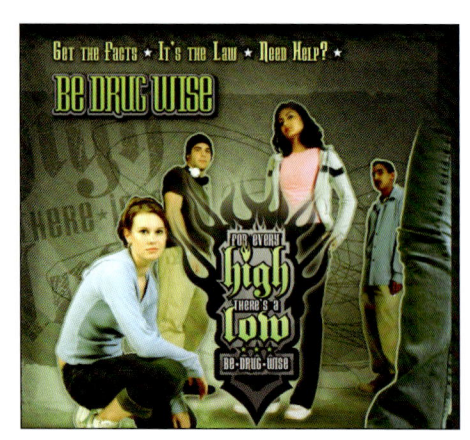

FIGURE 5.5 Health Canada's "Be Drug Wise" campaign aims to increase young people's awareness about drug use. Is this an example of influence or coercion?

PEOPLE POWER, CIVIL SOCIETY, AND A HEALTHY DEMOCRACY

In a democracy, citizens also have power. To thrive, a democracy must be open and accountable to its citizens. For that to happen, citizens must use their power effectively and responsibly.

In a democracy, citizens can do more than vote. Citizens are free—to express opinions, both for and against government. If people disagree with government, they can

- contact government representatives
- write letters to newspapers and other media
- put up a Web site
- gather support from other citizens
- form or join organizations that oppose a law or action
- organize and participate in demonstrations.

Civil society is composed of organizations and movements that citizens create outside government. People and organizations involved in civil society monitor governments. They also work for the common good by addressing social problems and needs. The focus can be as local as your schoolyard or as global as an international crisis, such as the conflict in Darfur. You will learn more about these **non-governmental organizations** in later chapters.

CIVIL CONFLICT AND THE RULE OF LAW

Societies experience conflicts when basic needs and wants are not met. As you learned earlier, basic needs and wants include items necessary for survival. Wants can also be more complex, such as the desire for recognition or achievement.

Governments, groups, and individuals use different methods to resolve conflicts. Authoritarian governments often use force to impose order. Democracies must rely on the institutions of government and the **rule of law** (the principle that all governments, groups, and people in society must obey the law).

Aboriginal cultures had their own unique ways of resolving disputes among citizens. When two people came into conflict, they first attempted to resolve the problem themselves. If they were unable to do so, they asked an elder to intervene. If this failed, the community applied its collective

> **DID YOU KNOW**
> University College of the North in The Pas, Manitoba offers a two-year program called "Restorative Justice and Conflict Resolution." The program prepares students to become facilitators in this Aboriginal method of resolving disputes. (To explore restorative justice, see Chapter 10, pages 213–215.)

public opinion to force the offenders to resolve their problem. In most cases, community disapproval was enough to prompt the disputing parties to make peace. Aboriginal justice often required **restitution**, in which one party was required to compensate the other for a loss or injury.

Different Ways to Resolve Disputes

Parties and groups involved in a conflict can **negotiate** by discussing the issues. Sometimes this leads to an agreement. If not, the disputing parties may call in a third party (not involved in the dispute) to referee and **mediate** an agreement between them. This is known as *mediation*. If the conflict still cannot be resolved, a third party may be given the power to **arbitrate**, or impose, a solution. This process is called *arbitration*. These methods are used increasingly in schools. Students are trained as peer mediators to help other students resolve conflicts. Mediators and arbitrators are also often used in labour disputes between employees and their employers (see Chapter 11).

PAUSE, REFLECT, APPLY

1. Define authority, influence, and coercion in terms of how power is exercised.
2. Decide whether authority, influence, or coercion is being used in each of the following situations:
   a) a music star urges young people to read more
   b) a mother forbids her children to watch a television show
   c) a movie is rated "restricted"
   d) a hockey player is ejected from a game after fighting with another player
   e) police "read the riot act" to demonstrators
   f) a penalty is charged on late income tax returns
3. Do you think people are more likely to obey a law if they a) are convinced it is right or b) fear its being enforced? Support your opinion with an example of a law.
4. In what sense does "civil society" act as a check on the power of government?
5. In your own words, describe how negotiation, mediation, and arbitration can be used to resolve conflicts.

> **KEY QUESTION**
> How has democracy absorbed influences and adapted to change?

Democracy: Yesterday and Today

The origins of democracy go back to the mid-5th century BCE and the polises of ancient Greece. "Polis" means "city" or "city-state" in Greek. By today's standards, polises were actually small towns. Each polis, which included the surrounding countryside, governed itself. Athens was the most famous. Only free-born males over a certain age were citizens—women and slaves were excluded from political participation.

Democracy emerged slowly in Athens. At first, when it was considered a very radical idea, democracy was supported by the philosopher Pericles (c. 495–429 BCE), among others. Because polises were small, all citizens knew one another. This was considered essential for democracy to work. All citizens could speak out and vote on issues, which were discussed in central assemblies in each polis. Because citizens directly made the laws themselves, this system was called **direct democracy**.

As states grew in size, and it became impossible for all citizens to know one another, direct democracy no longer worked. Citizens began to vote for representatives to hold political office and voice their interests in law-making assemblies. The term **representative democracy** applies to this kind of indirect democracy.

Today, most democracies are representative. Voters have no control over elected representatives after the election. Some democracies have experimented with the **recall election**. This gives electors the chance to vote to recall a representative before his or her term is up.

As you can see in Figure 5.6, democracy emerged in other places and changed over time.

FIGURE 5.6 Important events in the development of democracy

■ **c. 500 BCE: Greek polises**

origins of democratic ideas; direct democracy used to decide public policy

■ **1st–5th centuries CE: Roman Empire**

citizenship concept develops; non-Romans in Empire can become citizens

■ **c. 1150–1450: Iroquois Confederacy**

(date in dispute) five First Nations (North American Aboriginal groups) unite politically in a democratic form of government based on consensus decision making; eventually became the Six Nations Confederacy and influenced drafting of the US constitution

■ **1215: England, Magna Carta**

under threat of civil war, King John signs the "Great Charter"; the once absolute (unlimited) power of the monarch is now limited by law

■ **1775–1783: American Revolution**

Declaration of Independence (1776) states that "all men are created equal"; government of the people, by the people, for the people

(Figure 5.6 is continued on the next page.)

FIGURE 5.6 *Continued*

- **1789–1794: French Revolution**

the people overthrow an absolute monarch, establish a **republic** (a country with an elected president as head of state) based on equality; demands for civil rights spread across Europe

- **1876: The *Indian Act***

Canadian Parliament assumes exclusive power over First Nations and their lands, in violation of their constitutional treaty rights; this imposition of a foreign system of governance on Aboriginal peoples was a major setback to democracy in Canada, and an issue that continues today (see Figure 5.7)

- **19th–early 20th centuries**

political rights (the right to vote, run for office, participate in elections) steadily extended to more citizens (especially women) in Britain, United States, Canada, and Western European democracies

- **1918–1989**

spread of democracy to non-European states; setbacks caused by rise of authoritarian governments in 1930s, World War II (1939–1945), the Cold War (1945–1989)

- **1960**

extension of **franchise** (right to vote) to status Indians in Canada

- **1989–present**

democratic movements topple communist governments in the Soviet Union and countries under its influence in Eastern Europe (such as Ukraine); democracy spreads further into Asia and Africa; indigenous peoples worldwide seek greater self-determination

FIGURE 5.7 Aboriginal Canadians demonstrate in Winnipeg in March 2003 to protest Bill C-7, the federal government's proposed *First Nations Governance Act*. Critics said the bill was developed without meaningful consultation with Native communities on Aboriginal self-determination. Bill C-7 was defeated in Parliament the following October.

PAUSE, REFLECT, APPLY

1. What conditions allowed the Greeks to have direct democracy?
2. Why would electors want to use a recall?
3. What forms of technology could be used today to allow all citizens to vote on issues rather than just elect representatives? What form of democracy would this be?
4. Perhaps the last group in Canada yet to be given the political rights to vote and to hold public office is you, the 14- to 15-year-old age group. Make a case for or against the idea.
5. Is direct democracy desirable today, in your opinion?

Becoming Democratic

No one pretends that democracy is perfect or all-wise. Indeed, it has been said that democracy is the worst form of government except for all those other forms that have been tried.

—Winston Churchill (1874–1965),
British politician and statesman

> **KEY QUESTION**
> How and in what forms has democracy spread to countries across the world?

The above quotation leaves no doubt that democracy is imperfect. Nevertheless, it has become the most common form of government in the world today. Many factors account for its powerful global appeal.

THE ELEMENTS OF DEMOCRACY

1. Democratic decisions are made for the good of most people, most of the time

Citizens in democracies vote for representatives to make decisions and pass laws that they, the citizens, support. Frequent elections are an essential condition of a democracy. This means that elected representatives who defy the wishes of citizens may soon lose office.

What happens if representatives support decisions that they believe to be in the public interest, but that the voters who elected them do not support? The representatives can hope that voters come around—or forget—before the next election.

2. Democracy emphasizes legal and political equality

Ideally, all citizens in a democracy are equal before the law and in political life. All citizens, rich or poor, are equal in a court of law. All can vote. All can hold office.

Most democracies have a constitution. As the central law of the country, the constitution lays out the rules and principles of government power and the rights of the people. It also describes the organization of government, how it is elected, and the duties of elected representatives.

One part of Canada's written constitution is the *Canadian Charter of Rights and Freedoms*. The Charter outlines the basic rights and responsibilities of Canadians. It acts as a constant reminder to citizens, the courts, and the government to safeguard and respect individual rights.

3. Democracy protects minorities

The idea that minorities must be protected from the majority can be difficult for citizens to accept. This is especially true if the minority has very different values from the majority. It is often said that democracy means much more than "50 percent plus one." In other words, majority opinion must not always triumph, especially if it might crush the rights of minorities.

Because democracies favour the majority, they have not always treated minorities well. During World War II, for example, thousands of Japanese Canadians were incarcerated as "threats" to national security (see Chapter 13). Many of the families had lived and prospered in British Columbia for generations.

4. Democracy encourages peace, respect, and tolerance in citizens

How can people create and adapt to change in a democracy? The systems and methods of democratic government require people to persuade others to accept their points of view. This often means that citizens must learn to compromise. Democratic decision making can also be used in families, schools, and workplaces to reduce disagreements and eliminate serious conflicts.

OBSTACLES TO DEMOCRACY

Can any country become a democracy? This question is controversial.

It was once believed that democracy took a long time to become established. In countries in Western Europe, the process took centuries. It was also thought that democracy did not suit some countries in Eastern

FIGURE 5.8 A Hutterite school near Veteran, Alberta, March 2005. Canada's Charter protects minorities from discrimination based on race, national or ethnic origin, colour, religion, sex, age, or mental or physical disability.

Europe, Africa, Asia, and South America. However, many countries in those areas have become democracies in recent years.

Perhaps a better way to look at the question is to consider what obstacles may prevent democracy from taking root.

1. Ethnic differences and conflicts

Differences among ethnic groups (groups of people who share common customs and values based on language, religion, or homeland) can create disunity. In the central African country of Rwanda, for example, ethnic tensions between the majority Hutu and the minority Tutsi groups led to mass murder in 1994. Iraq is also divided—between Kurdish and Arab ethnic groups, and between Sunni and Shiite religious sects. These divisions have led to extreme violence amidst efforts to create democracy.

Some people say that authoritarian government is better than democracy in uniting countries that are ethnically divided. Often, a military leader will head such a government. Obviously, disunity will not be tolerated when there can be no disagreement with the leader.

2. A large gap between rich and poor

It has been said that democracy requires a large middle class to work fairly. The daily struggle of the poor to survive leaves them little time for democratic involvement. Without a large middle class, the rich few dominate government and use it for their own benefit. This pattern is common in less developed countries (countries with low average income).

3. A low literacy rate

Any country with a low literacy rate will face problems maintaining democracy. A free press is important to democracy. It allows public issues to be examined and discussed. People who cannot read cannot participate in this activity. They will also have trouble in understanding candidates' literature, voting procedures, and reading and marking ballots.

THE SPREAD OF DEMOCRACY

Regardless of imperfections and obstacles, democracy has spread quickly in the last two decades. That may be because the concept of personal freedom is a cornerstone of democracy and has wide appeal. By 2006, it was estimated that 122 of the world's 192 countries were democracies, although they differed in the degree of freedom their citizens enjoyed. In total numbers, that is about one-half of humankind.

108 CANADA IN THE CONTEMPORARY WORLD

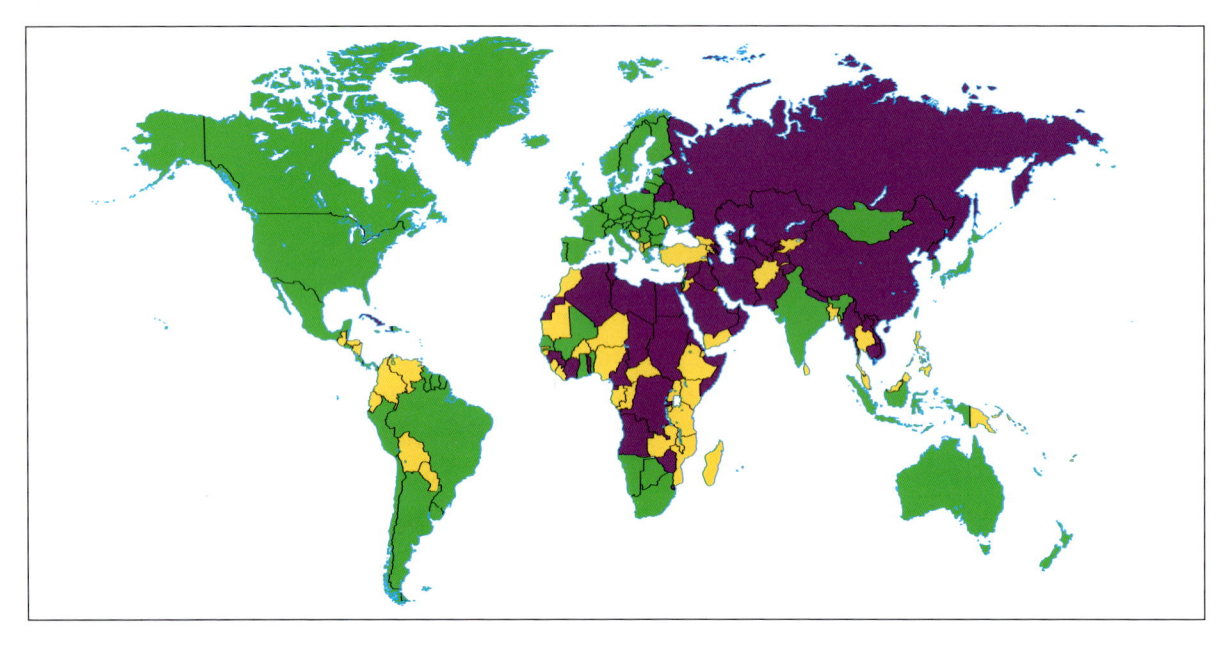

■ **Free:** High degree of political and civil freedom

■ **Partly Free:** Some restrictions on political rights and civil liberties; countries often prone to corruption, weak rule of law, ethnic strife, civil war

■ **Not Free:** Political process tightly controlled; basic freedoms denied

Free
Andorra
Antigua and Barbuda
Argentina
Australia
Austria
Bahamas
Barbados
Belgium
Belize
Benin
Botswana
Brazil
Bulgaria
Canada
Cape Verde
Chile
Costa Rica
Croatia
Cyprus (Greek)
Czech Republic
Denmark
Dominica
Dominican Republic
El Salvador
Estonia
Finland
France
Germany
Ghana
Greece
Grenada
Hungary
Iceland
India
Indonesia
Ireland
Israel
Italy
Jamaica
Japan
Kiribati
Korea, South
Latvia
Lesotho
Liechtenstein
Lithuania
Luxembourg
Mali
Malta
Marshall Islands
Mauritius
Mexico
Micronesia
Monaco
Mongolia
Montenegro
Namibia
Nauru
Netherlands
New Zealand
Norway
Palau
Panama
Peru
Poland
Portugal
Romania
Samoa
San Marino
Sao Tome and Principe
Senegal
Serbia
Slovakia
Slovenia
South Africa
Spain
St. Kitts and Nevis
St. Lucia
St. Vincent and Grenadines
Suriname
Sweden
Switzerland
Taiwan
Trinidad and Tobago
Tuvalu
Ukraine
United Kingdom
United States
Uruguay
Vanuatu

Partly Free
Afghanistan
Albania
Armenia
Bahrain
Bangladesh
Bolivia
Bosnia-Herzegovina
Burkina Faso
Burundi
Central African Republic
Colombia
Comoros
Congo (Brazzaville)
Djibouti
East Timor
Ecuador
Ethiopia
Fiji
Gabon
Gambia
Georgia
Guatemala
Guinea-Bissau
Guyana
Honduras
Jordan
Kenya
Kuwait
Kyrgyzstan
Lebanon
Liberia
Macedonia
Madagascar
Malawi
Malaysia
Mauritania
Moldova
Morocco
Mozambique
Nicaragua
Niger
Nigeria
Papua New Guinea
Paraguay
Philippines
Seychelles
Sierra Leone
Singapore
Solomon Islands
Sri Lanka
Tanzania
Thailand
Tonga
Turkey
Uganda
Venezuela
Yemen
Zambia

Not Free
Algeria
Angola
Azerbaijan
Belarus
Bhutan
Brunei
Burma (Myanmar)
Cambodia
Cameroon
Chad
China
Congo (Kinshasa)
Côte d'Ivoire
Cuba
Egypt
Equatorial Guinea
Eritrea
Guinea
Haiti
Iran
Iraq
Kazakhstan
Korea, North
Laos
Libya
Maldives
Nepal
Oman
Pakistan
Qatar
Russia
Rwanda
Saudi Arabia
Somalia
Sudan
Swaziland
Syria
Tajikistan
Togo
Tunisia
Turkmenistan
United Arab Emirates
Uzbekistan
Vietnam
Zimbabwe

FIGURE 5.9 Democratic freedoms: civil and political liberties, 2006. In that year, 2.97 billion people (46 percent of the world's population) lived in Free societies; 1.16 billion (18 percent) lived in Partly Free societies; and 2.33 billion (36 percent) lived in Not Free societies. How does this map look today? *Source: Freedom House, www.freedomhouse.org*

such as highways, water, parks, and police. The definition of marriage, which includes the privileges and rights of marriage, is a federal responsibility. It is the provinces, however, that issue marriage licences, authorize individuals to perform marriages, and register marriages. The grounds for divorce are set by federal law. But the rules that say how property is to be divided after divorce are set by provincial law.

▶ **DID YOU KNOW** ◀

In 2004–2005, the territories' operating revenues came mostly from federal transfer payments: Yukon, 78%; Northwest Territories, 80%; and Nunavut, 91%.

Responsibilities of Provincial and Territorial Governments

The responsibilities of the provinces and territories are not identical, but they all make decisions relating to

- property and civil rights
- marriage licences
- alcohol consumption
- natural resources and environment
- hospitals
- health and welfare
- education
- driver education and licensing
- motor vehicle operation and licensing
- provincial or territorial highways

Provincial and Territorial Revenue

To pay for the services they provide, provincial and territorial governments can collect income tax, sales tax, and hidden "sin taxes" on alcohol and tobacco products.

Territorial governments raise money in all the ways that provinces do. Most of their money, however, comes from the federal government in transfer grants. They receive a greater proportion of federal assistance because territories have much smaller populations than most provinces.

Responsibilities of Local Governments

Local governments are responsible for services that affect the daily lives of people, such as

- police and fire departments
- streets and roads
- water and sewage
- transit
- garbage and recycling
- libraries
- recreation
- local programs

FACE OFF: Should Governments Sponsor Gambling?

"You can't win if you don't play." "It's about entertainment. It's about good times." "Winning means a life of luxury and happiness." These are just a few slogans that governments in Canada use to advertise gambling.

In 1969, new laws allowed provincial and territorial governments to run lotteries to raise money. Soon they were also running casinos, video lottery terminals (VLTs), and slot machines. By 2006, legal gambling was estimated to bring in $20–$27 billion a year in Canada.

Some people say, fine. Adults can decide for themselves about gambling. And for many Canadians, it is harmless fun. Besides, government-run gaming creates jobs and revenue to support community organizations.

> Ten percent of the revenues from video lottery terminal operations is paid ... to Manitoba municipalities. ... 25 percent of VLT revenue is dedicated to community economic development projects. ... The remainder of our net income ... is given to ... programs that provide health care, education, community and social services ... .
>
> —Manitoba Lotteries Corporation

Other people say governments are promoting a destructive activity. Gambling addiction destroys marriages and families. It leads to theft and suicide. Casinos and slots may be adult-only entertainment—but children are exposed to gambling when parents gamble. And online gambling is a growing problem. Governments should protect citizens, not exploit them. Studies have shown that a "substantial portion of ... gaming revenue comes from problem gamblers."

> Government-sponsored gambling is therefore contrary to the interest of the general populace, and therefore contrary to the purpose of government.
>
> —Robert Williams, University of Lethbridge, Alberta, November 2004

Another opinion acknowledges that people will gamble, whether it is legal or illegal. Government should continue to supervise the activity but limit its advertising and ill effects.

What Do You Think?

1. Describe the advantages and disadvantages associated with the different viewpoints on government-sponsored gambling.
2. After answering question 1, which view of government-sponsored gambling do you agree with? Why?
3. The Manitoba government controls all gaming in the province. One initiative of the Assembly of Manitoba Chiefs (AMC) is to run casinos and "find ways to assist First Nations in gaining meaningful and profitable access to the gaming industry." The goal is to attain "revenues, jobs and economic benefits and opportunities for First Nations." Would you support the AMC? Explain. Consider the historic disadvantages First Nations have experienced.

DEMOCRACY IN CANADA

Democracy in Canada now is very different from what it was at Confederation, when Canada became a country. In 1867, only property-owning men who were British subjects could vote and hold public office. Women, Aboriginal people, and most minorities could do neither. All these groups would struggle for decades to gain basic democratic rights. Japanese and Chinese Canadians, for example, did not receive voting rights until 1948. It would be 1960 before Aboriginal Canadians could vote in federal elections without restrictions. (You will learn more about the history of the vote and elections in Canada in Chapter 9.)

CivicStar

ELIJAH HARPER

Elijah Harper has served his people, the Ojibwe–Cree of northern Manitoba, and other Aboriginal peoples in Canada, for decades. Born on the Red Sucker Lake reserve in 1949, his political career began in 1978 when he was elected chief. He held that post until 1981.

Harper was the first status Indian to be elected to the Manitoba Legislative Assembly (1981–1992). In government, he served as both Minister Responsible for Native Affairs and Minister of Northern Affairs.

Harper became famous across Canada when—holding an eagle feather for spiritual strength—he rejected the Meech Lake Accord in the Manitoba Legislative Assembly in 1990. The accord had been negotiated by federal and provincial governments to amend (change) Canada's constitution. It would have recognized Quebec as a "distinct society." It would also have given the provinces greater powers. However, the accord did not include rights for Aboriginal peoples. Harper felt that the accord treated Aboriginal peoples like "second-class citizens." Because of Harper's stand, the accord could not become law.

Harper explained his reasoning: "The [Meech Lake] gatherings clearly showed that little had changed since European settlers first came to our land. There was still no representation by or consultation with Aboriginal peoples. Building the future is more than saying no to that which is wrong. It is also saying yes to that which is fair and just." Harper's action spoke strongly and clearly for Aboriginal peoples across Canada.

Harper was later elected a federal member of Parliament for the Manitoba riding of Churchill (1993–1997). He organized Sacred Assemblies in 1995 and 1997. These events brought together Aboriginal and non-Aboriginal people from across Canada to find a basis for healing and understanding. He and others at the 1995 Sacred Assembly encouraged the federal government to proclaim June 21 National Aboriginal Day.

Harper's efforts have been recognized with the Stanley Knowles Humanitarian Award in 1991 and the National Aboriginal Achievement Award in 1996. In 1999, he was appointed a commissioner of the Indian Claims Commission.

THE WEB

Listen to an interview with Elijah Harper on the day he rejected the Meech Lake Accord at www.emp.ca/ccw

Your Play

1. Describe how Elijah Harper's rejection of the Meech Lake Accord is
   a) an example of democracy in action
   b) an example of a non-violent resolution to conflict.
2. In your view, what are the responsibilities of Aboriginal citizens in Canada? Are they different from the responsibilities of non-Aboriginal citizens? Explain.

PAUSE, REFLECT, APPLY

1. Why are frequent elections and legal equality essential to democracy?
2. Explain the purpose of a constitution in a democracy.
3. Which element of democracy do you think is the most important? Explain why.
4. Which obstacle to democracy do you think is the most serious? Explain why.
5. What does "50 percent plus one" refer to?
6. Explain this statement: "A democracy is defined by the way it treats its minorities."
7. How has democracy in Canada changed since Confederation?

REPLAY

In this chapter, you have explored these concepts:

1. Government is a system of making and enforcing decisions to guide the affairs of a community.
2. Authoritarian governments use coercion to enforce decisions.
3. Democracies rely on authority and influence to persuade citizens to accept decisions.
4. Most Aboriginal societies governed themselves based on consensus.
5. Democracy has evolved from a direct form to a representative form.
6. Citizens in a democracy can use their power to achieve change.
7. Democracies strive to guarantee equality, protect minorities, and encourage tolerance and compromise.
8. Ethnic conflict, economic inequalities, and low literacy levels are obstacles to democracy.

SKILLS TOOLKIT: How to Identify Bias

Suppose you were given a social studies assignment to cover a public meeting about the use of the local arena by minor hockey leagues. The issue is controversial, and public interest is high. The local cable television station and the local newspaper cover the meeting. You want to cover the story without **bias** (the slant or emphasis on certain facts that a news story or person expresses). Sources can reflect bias in

- choice of headline to draw attention to the story
- placement of a story (headline or byline)
- choice of visuals
- omission or inclusion of certain facts
- unwarranted or unsupported assumptions
- omission or labelling of some individuals or groups.

You write your account of the meeting as you saw it. Afterwards, you compare your account with the television and newspaper coverage. You might find that your memory and account differ from the other two sources. All three accounts reflect bias.

Bias can be intentional or unintentional. Unintentional bias sometimes happens because of the nature of the medium. Television is biased in favour of a good visual story, or evidence of conflict between individuals. Newspaper stories are biased in their choice of headline and their selection of facts in the lead paragraph intended to capture readers' attention. A newspaper editorial may go further, being intentionally biased in its selection of facts to support the point of view of the publishers.

With practice and awareness, you can learn to choose sources that give the fair and balanced coverage you need to make informed decisions.

Skill Practice

1. Bias can occur in news accounts by choice of words. Contrast the bias demonstrated by each of the following pairs of statements:
   a) "a handful of people protested the speaker's remarks" versus "loud jeers occurred when the speaker stated ..."
   b) "a former convict was apprehended" versus "an individual charged a number of years ago for an offence was arrested"
   c) "a group of terrorists attacked a compound" versus "a group of rebels engaged in a fight with government forces"
2. Arrange with a classmate to buy two different newspapers on the same day. Compare the headlines and coverage of three events. Identify the slant or bias each newspaper brings to the story.
3. What impact might the ability of citizens to detect bias have on democracy? Give specific examples.

STUDY HALL

Be Informed

1. Consider your student council.
   a) In what sense is it a government?
   b) What characteristics of a democratic government does it have?
   c) What type of power does it use the most? Give an example of a successful use of that power.
   d) What type of power does it not use, and why?
   e) Can you think of any restraints or limits to its decision-making power?

2. Rank order authoritarian, democratic, and consensus methods as to a) speed of decision making and b) acceptance by those affected.

3. Why do most democracies and their citizens regard a constitution as necessary to protect individual freedom? (Consider what could happen if a nation does not have one.)

4. Draw up a chart comparing authoritarian, democratic, and consensus decision making. The chart should have three columns: advantages, disadvantages, and an example of a good use of the method. Add any advantages or disadvantages that you can think of.

Be Purposeful

5. a) How can politics occur within i) a family? ii) a group of friends? iii) a sports team? Do you think such informal politics is bad, good, or neither good nor bad?
   b) Politicians are sometimes viewed unfavourably. From the way that politics is defined in this chapter, do you think this view is justified?

6. a) Do you think that i) families, ii) classrooms, and iii) workplaces can be run on a democratic basis? Should they be? Explain.
   b) "Authoritarian parents create authoritarian children; democratic parents create democratic citizens." Do you agree? Explain.

7. Increasingly, parents are urged not to use corporal punishment (inflict physical pain) on their children.
   a) What kinds of power are parents then forced to rely on?
   b) Do you agree with this idea?
   c) Does it "fit" with democracy?

8. When is a democratic government justified in using authoritarian decision making? Defend your answer and use examples.

9. Explain why each of the following is essential to a democracy:
   a) equality of all before the law
   b) free media
   c) minimal use of force to maintain order
   d) free and frequent elections
   e) multiple political parties
   f) minority rights
   g) judicial independence from government
   h) common good

Be Active

10. Study your school's student conduct policy. Find out
    a) who drew it up
    b) how it was drawn up and decided
    c) whether it allows for frequent change and review
    d) whether it includes rights as well as responsibilities.

11. Contrast the idea of an individual as a subject with that of an individual as a citizen. What do citizens today expect of a democratic government, such as Canada's, that was not expected in the past? Are citizens asking too much or too little of their governments today? Support your answer with examples.

CHAPTER 6
What Is Government?

Who's in charge here?

At Maple Leaf High School, the student council and the principal cannot agree on a new dress code for school dances. The student council likes the old dress code. The principal says that recent gang-related violence requires a stricter dress code. Students wearing bandanas or gang colours will not be allowed into the dance.

The principal has the authority to override the student council on this issue. But she does not want to create bad feelings, even though she has the best interests of all students in mind. What advice would you give her? What would be the ideal division of powers between the student council and the principal?

What You Need to Know
- What is a parliamentary democracy?
- Why does Canada have levels of government?
- Why does Canada have branches of government?
- What are the responsibilities and processes of each level and branch?
- Who carries out responsibilities in each branch?
- How does Aboriginal self-determination express itself in government?
- How can you locate and assess information?

Key Terms
executive
legislative
judicial
constitutional monarchy
governor general
members of Parliament
House of Commons
cabinet
minority government
Official Opposition
Senate
councillors

Key Question
How does the organization of government help democracy?

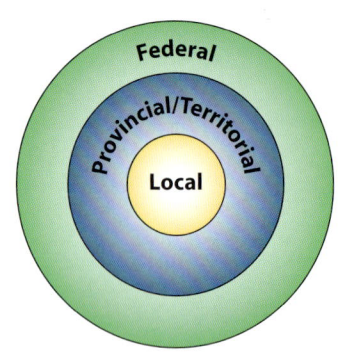

FIGURE 6.1 Levels of government in Canada

> **THE WEB** ▶▶▶
> Find your Manitoba municipality profile at www.emp.ca/ccw

> **THE WEB** ▶▶▶
> Explore governance in Manitoba's Aboriginal communities and take a virtual tour of Aboriginal Canada at www.emp.ca/ccw

Why Does Canada Have Different Levels of Government?

Canada has three levels of government:

- federal government (for all of Canada)
- provincial or territorial government (for a province or territory)
- municipal or local government (for local communities).

At Confederation in 1867, Canada's constitution created two levels of government—**federal** (national) and provincial. This system of government is called **federalism**.

Territorial governments were not mentioned in the constitution because that land was then controlled by the Hudson's Bay Company. The territories were created through later acts of Parliament. Canada's territories are the Northwest Territories (1870), Yukon (1898), and Nunavut (1999).

Local or municipal governments are created by provinces or territories to govern local communities. These include cities, towns, villages, and **rural municipalities**. Local governments can also be changed by provincial or territorial governments.

Aboriginal bands, or settlements, are considered by many people an additional "level" of government. They are self-governing bodies that may be created and changed by the federal or provincial/territorial government that established them.

ABORIGINAL SELF-GOVERNMENT

In Canada, Aboriginal peoples have an inherent (existing) right to **self-determination**. As you have seen, First Nations had systems of government and justice before European contact. Many of these systems were democratic, for example, the Anishnaabe–Ojibwe clan system in Manitoba and elsewhere and the Iroquois Confederacy (or Six Nations Confederacy) in the Great Lakes–St. Lawrence Lowlands region.

Today, Aboriginal communities can be self-governed at the local and the territorial levels. **Self-government** may include advice from tribal councils (voluntary groupings of bands sharing common interests) in such areas as economic development and community planning. For groups such as the Assembly of First Nations, Aboriginal self-government is equal in status to that of the provinces within Canada's federal system.

Aboriginal self-government depends on the demographic concentration of Aboriginal people living in an area. Because 85 percent of the citizens of Nunavut are Inuit, the whole territory is self-governed. Aboriginal communities in Manitoba have achieved varying degrees of self-government at the local level.

RESPONSIBILITIES OF DIFFERENT LEVELS OF GOVERNMENT

Each level of government in Canada has different responsibilities and provides different services. Only the federal and provincial governments have their responsibilities outlined in Canada's original constitution, as set out in the *Constitution Act, 1867* (formerly called the *British North America Act*).

Responsibilities of the Federal Government

The federal government makes decisions related to matters of nation-wide importance, such as

- foreign trade and relations
- Aboriginal peoples
- defence
- postal service
- immigration
- communications
- unemployment
- criminal law (*Criminal Code*)
- currency (money)

Federal Revenue

To pay for all the services it provides, the federal government collects income taxes, the goods and services tax (GST), and excise taxes (taxes on certain domestic and foreign goods that are not apparent to the consumer). The federal government transfers a portion of its revenues directly to individuals and to the provinces and territories.

Federal transfers to individuals include payments for pensions, family allowances, employment insurance, and so on. Federal transfers to the governments of the provinces and territories fund such areas as post-secondary education, health care, and other programs. Federal "equalization" payments are made to reduce the economic disparity (gap) between "have" and "have not" provinces. (See Figure 6.2 on the next page.)

> **THE WEB**
> Taxes are often a "hot-button" issue. To get an idea of the enormous amounts of money involved in federal revenues and expenditures, go to www.emp.ca/ccw

Where Do Federal and Provincial Responsibilities Overlap?

Federal and provincial governments share responsibilities in some areas, such as agriculture and environmental protection. Other areas also overlap,

FIGURE 6.2 Manitoba's provincial revenue (top) and provincial operating expenditure for 2006–2007 (forecast). How big a piece of the pie is health spending? How does this compare to federal transfers? *Source: Manitoba Finance at www.gov.mb.ca/finance/budget06/papers/finstats.pdf*

Provincial Revenue, 2006–2007
Major Sources (percentage of total)

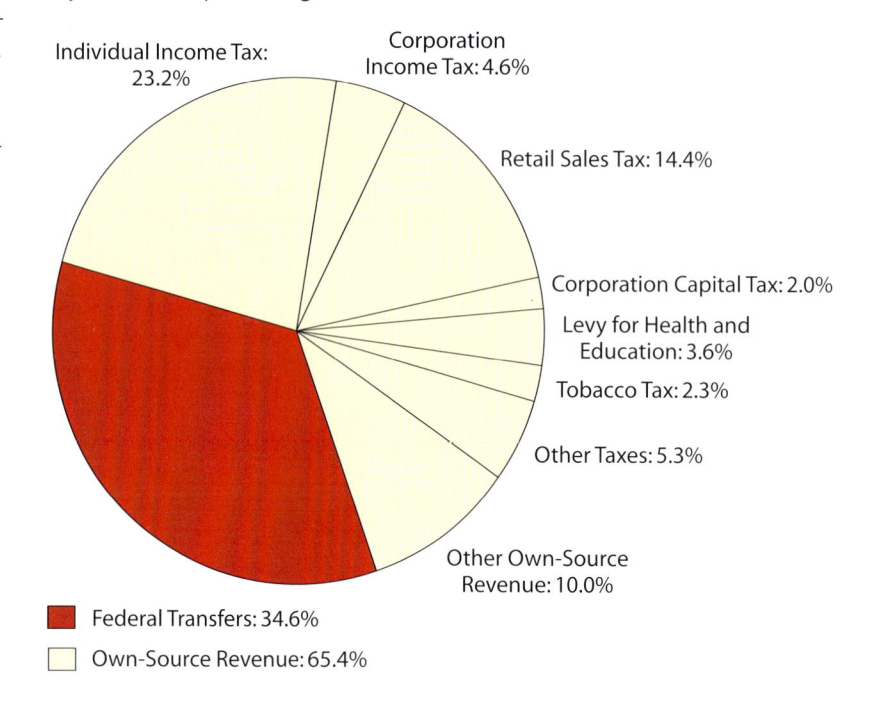

- Individual Income Tax: 23.2%
- Corporation Income Tax: 4.6%
- Retail Sales Tax: 14.4%
- Corporation Capital Tax: 2.0%
- Levy for Health and Education: 3.6%
- Tobacco Tax: 2.3%
- Other Taxes: 5.3%
- Other Own-Source Revenue: 10.0%
- Federal Transfers: 34.6%
- Own-Source Revenue: 65.4%

Provincial Operating Expenditure, 2006–2007
Major Categories (percentage of total)

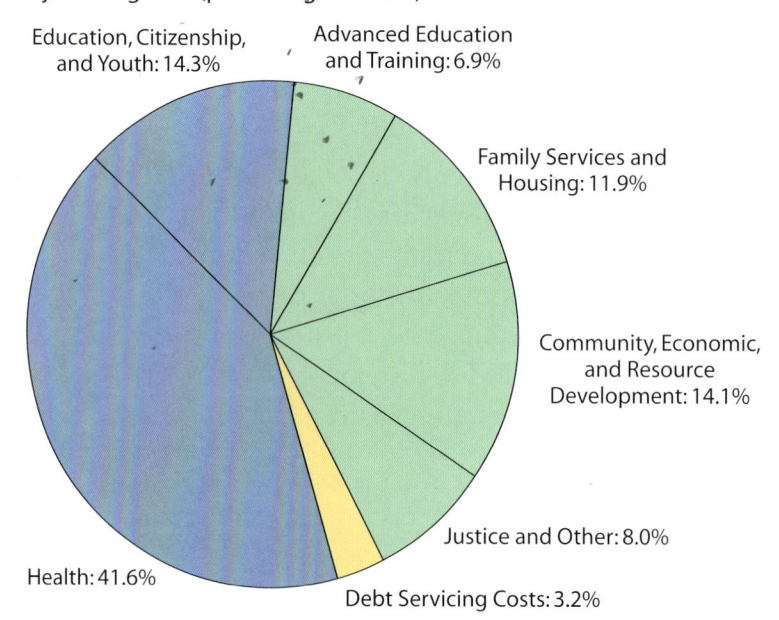

- Education, Citizenship, and Youth: 14.3%
- Advanced Education and Training: 6.9%
- Family Services and Housing: 11.9%
- Community, Economic, and Resource Development: 14.1%
- Justice and Other: 8.0%
- Debt Servicing Costs: 3.2%
- Health: 41.6%

Aboriginal local governments often have wider responsibilities than typical local governments. For example, they may be responsible for housing, oil and gas development, and education, in addition to providing the services listed above.

Local Revenue

Local governments receive grants from the provincial government. They also raise revenue through property taxes. These are paid by both homeowners and businesses. The average family in Canada paid between $2,400 and $3,000 in property taxes in 2006. Municipalities also raise money through fees they charge for parking and for various licences.

Aboriginal councils receive funding from the federal government. The amount is determined by geographic location, distance from major population centres, and local climate. Some First Nations communities are exploring the idea of creating their own tax systems. This would allow them to raise money to pay for services and also to invest in economic development.

PAUSE, REFLECT, APPLY

1. Find out about two decisions made by your school's student council or school council. In your opinion, were these good decisions? Why?
2. Briefly describe the three levels of government as outlined in this section.
3. List what you consider to be the three most important responsibilities of your provincial government.
4. List what you consider to be the three most important responsibilities of the federal government.
5. Create a chart to compare how governments at different levels raise money to provide services.

Branches of Government in Canada

In Canada, government powers are separated into branches. This idea goes back to French political thinker Montesquieu (1689–1755). Montesquieu thought that by separating government powers into branches, each would be checked and balanced by the others. Most democratic governments have this three-branch structure, including Canada, the United States, and Britain.

> **KEY QUESTION**
> Why does Canada have different branches of government?

The branches of Canadian government are the **executive** (to carry out the business of government), the **legislative** (to make laws), and the **judicial** (to interpret and enforce laws).

Figure 6.4 shows how each branch of government functions at the federal and provincial/territorial levels. Usually, the term "branch of government" is not used at the local level. However, local governments do have different branches to make and enforce laws.

LITERACY COACH

This chapter includes many diagrams and tables. These graphically summarize key information, so don't ignore them as you are studying. Diagrams can show you the "big picture" and the relationships of parts to the whole. For example, Figure 6.3 helps you see how the branches of government and the judiciary work together.

Canada's System of Government

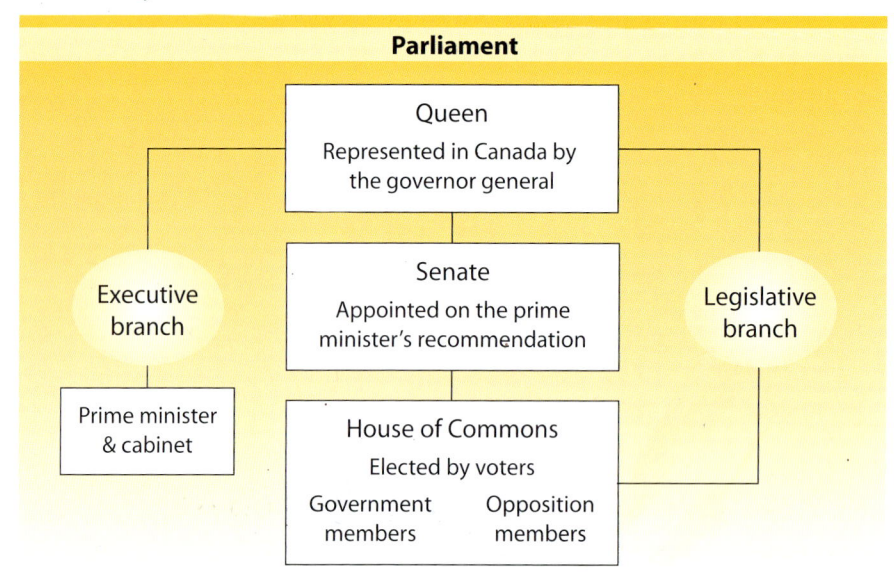

Parliament

- Queen — Represented in Canada by the governor general
- Senate — Appointed on the prime minister's recommendation
- House of Commons — Elected by voters (Government members, Opposition members)

Executive branch: Prime minister & cabinet

Legislative branch

Judiciary

- Supreme Court of Canada — Nine judges appointed by the governor general
  - Federal Court of Canada
  - Provincial courts

FIGURE 6.3 Branches of Canada's federal government

Branch	Function	Key People
Executive	Make and implement decisions Carry out policies and run government departments	Queen, represented by governor general (federal), lieutenant governor (provincial), or commissioner (territorial) Prime minister (federal) or premier (provincial) Cabinet ministers Civil servants
Legislative	Introduce, debate, and pass laws	Elected representatives Appointed senators (federal level only)
Judicial	Interpret and enforce laws	Judges and courts

FIGURE 6.4 Branches of government, their functions, and key people. The Queen is head of state, but does she have real political power?

The Executive Branch

The executive branch of government is its leadership. The word "execute" means "to carry out." (For example, "She executed a perfect dive.") The executive in a government carries out the business of the government. This includes developing policies and implementing laws. In a school, the principal and vice-principal would be known as the executive.

THE GOVERNOR GENERAL

Even though the "fathers" of Confederation represented both anglophone and francophone interests, it was agreed that Canada would be a **constitutional monarchy**. The British monarch became the official head of state of Canada. Today, Queen Elizabeth II is monarch of Canada. However, the constitution limits the monarch's power. The monarch is represented in Canada by the **governor general**, who is head of government.

Until 1952, the governor general was always British and came to Canada to represent the monarch. For example, Lord Stanley of Preston was governor general from 1888 to 1893. He fell in love with hockey and donated the famous cup for hockey supremacy that still bears his name. However, Lord Stanley went back to England before he could present the cup to a winning team.

Today, the prime minister recommends the candidate for governor general to the monarch. Since Vincent Massey was appointed in 1952, all of Canada's governors general have been Canadian citizens.

> **KEY QUESTION**
> How does the executive branch make decisions in Canada?

> **DID YOU KNOW**
> In 2005, then governor general Adrienne Clarkson donated the Clarkson Cup to recognize excellence in women's hockey. She came up with the idea during a prolonged NHL lockout.

At the federal level, the governor general

- signs all bills into law, a process known as giving **royal assent**
- officially welcomes representatives of foreign governments to Canada
- reads the Speech from the Throne (government plans in a new session of Parliament)
- promotes pride in and awareness of Canada.

> ▶ **DID YOU KNOW** ◀
> Two Manitoba high schools were named to honour former Governor General Vincent Massey: Vincent Massey High School in Brandon, and Vincent Massey Collegiate in Winnipeg.

The governor general is a **figurehead**, head of government in name only. The position, like the monarch's, is symbolic. It is meant to reflect the best traditions rooted in Canada's past. Still, it is the governor general who officially appoints the prime minister and who dissolves Parliament. In most cases, the prime minister appointed is the leader of the party with the most seats in the House of Commons (see page 123).

THE LIEUTENANT GOVERNOR

In each of Canada's 10 provinces, a lieutenant governor represents the monarch. The lieutenant governor is appointed by the governor general on the recommendation of the prime minister, usually for a term of five years. Provincial duties include signing bills into law, reading the Speech from the Throne, and promoting the province.

FIGURE 6.5 (Left to right:) Lincoln Alexander was the first black lieutenant governor (Ontario, 1985). W. Yvon Dumont, a Métis, was the first Aboriginal lieutenant governor (Manitoba, 1993). Michaëlle Jean, an immigrant from Haiti who worked as a journalist before being installed as Canada's 27th governor general in 2005, is the youngest person, the third woman, and the first black person to hold the job. What does this say to you about Canadian pluralism?

THE PRIME MINISTER AND CABINET

The prime minister is the most powerful political leader in Canada. He or she is leader of the political party with the most elected representatives, or **members of Parliament** (MPs), in the **House of Commons** (see Figure 6.6, page 127). A political party is an organization of people with similar ideas (as discussed in chapters 8 and 9).

Following an election, the prime minister chooses a group of advisers known as the **cabinet**. The prime minister and the cabinet hold the real power of the federal executive branch.

In most cases, the prime minister chooses cabinet ministers from MPs from his or her party. The cabinet is part of the executive team. As with most teams, the prime minister selects the best "players" for positions in the cabinet. In choosing these MPs, the prime minister must reflect Canada's diversity and strive for gender equality.

Most federal cabinets include 20 to 30 members. Aside from advising the prime minister, cabinet members look after departments, or **portfolios**, such as Finance, Justice, Health, and Defence. For example, in consultation with the prime minister,

- the minister of finance might balance the budget
- the minister of justice might propose changes to the criminal law related to marijuana
- the minister of health might introduce a teen sports program
- the minister of defence might change the size of Canada's armed forces.

As you can see, cabinet ministers have political power. This is perhaps why they occupy front seats in Parliament. The majority of MPs in the governing party are not in the cabinet. They sit in seats behind the cabinet and are known as **backbenchers**. Usually, backbenchers work to represent the interests of their constituents. As a group, they can have a major influence on policy, particularly if the issue is controversial (for example, same-sex marriage, the gun registry, and the US Missile Defense program).

The Canadian cabinet follows the British principle of **cabinet solidarity** (acting together). This means that all members of the cabinet must publicly support all cabinet decisions or resign from cabinet.

▶ **DID YOU KNOW** ◀

Political parties appoint one of their elected members to be the "party whip." The name says it all. It is the party whip's job to make sure that elected party members attend the legislature and vote as the party leadership wants them to vote.

THE WEB ▶▶▶

The salaries of MPs, MLAs, MPPs, PMs—and premiers—heat up debates inside and outside legislatures. Check out the figures at www.emp.ca/ccw

THE PREMIER AND CABINET

The premier leads the executive branch of the provincial government. Like the prime minister, he or she leads the political party elected by the people to govern the province.

The federal principles of majority support, cabinet selection, and cabinet solidarity apply provincially as well. However, there are no provincial or territorial portfolios for defence, foreign affairs, Indian affairs, or veterans' affairs. These are areas of federal responsibility.

CivicStar

ERIC ROBINSON

Eric Robinson was born in Cross Lake First Nation (or Pimicikamak Cree Nation) in Northern Manitoba, in 1953. His Cree name is Ka-Kee-Nee Konee Peewonee Okimow (Chief of the Whirlwind Blizzard).

Robinson has served his people for many years in many ways. From 1981 to 1982, he was Grand Councillor of the Four Nations Confederacy of Manitoba. He also co-chaired the National Indian Brotherhood and served with the Assembly of First Nations.

Robinson became a skilled writer. *The Infested Blanket*, a book he co-wrote, was published in 1985. It exposed how Canada's constitution devastated the First Nations. Robinson was also a radio broadcaster and producer. He often worked the social justice "beat."

Robinson became officially involved in Manitoba's Aboriginal Justice Inquiry. The Manitoba government set up the inquiry in 1988, after years of protests and demands. It investigated two killings: the 1971 murder of teenaged Cree student Helen Betty Osborne, in The Pas; and the 1988 killing by a Winnipeg police officer of J.J. Harper, a young Aboriginal leader (see Chapter 10, pages 211–212).

After two years, the inquiry reported that Manitoba's justice system was failing Aboriginal peoples in a big way. Robinson helped write that report. He also served on the Aboriginal Justice Implementation Commission, which recommended changes to the system.

In 1993, Robinson was elected to the Manitoba Legislative Assembly. He was re-elected in 1995, 1999, and 2003. After the 1999 and 2003 elections, he was appointed to the provincial cabinet.

In 2003, CBC Manitoba interviewed people about what the inquiry and commission had achieved. Reactions were mixed. Winnipeg Police Chief Jack Ewatski was proud of hiring 111 Aboriginal officers (9 percent of the total force). Assembly of Manitoba Chiefs Grand Chief Dennis White Bird was unimpressed: "The police are still having their confrontations and conflicts with First Nations people. Nothing has really changed."

Robinson summed it up this way:

I believe that the change is coming. We would like to do it, like, 10 years ago, but unfortunately the way things work out, we're just getting to these issues, the critical ones. There's much more work to be done, let's not fool ourselves.

Your Play

1. If you were premier of Manitoba, which of Eric Robinson's skills and qualities do you think would make him "cabinet material"?
2. What was the purpose of a) the Aboriginal Justice Inquiry? b) the Aboriginal Justice Implementation Commission?
3. Go to the Web site of the Assembly of Manitoba Chiefs and write a brief report on a) who the Grand Chief is today and b) one of the AMC's initiatives.

Canada's three territories also have premiers. In Yukon, the premier leads the political party in power. In the Northwest Territories and Nunavut, however, a **non-partisan** (not affiliated with any political party) council selects premiers.

PAUSE, REFLECT, APPLY

1. Briefly describe what "federalism" and "constitutional monarchy" mean and how they work.
2. What is meant by the "executive branch" of government?
3. Describe the government level and major responsibilities of a) the governor general and b) the lieutenant governor.
4. Explain a) the importance and b) the functions of the cabinet at both the federal and provincial levels.
5. Identify the following people and something significant that each accomplished: Lincoln Alexander, W. Yvon Dumont, Michaëlle Jean, and Eric Robinson.

The Legislative Branch

In democracies, the legislative, or lawmaking, branch of government is elected by the voting public. In Canada, if the executive branch loses the support of the elected legislature, it must resign.

> **KEY QUESTION**
> How does the legislative branch represent Canadians?

THE HOUSE OF COMMONS

Canada is a parliamentary democracy. The House of Commons in Ottawa is our federal legislative body. It is composed of the members of Parliament elected in 308 separate **ridings** (2006) across Canada. Ridings are defined geographical areas.

Think of each riding as a homeroom. In a student council election, each homeroom votes for one of its members to represent the homeroom in the student "parliament." Similarly, each MP represents the interests of the **constituents** (voters and non-voters) in his or her riding. Ridings are also known as **constituencies**, and most have about 100,000 voters. Manitoba has 14 federal ridings (2006).

MPs assemble in the House of Commons to do the country's business. Most belong to political parties. If an elected representative is not affiliated with a political party, he or she is an **independent**. The political party with the largest number of MPs becomes the government of

Canada. To pass a bill, the government needs the support of "one-half plus one" of the total MPs ($\frac{1}{2} \times 308 + 1 = 155$).

After the 2004 federal election, the Liberal Party formed a **minority government**. That means it had more MPs than any other party (135), yet fewer than 155. As in any minority government, the Liberals needed support from another party or parties to pass bills. The Liberal government did not last long. Another federal election was held in January 2006. This time the Conservative Party won, but with 124 seats: another minority government.

Ideas for new bills are usually introduced by cabinet ministers. To become law, a bill must be approved by a majority of MPs. If the government loses an important vote in the Commons—on a budget, for example—it loses the **confidence** of the House and will probably have to resign (see Chapter 8).

After a government is defeated, the governor general may call a new election or invite the **Official Opposition** (the party with the next largest number of seats) to form a government. In any case, a federal election must be held at least every five years.

The Speaker of the House of Commons is an MP who acts like a referee to enforce the rules of parliamentary debate

The **Speaker of the House** is elected, by secret ballot, by all MPs. He or she is expected to be non-partisan. The job was once very dangerous (over the centuries, at least nine Speakers in the British Parliament were executed after their reports upset the monarch). Today, the Speaker of the House is still ritually dragged to the Speaker's Chair.

The Speaker sits on a raised platform in the House of Commons, as you can see in Figure 6.6. Members of the governing party sit in rows to the right of the Speaker. In the front row sit the prime minister and cabinet. Across the aisle are the opposition parties. Members of the Official Opposition sit in the front seats directly opposite the government.

▶ **DID YOU KNOW** ◀

The Commons Mace is carried by the Sergeant-at-Arms to open or close every sitting of Parliament. It symbolizes the authority given to the House of Commons by the monarch. Long ago, the mace was a weapon of war. This is why it is shaped like a club.

CHAPTER 6 WHAT IS GOVERNMENT? **127**

1	Speaker	**13**	Interpreters
2	Pages	**14**	Press Gallery
3	Government Members*	**15**	Public Gallery
4	Opposition Members*	**16**	Official Gallery
5	Prime Minister	**17**	Leader of the Opposition's Gallery
6	Leader of the Official Opposition	**18**	Members' Gallery
7	Leader of the Second Largest Party in Opposition	**19**	Members' Gallery
		20	Members' Gallery
8	Clerk and Table Officers	**21**	Speaker's Gallery
9	Mace	**22**	Senate Gallery
10	Hansard Reporters	**23**	TV Cameras
11	Sergeant-at-Arms		
12	The Bar		

* Depending on the number of MPs elected from each political party, government members may be seated on the opposite side of the Chamber with opposition members (or vice versa).

FIGURE 6.6 Canada's House of Commons. *Source:* Guide to the Canadian House of Commons *(3rd ed.)*. Ottawa: Government of Canada, 2005, p. 6

Question Period takes place each day the House is in session

For 45 minutes, opposition members can question the prime minister and cabinet during Question Period, or Oral Questions. The opposition usually tries to embarrass the government with queries on almost any issue. Often, cabinet ministers do not answer questions directly. They may also criticize the opposition. The period is often full of political posturing and theatrics.

Everything everyone says in the Commons is recorded and published in an official document called Hansard. MPs cannot speak directly to one another. They must address their remarks through the Speaker, referring to one another as "the Honourable member from (name of riding)."

Anything MPs say in the House is protected from legal action. But if an MP uses "unparliamentary language" (calling another MP a liar, or swearing, for example), the Speaker can insist that the MP apologize. If the MP refuses, he or she can be ejected from the House.

> **THE WEB**
> Learn more about Hansard and find webcasts and podcasts of Question Period and House of Commons committee meetings at www.emp.ca/ccw

THE SENATE

The **Senate** is the Upper House of the legislative branch of the federal government. "Upper" suggests that it is more important than the House of Commons, which is the Lower House. In 1867, many people believed this was true. Senators were expected to be upper-class gentlemen, only.

A major purpose of the Senate was to **veto** (block) "irresponsible" bills passed by the House of Commons. It was thought that the democratically elected representatives of the common people could not be trusted to run the government without being overseen by the upper classes.

The Senate has changed. In 1930, after the important decision in the Persons Case (see CivicStar, page 129), the first woman senator, Cairine Wilson, was appointed. Since 1965, senators have been required to retire at age 75.

Because all bills must pass through the Senate to become law, it still serves as a chamber of "sober second thought." Now, however, the appointed Senate rarely vetoes legislation passed by the elected House of Commons.

The Senate usually has 105 senators, or "seats." The constitution dictates the distribution: Ontario 24, Quebec 24, Nova Scotia 10, New Brunswick 10, Prince Edward Island 4, Manitoba, British Columbia, Saskatchewan, Alberta, and Newfoundland and Labrador 6 each, and the Northwest Territories, Nunavut, and Yukon 1 each.

> **DID YOU KNOW**
> Georges-Casimir Dessaulles was appointed to the Senate at the age of 80. He served until he died, age 102, in 1930. Dessaulles spoke only twice in the Senate: once to deny his appointment was corrupt, and once to acknowledge the celebration of his 100th birthday.

CivicStar

EMILY MURPHY AND THE FAMOUS FIVE

Emily Murphy (1868–1933) was born into a wealthy legal family. As a curious child, she taught herself all about law and government.

Under the pen name Janey Canuck, Murphy wrote travel pieces about Canada. She became famous. And she used her fame to write about serious social issues.

Moving to Alberta in 1903, Murphy campaigned so that married women would have property rights. She wrote articles. She criticized laws and lawmakers. She inspired other women. By 1911, a new Alberta law recognized a wife's property rights.

In 1916, a court case involving a group of prostitutes caught Murphy's attention. She and a group of reformers were barred from entering the court. The evidence was "not fit" for women's ears. Outraged, Murphy started another campaign against an injustice. She took her demands all the way to the top: the attorney general of Alberta. The result? She became the first woman ever to be appointed a police magistrate in the British Empire.

In 1917, a lawyer challenged that appointment. The *British North America Act* stated: "Women are persons in matters of pains and penalties, but are not persons in matters of rights and privileges." In other words, women were not legal "persons." Therefore, Murphy could not be appointed a magistrate or to any public office. The same argument barred women from the Senate.

For 12 years Murphy guided a legal battle: the Persons Case. She was joined by four other Alberta women: Nellie McClung, Louise McKinney, Henrietta Edwards, and Irene Parlby. Together, they took the legal battle all the way to England and became known as "the Famous Five."

Finally, on October 18, 1929, the Privy Council of Britain declared that, under the BNA Act, women were legal "persons." The Famous Five had changed Canada.

Your Play

1. Do you think Emily Murphy saw herself as a victim? Explain.
2. How can groups, or teams, accomplish more than individuals in influencing political and social systems?
3. The photograph shows how the Famous Five live on. How does it speak to you about the rights of women and democratic ideals?
4. Research and analyze other artworks that commemorate Murphy and the Famous Five. A good place to start online would be the Famous 5 Foundation.
5. The figure on the far left of the photograph is Nellie McClung. Research her strong Manitoba connections.

FIGURE 6.7 This larger-than-life bronze sculpture by Barbara Paterson stands on Parliament Hill in Ottawa. It depicts an imaginary moment when the "Famous Five" received word that women were indeed "persons" under the BNA Act.

FIGURE 6.8 The Senate. The Speaker of the Senate is recommended by the prime minister and appointed by the governor general. How is this different from the Speaker in the House of Commons?

> **DISCUSSION POINT**
> Some Canadians are demanding a "triple E" Senate. They want "elected" senators, seats divided "equally," and a more "effective" Senate. Canada's demographic changes are being ignored, they say. Would a "triple E" senate be better for Canada and more democratic?

Senate appointments are often based on **political patronage** (the granting of political favours). A prime minister may appoint an individual to reward earlier political support, for example. Regardless, many senators are hard-working public servants. Aside from suggesting improvements to bills, they may serve on parliamentary committees and commissions that investigate important issues such as child poverty. Senators also make recommendations for further action or study.

THE LEGISLATIVE ASSEMBLY

The legislative branches of Canada's 10 provinces are almost mirror images of the House of Commons.

In Manitoba, as in most provinces, elected representatives are known as members of the Legislative Assembly (MLAs). In Quebec, they are members of the National Assembly (MNAs). Ontario has MPPs, or members of the Provincial Parliament. Manitoba has 57 provincial electoral divisions, or ridings (2006).

FIGURE 6.9 Manitoba's Legislative Assembly meets in the Chamber, at the centre of the Manitoba Legislative Building in Winnipeg. The layout is unique in Canada. Would you say the design is more or less "democratic" than that of the House of Commons? Explain.

Elected representatives in provincial legislatures follow procedures similar to those followed by federal MPs. There is a Speaker, the government party, the Official Opposition, Question Period, the mace, parliamentary etiquette, and so on. There is one significant difference: provincial governments have no senates. (See Figures 6.3 and 6.4.)

TERRITORIAL LEGISLATIVE ASSEMBLIES

About 100,000 people in total live in Canada's three territories: Yukon, the Northwest Territories, and Nunavut. In the latter two territories, most of the people are Inuit.

Each territory has a **commissioner** (who is similar to a lieutenant governor), a premier, and a legislative assembly that functions similarly to a provincial legislature. However, territories have less power than provinces in such areas as land ownership and control over school curricula. Because of an agreement between the Inuit and the federal government, Nunavut has more control over land and resources than the other territories.

▶ DID YOU KNOW ◀
Nunavut means "our land" in the Inuit dialects of the eastern Arctic. It was once part of the Northwest Territories.

The legislatures of the Northwest Territories and Nunavut maintain Aboriginal political traditions. Decisions are based on consensus, and legislatures are non-partisan. Each issue is considered on its merits, and the elected members vote to reach an agreement by the group as a whole. Elders are consulted before any policy or bill is passed into law.

LOCAL GOVERNMENT COUNCILS

▶ DID YOU KNOW ◀
Glen Murray was the first openly gay candidate ever to become the mayor of a major North American city when he was elected mayor of Winnipeg in 1998.

The head of a municipal government in a town or city is a **mayor**. In rural areas, this person is called a **reeve**. He or she is directly elected by the people. This person leads a government of **councillors**, who are elected by the voters in geographic areas known as **wards**. In areas of low populations, councillors are elected to represent the entire municipality. Each member of the locally elected council, including the mayor or reeve, has one vote.

Citizens can often have the most direct contact with and the biggest impact on government at the local level. For this reason, social reforms and change often occur here first.

The federal *Indian Act* recognizes the right of certain groups of Aboriginal peoples in Canada to elect and form local governments. These **band councils** pass bylaws similar to those of municipalities and provinces and make decisions. Under the *Indian Act*, certain bylaws passed by band councils may be disallowed by Indian and Northern Affairs Canada.

PAUSE, REFLECT, APPLY

1. How many ridings or constituencies are there at the federal level? How many members of Parliament?
2. Describe a) how a government is formed, and b) how that government passes bills.
3. Why do you think the Speaker of the House is elected by secret ballot, as opposed to a show of hands?
4. Describe the structure and purposes of the Senate.
5. Define the following: minority government, Speaker of the House, Question Period, Hansard, MLA, and patronage.
6. How do the structure and political power of the territories' legislatures differ from those of the provinces?
7. Create a comparison chart: list four features of Aboriginal political traditions and compare them to federal–provincial parliamentary traditions.

The Judicial Branch: Federal and Provincial/Territorial Levels

The judiciary (judicial branch) of government deals with the law courts and the administration of justice. Canada's courts are also called upon to interpret the country's laws.

Do governments have the right to regulate tobacco advertising? Does a province have the right to separate from Canada? What is meant by "freedom of expression" or "unreasonable search or seizure"? Answers to these and many other questions are provided by the judicial branch of government.

> **KEY QUESTION**
> How does the judiciary administer justice in Canada?

THE SUPREME COURT OF CANADA

The Supreme Court of Canada is the highest court in the land, and the court of last appeal. That means that if you are appealing your case, the Supreme Court is your last stop. Its ruling is final.

The court consists of a chief justice and eight other judges (three from Quebec), all appointed by the prime minister. (See Figure 6.10 on the next page.) Upon request, the Supreme Court may review the criminal or civil law decision of a lower court. It may also interpret the constitution.

Among other decisions in the past two decades, the Supreme Court has declared that certain restrictions on abortion are illegal, that Sunday shopping prohibitions are illegal, and that same-sex marriages are constitutional.

PROVINCIAL AND TERRITORIAL COURTS

Each province and territory has courts to enforce federal and provincial laws in criminal and civil issues. Each province and territory also has a court of appeal. (See Figure 6.11 on the next page.) This court may review the decision of a lower court and interpret the constitution.

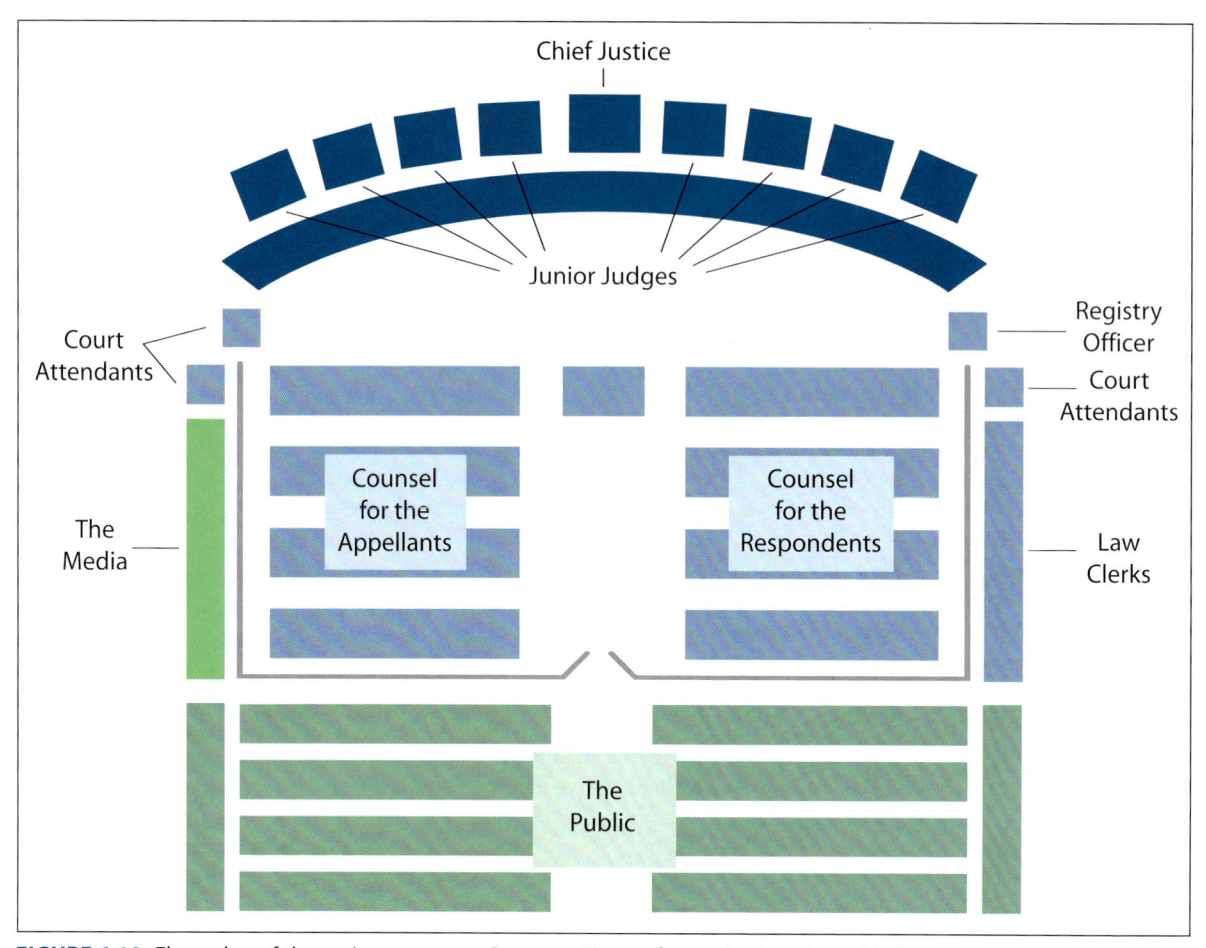

FIGURE 6.10 Floor plan of the main courtroom, Supreme Court of Canada. How does this floor plan compare to layouts for the House of Commons, the Senate, and the Manitoba Legislative Assembly? Does it reflect a commitment to democratic ideals? Explain. *Source: Supreme Court of Canada, www.scc-csc.gc.ca*

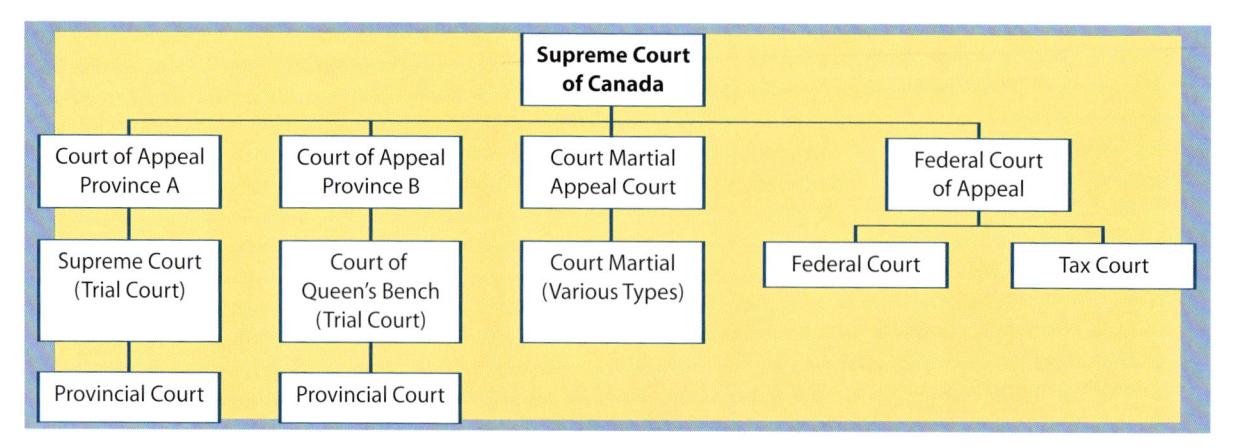

FIGURE 6.11 The structure of Canada's court system. The Court Martial Appeal Court hears appeals from military courts. *Source: Department of Justice Canada, www.justice.gc.ca*

PAUSE, REFLECT, APPLY

1. Explain the role of the judicial branch at the federal level.
2. Explain the role of the judicial branch at the provincial level.
3. What do you think is the purpose of having different courts at different levels of government?

REPLAY

In this chapter, you have explored these concepts:

1. Canada has three levels of government—federal, provincial/territorial, and local. Aboriginal self-government can occur at the local and territorial levels.
2. Each level of government has different responsibilities and different sources of revenue to pay for services.
3. Canada has three branches of government—executive, legislative, and judicial.
4. Each branch of government facilitates the democratic process in a different way.
5. Canada's governments continue to evolve to reflect the diversity of its peoples and their democratic heritage.

SKILLS TOOLKIT ▶ How to Locate Information

Do you need facts, figures, names, dates, opinions, pictures—information of any sort for your essay or debate? It is there for you, at your local library or on the Internet. However, using the library or the Internet is a bit like stepping into a huge information warehouse. How do you find the exact information you are looking for? Here are some tips. (All highlighted names can be accessed by visiting www.emp.ca/ccw.)

At the Library

Ask a librarian to help you locate main information sources, such as books, newspapers, CD-ROMs, and videos. Ask to see the catalogue files that summarize stories and articles from local, national, and international newspapers and magazines.

Can't get to the library in person? Have access to a computer or telephone? Many libraries now offer members "virtual reference libraries" in the form of online databases. Check out **Manitoba Public Library Web Sites** at www.emp.ca/ccw. Assistance from a librarian is also usually available, online and by telephone, at select times.

Online

Access your local newspaper archives (files of past issues) by typing the name of the newspaper into a search engine. Once you are at the paper, use its search button to search for your person or topic.

You can find links to magazines and newspapers around the world at **World Newspapers**.

Government of Canada Web sites offer reliable and accurate information. For information on the laws and courts, and even actual trials, go to **Manitoba Justice**. It has lots of information and links.

For information on voting and elections, go to **Elections Canada**. It will also send you information at no cost. Use **The Canada Page** to find other sites of interest.

Direct Contact

Sometimes the best way to get information is to visit, telephone, or e-mail local experts—community workers, politicians, government officials, philanthropists, and so on.

Before you make contact, think about what you want to find out. Then focus your questions. Ask yourself: Is this the right person or group to contact? Should I also contact other persons or organizations to get other perspectives?

When making contact, be sure to be

- polite
- brief
- clear
- to the point.

Checking Sources

Always consider your sources. Ask yourself questions such as:

- Is this fact or opinion?
- Is this source reliable?
- What is the source's connection to the issue?
- How current is the information?
- Can I check this against another source?

Skill Practice

1. Take an inventory of your upcoming assignments for the next month and make a list of the issues, ideas, or people that you will need to research or contact. Search the Internet. Tour the local library and ask for assistance in researching your material. Try not to focus on answering a specific question, but on becoming more independent at research.
2. What resources and methods did you learn to use by taking this advance tour?

STUDY HALL

Be Informed

1. Working in small groups, find the names and pictures of the following people that represent you in government: municipal councillor, mayor or reeve, school trustee, member of your provincial legislature, premier, lieutenant governor, federal member of Parliament, prime minister, and governor general. Create a classroom display.

2. Explain why territories in Canada do not have the same rights and responsibilities as provinces.

3. Using the library or the Internet, find a story that tells you something important about the recent activities of your local government, your provincial government, and your federal government.

4. In this chapter you have met reformers, lieutenant governors, governors general, and cabinet ministers. Sometimes circumstances have empowered these people to make different choices. Ontario's Lieutenant Governor (1997–2002) Hilary Weston, for example, was wealthy. She donated her salary to job-training programs for high school students and street kids. Emily Murphy also contributed some of her wealth to social causes. These are examples of *philanthropy*. Find examples of philanthropy in your community and explain them to your class.

Be Purposeful

5. With a partner, find three rules in your student council's constitution that you might wish to change. Find out how this constitution can be changed (the process is called the "amending formula"). Report your findings to the class.

6. Organize a mock federal cabinet meeting. Assign roles to the prime minister and approximately 14 different cabinet ministers and their assistants. In the meeting, each cabinet minister (and assistant) argues for money to support a program under his or her portfolio. What rules are used in the meeting? How are conflicts resolved?

7. After appropriate research, conduct a debate on one of the following resolutions:
   - The monarchy should be abolished in Canada.
   - The Canadian Senate should be abolished.

Be Active

8. Invite one or more of the people profiled in activity 1 to visit your class and to speak about their concept of active citizenship.

9. Identify an issue that concerns you at the local, provincial, or federal level. Write a letter to either your municipal councillor, MLA, or MP to express your point of view. Support your point of view with evidence. Politely request a response from the person to whom you are writing.

10. Eric Robinson, Nunavut premier Paul Okalik, and many other Aboriginal leaders have spoken out about the high suicide rate among Aboriginal youth in certain communities. With a partner, research and present to the class measures being taken by government and non-governmental organizations to address this concern. Visit www.emp.ca/ccw for links to resources.

11. In small groups, investigate the concept of citizens paying for the services they use. State whether or not the idea is worthwhile, and explain your reasons. Here are some ideas:
    - tolls to pay for roads
    - user fees for medical services
    - book fees for public schools

CHAPTER 7
How Do Laws and Regulations Affect You?

A factory worker in England tests a cane in 1965. Teachers used canes to punish and discipline students. In 2004, the Supreme Court of Canada ruled that "corporal [physical] punishment by teachers is unacceptable." It also said that teachers could use "reasonable" force to restrain or remove unruly students. What do you think is "reasonable"?

What You Need to Know
- How do government laws and regulations affect your daily life?
- What ideals, beliefs, and values shape laws and regulations?
- How can citizens disagree with a law responsibly?
- What are the responsibilities and processes of the justice system?
- What are the conservative, liberal, and centrist philosophies?
- How do citizens and governments deal with the disadvantages of democracy?
- How can you identify main and supporting ideas?

Key Terms
values	right-wing
beliefs	left-wing
bylaws	conservative
discrimination	liberal
harassment	political spectrum

Key Question
Are Canadians over-regulated?

Imagine a time in which a student who misbehaves is beaten with a rubber strap. A world in which a 14-year-old boy is accused of killing a classmate and sentenced to hang. A society where Aboriginal people are monitored by government agents, where black children are segregated in their own schools, and where gay people are labelled criminals.

Imagine that it is illegal to advertise or display birth control devices, such as condoms. People do not wear seat belts in cars. The penalty for driving intoxicated (proven by the inability to walk a straight line or to touch one's nose) is a small fine. A cigarette and ashtray are offered at a parent–teacher interview. Teenagers may drive at age 16, but must wait until they are 21 to vote or drink.

How would you like to live in this world? Some of your parents and grandparents did—in Canada in the 1950s. Laws and regulations touched every area of their lives. How are things different for teenagers living today? Do laws affect you? How?

Where Do You Encounter Laws and Regulations?

It may surprise you to learn that the law affects you as much as it did your parents and grandparents. While many laws and regulations from the 1950s no longer apply, some remain, and new laws have been introduced. Today, government still plays a major role in your life.

WELCOME TO YOUR LIFE

If you were born here, your parents had to get a birth certificate for you. If you joined your family through international adoption or if your family immigrated to Canada, you had to obtain a Permanent Resident Card (PRC) to stay here. Later, you applied for a Social Insurance Number (SIN).

The food and liquids you consumed were checked and regulated by inspectors. The toys you played with and the car seat you occupied had to meet Canadian safety standards. As you grew, you had to wear a helmet when riding a bicycle. The public places you entered were smoke-free zones. At a certain age, you were required to be schooled and immunized against certain diseases. When you entered or left your school bus, other vehicles on the road had to stop to allow you to cross the street safely.

These are just some examples of how government has entered your life on a regular basis for years and years.

In some ways, government acts as a super-parent. It is concerned with everyone's well-being. At times, you probably disagree with your parents about rules they set. Similarly, Canadians often disagree with government about what it is doing on their behalf.

However, because Canada is a democracy, citizens have a say in how government will operate.

How can you have your say? You can become informed about government by reading, viewing, and listening. You can be involved in government activities such as attending meetings and voting. If you disagree with a government, you can e-mail an elected official or attend a protest demonstration. You can support the government by taking part in recycling programs, by protecting the natural environment, by respecting human rights, and by acting to preserve Canada's heritage.

Most importantly, you can get involved by learning about which Canadian laws and regulations affect you. Knowing how far government

> **LITERACY COACH**
>
> Effective readers "preview" several paragraphs of information at a time by skimming before they read. They also draw on their own knowledge to figure out where the text is going. Where do you think this section is going? Read the first sentence again and skim the next six or seven paragraphs. Check, confirm, or revise your prediction at the end of the section.

FIGURE 7.1 Some schools ban all scarves, caps, and do-rags during class. In these schools, such items must be stowed in a locker during school hours.

THE WEB

The Manitoba Human Rights Commission has brochures describing your rights at school and work. Read them at www.emp.ca/ccw

DISCUSSION POINT

Many young people argue that a school ban on headgear is a pointless intrusion. They say their fashion choices have nothing to do with learning. What do you think?

reaches into your life is a first step toward being an active citizen. And you don't have to agree with what the government is doing.

RULES AT HOME AND AT SCHOOL

At home and school, rules daily remind us about manners, chores, privileges, curfews, communication, and clothing. Some rules are made specifically for emergencies and safety. Other rules are meant to keep households and schools running as smoothly as possible. Because not all families and classrooms are the same, the rules they agree to impose also differ. Each family or classroom may have somewhat different **values** (what you find important) and **beliefs** (what you believe in). The different rules reflect that diversity.

In Manitoba, some laws affect every student. By law, you must enter school or be home-schooled from age 7 to 16. (However, with permission from your parent or guardian, you may quit school at 15.) At secondary school, you must complete a certain number of courses in order to graduate. When you turn 18, you gain the right to look at your school records. These are just a few laws passed by the Manitoba government that affect you directly.

Other regulations—regarding behaviour, dress codes, and policies around lateness—are set by your school or school board. In some cases, these rules must be interpreted before they can be enforced. Some schools, for example, ban T-shirts with slogans that are "offensive" or that "promote violence." If you were going to define these terms, how would you do so?

Other schools have more extensive dress codes that spell out exactly what types of jewellery, headgear, tops, pants, and shoes you can wear.

PAUSE, REFLECT, APPLY

1. Identify six ways in which the government has affected your life to date.
2. Why do you think different provinces have different school-leaving ages?
3. What is your school's dress code? How was it created? Do you ever find it difficult to interpret or follow? Explain why.
4. Develop three or four criteria for a "reasonable" dress code for high school students.

City and Town Bylaws

The community in which you live also passes laws. Laws passed by local governments are called **bylaws**. Different cities and towns have different bylaws.

Municipal bylaws often reach into your daily routines. There are bylaws about how much noise you can make with your garage band or stereo, and where your parents can park their car. There are zoning bylaws about how land can be used. For example, a business that features video arcades or adult entertainment cannot be established within a certain distance of schools.

SAFETY-CONSCIOUS BYLAWS

Many bylaws are passed to protect the safety, security, and comfort of different people moving around the community. For example, some communities have a bylaw that prohibits the playing of games, such as skateboarding or road hockey, on public streets. This bylaw protects the safety of players and also reduces inconvenience to drivers.

Some bylaws are aimed at the safety of young children playing outside. For example, many towns and cities have bylaws that say you must remove the inside lock or door of any freezer or refrigerator before placing it outside for collection. This protects children from accidentally locking themselves inside.

PET SMART

Pet lovers are also restricted by bylaws so that everyone can enjoy community parks and sidewalks. In most communities, pets must be leashed outdoors, and "pooper scooper" laws require you to clean up after them. Some communities ban certain kinds of pet ownership. For example, want to buy or adopt a pit bull in Manitoba? First you will have to agree to keep the dog outside the capital. Winnipeg has banned pit bull ownership since 1990. Other Manitoba communities allow pit bulls.

> **KEY QUESTION**
> Are bylaws more concerned with protecting individuals or protecting communities?

> **THE WEB** ▶▶▶
> You can search Winnipeg's many bylaws at www.emp.ca/ccw

FIGURE 7.2 Not allowed near a Winnipeg sidewalk—unless the lock has been removed! What might happen if a young child used the refrigerator as a hiding place?

SOURCES

Sometimes, global concerns have a way of affecting people at home in their own communities. For another view, see Sources, Chapter 14, page 310.

Many communities also forbid the ownership of "exotic" pets. An exotic animal is usually defined as a species that is not a dog, or a cat, or a traditional pet, and is not native to Manitoba.

ENVIRONMENT FRIENDLY

In recent years, municipalities have passed more bylaws related to the environment. Many ban or limit pesticide and herbicide use on lawns. They also require you to sort your garbage into recyclables and landfill material. Some municipalities also have separate collections for biodegradable scraps or food wastes, or have started compost programs.

PAUSE, REFLECT, APPLY

1. Name three ways in which local bylaws affect your daily life.
2. Have you ever encountered a local bylaw you disagreed with? What was it, and what action, if any, did you take to protest or change it?

Provincial and Territorial Laws and Regulations

KEY QUESTION

What provincial or territorial law has the greatest impact on your life?

Provincial and territorial laws also affect your daily life. For example, Manitoba applies a 7 percent sales tax on most goods and some services. Some essential goods and services (for example, basic groceries, medicines, children's clothing, dental services, and so on) are exempted. The province also prevents you from buying cigarettes or consuming alcoholic beverages until you are 18 years old.

The Manitoba government also has strict laws about who gets to drive. The Graduated Driver Licensing (GDL) program requires you to pass a written test. Then you are monitored for three years, in stages.

First you are a learner, then a supervised driver, and finally, if you pass, a full-stage driver, with full driving privileges.

What if your primary language is French? The Manitoba government guarantees you access to government services in French. As a francophone, you can contact francophone school board representatives and receive an education in French, along with other francophone students.

Provinces also pass laws that affect the environment and the health of their citizens. Manitoba and New Brunswick were the first provincial governments to ban smoking in all public places, including bars and restaurants. That ban went into effect in 2004. This strict law leaves only one indoor location for smokers: their own homes.

Manitoba is also a leader in reducing gas emissions from vehicles that cause problems such as global warming. Under Premier Gary Doer, Manitoba pledged to reduce gas emissions by 23 percent. That is almost four times the amount targeted by the *Kyoto Protocol*, the international agreement to reduce global warming. Doer was named one of 20 "individual achievers" by *BusinessWeek Online* for his role in battling climate change.

FIGURE 7.3 Manitoba's Graduated Driver Licensing (GDL) program aims to keep new drivers in lower-risk situations before introducing them to more difficult driving situations. The program is credited with saving lives and reducing injuries.

THE MANITOBA *HUMAN RIGHTS CODE*

A smoke-free Manitoba limits some people's freedoms. The province's *Human Rights Code*, however, guarantees certain rights and protections for young and old alike. The Code is a provincial law that guarantees equal rights and opportunities in specific areas such as jobs, housing, and services.

The Code's goal is to prevent discrimination and harassment based on different characteristics (things about you that you cannot change). Figure 7.4 lists some of the characteristics and activities the Code covers.

Think about it: How does the Manitoba *Human Rights Code* affect you, personally? For one thing, its protection is wide-ranging. The right to be free from **discrimination** and **harassment** applies to work; accommodation (hotels, motels, and hostels); housing; contracts; and membership in unions and trade or professional associations. (See Figure 7.5.)

▶ **DID YOU KNOW** ◀
In 1974, pressure from the francophone community led to the creation of the Bureau de l'éducation française, which oversees French-language instruction throughout Manitoba.

☐ **DISCUSSION POINT**
Some people say that the GDL program is too long and inconvenient. During the second year, drivers must always be accompanied by another driver. Is this a realistic requirement for teenagers?

Protected Characteristics

The Code prohibits discrimination based on the following characteristics:

- ancestry
- nationality or ethnic origin
- religion
- age
- sex (including pregnancy)
- gender-determined characteristics
- sexual orientation
- marital or family status
- source of income
- political beliefs
- physical or mental disability

Protected Activities

Protection from discrimination extends to

- any aspect of employment
- services available to the public or a section of the public
- legal contracts
- renting out spaces
- buying real estate
- signs and statements

Source: Adapted from www.gov.mb.ca/hrc/english/publications/reasonableaccommodation.pdf

FIGURE 7.4 The Manitoba *Human Rights Code*

When you apply for a job, you cannot be asked if you have a criminal record. You can only be asked for personal information that directly relates to the requirements of the job. Some jobs do require background checks. Even so, you must agree to one in writing before the employer conducts it.

If you experience discrimination or harassment, you can inform authorities at your place of work, residence, or wherever you receive services. If the activity does not stop, you may contact the Manitoba Human Rights Commission. This agency hears complaints and enforces the principles of the Code.

The Manitoba *Human Rights Code* also guarantees equal treatment for persons with disabilities. This applies whether the condition developed over time, resulted from an accident, or was present at birth.

Under the Manitoba *Human Rights Code*, schools must take reasonable steps to accommodate all students with disabilities. "Reasonable" means that 1) effort has been made and

FIGURE 7.5 In Manitoba, you cannot be prevented from renting a property because you are pregnant or attending school. Why do you think landlords want to exclude certain people from renting?

2) the measures taken are enough to help the student. Some examples of reasonable accommodations include:

- making the school wheelchair-accessible
- employing educational assistants
- modifying the curriculum to meet the needs of students with disabilities
- offering special technologies that aid learning.

PAUSE, REFLECT, APPLY

1. List the three provincial laws that affect your life the most and explain your choices.
2. Examine the cartoon in the Sources feature, page 142. What is a "ramification," and why does the cartoonist say major ones are ahead?
3. a) What rights does the Manitoba government recognize for francophones?
   b) How did these come about?
4. Do you know someone who has encountered discrimination or harassment in employment or in some other area? In your opinion, did the person have grounds for contacting the Manitoba Human Rights Commission? Explain.
5. Why is the right of renters not to be discriminated against placed above the freedom of landlords to choose tenants however they see fit?

Federal Laws and Regulations

In many respects, you may think of the federal government as the level most removed from your life. Yet, at times, it can have a dramatic impact on a young person.

> **KEY QUESTION**
> Should there be one set of laws for adults and another for teenagers?

CRIMINAL LAW

Criminal law is the responsibility of the federal government. It is the branch of law that deals with acts or offences against society that have been classified as crimes.

Youth Justice

The *Youth Criminal Justice Act* (2003) determines how lawbreakers between the ages of 12 and 17 are treated. The youth justice system reflects the idea that young people are still maturing and do not yet possess the judgment of adults. In Canada, justice for youth differs from adult justice in many respects, including

- degree of accountability (to what extent the person can be held responsible for the crime)
- length of sentences
- approaches to rehabilitation.

Young people involved in the justice system must not be identified by the media. Punishments may range from custody (comparable to imprisonment for adults) to extra-judicial measures (measures outside the court system). Prison sentences are less severe than those for adults. They are served in youth detention centres, not adult jails.

Under a variety of extra-judicial measures, the young offender may meet a Youth Justice Committee composed of community members. The committee may recommend one or more of the following:

- restitution (paying back to the community, usually through service)
- community support for the youth
- a meeting between the victim and the young offender.

▶ **DID YOU KNOW** ◀

The death penalty was abolished in Canada in 1976 by Bill C-84. The bill was introduced in the House of Commons by Pierre Trudeau's Liberal government, and passed by a vote of 131–124. Shortly after that, the US Supreme Court reinstated the death penalty in the United States.

(You will learn more about the youth criminal justice system in Chapter 10.)

According to Statistics Canada, young adults aged 18 to 24 have the highest rates of drug offences. This is followed by those aged 12 to 17. In 2003 and 2004, the Liberal government introduced controversial bills to make possession of less than 15 grams of marijuana no longer a criminal offence. Instead, those offenders would have faced a fine of up to $400. They would not have been left with a criminal record. Both bills faced heavy

FIGURE 7.6 In 1959, 14-year-old Steven Truscott was found guilty of raping and murdering his 12-year-old classmate, Lynne Harper, and was sentenced to be hanged. Eventually, his sentence was reduced, and he was quietly paroled in 1969. Truscott has always maintained his innocence. Recently, he successfully applied to the minister of justice for a review of his case. How would justice be different for Truscott today?

opposition, and both died when elections were called. More than 600,000 Canadians have criminal records for simple possession of marijuana.

The Canadian Medical Association backed the government's reform of drug laws. It pointed out that a criminal record can bar young people from many jobs and opportunities, including getting into medical school. It called the negative health effects of moderate marijuana use "minimal." The Canadian Association of Chiefs of Police also advocated decriminalization. It said that prosecuting people for small amounts ties up scarce resources. Other groups, such as the Canadian Police Association and Mothers Against Drunk Driving, have opposed decriminalization. They argue that it will lead to increased use of hard drugs and more cases of impaired driving.

THE *CANADIAN CHARTER OF RIGHTS AND FREEDOMS*

At the federal level, rights are protected by the *Canadian Charter of Rights and Freedoms*. As you learned in earlier chapters, the Charter deals with a citizen's relationship with the government. Section 8 states: "Everyone has the right to be secure against unreasonable search or seizure." In practice, this section means that you and your possessions cannot be searched unless police officers have a search warrant or a good reason to search. Furthermore, your dwelling place (house or apartment) cannot be searched without a proper warrant issued by a judge.

School Searches

What about your right to privacy in an elementary or secondary school? You have fewer rights than you would in other circumstances. Teachers and other school authorities are responsible for providing a safe environment and maintaining order and discipline for everyone in the school. This may sometimes require searches of students, lockers, and personal belongings, as well as seizure of prohibited items. In this sense, a student's Charter protection stops at the schoolhouse door.

Equality Rights

Section 15(1) of the Charter states:

> Every individual is equal before and under the law and has the right to the equal protection and equal benefit of the law without

▶ **DID YOU KNOW** ◀
In the case *R v. M. (M.R.)*, the Supreme Court of Canada ruled in 1998 that a school official can search a student or student's locker without a warrant. The case involved a student suspected of selling drugs. When the vice-principal searched the student, drugs were found in the boy's socks.

discrimination and, in particular, without discrimination based on race, national or ethnic origin, colour, religion, sex, age or mental or physical disability.

While Manitoba's *Human Rights Code* deals with relationships between private individuals, section 15 of the Charter deals with the relationship between the government and the individual. All provincial and territorial human rights codes are subject to the terms of the Charter. If a section of a human rights code is found to be inconsistent with the Charter, the courts can declare that section to be no longer in force.

CivicStar

JUSTINE BLAINEY

In 1981, 10-year-old Justine Blainey was a skilled hockey player. She had just won a position on the Metro Toronto Hockey League team. Her victory was short-lived, however. League regulations did not allow girls to play.

Blainey brought a complaint to the Ontario Human Rights Commission. She was shocked to learn that Ontario's *Human Rights Code* allowed sexual discrimination in sports. Blainey thought the law was discriminatory, and appealed her case before the courts.

In 1986, the Supreme Court of Canada upheld Blainey's appeal, declaring that her equality rights under the Charter (section 15) had been violated. Ontario's *Human Rights Code* was changed so that athletic organizations could no longer restrict membership on the basis of gender.

In 1988, Blainey played her first minor-bantam league hockey game. She continued playing hockey with boys until the age of 19. At the University of Toronto, she played on the women's hockey team.

Blainey also fought back when the university tried to stop funding the women's team. Her "Save the Team" night raised $8,000, and the team had its funding increased.

▶ DID YOU KNOW ◀

Today, more Canadian girls and women are playing hockey than ever before. In the mid-1990s, about 10,000 were registered to play. By 2005, more than 60,000 girls and women were playing hockey—often with boys, on boys' teams. Female leagues are also being created across Canada, and the demand for female referees and coaches is up.

Your Play

1. Create a flow chart to illustrate the process Justine Blainey followed, and the government bodies she contacted, to redress her situation in 1981.
2. Justine Blainey was criticized for pursuing her Charter rights. What would you have done in her situation? How would you have answered your critics?

THE CANADIAN *COPYRIGHT ACT*

Every time a radio or television station plays a song or video, musicians, composers, artists, and music companies are paid a royalty fee for their creative work. In 2004, it was estimated that 51 percent of young Canadians between the ages of 12 and 19 downloaded music from the Internet without paying a penny. Should royalties be paid for the millions of songs downloaded each year?

Canada's federal government is responsible for both communications and copyright protection. In 1998, it changed the Canadian copyright law to apply a levy (fee) on all blank audio recording media, including CDs, and even hard-disk–based MP3 players.

The money collected is distributed to copyright holders (including artists, composers, and record companies) for revenue "lost" through Internet downloading.

In 2004, the Federal Court of Appeal ruled that the $25 fee imposed on iPods and other MP3 digital music players was illegal. That same year, the Supreme Court of Canada ruled that Internet service providers (such as Bell, Sprint, and AOL) are not responsible for paying royalties on music downloaded by users.

> **THE WEB**
> Learn more about levies introduced because of Internet downloading at www.emp.ca/ccw

FACE OFF: Downloading Music from the Internet

In 1999, 18-year-old Shawn Fanning invented an Internet file-sharing service. He called it Napster, after his own nickname. Fanning's invention allowed millions of users to download music from a server that was part of a Web site.

For Napster fans, technology was being used to do the same thing that had been done for years in neighbourhoods, schoolyards, and concerts: they were swapping music. What was wrong with sharing music with a friend, even if that friend was online? Young people argued that bands like Metallica made so much money from concerts that they would not miss the revenue from lost CD sales.

Fanning has conceded that the music industry has suffered, but offers a justification:

> It may be hurting the music industry at this point, but my view is when consumers have the ability to learn about new and interesting music—and the barrier is lowered in a way that gives them control over how they experience it—I think those are positive things.
>
> —Shawn Fanning

FIGURE 7.7 Who in this cartoon is the victim of crime?

Many in the music industry saw things differently. They viewed each musical creation as their intellectual property and that of the composer, artist, and producer. Under copyright law, an artistic creation cannot be reproduced or distributed without the owner's permission. Industry spokespeople charged that downloading music from the Internet was theft, pure and simple. And in 2000, Metallica sued Napster for copyright infringement.

> It is ... sickening to know that our art is being traded like a commodity rather than the art that it is. From a business standpoint, this is about piracy, i.e., taking something that doesn't belong to you; and that is morally and legally wrong.
>
> —Metallica lawsuit against Napster

Not all musicians agree. In 2006, some Canadian musicians formed the Canadian Music Creators Coalition. The coalition believes that copyright law might need reforms because of new technology, but not at the expense of fans.

> [W]e believe that suing our fans is destructive and hypocritical. We do not want to sue music fans, and we do not want to distort the law to coerce fans into conforming to a rigid digital market artificially constructed by the major labels.
>
> —Steven Page, The Barenaked Ladies

FIGURE 7.8 Barenaked Ladies frontman Steven Page.

What Do You Think?

1. Copyright laws also apply to "intellectual property" other than music and videos—for example, plays, books, and sheet music. Create a table in which you list the advantages and disadvantages of copyright laws.
2. On the Internet, research the 2000 Metallica lawsuit against Napster. Summarize Metallica's arguments in an argumentative paragraph.
3. Why do you think Steven Page calls suing music fans "destructive and hypocritical"? Explain your answer.
4. What is your opinion about free music downloading? Give two reasons for your viewpoint.

PAUSE, REFLECT, APPLY

1. Explain how young people and adults receive different treatment from the Canadian justice system today.
2. Give reasons why you think that "different treatment" is a good or bad idea.
3. Describe two federal laws that you would like to see changed or adjusted. Explain why you would like the change.
4. a) How did Justine Blainey effect change in the sports system?
   b) In what other ways can individuals and groups influence social and political systems?

The Political Spectrum

At every level of government, laws and regulations have some impact on your life. Sometimes you may support those laws. Sometimes you may disagree with them. Maybe you feel that pit bulls should not be banned, or that possession of small amounts of marijuana ought not to be decriminalized, and your best friend holds opposing views.

Your right to do something may also clash with what the larger group wants. For example, your "right" to keep your pit bull may conflict with your neighbour's right to feel secure. Your "right" to display a certain T-shirt slogan may ridicule a whole group of people whose ethnic background or sexual orientation is different from your own. It is the role of government and the courts to resolve conflicts. The courts often use the guideline of what a "reasonable person" would do. Section 1 of the Charter refers to "**reasonable limits**" on rights and freedoms.

RIGHT, LEFT, WHAT?

You may have heard references to **right-wing** and **left-wing** in discussions about politics and society. These terms are used as convenient ways to describe bodies of beliefs. Your opinions and beliefs place you somewhere on an imaginary line called the **political spectrum**.

Being a conservative places you on the right side; being a liberal places you on the left. The concept of the left–right political spectrum dates back to the French Revolution (1789). In the French Assembly, elected conservative politicians sat to the right of the Speaker's chair; elected liberals sat to the left.

Note that the term "conservative" does not necessarily mean the same as the term "Conservative Party." Similarly, "liberal" does not necessarily mean the same as "Liberal Party." For example, in Canada, it is possible for someone to be a **centrist** (one whose political beliefs lie in the middle of the political spectrum) and a member of the Conservative Party, and it is possible for someone to have conservative views on many issues and be a member of the Liberal Party.

So what do these labels mean? Figure 7.9 lists some ways to describe the two sides of the spectrum.

> **KEY QUESTION**
> Is there one "best" political philosophy?

> **DISCUSSION POINT**
> A Canadian political movement called "Unite the Right" worked for six years to merge the Canadian Alliance and Progressive Conservative Party. In 2003 it happened, and the Conservative Party of Canada was created. What kind of policies would you expect the new party to promote?

◀ Left-wing	Right-wing ▶
Liberals tend to believe in	**Conservatives tend to believe in**
■ government involvement in people's lives	■ minimal government involvement in people's lives
■ ensuring equal opportunities through law	■ individuals being responsible for themselves
■ the inevitability of social change	■ maintaining traditional values and social patterns
■ generous subsidies such as welfare, medicare, and pension benefits	■ emergency relief and personal charity
■ higher taxation to guarantee social services	■ lower taxation to encourage individual spending and entrepreneurship
■ a small military, especially in peacetime	■ a strong military defence of the nation

FIGURE 7.9 The left–right political spectrum. In the centre are many people who would describe themselves as moderate, and who blend the two sides of the spectrum.

WHEN PHILOSOPHIES CLASH

When citizens clash in their political views, government's role is to address those differences. Governments try to accommodate opposing ideas by using study groups, public hearings, opinion polls, and information sessions. Citizens may express their viewpoints on an issue through e-mails, letters, and Web sites. By means of education and discussion, differing views may be understood and reconciled.

In Canada, the three levels of government follow the will of the majority, but also recognize the rights of minorities. Citizens are aware of the rights of minority groups in various ways. A Sikh citizen is permitted to wear his traditional turban and beard as a member of the Royal Canadian Mounted Police. A francophone citizen can communicate with government and educate her children in the French language. A citizen with physical handicaps is able to attend school, theatre, and other facilities without facing barriers.

FIGURE 7.10 Left and right, two means of protest. Citizens in Manchester, England, march to protest their country's involvement in the war in Iraq. A bystander's shirt expresses an entirely different view, another form of protest. Where on the political spectrum would you place the bystander and the marchers? Explain your reasons.

Sometimes differences and conflicts are settled in an elected parliament. Sometimes they are settled in a judicial court, or through a government agency such as a human rights commission or tribunal. In each setting, opposing sides are permitted to present their ideas and philosophies. They present arguments and counterarguments. After a decision is made, all sides accept that decision. By resolving conflicts using these methods, Canadians have been able to build one of the world's most inclusive societies.

PAUSE, REFLECT, APPLY

How do you think liberals and conservatives would view each of the following issues? Examine all the characteristics of each philosophy before deciding. Offer a reason for each of your choices.

- Subsidized child care
- Same-sex marriage
- Children's rights
- Film censorship
- Guaranteed annual income for the poor
- Low taxes for business
- Environmental regulations
- The death penalty

REPLAY

In this chapter, you have explored these concepts:

1. Laws and regulations at every level of government affect your life.
2. Laws and regulations balance the rights of the individual with the needs of society.
3. The *Canadian Charter of Rights and Freedoms* protects individuals from unfair laws.
4. The justice system recognizes two groups of people: adults and youths.
5. The political spectrum is an integral aspect of democracy.
6. When philosophies clash, government's role is to help resolve the differences.

SKILLS TOOLKIT

How to Identify the Main Idea and Supporting Evidence

When you read information you have located, are you faced with a "wall of words"? The challenge for you is to spot the most relevant pieces of information.

The *main idea* in what you are reading is the most important piece of information. Why did the author bother writing this? The reason is usually the main idea. The details or examples that support that idea are called the *supporting evidence*.

The passage at right is about Canadian political writer Naomi Klein. Imagine that your teacher has assigned this piece for reading. The goal is to read the passage and identify the main idea and supporting evidence.

- Make sure you understand what you are looking for. Review the definitions of main idea and supporting evidence (above).
- Look for key words that tell you about the person or issue. For example, find words that express attitudes, beliefs, or decisions.
- Find a statement that expresses Klein's point of view. Then find a statement that supports that point of view. Sometimes supporting statements are specific examples.
- Be prepared to ignore information that may be interesting, but not relevant to your assignment.

Skill Practice

1. Select the one statement that best illustrates the main idea of this passage. Explain why you selected this particular statement.
2. Select another statement that offers further evidence to support your choice.
3. Identify four statements that are not relevant to this particular reading assignment.

Naomi Klein was born in Montreal to American parents who came to Canada in protest at the Vietnam War. She always had a love for designer labels. In her teenage years, she was a "mall rat," and in her high school yearbook she was described as "most likely to go to jail for stealing peroxide."

In university, Klein, herself Jewish, wrote in a newspaper article that the Jewish state of Israel should stop its occupation of Palestinian land. In 2000, she published a book that criticized large corporations such as Nike, McDonald's, and Starbucks for taking over world markets with their brand-name advertising. For example, her book pointed out that Indonesian workers are paid $2 a day to make Nike running shoes that sell for $120.

Although concerned about the living and working conditions in the world's poor countries, she also criticized North American "McJobs" that have low wages, no worker protection, and no future. Klein, who is married to television personality Avi Lewis, considers herself a feminist. She has succeeded in bringing attention to the manner in which large corporations take advantage of people in both less developed and more developed countries (countries that are technologically advanced and wealthy).

STUDY HALL

Be Informed

1. Identify some of the ways in which a young person can become involved in government.
2. What is a bylaw? List two examples of bylaws.
3. As members of Canadian society, we have both rights and responsibilities. At the local level, we have the right of pet ownership. List at least four responsibilities associated with pet ownership.
4. Explain, with examples, three ways in which provincial laws affect young people.
5. What is section 8 of the *Canadian Charter of Rights and Freedoms*, and how does it apply to a young person's life inside and outside school?
6. What is section 15 of the *Canadian Charter of Rights and Freedoms*, and how was it applied to the case of Justine Blainey in 1986?

Be Purposeful

7. a) Organize a classroom debate on each of the topics listed below.
   b) Before the debate, research your position and your opponent's position.
   c) After the debate, summarize your position on each debate topic in a well-written paragraph.

   Debate topics:
   - Pit bulls and other dogs deemed dangerous should be outlawed.
   - Smoking should be outlawed in all public places.
   - The possession of small amounts of marijuana should be decriminalized.
   - There should be no restrictions on downloading music from the Internet.

8. Read about Manitoba's *Human Rights Code* and the Manitoba Human Rights Commission at www.emp.ca/ccw. Study each of the following examples, and decide whether the situation described is a legitimate case of discrimination for the Manitoba Human Rights Commission. Provide reasons for your answers.
   - A male student notices that he is paying five times as much for automobile insurance as a female student who is the same age and has the same driving record.
   - After a complaint from a customer, a restaurant owner asks a nursing mother to breast-feed her child in the women's washroom.
   - An advertisement for a receptionist's job asks for female applicants who speak "unaccented English."
   - During a job interview for the position of childcare worker, you are asked to submit to a criminal record check and to supply the names of two references.

9. Select a current politician in Canada or in the world, and research that person's political ideas. In a well-written short paper, explain why the person is a conservative, liberal, or centrist.

Be Active

10. With a partner, research and present to the class the measures that are being taken by your local community to improve the environment.
11. Research and report on Manitoba's Environmental Youth Corps (EYC). Include descriptions of recent EYC projects in several Manitoba communities. If you feel strongly about what you discover, make a pitch for your class to undertake a project in your community. Find out about EYC at www.emp.ca/ccw.
12. Outline the steps you would take to convince your community to adopt what you consider to be a new and worthwhile environmental protection measure.

CHAPTER 8
How Do Governments Make Policy?

Soon after the Conservative Party won a minority government in 2006, Prime Minister Stephen Harper visited Canadian troops in Afghanistan. What is the cartoonist saying about politics?

What You Need to Know
- What is public policy, and how is it made?
- What are the major influences on policy?
- How can public policy makers and citizens address social injustices in Canada?
- How do minority governments affect the advantages and disadvantages of Canada's democratic systems?
- Why must public policy makers recognize many perspectives?
- How can you find and identify different points of view?

Key Terms
policy	petitions
platform	bill
grassroots	standing committee
interest groups	non-confidence
referendum	youth wings
stakeholders	polls

Key Question
In a democracy, should government lead or follow public opinion?

AcmeAthletic has offered to pay half the cost to build athletic facilities on the property of Applecity High School. City council will pay the other half, as long as the facilities are open for community use on weekends and evenings. The area has no community centre and has had problems with youth gangs for years.

AcmeAthletic and the city want the school board to donate the property. AcmeAthletic also wants the school to display its "Flash" logos. In exchange, the school can use the facilities during school hours, up to 6 p.m.

There is another problem, too, besides advertising Acme products in school. AcmeAthletic has used child labour in Southeast Asia. Student council has been leading a consumer boycott (refusal to buy) of AcmeAthletic products. The student council has no say in the decision.

Should the school board approve this offer? Who are the winners and losers if it decides yes? If it decides no?

Platforms and Policies

Policy is the plan of action of a political party or government to achieve certain goals. During an election, each party promotes its **platform** to the public. This is the group of policies it promises to pursue if elected. Policies have to deal with issues and problems in the real world. Citizens vote for the candidates and parties that best represent their own views and wants.

The party that wins becomes the government and is then expected to turn its policies into laws and actions.

Sound simple? It's not.

DO CITIZENS REALLY WANT TO HEAR ABOUT POLICIES?

Sometimes people care passionately about policy; often, it seems, they do not. In his memoirs, Pierre Trudeau described his campaign in the 1972 federal election. Trudeau won a second term as prime minister, but the Liberal Party won fewer seats than it did in 1968:

> I described the exercise as "a conversation with Canadians." "Here's what we've accomplished in the past four years," I said to them, "and here are our plans [policies] for the next four years. If you like them—then vote for us." … The electorate was eager for cheers and rallies, and there I was giving them calm, lucid propositions [clear ideas]. That is not how you win elections.

Bad things can happen when people pay too little attention to policy. In the 1930s, for example, a different kind of leader came to power in Germany. Like Trudeau, Adolf Hitler was *charismatic*—that is, he had a personal "magic" that aroused loyalty and enthusiasm among his followers. Hitler's powerful speeches inspired thousands at mass rallies by appealing to their love of Germany and their fears of others. Behind Hitler's stirring words were hateful plans and policies. These eventually led to World War II (1939–1945) and terrible war crimes, including the Holocaust and other genocides:

> It might be argued that had more non-Nazi Germans read [*Mein Kampf*, Hitler's autobiography] before 1933 [when he came to power] and had the foreign statesmen of the world perused it carefully while there was still time, both Germany and the world might have been

▶ **DID YOU KNOW** ◀

In 1933, *Mein Kampf* sold 1.5 million copies. It made Hitler rich. Every German couple intending to marry had to own a copy. Some historians suggest that few people read the book very carefully.

saved from catastrophe. For whatever other accusations can be made about Adolph Hitler, no one can accuse him of not putting down in writing exactly the kind of Germany he intended to create if he ever came to power and the kind of world he meant to create by armed German conquest.

—William L. Shirer, *The Rise and Fall of the Third Reich* (1959), p. 81

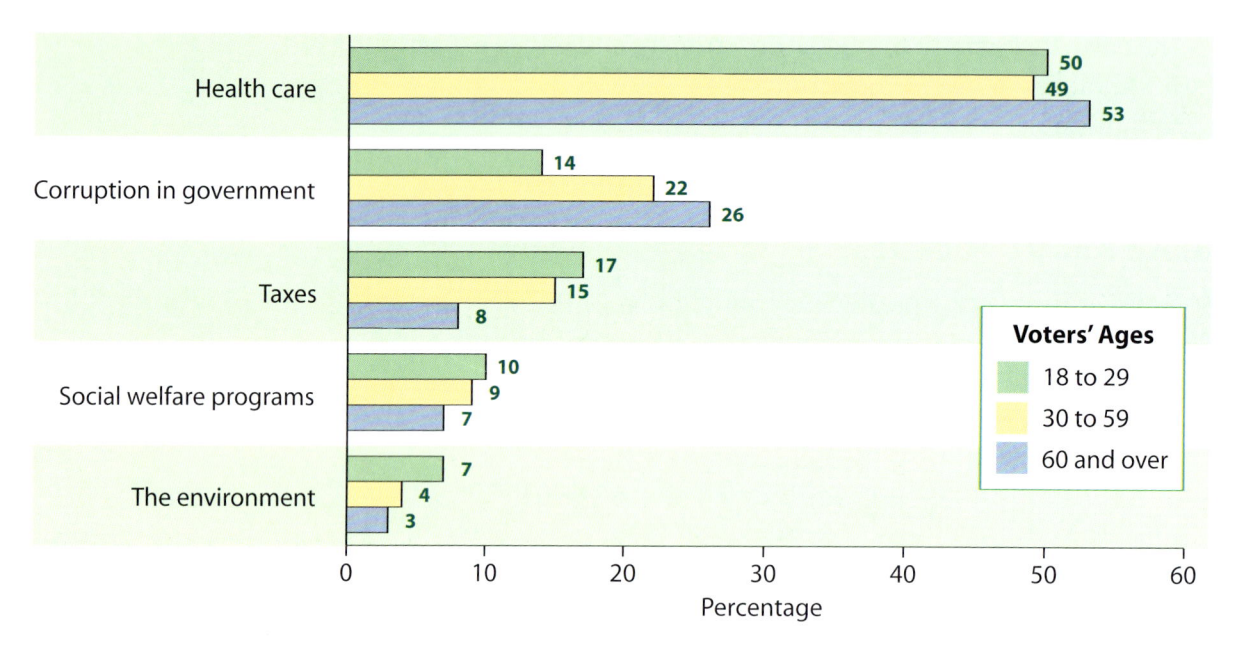

Issue	18 to 29	30 to 59	60 and over
Health care	50	49	53
Corruption in government	14	22	26
Taxes	17	15	8
Social welfare programs	10	9	7
The environment	7	4	3

FIGURE 8.1 In a study of the 2004 federal election, Canadians were asked which issues were most important to them. What issues were most important to the youngest voters? Do you think this is still true? *Source: Elections Canada*

PAUSE, REFLECT, APPLY

1. a) What is policy?
   b) How does policy relate to platform?
2. a) Trudeau wrote that he nearly lost the 1972 election for what reason?
   b) Is Trudeau being insulting to voters or realistic? Explain.
3. a) List three facts you know about Adolf Hitler.
   b) List three results of Hitler's election.
   c) What lessons can be learned from Hitler's ideas, election, and subsequent policies?
4. a) How important is it to have a charismatic leader to communicate a political party's platform?
   b) What responsibility do voters have to question those policies?
5. What characteristics make a good leader?

How Are Policies Developed?

In Canada, governments collect and spend billions of dollars in taxes each year. Government decisions touch every aspect of life—from homes to homelessness, from schools to threats of military attacks from outer space.

Government policy falls into several areas:

- social (health, education)
- financial (taxes, money supply)
- international (defence, trade, foreign relations)
- public works (transportation, construction)
- resources (fisheries, agriculture, energy)
- legal (justice)

Each policy area is managed by a different department or ministry.

Policies deal with the wants and needs of our complex society. Large numbers of people are involved and consulted as opinions, facts, and information are researched.

Policies have consequences—good and bad, long-term and short-term. A policy may look good on paper. Once put into action, however, it may produce unexpectedly bad consequences. New policies must then be created to correct mistakes.

> **KEY QUESTION**
> Why is it often difficult, complicated, and slow to pass laws in a democracy?

MAJOR INFLUENCES ON POLICY

Governments and political parties create policies around their core beliefs. They must also respond to many influences. Some of the most important influences are described next.

Political Party Membership

Across Canada, thousands of ordinary Canadians join and work for political parties locally. This is referred to as the **grassroots** level. Why would people want to get involved?

Even at this level, party members can strongly influence a party's goals. Members from each riding

FIGURE 8.2 Manitoba NDP Premier Gary Doer jokes around with youth supporters during a campaign stop in June 2003. The NDP won 35 of Manitoba's 57 ridings. How important to you is it for youth to be represented in the political process?

can become delegates to party conventions and conferences. Delegates can discuss policy with party leaders and elected representatives. Delegates' directions are put forward in **resolutions**. If passed, resolutions become policies. In other words, through grassroots involvement, ordinary people can have some influence and power.

Civil Service Advice

The executive branch of government employs thousands of civil servants. Top civil servants are experts and advise government on policy details. It is not enough to say, "We want everyone to have a good education." Costs must be calculated, options developed, and a plan of action devised.

Judicial Opinion

The influence of the courts on public policy has increased since the passage of the *Canadian Charter of Rights and Freedoms* in 1982. Government legislation must comply with the Charter. If it does not, the courts can override laws that contravene (do not respect) the Charter. In 2004, for example, the federal government went to the Supreme Court of Canada for a constitutional opinion on proposed changes to marriage laws to recognize same-sex couples. The issue was extremely controversial.

Economic Realities

Economic conditions also affect policy decisions. Once a party is elected, voters expect it to deliver on its platform and promises. The key economic question: Is there enough money to keep all those promises?

Intergovernmental Concerns

Policies in one level of government are influenced by the demands and needs of other levels of government. For example, Manitoba may need federal funds to build new hospitals. The city of Flin Flon may need provincial funds to support public transit. The federal government may want municipal land to build a new airport. The three levels of government will have to communicate and reach agreements so that as many groups as possible can benefit.

International Pressures

Political borders cannot keep out international influences. Foreign policy, defence, and trade all depend on relationships with other countries. Policies must reflect this reality. As you learned in Chapter 1, most important for Canada is the relationship between its policies and the reactions of the United States. This relationship is important because the US is Canada's closest ally and trading partner—and the world's most powerful country.

Interest Groups

In democracies, informed people can come together to pursue common causes or goals. The groups they form are called **interest groups**. To achieve their goals, interest groups try to influence policy makers. Many groups focus their efforts on the courts and interpretation of the Charter.

> ▶ **DID YOU KNOW** ◀
> The International Joint Commission has been settling trans-border water disputes between Canada and the United States for 100 years. One continuing dispute is North Dakota's plan to redirect water from Devil's Lake into Manitoba to prevent flooding. Manitoba and Canada have a problem with that: the water is highly polluted.

CONSEQUENCES OF A POLICY

Most policies are created with good intentions. Criteria to assess what "good" is would include policies that are designed to

- do what is best for the most people
- protect the weakest in society
- provide fairness and equity
- create a cleaner, healthier community.

Policies intended to improve or protect society may have the opposite effect. What is good for "most people" may harm others.

For example, in 1916, Manitoba prohibited the sale and consumption of alcohol. A large majority voted in favour of such a law in a public **referendum** (a direct vote on an issue or policy). Alcohol was seen to cause many social ills. There were social benefits to "prohibition." Crimes related to drunkenness and family violence decreased. But criminals and bootleggers took over the production and sale of alcohol. Manitoba experienced a crime wave. Government taxes on liquor sales vanished.

Prohibitionists argued that by using grain for food, not liquor, Canadians were supporting the soldiers fighting in World War I (1914–1918). Many veterans returning from the war disagreed. They felt they had earned the right to choose whether or not to drink. The law became very unpopular. In 1923, Manitoba changed it. Alcohol would

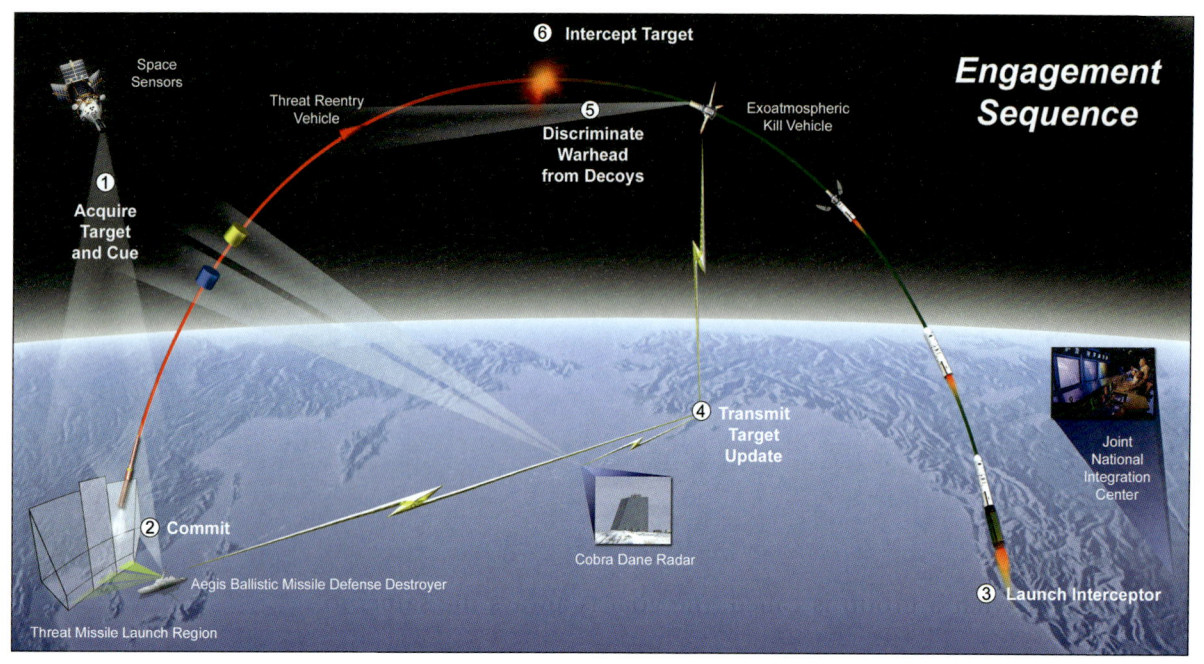

FIGURE 8.3 In 2005, Prime Minister Paul Martin rejected the US Ballistic Missile Defence program. Canada opposed putting weapons into space. In the 2006 election campaign, Stephen Harper was open to Canadian participation. How might this affect Canada–US relations? With whom do you agree? *Source: Canadian Broadcasting Company*

be sold and controlled by the government. Today, the Manitoba Liquor Control Commission still fulfills that function.

Stakeholders

Individuals or groups that have something to gain or lose from a policy or law are known as **stakeholders**. In the case of prohibition, for example, stakeholders included liquor producers, the government, veterans, bar owners, police, drinkers, and so on. Other stakeholders included spouses and children of violent drinkers.

PAUSE, REFLECT, APPLY

1. Who is allowed to belong to a political party?
2. Which of the following must be democratically elected: a civil servant, a party member, a member of Parliament, a member of an interest group, a judge?
3. What is a "stakeholder"?
4. What criteria does (or should) a government use in forming a policy that will affect the interests of different stakeholders?
5. Make a web diagram. In the centre, write "policy." In the outer circles, name (in one or two words each) all the stakeholders or influences that might affect policy makers.

Interest Groups and Policy Makers

In a democracy, many individuals and interest groups try to influence parties and governments. Interest groups are diverse. Business people form interest groups. So do labour unions and religious organizations. Students form interest groups, as do parents and educators, lawyers, prisoners, social agencies, ethnic and cultural groups, monarchists, artists—the list goes on.

Interest groups use different methods and media to try to influence policy decisions: mailings, **petitions** (written demands signed by many people), media interviews, appearances before government committees, advertising campaigns, demonstrations, meetings with government and party officials, and so on. (See the Skills Toolkit on petitions in Chapter 9.)

Interest groups can also be called **lobby groups** and **pressure groups**. Regardless of what a group is called, the goal is always the same: to influence policy makers to support the group's position.

> **KEY QUESTION**
> How much influence should interest groups have in a democracy?

COMPETING INTERESTS

The more contact an interest group has with government, the greater its chances of influencing policy. Pressure/lobby groups compete to communicate regularly with government.

For example, while first developing its policies on the *Kyoto Protocol*, the Canadian government was lobbied by Greenpeace and the Canadian Environmental Law Association. These groups strongly supported Kyoto. The Canadian Council of Chief Executives

FIGURE 8.4 This 2005 Greenpeace protest urged the federal government to apply the *Kyoto Protocol*. In 2006, the new government under Stephen Harper said it supported an alternative to Kyoto. What has happened since?

FACE OFF: Homelessness and Public Spaces

Policy Issue: A municipal government must decide how to deal with homeless people sleeping in public places.

Policy Background: In the 1980s and 1990s, governments adopted policies to reduce spending. Social programs—including housing, education, employment insurance and retraining—were cut back. In big Canadian cities, large numbers of homeless people began to appear. This hadn't been seen in decades.

Today, across Canada, homeless people are sleeping on street grates and in building entries, parks, and public squares. The Federation of Canadian Municipalities has declared homelessness a "national disaster."

Policy Options: As many as 1,000 homeless people sleep on the streets of Anycity each night. Another 2,000 sleep in emergency shelters. More than 100 people sleep in the city hall square. City council meets to find a solution. Two sides emerge during the debate: "Tough Love" and "Have a Heart."

Tough Love

- Short-term help isn't enough. Deal with the causes of homelessness (abuse, addiction, physical and mental illness, unemployment).
- Volunteers who give blankets and food only encourage homeless people to stay on the streets.
- People have a right to walk in public places without stepping around bodies.
- Homeless people make public places unsafe and unclean.
- Homeless people victimize businesses, tourists, and residents.
- Sleeping in public places should be outlawed.
- Police should take vagrants to shelters. If vagrants refuse, they should be taken to jail.

Have a Heart

- Forcing homeless people into shelters or jail violates the rights of society's most vulnerable members.
- Forcing homeless people out of public spaces puts them at risk in unsafe hiding places.
- Government should build affordable housing or subsidize (help to pay) rents.
- Many of the homeless fear theft, fights, or disease in shelters.
- Governments must provide more medical, counselling, and social services.
- Spending 1 percent of government budgets on affordable housing would end homelessness.
- "Charity begins at home."

FIGURE 8.5 Karen Christiansen watches Canadian Pacific's Holiday Train stop outside Brandon in December 2005. The cross-Canada train raises money for food banks every year. Which side of the debate would you say Christiansen is on?

What Do You Think?

1. Good policy making requires consultation. List at least 10 stakeholders that councillors should consult before making a decision. Try it alone, then work in pairs, and share your results.
2. In creating policy, politicians need to look for solutions, not arguments. Working in pairs or in groups, make three lists (or do a Venn diagram of three interlocking circles):
    a) List all the points on which Tough Love and Have a Heart agree.
    b) List points on which they absolutely disagree.
    c) In the middle, make a list of points where you find parts of the policy may be acceptable to both sides.
    d) Come up with a three- to five-point policy based on your "middle way."

and the Alliance of Manufacturers and Exporters also lobbied, but against Kyoto. They feared that the *Kyoto Protocol* would unnecessarily cost businesses billions of dollars and lead to huge job losses. The interests of both sides had to be balanced.

An interest group may be non-partisan (have no formal ties with political parties) yet include people with similar political views. The National Citizens Coalition (NCC) and the Canadian Centre for Policy Alternatives (CCPA) are two examples. Both represent large numbers of voters, but at opposite ends of the political spectrum. Both groups study policy and government very closely.

A SPECTRUM OF INFLUENCE

Some interest groups can afford to hire professional lobbyists, who make their living representing interest groups. Some professional lobbyists are former politicians or civil servants—insiders who know whom to talk to and how to contact them.

Sometimes interest groups are umbrella organizations. For example, the Insurance Bureau of Canada promotes the interests of many insurance companies. The bureau gives member companies a stronger voice influencing policies than each would have separately. Insurance companies may want limits on the amount a person can collect (liability) on a claim, or new rules on investments.

Ordinary citizens form interest groups, too. Neither rich nor powerful, these people join together to make a difference. For example, young drivers form an organization to pressure insurance companies to lower automobile insurance rates. People in St. Boniface organize for bilingual road signs. College and university student associations lobby to prevent tuition rates from rising.

THE WEB
Learn more about the NCC and CCPA and where to place them on the political spectrum at www.emp.ca/ccw

☐ **DISCUSSION POINT**
Stephen Harper dropped out of federal politics from 1997 to 2002 and headed the National Citizens Coalition. What kinds of policies would you expect him to introduce as Canada's prime minister?

LITERACY COACH

Use the "think-aloud" method as you read about CivicStar Hannah Taylor on page 166 or any other CivicStar in this book. To use this method, write down what you are thinking about as you read. This is a way of taking notes about the text. Here is an example:

On a cold winter day in 2001 [I was 9], Hannah Taylor saw something on a Winnipeg street that shocked her: a man eating out of a garbage can [it shocked me too, the first time]. Very upset, she asked her mom, "Why?" [That's weird; I was with my uncle, and I asked "why"] ...

CivicStar

HANNAH TAYLOR: LADYBUG LADYBUG

On a cold winter day in 2001, Hannah Taylor saw something on a Winnipeg street that shocked her: a man eating out of a garbage can. Very upset, she asked her mom, "Why?" Weeks later, the image still haunted her. She kept asking, "why?"

Hannah was five years old. It's not unusual for kids to keep asking questions. Besides, nobody likes to see anyone eating out of a garbage can, do they? Then why was this happening? "If everybody shared, wouldn't there be … ?" You get the idea: Hannah's questions continued.

Hannah started school. One day, she saw a homeless woman pulling a banged-up grocery cart. Hannah became more upset and asked more questions. Finally, her mother said that Hannah might not feel so sad if she did something about the problem.

Hannah did. She met more homeless people. She went to shelters. She talked about homelessness to anyone and everyone who would listen. She did a grade 1 class project.

On a trip to Toronto, she met a homeless man and accidentally dropped her lucky ladybug charm in his cup along with some money. The man, Carey, caught up with her and returned the charm. Carey thought it important. Something clicked for her in that moment, something about "family" and respect, regardless of social divisions.

Inspired and helped by people in the homeless community, Hannah started the Ladybug Foundation to raise awareness and funds for other organizations dealing with homelessness. One campaign uses jars painted to look like ladybugs "because ladybugs bring luck and homeless people need good luck." Hannah's campaign caught on with the media.

Hannah has since spoken to thousands across Canada—from the homeless to the wealthiest business leaders. Her message is simple: "I believe that if people know about homelessness—they will want to help."

Within five years, the Ladybug Foundation had raised more than $500,000. Even prime ministers Jean Chrétien and Stephen Harper have had Ladybug jars on their desks.

Now … how do you think that might affect government policies?

Your Play

1. What motivated Hannah Taylor to take action?
2. a) What steps did she take?
   b) How effective were these steps?
   c) Why are catchy names, slogans, and logos important tools for interest groups?
3. Visit the Ladybug Foundation Web site at www.emp.ca/ccw and explore its vision, mission, and goals. How useful might these be as models for doing something about other social issues?

PAUSE, REFLECT, APPLY

1. What is a lobbyist?
2. Interest groups try to inform and influence the public as well as politicians. Why is this important to them?
3. What is the difference between a professional lobbyist and someone like Hannah Taylor?
4. By law, all professional lobbyists in Canada must sign up on a lobby registry. This allows the public to know who is lobbying and for what.
   a) Why is this law necessary?
   b) Why might the government do what a lobby wants, even if it is not a good policy for the majority of people? (Brainstorm and record examples.)
5. Identify poverty issues (local, provincial, or national) that concern you and then propose some policies and actions to deal with them. Your goal? To create a more equitable society.

How Policy Becomes Law

Have you ever had strong feelings about a social problem, government program, or law? Have you had ideas about how to fix the problem, or for better laws and programs? What about the gun registry, or government apologies and payments for past injustices? What about crop insurance to protect farms? And post-secondary education: should tuition fees be higher, or lower? Or should post-secondary education be accessible to all, like universal health care?

This is how bills and laws originate, as ideas in people's heads. In a democracy, ideas can come from many different sources: political party policy, government administrators, interest groups, individual citizens, and advisory bodies. In other words, if you have an idea and believe in it, there are ways you can take action.

An idea or feeling, however, isn't enough in itself. It has to be turned into a proposal. Then that proposal must travel through a complex legislative process.

THE STAGES IN PASSING A FEDERAL BILL INTO LAW

Chapter 6 described the three levels of government: federal, provincial, and municipal. The process for creating laws is carefully set out in all three levels and is similar in each. Only the federal government, however, has a Senate. With this background, it is possible to trace how a policy becomes a law in the provincial and federal governments by studying the federal stages.

> **KEY QUESTION**
> What safeguards are in place to make sure that policies are well thought out before becoming law?

THE WEB ▶▶▶
Follow the stages a bill must pass through to become Manitoba law at www.emp.ca/ccw

Flow chart stages

1. **FROM IDEA TO BILL** — Cabinet minister or prime minister, senator, or private member proposes a bill.
2. **FIRST READING** — The bill is read for the first time and is printed.
3. **SECOND READING, DEBATE, AND VOTE**
4. **COMMITTEE STAGE** — Committee members study the bill, clause by clause.
5. **REPORT, AMENDMENTS, AND VOTE**
6. **THIRD READING, DEBATE, AND VOTE**
7. **THE SENATE** (federal level only) — The bill follows a similar process to that of the House of Commons.
8. **ROYAL ASSENT** — The bill receives royal assent after being passed by both Houses.
9. **IN FORCE** — The bill becomes an act, and law. It takes effect immediately or at a later date or dates.

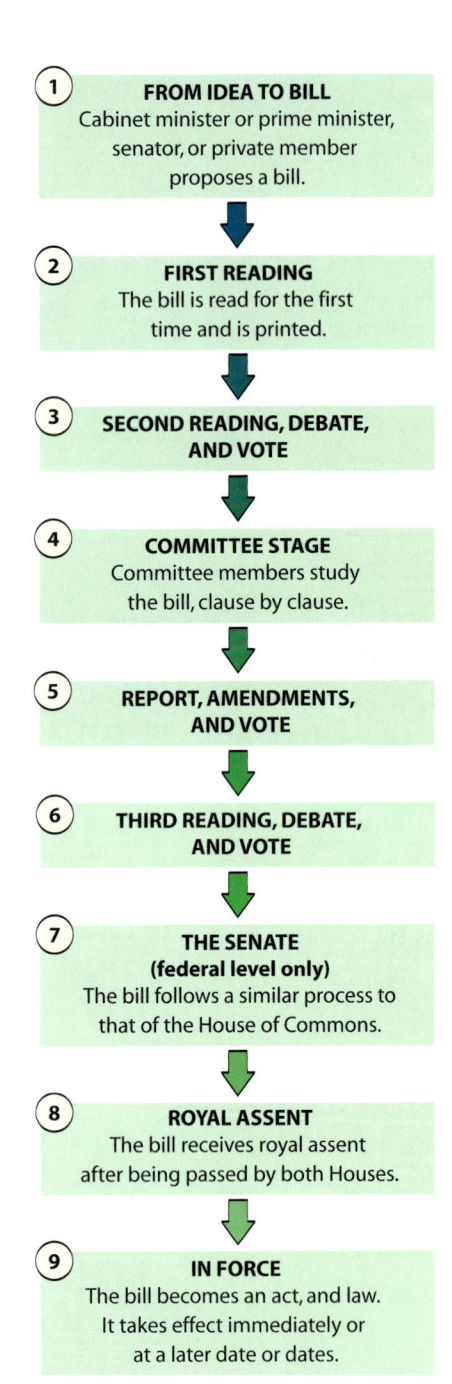

FIGURE 8.6 Flow chart of how a bill becomes law: the legislative process

1. From idea to bill

In Parliament, most proposals for laws begin with the prime minister (PM) and cabinet ministers. The PM and cabinet discuss and decide which policies they want as law. Cabinet ministers are responsible to see that policies are carefully examined by public servants in their departments. A policy on taxes, for example, would go to the finance minister.

The minister ensures that the policy is drafted and checked by government lawyers. The legal document they produce is known as a **bill**. Cabinet solidarity requires all cabinet members to support a bill, even if personally they disagree with it.

If a senator feels it necessary, he or she may introduce an individual bill. Like any bill, it must go through the legislative process (see Figure 8.6). Private members of Parliament (MPs who are not in cabinet and who can belong to any party) may also introduce bills. This is known as a "private member's bill." In both cases, the bill does not have cabinet solidarity behind it. Thus, it is less likely to make it through all the stages and become law.

2. First reading

The cabinet minister (or private member or senator) presents the bill to the House of Commons. There is no discussion, debate, or vote.

3. Second reading

At this critical stage, all MPs can question the bill's purposes and consequences. The debate can take hours, days, or weeks. The government can set a time limit, but the opposition parties must agree. After debate, the bill is voted on. If passed, it means that the bill is approved in principle. The bill then moves on to committee.

4. Committee stage

The bill is studied, clause by clause, by a **standing committee**. This group of MPs from all parties asks questions and invites public and expert input.

5. Report stage

After completing its work, the standing committee issues its report and may recommend **amendments** (changes). The bill is sent back to the House of Commons. Any amendments are introduced, debated, and voted on. If it passes, the bill moves on.

6. Third reading

The amended bill is debated, and more amendments can be proposed. Finally, a vote is taken. If the bill passes, it moves on to the Senate.

7. The Senate (federal level only)

The bill goes through the same stages in the Senate as it did in the Commons. The Senate, which is appointed, can delay or defeat the bill. (In 1988, for example, the Senate refused to pass the Canada–US *Free Trade Agreement* so that a federal election could be held on the issue. An election was called, and the agreement was eventually passed.) By tradition, however, the Senate usually approves bills. After all, by this point bills have been approved by elected representatives. If the Senate proposes amendments, the revised bill returns to the Commons for another vote.

8. Royal assent

Finally, the governor general signs the bill, turning it into an act, which becomes a **statute** (law that is written and passed by a legislature). The assent reads, "Her Majesty, by and with the advice and consent of the Senate and House of Commons, enacts as follows … ." Because the governor general is appointed, not elected, he or she traditionally will not refuse to give assent. (At the provincial level, the lieutenant governor signs the bill.)

9. In force

The law comes into force upon **royal assent** or at a date (or dates) specified in the Act.

THE PASSAGE OF MUNICIPAL BYLAWS

Although there are different systems of municipal government across Canada, all are non-partisan. To become bylaws, municipal policies follow a process similar to the federal one.

> **DID YOU KNOW**
> If important legislation (often about money, such as the budget) is defeated in second or third reading, it may be considered a vote of **non-confidence**. Because the majority of MPs have not supported the government, the prime minister and cabinet must resign. Traditionally, an election is called.

> **THE WEB**
> Find out why the Liberal minority government lost the confidence of the House of Commons and lasted only five months in 2005 at www.emp.ca/ccw

> **THE WEB**
> To see different kinds of federal bills, go to www.emp.ca/ccw

CANADA IN THE CONTEMPORARY WORLD

1. Elected councillors (or alderpersons) sit on various committees that oversee such areas as parks and recreation, planning and transportation, community services, and budget and finances.
2. Committees study policy proposals. Citizens are free to contact their councillors, attend committee meetings, and ask to address council meetings.
3. Bylaws pass through stages similar to the provincial and federal process: first reading; second reading, with debate and public input; committee; final reading; vote. There is no Senate or royal assent.

PAUSE, REFLECT, APPLY

1. a) Why is a bill more likely to be defeated in a minority than in a majority government?
   b) Why is a senator's or private member's bill less likely to become law than a government bill?
2. Who is responsible for the formal writing and preparing of a government policy into a bill?
3. Who is responsible for presenting a government bill to the House? What is this stage called?
4. A "standing committee" is basically the same in all three levels of government. Describe it.
5. The Senate has been called the "house of sober second thought." Do you think this is a benefit in the passage of bills? Explain.
6. Judging from the quotation from the royal assent (page 169), who might you think makes laws in Canada?

▶ KEY QUESTION
Can ordinary citizens still influence government policies after elections?

Where Do I Come In?

Some people feel that one must be part of a larger group in order to be heard. They are mistaken. Here are some strategies you can use as an individual to be heard by governments.

CONTACT YOUR REPRESENTATIVE

The most direct access to government is through your local elected representative. You can contact him or her in various ways. Many organizations offer advice on how to do this effectively. Here are a few tips:

1. E-mails and faxes are easy to send (and easy to ignore).
2. Handwritten or typed letters to federal and provincial representatives are more personal and more effective:
   - Briefly, respectfully, and clearly relate your experience and concern.

- Identify the specific law, regulation, policy, or program, and how you want it changed.
3. Copy your letter to the minister or councillor responsible for the area that concerns you. He or she has great political power and needs to hear from citizens directly.

> **THE WEB** ▶▶▶
> For extensive federal and provincial contact information, go to www.emp.ca/ccw

GET INVOLVED AT THE GRASSROOTS LEVEL

How can young people change the system, improve opportunities, or fight injustice if only older people pick the leaders—and are the leaders?

Earlier in this chapter, the grassroots membership of political parties was identified as a major influence on policy. It is a route that is open to all citizens, including youth. Most major political parties in Canada accept members from the age of 14.

Most parties have **youth wings**. These are meant to increase access for young members into the party. They can also focus youth power within the larger party. As convention and conference delegates, young members can influence leadership choices. They can also put forward resolutions.

Members of youth wings often become party leaders. Former prime ministers Brian Mulroney and Jean Chrétien—and Stephen Harper—were all members of youth wings.

> **THE WEB** ▶▶▶
> Find links to youth wings of major parties at www.emp.ca/ccw

THE ROLE OF PUBLIC OPINION POLLS

To win elections, parties like to know what citizens want. One way to do that is through surveys, or public opinion **polls**. Compas, Ekos, Environics, and Ipsos-Reid are among Canada's best-known polling companies and are often quoted in news reports.

By contacting as few as 1,000 people, pollsters can get an accurate snapshot of how all Canadians feel on an issue. The sample (the people interviewed) must be selected at random (not biased or skewed). **Random sampling** statistically ensures that each individual in a population has an equal chance of being selected.

Poll questions must be carefully designed. They must not lead people to respond in a certain way. To test the popularity of Prime Minister X, a pollster might ask: "Who is your favourite politician?" or "Do you prefer X, Y, or Z for prime minister?" or "How would you rate X's effectiveness as prime minister: very good, good, fair, or poor?"

Polls have a margin of error. For example, a poll shows that party leader X has 52 percent approval and Y has 48 percent. The **margin of**

> **LITERACY COACH**
>
> Whenever you read poll results, check the questions asked, the sample size, and the margin of error.

> **THE WEB** ▶▶▶
>
> For more information on pollsters and polling, go to www.emp.ca/ccw

error is plus or minus 5 percent. In other words, X might actually have 47 percent to Y's 53 percent! It is wise to view polling data as having a range.

A poll is very different from an election or a referendum. Polls do not involve ballots, and governments are not obliged to make laws based on poll results.

Government by Numbers?

Would government based on polls be good government? Chapter 3 described how majority opinion does not always lead to achieving the common good. Besides, public opinion changes, sometimes overnight. Polls cannot predict how people will feel in the future.

In the end, citizens expect parties and governments to stay informed about issues. Then, representatives and leaders must do what they feel and reason is right—even if it is unpopular. As US President Harry Truman once advised a young politician: "Always do right. This will please some and surprise the rest."

FIGURE 8.7 Each year, 40 high school students from across Canada are hired in the House of Commons Page Program. The paid position is part-time. Pages do everything from act as messengers for members of Parliament, to manage files and documents, to speak to groups of high school students.

CivicStar

LESTER PEARSON: SUPERMAN IN A BOW TIE?

Lester Pearson (1897–1972) was often modest in person. But as a Canadian diplomat, policy maker, and politician, he was a world giant.

The government under Prime Minister Lester Pearson (1963–1968) achieved the extraordinary. It showed politicians taking account of different perspectives and popular opinion and still making major policy decisions based on principles.

Pearson never led a majority government. His policies had to win support from at least one other party. Usually, this was the New Democratic Party.

Pearson governed at a time when groups that had felt powerless were speaking out. Francophone Canadians, Aboriginal peoples, and women were all demanding political change. Immigration was overturning traditions. Canada was becoming multicultural.

Already a Nobel Prize–winning diplomat, Pearson was trained to listen and to try to satisfy all stakeholders. That can be a superhuman challenge in politics. Pearson was criticized for being indecisive or too easily influenced.

In 1963, Pearson set up the Royal Commission on Bilingualism and Biculturalism. Eventually, it opened up opportunities for francophone Canadians in the public service, society, business, and education. Pearson brought prominent Quebeckers into cabinet, such as Pierre Trudeau.

The 1967 Royal Commission on the Status of Women sought to give "women equal opportunities with men in every aspect of Canadian society."

Pearson introduced major new social welfare policies, including the Canada Pension Plan and the Canada Assistance Plan. Most controversial of all, the *Medical Care Act* provided medical coverage for every Canadian. Today, universal health care is as much a part of the Canadian identity as the Maple Leaf flag.

Facing fierce opposition, Pearson unified the Canadian navy, army, and air force into the Canadian Armed Forces. Finally, under Pearson, and after furious debates, Canada adopted the Maple Leaf flag, replacing the British Union Jack.

Pearson retired in 1968. At the Liberal leadership convention that year, he said, "[A leader is] expected to be a combination of Abraham Lincoln and Batman, to perform instant miracles. Then, when the poor chap can't live up to this, the process of demolition begins so that another superman can be erected in the ruins."

FIGURE 8.8 Lester Pearson at a Montreal Expos baseball game in 1970

Your Play

List Pearson's new policies. Beside each, describe three stakeholders that were affected, and explain in what ways.

PAUSE, REFLECT, APPLY

1. Find the names of your municipal, provincial, and federal elected representatives.
2. Why is a letter more effective than an e-mail in getting the attention of a member of Parliament or a cabinet minister?
3. a) What is a public opinion poll?
   b) What features ensure a poll's accuracy?
4. Identify two major differences between a poll and a referendum.
5. Politicians use polls to see what voters like and dislike. Why are non-politicians interested in polls?
6. Search the Web sites of the polling companies named on page 171. Select one or two polls being reported. Describe what the information says to you about an issue or policy.

REPLAY

In this chapter, you have explored these concepts:

1. Effective policy makers consult large numbers of stakeholders and experts.
2. Government policies are affected by many influences.
3. Policies are seldom a choice between right and wrong; they are usually a choice between what is better under the circumstances.
4. Bills pass into law in the federal, provincial, and municipal levels of government through a series of steps.
5. Citizens can use a variety of means and strategies to influence government, both individually and collectively.

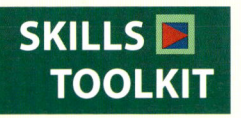

SKILLS TOOLKIT: How to Look for and Detect Different Points of View

When looking for information about an issue, it is important to know the points of view of the sources you find. Consider this ancient parable (story) from India:

> Six blind people are asked to describe an elephant by touching the elephant's body. Each one touches a different part: the side, the tusk, the trunk, the leg, the ear, and the tail. In turn, each declares the animal to be like a wall, a spear, a snake, a tree, a fan, and a rope. The moral of the parable? Though each person is partly right, all of them are wrong.

All sources have a perspective and thus some bias (one-sidedness). You cannot eliminate it. However, you can recognize the perspectives of your sources. You can also look at an issue from many different perspectives.

Here is a checklist to help you find different perspectives:

- Identify a variety of stakeholders.
- Locate different reports and source different media, including newspapers, magazines, books, radio, television, and the Internet.
- Find sources from different regions.
- Opinions change over time; look at sources from different time periods.

Here is a checklist to assess perspective and bias:

- What do stakeholders have to gain or lose?
- How knowledgeable is the source?
- What is the source's reputation?
- Is the source connected to a political party or group?
- Do an Internet search to check the credentials of unfamiliar sources.
- Is the source primary (original) or secondary (interpretive or analytical)?
- Is the perspective subjective (opinion) or objective (unbiased, fact)?
- Check where and when news items were written.

Skill Practice

1. Review the Face Off feature on page 164. Identify the stakeholders. Playing the role of a reporter, identify a new stakeholder that you would wish to speak to. Explain that new perspective.

2. In 1995, the Liberal federal government introduced Bill C-68 in response to the 1989 mass killing by a gunman of 14 female students in Montreal. Enacted in 1995, the *Firearms Act* required all firearms owners in Canada to register them. The original cost of the gun registry was estimated at $119 million. By 2006, it had cost more than $2 billion. The Conservative government made changes to the registry in 2006. Describe the possible perspectives of these stakeholders on the *Firearms Act*:
   a) an MP
   b) a gun collector
   c) a hunter
   d) the sister or brother of one of the women killed in Montreal
   e) the Canadian Association of Chiefs of Police
   f) the Law-abiding Unregistered Firearms Association.

3. Find three very different perspectives on a current news event from very different sources. Consider using news media, Web sites of parties and interest groups, and so on. Identify different viewpoints. Think: why do these differences occur? Describe your personal assumptions and how they have or have not changed based on the new information and ideas you have researched.

STUDY HALL

Be Informed

1. Explain the relationship among policy, platform, bill, and act.
2. Identify five different factors that influence policy decisions. Explain how each factor exerts influence.
3. A municipal bylaw to force street people to sleep in shelters has been proposed. As a municipal councillor, write a) an argument in favour of the policy, b) an argument opposed to the policy, and c) an argument to change the policy to respect both perspectives.
4. a) What is a lobby group?
   b) Why does the government have a lobby registry that is accessible to the public?
5. a) Review the stages of passing a bill into law. At what points do you, as a citizen, have the best opportunity to be heard?
   b) What would you have to do to be heard?
   c) How would you know if anyone was listening?

Be Purposeful

6. Canadian society faces the same issues again and again. Using one of the following issues, prepare a two- to three-minute speech or audio-visual presentation. The topic: "How do policy choices we face today compare with policy decisions made in the past?" Research the issue using history textbooks, the library, and the Internet. State your position clearly. Use the past as an example of a policy's good or bad consequences.

   Issues
   - (80 Years Ago) Should marijuana use be decriminalized today? Compare today's debates with prohibition debates in Canada during and after World War I into the 1920s. What can be learned from the past?
   - (70 Years Ago) What policies are needed to deal with the homeless today? How do they compare with homeless policies during the Great Depression of the 1930s?
   - (40 Years Ago and Recent) What should Canada's policy be regarding participation in US missile defence? Compare the decision of Paul Martin's government in 2005 with the Bomarc debates of 1963. Compare the positions of Lester Pearson, John Diefenbaker, and Tommy Douglas with those of Paul Martin, Stephen Harper, and Gary Doer. Compare Canadian attitudes toward President John F. Kennedy and President George W. Bush. How did these attitudes influence policy decisions?

Be Active

7. Conduct a poll in two classes other than your own. Try two questions: a closed question, such as, "Should students be able to elect their principal?" and an open question, such as, "If an election were held today, whom would you vote for as principal of your school?" Select a scale and make a graph of the poll results. Do you believe that the school board would follow your wishes?

8. Your instructor will divide the class into three groups: Liberal, Conservative, and New Democrat. You and the other members of your group must use the Internet or telephone to contact a party, youth wing, or riding association. Find out
   a) how to join
   b) membership requirements
   c) youth group activities
   d) how young members and youth groups get their issues into party platforms.

   A possible followup: Write a letter to the party leader about whether your research experience was helpful or unhelpful in finding out about the party's policies.

CHAPTER 9
How Do Citizens Elect Governments?

Iraqi citizens line up to vote in spite of the threat of attacks by armed rebels intent on disrupting the election.

On January 30, 2005, the people of Iraq voted in an unusually important election: it gave them their first democratically elected government in more than 30 years.

For decades, Iraq had suffered under the brutal regime of a dictator, Saddam Hussein. Then in 2003, US and British forces invaded Iraq, defeated the Iraqi military, and occupied the country. When elections were held for the new, democratic government, people turned out to vote in surprisingly large numbers, under conditions of great danger.

Why do you think people would take such risks to elect leaders democratically?

What You Need to Know
- How are governments elected in Canada?
- What is the role of political parties in the parliamentary process?
- How do the roles of political parties differ in majority and minority governments?
- Who are some political leaders in Canada today?
- How do voting and elections influence Canada's political systems?
- What are the advantages and disadvantages of the Canadian system?
- How can you be more effective as a petition signer and petition maker?

Key Terms
representative democracies
direct democracies
chief electoral officer
platform
constituency
franchise
majority government
minority government
first past the post (FPTP)
proportional representation (PR)
petition

Key Question
Do elections produce governments that truly represent the people?

Voting

Democracy is the process by which people choose the man who'll get the blame.

—Bertrand Russell (1872–1970), English philosopher

☐ **DISCUSSION POINT**
About 65 percent of Canadians voted in the 2006 federal election. During some elections, the percentage of voters has been even lower. Is it really a democracy when so many people don't vote?

Voting in an election has been called the single most important act of political participation in a democracy. Democracies today are **representative democracies**, not the **direct democracies** first developed in the small cities and towns of ancient Greece. Modern nations are too large to assemble all citizens to debate and vote on all laws affecting them. Instead, citizens elect representatives to do these things on their behalf.

Democratically elected governments have considerable powers. However, the government must always be accountable to the people. If the people do not like what the government is doing, they can vote leaders out of office and elect a new government.

CHECKS ON REPRESENTATIVES' POWERS

Candidates make promises to the electorate during election campaigns. Not all such promises will be kept. It is important that elections be held frequently to ensure that representatives are responsive to the electorate. Canadian federal and provincial representatives must hold an election at least every five years. Municipal politicians are elected every three years.

Additional methods have been suggested to make elected representatives more accountable. These will be considered later in the chapter. First, let's look at how elections are run today.

THE ELECTION PROCESS

The prime minister (in the case of a federal election) or premier (in a provincial or territorial election) chooses the best time to call an election within the five-year limit.

☐ **DISCUSSION POINT**
What happened with Bill C-16? Do fixed election dates "improve the fairness of Canada's electoral system"? Explain.

In 2006, Prime Minister Stephen Harper's minority government introduced Bill C-16 to amend the *Canada Elections Act*. If the bill passes, federal elections will be held on a fixed date: the third Monday in October, every four years. The bill also sets out Monday, October 19, 2009 as the date of the next general election. Once the next general election is held, the following election would be set for the third Monday in October, four calendar years in the future.

In announcing the bill, the government said: "Fixed election dates will improve the fairness of Canada's electoral system by eliminating the ability of governing parties to manipulate the timing of elections for partisan advantage."

Elections also occur when a government is defeated in the legislature on a vote of non-confidence (see Majority and Minority Governments, page 187).

For a federal election, the prime minister asks the governor general to call a general election. It must be held within 36 days of that announcement. Election day is always on a Monday unless there is a statutory holiday, which moves it to a Tuesday. Provincial and territorial elections operate in a similar fashion and are called by the lieutenant governor.

> **DID YOU KNOW** <
> Elections are expensive. The 2004 federal election cost Canadian taxpayers $200.3 million.

The chief electoral officer, who is head of Elections Canada, mobilizes thousands of permanent and temporary workers to prepare for the election. Voting locations are reserved in schools and community centres, individuals are hired to supervise voting, and ballot boxes are sent out to the 308 ridings across Canada.

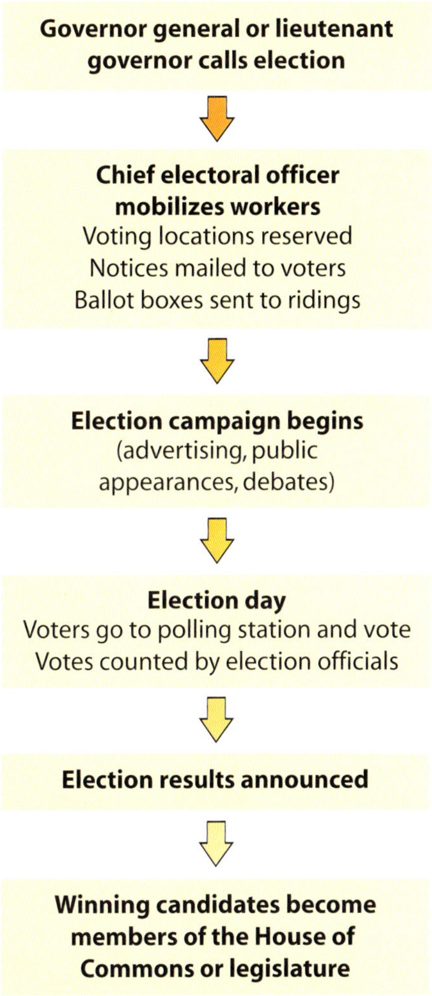

Notices are delivered or mailed to voters telling them where to go to vote. Instructions on where to vote are included for people who may be travelling on election day and wish to vote ahead of time in advance polls. Canada has a permanent voters' list drawn from government income tax information, driver's licences, and other sources containing citizens' addresses.

The campaign begins in earnest as the candidates and their political parties use newspapers, radio, and television advertisements to promote their **platforms** (the policies they will introduce if elected). Party leaders also travel the country to support their candidates, speak at rallies in towns and cities, and engage in television debates.

Governor general or lieutenant governor calls election
⬇
Chief electoral officer mobilizes workers
Voting locations reserved
Notices mailed to voters
Ballot boxes sent to ridings
⬇
Election campaign begins
(advertising, public appearances, debates)
⬇
Election day
Voters go to polling station and vote
Votes counted by election officials
⬇
Election results announced
⬇
Winning candidates become members of the House of Commons or legislature

FIGURE 9.1 Flow chart of the election process in Canada

LITERACY COACH

A flow chart is another great way to organize information that occurs in a sequence. Placing events described in the text into a flow chart can make that information easier to understand, and easier to study, too.

▶ DID YOU KNOW ◀
The chief electoral officer cannot vote in general elections.

☐ DISCUSSION POINT
Should Canadians be given the right to vote at age 16?

▶ DID YOU KNOW ◀
Canada regularly monitors democratic elections in other countries and regions. In 2006 alone, Canadian representatives monitored elections in Haiti, Ukraine, and West Bank and Gaza.

By law, Canadian broadcasters must make some free air time available to each party for the purpose of promoting candidates. Other forms of campaign advertising include lawn signs, door-to-door campaigning, and all-candidates' meetings, at which candidates meet the voters and answer questions.

On election day, polling stations are open for 12 hours. By law, all employees are allowed three consecutive hours to vote with no loss of pay. After showing some identification, voters are given a ballot by the deputy returning officer who is in charge of the polling station.

The voter moves to a booth and chooses one of the candidates by marking an X on the ballot in secret. The voter then returns the folded ballot to the deputy returning officer, who checks that it is the same ballot originally given to the voter. This step is taken to ensure that only the voter has marked the ballot.

Once satisfied that the ballot is the same, the deputy returning officer returns the folded ballot to the elector. The voter then places the ballot in the ballot box. Finally, a poll clerk strikes the voter's name off the voters' list.

After the polls close, the votes are counted by the deputy returning officer and poll clerk. The deputy returning officer and the poll clerk have also ensured that the election has been conducted properly. Scrutineers—members of political parties whose candidates are on the ballot—are also present to witness the count. Their role is to ensure that the election has treated their particular candidate fairly.

The candidate with the most votes becomes the member of Parliament (MP) for that riding. If the vote is especially close between candidates, the ballots may be recounted.

FIGURE 9.2 A prisoner in the Montreal Detention Centre casts his ballot in a federal election. All inmates in federal and provincial prisons have the right to vote.

Who Can Vote?

Qualifying to vote in a federal election is simple: one must be a Canadian citizen over the age of 18. The same rule applies to provincial or territorial elections, with the further requirement that the citizen be a resident of the riding or **constituency** where the vote is taking place.

PAUSE, REFLECT, APPLY

1. Who, in theory, has the power to call a federal election? Who actually makes the decision?
2. What circumstances might require a voter to use an advance poll?
3. Why is a voters' list necessary for a proper election?
4. All ballots are numbered with a set number given to each polling station. Why is this measure necessary?
5. What purpose is served by scrutineers?
6. All ballots judged to be spoiled (improperly marked) are kept in case of a recount. What kinds of mistakes might a voter make in marking a ballot, causing it to be judged spoiled?
7. Are Canadian elections fair and free of fraud? Do they produce a government that represents our wishes? Give your opinion from what you have studied so far.

Elections in Canada

Compared with today, voting at the time of Confederation was undemocratic, and election practices were corrupt. In 1867 the vote was limited to male, British citizens over the age of 21 who owned property. This excluded large numbers of people—women, renters, minorities, and Aboriginal people—who can vote today.

There were also several voting days across Canada instead of one. The government would choose ridings where it stood the best chance of winning for the first election day. Then it would spread the news of the government's win to other areas to encourage voters to elect government candidates! In addition, balloting was not secret. Because the number of voters in a riding was small—about 750 on average—candidates knew most voters personally and could influence their vote.

Denying the **franchise** (the right to vote) was also used as a weapon against minorities. In 1885, for example, Asians were denied the right to vote. During World War I (1914–1918), the government extended the vote to groups likely to support its policy of conscripting men into military service, and took away the vote from groups likely to oppose it. Women were finally permitted to vote in federal elections in 1918. Various provinces took longer to grant that right. Hindus, Chinese, and Aboriginal people in Canada were excluded from voting for the first half of the 20th century.

Today, the vote has been extended to all Canadian citizens over 18 years of age, including prison inmates and the mentally challenged. Voting stations everywhere must accommodate blind and disabled citizens.

> **KEY QUESTION**
>
> Is Canada a vigorous democracy with widespread voting participation, and political parties that excite and engage Canadians?

> **DID YOU KNOW**
>
> Canadian elections were not always conducted by secret ballot. In centuries past, voters often had to declare whom they were voting for. Some candidates "bought" votes with bribes. Brawls regularly broke out at polling booths, sometimes fuelled by alcohol.

FIGURE 9.3 Important events in the franchise in Canada

- **1867** Only property-owning males of British ancestry may vote

    Provinces produce voters' lists (women, minorities, Aboriginal people cannot vote)

- **1885** Federal government takes control of national vote, removes property qualification

    Provinces continue to exclude some people from voting

- **1916** Women gain vote in Manitoba, Saskatchewan, Alberta

- **1917** Women related to soldiers, Aboriginal soldiers gain national vote

    National vote taken from central Europeans

- **1918** All women gain national vote

- **1920** Federal government extends the franchise to Canadians 21 years of age, except minorities and Aboriginal persons

- **1934** Inuit lose vote

- **1948** Asians gain vote

- **1950** Inuit gain federal vote

- **1960** Status Indians gain federal franchise

- **1969** Manitoba lowers voting age from 21 to 18

- **1970** Federal voting age and age at which a person can run for federal office lowered from 21 to 18

- **1982** Right to vote embedded in new constitution

- **1993** Mentally disabled persons and prisoners serving less than two years gain vote

- **2002** Supreme Court strikes down law barring penitentiary inmates from voting in federal elections

▶ DID YOU KNOW ◀

In 1914, the Manitoba chapter of the Canadian Women's Press Club put on a show to publicize the movement for women's **suffrage** (the right to vote). The women ridiculed anti-suffrage arguments by reversing reality. They set up a mock legislature where women occupied most of the seats and where men were pleading for the vote. In this way, they made the anti-suffrage arguments appear absurd.

FIGURE 9.4 The Political Equality League was founded in 1912 in Manitoba. Its purpose? To enfranchise women. Members often poked fun at the premier, Rodmond Roblin, for his firm stand against women's right to vote.

CANADA'S RECENT VOTING RECORD

The percentage of Canadians voting in federal elections has been in steady decline for a number of years.

Mandatory Voting

Following the 2000 federal election, Canada's chief electoral officer said that Parliament might have to pass a law requiring citizens to vote if the rate of voter participation continues to fall.

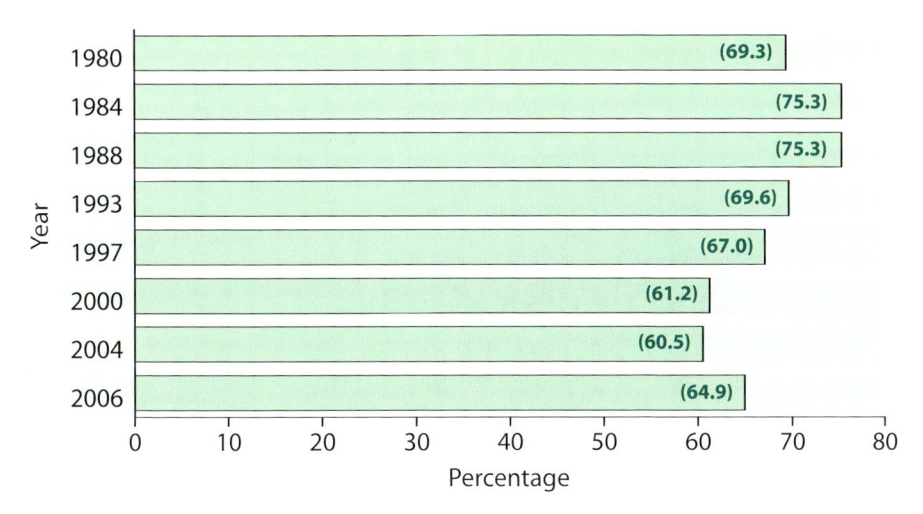

Year	Percentage
1980	69.3
1984	75.3
1988	75.3
1993	69.6
1997	67.0
2000	61.2
2004	60.5
2006	64.9

FIGURE 9.5 Election turnout rates (1980–2006). *Source: Data from Elections Canada, A History of the Vote in Canada*

Voter turnout for the 2004 election was little more than 60 percent, the lowest since the election of 1898. In 2006, voter turnout was up somewhat—to 64.9 percent. This poor participation rate gives Canada one of the worst records among the 29 industrialized countries in the Organisation for Economic Co-operation and Development, ahead of only Poland, Switzerland, and the United States.

According to a 2004 study published in the *Canadian Parliamentary Review*, the participation rate in Australia, where voting is mandatory, is 94 percent. Voting is also compulsory in Belgium and Greece, where the turnout rates are 92 percent and 80 percent, respectively.

► **DID YOU KNOW** ◄
Women did not receive the right to vote in Quebec provincial elections until 1940, more than 20 years after they received the right in other provinces.

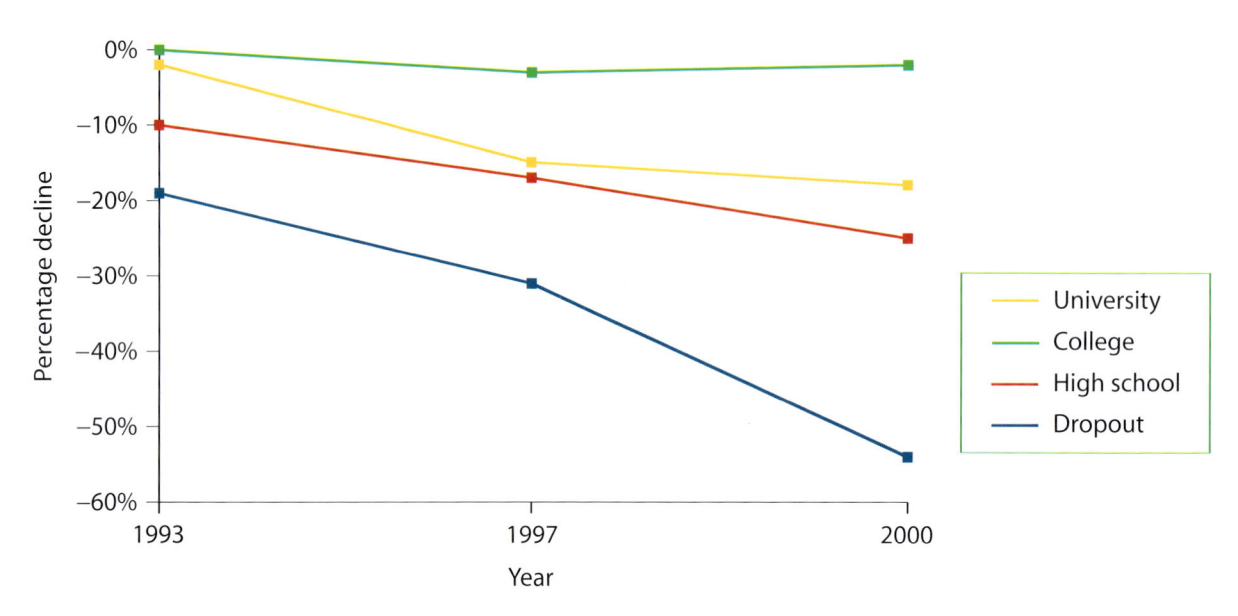

FIGURE 9.6 Tuned out or turned off? Percentage decline in youth participation in voting, by level of education. The turnout in 1993 among those with some college education is used as the benchmark. *Source: Elections Canada,* Electoral Insight, *July 2003, p. 10*

WHO CAN RUN FOR OFFICE?

Any Canadian citizen can run for political office. The candidate

1. must be 18 years of age or older
2. must collect the signatures of at least 100 other citizens on the nomination form
3. must deposit $1,000 with an election official called a returning officer (this amount is refundable if the candidate submits receipts for allowable election expenses)
4. does not have to live in the riding or constituency he or she intends to represent
5. does not have to be a member of a political party. However, most candidates are, and must show proof of their official party nomination. A candidate who is not a member of a political party is classified as an independent.

WHAT DO POLITICAL PARTIES STAND FOR?

A political party is built around a central core of beliefs. The differences in beliefs among political parties are described by the terms "left," "right,"

☐ **DISCUSSION POINT**

History books talk about the Fathers of Confederation in 1867. Why were there no Mothers of Confederation?

and "centre." A good way to understand the differences in positions is to consider attitudes toward change.

A party on the left is usually dissatisfied with the present conditions of society (the status quo). It sees inequalities of income between people as too great. It believes that government should actively reduce these inequalities, regulate business behaviour, and provide more social programs.

A party on the right is cautious about change, particularly when it comes to government spending and regulation. It values social order and tends to support traditional institutions such as the conventional family, religion, the military, and the police.

A party at the centre combines beliefs from both left and right, depending on the issue. It is generally satisfied with the status quo, but will advocate change it deems beneficial.

Parties on the left criticize centrist parties for not going far enough for needed changes. Parties on the right criticize centrist parties for going too far for change.

No Canadian political party today can be placed on the extreme left or right. In fact, the policies of the main parties often overlap. (See also Figure 7.9 on page 152.)

FIGURE 9.7 The Canadian political spectrum

Left — NDP — Bloc Québécois — Centre — Liberal Party — Conservative Party — Right

PAUSE, REFLECT, APPLY

1. a) Consider requirements 1, 2, and 3, governing who can run for political office. Think of a reason why each requirement helps ensure that only serious candidates run for office.
   b) Give your opinion on requirement 4. Should candidates have to live in the riding they seek to represent?
2. Predict where a party of the left, right, or centre might stand on each of the following issues:
   a) a nationally funded daycare system
   b) lower tuition fees for post-secondary students
   c) same-sex marriage
   d) lower business taxes
   e) greater search powers for police.
3. Does having a choice of political parties help citizens elect governments that truly represent their wishes? What if there were no political parties?

186 CANADA IN THE CONTEMPORARY WORLD

▶ **KEY QUESTION**

Is Canadian democracy better served with multiple political parties, or with two? Does our electoral system need to be changed?

☐ **DISCUSSION POINT**

After the 1993 election, the federal Parliament was nicknamed "the pizza Parliament." Why did the nickname stick?

Political Parties in Canada

Political parties are organizations that try to elect individuals to public office to control the machinery of government. A person nominated by a party receives publicity, campaign workers, and financial help in an election. Parties are not mentioned in the constitutions of most democracies. Their powers do not come from laws but from the support of voters. Voters can eliminate a party in an election, or create new parties. Canada has done both.

For most of Canada's history, two political parties dominated federal politics: the Liberals and the Conservatives. The Conservatives held power for most of the period from Confederation in 1867 to the early 1900s. For most of the 20th century, the Liberal Party held power.

A smaller party, the Co-operative Commonwealth Federation (CCF), later renamed the New Democratic Party (NDP), was formed in the 1930s. Then in the 1993 election, two new parties—the western-based Reform Party (later the Canadian Alliance) and a Quebec-based separatist party, the Bloc Québécois—won more than 50 seats each, while the Progressive Conservatives won only two. Until 2004, there were five major political parties (with the Liberals holding the majority of seats). Today, four major political parties contend for power at the federal level.

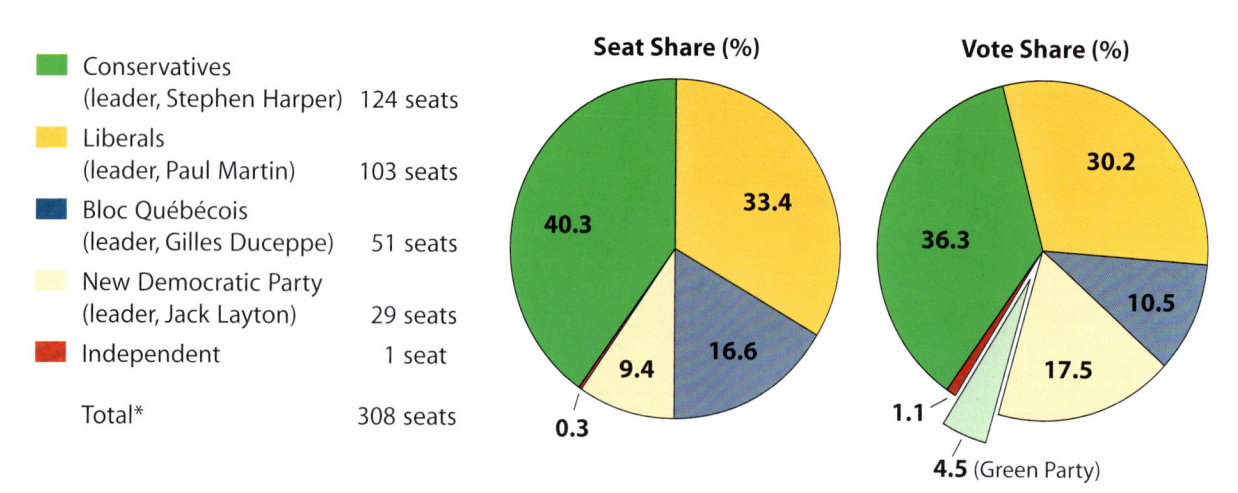

■ Conservatives (leader, Stephen Harper)	124 seats
■ Liberals (leader, Paul Martin)	103 seats
■ Bloc Québécois (leader, Gilles Duceppe)	51 seats
■ New Democratic Party (leader, Jack Layton)	29 seats
■ Independent	1 seat
Total*	308 seats

Seat Share (%): Conservatives 40.3, Liberals 33.4, Bloc Québécois 16.6, NDP 9.4, Independent 0.3

Vote Share (%): Conservatives 36.3, Liberals 30.2, Bloc Québécois 10.5, NDP 17.5, Independent 1.1, Green Party 4.5

* While the Green Party received 4.5% of the vote, no Green Party candidate won a seat.

FIGURE 9.8 Federal election results, 2006, by party: percentage of seats in the House of Commons and percentage of vote

CHAPTER 9 HOW DO CITIZENS ELECT GOVERNMENTS? 187

MAJORITY AND MINORITY GOVERNMENTS

To form a **majority government**, a party must win one-half of Canada's 308 ridings, plus one more (155). With this number, the party forms the government and has enough votes to pass legislation it wishes to see made into law. Most of the time, party members vote to support their party's legislation. If important legislation proposed by the government is defeated in Parliament, the prime minister and cabinet must resign (see **non-confidence**, Chapter 8, page 169). Majority governments are seldom forced into an election.

Because Canada has several major parties, it is possible for one party to win more seats than each of the others, but not win a majority of seats. This is exactly what Canada faced after the 2004 and 2006 federal elections. In 2004, the Liberals had 135 seats, 20 short of a majority. In 2006, the Conservatives won 124 seats, 31 short of a majority.

These **minority governments** must depend on the support of other parties, and any legislation that they propose can be easily defeated. For this reason, minority governments are often viewed as unstable, easily leading to crises, resignations—and early elections.

FIGURE 9.9 What statement is the cartoonist making about minority governments?

TWO-PARTY AND MULTIPARTY SYSTEMS

▶ **DID YOU KNOW** ◀
From 1957 to 2006, Canada had eight federal minority governments.

If Canada had only two parties, every government would be a majority government (the chances of a tie with an even number of seats out of 308 are remote). A two-party system has the advantage of offering a clear choice between two leaders and two party platforms. It offers stability by avoiding the uncertainty of a minority government. The United States has a two-party system. Britain, New Zealand, and Australia used to have two-party systems but have all moved to multiparty systems.

The multiparty system offers the public a wider choice of policies, even if it produces less stable minority governments. But there is another argument used against both two-party and multiparty systems. It is that our voting system, called **first past the post** (**FPTP**), is unfair and undemocratic and should be replaced by **proportional representation** (PR) (see Face Off, page 192).

All of Canada's provinces and territories follow the party system except one—Nunavut. Why? Because the members of the Nunavut legislature use consensus to make decisions. In a party system, the parties are seen as adversaries (people opposing one another). They argue their respective positions and take a vote to reach a decision on House business. With a consensus system, however, discussion proceeds until all members can come to an agreement.

Interest Groups

Voting in an election is not the only way that citizens can make changes in a democracy. Another way is to form a pressure or **interest group**. This is a group of citizens who hold a common goal (such as Greenpeace, which pressures government to pass laws to preserve the environment) or are members of a particular occupation (such as the Canadian Medical Association, which represents Canadian doctors on health care issues). Pressure groups try to influence governments to pass laws favouring their goals or interests. (See also Chapter 8, pages 163 and 165.)

Interest groups hold private meetings with top civil servants in government, send representatives to parliamentary committees, and advertise in the media to try to influence government.

Supporters say that interest groups provide specialized information that representatives need to make important decisions and pass laws. Critics say that some groups are too powerful and enjoy unfair influence on government decision making.

CivicStar

FIGURE 9.10 A student "prime minister" (left) speaks as the New Brunswick and British Columbia "premiers" look on during a Forum for Young Canadians. The forum gives students a balanced overview of Canada's political system.

LAC DU BONNET SENIOR SCHOOL

Lac du Bonnet Senior School in Lac du Bonnet, Manitoba, takes government seriously. Instead of electing a student council, students elect a real parliament, and the leader answers to "prime minister."

That's right; the school has a prime minister! The student council is much like other student councils, except that it follows the parliamentary system. Besides a PM, the school has a Speaker of the House, a minister of finance, ministers of entertainment, a minister of the environment, and ministers of yearbook—to name a few.

Although each minister has a portfolio, members of parliament work together as a team—planning, promoting, and participating in all meetings and sponsored activities. Teachers also have a member to represent them, and the student parliament shares the minutes of its activities with the teacher member.

Many students involved with the student parliament have developed a keen appreciation of politics. Some have even been appointed to the local municipal council. That was the case with former PM Markie Towers, who observed, "I wanted to be more involved in the community, and what better way than to have a voice on council?"

And a few years back, Riva Karklin's involvement in the Lac du Bonnet parliament sparked an interest in travelling to Ottawa to see the "other" Parliament up close. Lucky for Riva, she was selected to attend the Forum for Young Canadians, in Ottawa, and got her wish.

Your Play

Other schools in Manitoba also elect prime ministers. Would your school benefit from running its student council as a parliament? What might be the advantages and disadvantages of such a system? Explain your answer.

PAUSE, REFLECT, APPLY

1. a) How do political parties get candidates elected?
   b) Why does an independent candidate find it difficult to win an election?
2. a) State the difference between a majority and a minority government in terms of numbers.
   b) Why do multiparty systems sometimes produce minority governments?
3. Minority governments are sometimes criticized for being weak. Others say they are more responsive to the electorate as a whole. What do you think?
4. What is one advantage of a multiparty system? A two-party system?
5. What is an interest group? What value do interest groups have in the democratic process?

Electoral Reform

Since the 1990s, groups such as Fair Vote Canada (national), Every Vote Counts (Prince Edward Island), and Mouvement pour une démocratie nouvelle (Quebec) have lobbied for electoral reform. A number of factors have contributed to dissatisfaction with Canada's first-past-the-post voting system:

- *Lack of representation.* Since the 1993 federal election, many political parties have competed for Canadians' votes. Critics argue that voters who choose to support one of the smaller parties are not fairly represented in Parliament.
- *Declining voter turnout.* Voter turnout at federal elections has been declining steadily since 1988. An Elections Canada survey found that many people did not vote because they felt the election result was already decided. Supporters of electoral reform believe that people would be more likely to vote if they felt that the number of seats a party held more closely represented its percentage of the popular vote.
- *Controversial election results.* British Columbia's progress in electoral reform was fired by voter anger over the controversial results of the 1996 provincial election. In that election, the New Democratic Party won a majority of seats and formed the government despite the fact that the Liberal Party received a higher percentage of the popular vote. Similarly, the Parti Québécois won the 1998 Quebec election, even though the Liberal Party had a higher percentage of the votes.
- *Ineffective opposition.* The call for electoral reform has sometimes been a response to "landslide" election victories. Some voters feel unrepresented when the winning party is left to govern without effective opposition in Parliament. In the 1987 New Brunswick election, the Liberal Party won all 58 of the province's seats. In the 2000 election in Prince Edward Island, the Progressive Conservatives won 26 of 27 seats.

Electoral reform is a hot topic across Canada. In Prince Edward Island, voters rejected a proportional electoral system in 2005. They'll vote on it again in 2007. Shortly after being elected in 2006, the federal Conservative party made a commitment to electoral reform. In the same year, the Ontario Citizens' Assembly on Electoral Reform was formed. Its recommendations are due in 2007. In Quebec, the Citizens' Committee proposed a two-vote proportional representation system to the National Assembly in 2006. The committee rejected the government's proposed new system. And New Brunswick will hold a referendum on proportional representation in 2008.

WESTERN INITIATIVES

The BC government established the independent British Columbia Citizens' Assembly in 2003 to examine the province's first-past-the-post electoral system and to explore alternatives. It held public consultations to decide whether to keep the current system or to recommend a new system compatible with Canada's Parliament.

In 2004, the Citizens' Assembly proposed a new electoral system based on proportional representation. The new system, it said, would give voters more choice and control, and strengthen local representation. In a 2005 referendum, 57 percent of voters supported the new system, but 60 percent was required to make the results binding on government. Another referendum will be held during the 2009 provincial election.

In Manitoba, electoral boundaries are reviewed every 10 years to take into account population shifts. The most recent census data are used in these reviews. Members of the public are also consulted about where the boundaries should be. Each riding must have an "average population" based on the total population of the province. South of the 53rd parallel (latitude), this average can vary by 10 percent. North of the 53rd parallel, it can vary by 25 percent. This is another way to ensure that both rural and urban voters—and their concerns—are well represented in the legislature: referenda (see page 193).

THE WEB ▶▶▶
Learn more about your provincial electoral district at www.emp.ca/ccw

FIGURE 9.11 Manitoba's electoral districts, last reviewed 1998. *Source: Elections Manitoba*

FACE OFF: A New Electoral System for Canada?

A study by the Institute for Research on Public Policy released in July 2000 found that 49% of Canadians find the current voting system unacceptable, compared to 23% who favour the current system.

— Democracy Watch, www.dwatch.ca/camp/voterpt.html

Should Canada change its method of electing members of Parliament? Canada has always used the first-past-the-post (FPTP) election system, but criticism of it is mounting. Here is the problem. Suppose in a school with 500 students, four students ran for president of the student council. Candidate A received 200 votes; Candidate B received 100 votes; Candidate C received 125 votes; and Candidate D received 75 votes.

Under a FPTP system, Candidate A wins the election. He or she has the most votes and is first past the post, like the lead horse in a race. However, A has won only 40 percent (200/500 × 100 = 40%) of the votes cast. Sixty percent of the students did not vote for A (who does not have a majority of the votes, but still wins). Is this fair?

Critics say that FPTP is unfair. When there are more than two parties running, one party can gain the majority of seats with less than a majority of the total votes cast—just as in the school election. These critics advocate replacing FPTP with proportional representation (PR).

> In the 24 federal elections since World War I, only three have resulted in majority governments that were actually elected by a majority of the votes cast!
>
> — Democracy Watch, "The Right to Have Your Vote Count," November 2001, www.dwatch.ca/camp/voterpt.html

A PR system divides up the seats according to the total percentage of votes each party receives. Voters must vote for a party, not a candidate. A party that receives 20 percent of the vote receives 20 percent of the seats. Then the party chooses candidates from party lists to fill those seats. In effect, MPs are chosen not by voters in ridings, but by the parties.

> Having been in New Zealand at the time of their first election under proportional representation, I am disappointed that some in Canada are advocating the same system, which would see MPs chosen, not by voters in ridings, but from closed party lists. This is an insult to the intelligence of voters.
>
> — Letter to CBC during 2004 federal election, www.cbc.ca/canadavotes/yourview/letters_w5.html

British Columbia is thinking of combining the FPTP and PR systems. The ballot will allow voters to choose candidates, but the governing party will be the one with the greatest percentage of the total votes cast throughout the province.

Electoral reform proponents believe switching to an electoral system that uses ... [PR] will produce a fairer result and help voters feel that their vote matters. Today, most of the world's democracies use PR ... .

— From "What Else Can Be Done to Encourage Canadians to Vote," www.mapleleafweb.com/features/electoral/voter-turnout/what-can-be-done.html

What Do You Think?

1. Why is a PR system unnecessary if only two candidates or parties run in an election?
2. Explain how a PR system appears to be fairer when more than two parties are running in an election.
3. Some FPTP defenders say that PR encourages the formation of smaller parties and, thus, minority governments. Explain the link between the two. Do you think this is an argument in favour of PR or against it?

REFERENDA

A referendum is a form of direct democracy because it allows voters, rather than elected representatives, to vote on a particular issue. A referendum can take the form of a single question (requiring a yes or no answer) or a number of alternatives (from which voters must choose).

Dramatic examples are the Quebec referenda of 1980 and 1995. The Parti Québécois asked the Quebec electorate to decide—Yes/Oui or No/Non—whether to separate the province from the rest of Canada. The referendum campaigns were emotional and hard fought. In 1980, over 60 percent of Québécois voted No/Non, but in 1995, the margin of victory for the No/Non side was less than 1 percent.

Critics argue that referenda

- undermine the authority of elected representatives in Parliament who are entrusted to make the laws of the country, subject to removal in the next election
- simplify complex issues to a yes or no answer, making compromise difficult
- can be used to convince the rest of the world that the electorate supports the government (the government obtains the referendum result it wants by using propaganda and intimidation)
- can be used against minorities in the name of majority sentiment. For example, in Quebec, the northern Aboriginal population believes that Quebec's separation from Canada would be illegal because it would include lands they claim belong to them.

▶ **DID YOU KNOW** ◀
The *Referendum Act* came into force in 1992. It states that a federal referendum can be held only to obtain the opinion of voters on a question related to Canada's constitution.

THE WEB ▶▶▶
Find out what happened to protesting members of the Edible Ballot Society and other strange election facts at www.emp.ca/ccw

FIGURE 9.12 Montreal riot police watch a fire burn underneath a "Oui" sign after the No side won the 1995 Quebec referendum. What might be the emotional impact of this act on people who voted "oui"? How might it shape attitudes toward Canadian federalism?

PAUSE, REFLECT, APPLY

1. a) What does a voter vote for in a PR system?
   b) Whom does a voter vote for in a FPTP system? Which system do you think is fairer?
2. Why are referenda a form of direct democracy? Do you think they should be used more frequently or not? Explain.
3. Describe how democratic ideals and citizen participation are shaping electoral systems across Canada.

REPLAY

In this chapter, you have explored these concepts:

1. Frequent, fair elections are a check on the power that citizens give to their elected representatives to make decisions for them.
2. The standardized, careful procedures followed by election officials ensure that Canadian elections are fair and free of fraud.
3. Because Canada has evolved into a multiparty system, minority governments are more likely to be elected now than in the past.
4. Although the struggle to extend the vote to all Canadian citizens has been largely won, voter turnout is declining.
5. Voters are growing dissatisfied with the current (first-past-the-post) voting system and are looking at other systems, such as proportional representation.

SKILLS TOOLKIT: How to Avoid Petition Pitfalls

Have you ever signed a **petition** and then asked yourself, "I wonder what that's going to accomplish?"

Petitioning is one of the oldest and most popular forms of democratic protest. When King John signed the Magna Carta in 1215, he recognized the right of his barons to petition him—in other words, to bring their grievances to him. Out of this contract grew the right of English citizens to bring their grievances to Parliament.

Although petitioning is still one of the most popular forms of protest, it is not always effective. Here are some tips for maximizing petition success:

When writing petitions ...

- Open with a clearly stated, polite request. What do you need, and why? Give reasons why your request should be acted upon.
- Focus your request on one issue. Don't introduce points that may distract the reader.

Good
We, the undersigned, request that the school library hours be extended until 5 p.m. during the exam cycle. Students need the extra time to search the Internet, and the computers at the public library are often booked at this time.

Poor
We want the school library to stay open later during exams because nobody can get any work done at the public library and we want to protest removing the soda pop vending machines from the school, which is really stupid.

When signing petitions ...

- Beware of e-petitions. They can be hoaxes. What guarantees are there that anyone is collating the signatures or will even deliver the petitions? Beware attempts to solicit your name, telephone number, and address online.
- Even if you know a petition is legitimate, try to find out what obligation the intended party has to respond. Governments promise only to accept and consider petitions—not necessarily to act on them.
- When you present a petition, try to appear with as many signers as possible. That way, your petition makes a strong statement. That, in turn, can create more civic interest and action. The real value of a petition is its ability to mobilize (rally) people to action. When activists collect signatures, for example, people hear about the issue and may decide to become involved.

Skill Practice

Create a well-crafted petition statement about an issue that you think is important. (Use the guidelines above.) Who should receive your petition? What obligation do they have to act on it?

STUDY HALL

Be Informed

1. Consider the following quotation: "The people as a body cannot perform the business of government for themselves … . Limiting the duration of rule is … an old and approved method of identifying the interests of those who rule with the interests of those who are ruled." (James Mill, English political philosopher, 1825)
   a) What is Mill talking about? What does he think?
   b) Who actually has the power to make decisions—the people or their representatives?

2. How are frequent elections a check on the power that voters give their representatives?

3. Identify several procedures from the election process that are intended to ensure that elections are free from fraudulent practices.

4. Explain how the requirements for candidates in an election are intended to exclude individuals who are not truly serious about political office.

Be Purposeful

5. The 2002 Supreme Court decision granting the vote to all prisoners was highly controversial. What is your opinion? Explain.

6. Consider a mock riding with 10,000 voters and four candidates representing four different parties. Show how a candidate could win with fewer than 3,000 votes.

7. Polls are taken often during election campaigns to estimate the percentage of voters supporting a party or candidate at that time. Do you think polls tend to influence voters? If so, should they be limited or banned? Give a reasoned opinion on this issue.

8. Politicians are often criticized for not keeping their election promises once they are elected. Their defence is that sometimes circumstances change after they come to office. What do you think? Do voters have the democratic right to insist that politicians carry out all their promises?

9. Voting in Australia is compulsory for citizens. Non-voters are fined unless they present a reasonable excuse. What do you think of this idea, considering that less than 65 percent of Canadians eligible to vote did so in the 2006 federal election?

10. First Nations, Inuit, and Métis hold their own local elections to elect band council members and a chief. Find out how these elections are carried out and how they differ from other Canadian elections.

Be Active

11. Elections Canada is active in many new democracies, supervising or helping people to organize free and fair elections. Imagine you are part of an election team sent to a new democracy in a less developed country. The conditions are complex:
    a) Many citizens cannot read.
    b) Villages are remote, and few citizens own transportation.
    c) People are intimidated by authority and authoritarian figures.
    d) Women's votes are subject to male influence.
    e) Local citizens have difficulty obtaining information about candidates.

    Is the situation hopeless for a democratic election? Suggest some strategies for overcoming these problems.

12. Hold a mock parliamentary election in your classroom. Small groups of students can work together to represent different parties and put forward a candidate. Another group of students can work to prepare for voting day and oversee the vote to ensure that it is conducted fairly.

    - Launch your election with an announcement by a governor general or lieutenant governor.
    - Set an election date.
    - Review your campaign platform and strategy with your group and assign tasks to individual members, e.g., publicist, manager, and so on.
    - Campaign intensively!
    - Hold a vote.
    - Announce the results.

    See Figure 9.1 and pages 178–180 for information on the election process.

CHAPTER 10
How Does the Judicial System Work?

Led away in handcuffs

It was a beautiful fall night when a local gang severely beat two 15-year-olds walking in the park. Residents in a nearby house heard the disturbance and called 911. When police arrived, many young people were at the scene. Several were led away in handcuffs. One girl kept saying she was glad someone had finally made the victims "shut up for being so dumb."

Police suspected that more teens were involved in the incident. They knew they would be gathering more evidence in the coming weeks. Two teens were eventually arrested and charged with the beatings. You will meet them in the following pages. Before you read their stories, predict what might happen to them.

What You Need to Know
- What safeguards in the judicial system protect the rights of people accused of crimes, the victims of crime, and society?
- What roles do the police and the courts play in a democracy?
- What is the purpose of a youth criminal justice system?
- What is the origin of Aboriginal justice? What is its role today?
- How can you organize information before writing a paper or delivering an oral report?

Key Terms
burden of proof
prosecution
Aboriginal justice
young offenders
Youth Criminal Justice Act
warrant
Crown
adversarial system
incarceration
defendant
systemic racism
restorative justice

Key Question
How much should government interfere with people's rights and freedoms?

197

Canada's Judicial System

The Canadian judicial system tries to achieve two goals. First, it must ensure that society operates in a peaceful and orderly manner. Pedestrians and motorists need to know, for example, that drivers will stop at red lights. Homeowners must be assured that people will not trespass on their property. Everyone in society needs to know that people who harm others will be prosecuted for their offences.

Without such assurances, society would be chaotic and unpredictable. To quote philosopher Thomas Hobbes, life would be "nasty, brutish, and short." Law is the glue that holds society together by ensuring social order.

Second, the judicial system tries to balance the need for social order with respect for the individual rights of the citizen. Not all societies do this. As you learned earlier, authoritarian governments impose social order through harsh laws and the use of police and military force. Individuals can be arrested and imprisoned without trial.

☐ **DISCUSSION POINT**
Why do democracies balance the rights of individuals and society?

FUNDAMENTAL LEGAL RIGHTS

In a democracy, all citizens are equal before the law and accountable under the law for their actions. No citizen is above the law, and neither is any government. As you learned in Chapter 5, this guiding principle is called the rule of law.

Fundamental legal rights are clearly stated in the *Canadian Charter of Rights and Freedoms*. Canadians have

- the right to be free from unreasonable searches or seizures
- the right on arrest or detention (being put in custody) to be told of the reasons
- the right to be represented by counsel (a lawyer)
- the right to have a court decide if the detention is lawful
- the right, on being charged with an offence, to be told the details of the offence
- the right to a trial within a reasonable time
- the right to be presumed innocent until proven guilty (this **burden of proof** in a criminal trial rests on the **prosecution**, the lawyers working for the state, not on the person charged)
- the right not to be denied **bail** (temporary release from custody) without just cause

- the right not to have to testify against themselves (appear as a witness in their own trial)
- the right not to be subjected to cruel and unusual treatment or punishment.

THE CHANGING JUSTICE SYSTEM

Canadian society is constantly changing, and the legal system must change with it. Laws and legal procedures are always under review. Old laws may become outdated because of changing social values and new technologies.

In the past, the courts did not have to deal with crimes involving the Internet and high-tech digital information. There was no such thing as "theft of personal electronic information." Few people talked about decriminalizing marijuana possession. Concepts such as **victims' rights** (the rights of those people hurt by a criminal offence) and **Aboriginal justice** (a justice system managed by Aboriginal peoples) were unknown.

The justice system also has to deal with a growing case load. Many more cases are coming before Canadian courts today than in the past. It can take months to bring criminal cases to trial, and often years before civil disputes are settled. The judicial system is experimenting with newer ways to settle disputes and with ideas drawn from Aboriginal justice (see pages 211–215).

ATTITUDES TOWARD THE LAW

In many democracies, confidence in the justice system has waned. There are many reasons for this. As democratic societies become more open and less authoritarian, citizens are more willing to question their institutions. Also, several high-profile trials around the world have exposed corruption or mismanagement in police departments and in the courts.

Sometimes a case can highlight people's attitudes about a law, or a proposed change in law. In 2005, four RCMP officers were shot and killed while trying to repossess a pickup truck at an Alberta farm. The owner of the farm was also running an illegal marijuana growing operation.

The event shocked Canadians. It was the largest loss of RCMP life since the Northwest rebellions of 1885. Flags flew at half-mast across Canada. Many politicians and citizens called for tougher sentences for marijuana growing operations. Others said that if marijuana had been made legal, such a violent standoff would never have occurred and lives could have been saved. The event highlighted public attitudes toward three cornerstones of the Canadian justice system: the police, the courts, and the laws themselves. Most citizens have strong opinions about all three.

As you can see from Figure 10.2, many Canadians are confident in the justice system, but a sizable number are not. If you add the last three numbers together, you find that 46 percent of Canadians express confidence in the justice system. Those in the mid-range (22 percent) feel neutral about the justice system, while 32 percent (numbers 1–3) indicate a lack of confidence in the justice system.

The study's researchers found even lower levels of confidence in European nations and the United States. Is the justice system in trouble in Canada and other democratic countries?

FIGURE 10.1 At the funeral for the four slain RCMP officers, the fiancée of one officer accepts his Stetson hat from a fellow officer.

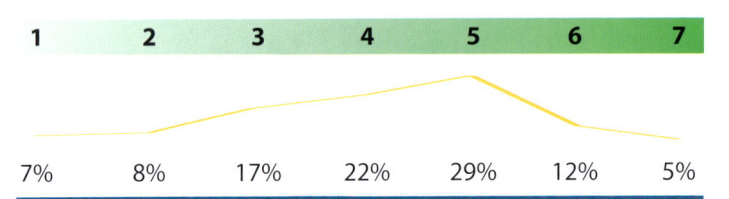

1	2	3	4	5	6	7
7%	8%	17%	22%	29%	12%	5%

FIGURE 10.2 This chart shows responses of Canadians to the question, "How much confidence do you have in the justice system?" 1 represents "no confidence"; 7 represents "a great deal." *Source: Data from Confidence in Justice: An International Review, Table 4.1; www.kcl.ac.uk*

The authors of the study, *Confidence in Justice: An International Review*, concluded the following:

- Most people believe that the crime rate is rising and blame the criminal justice system.
- Police receive the highest confidence rating; the courts and the parole system receive the lowest.
- People respect police officers more than they respect the courts and correctional authorities because they know them better.
- Correctional authorities do a better job at supervising prisoners than supervising offenders in the community.

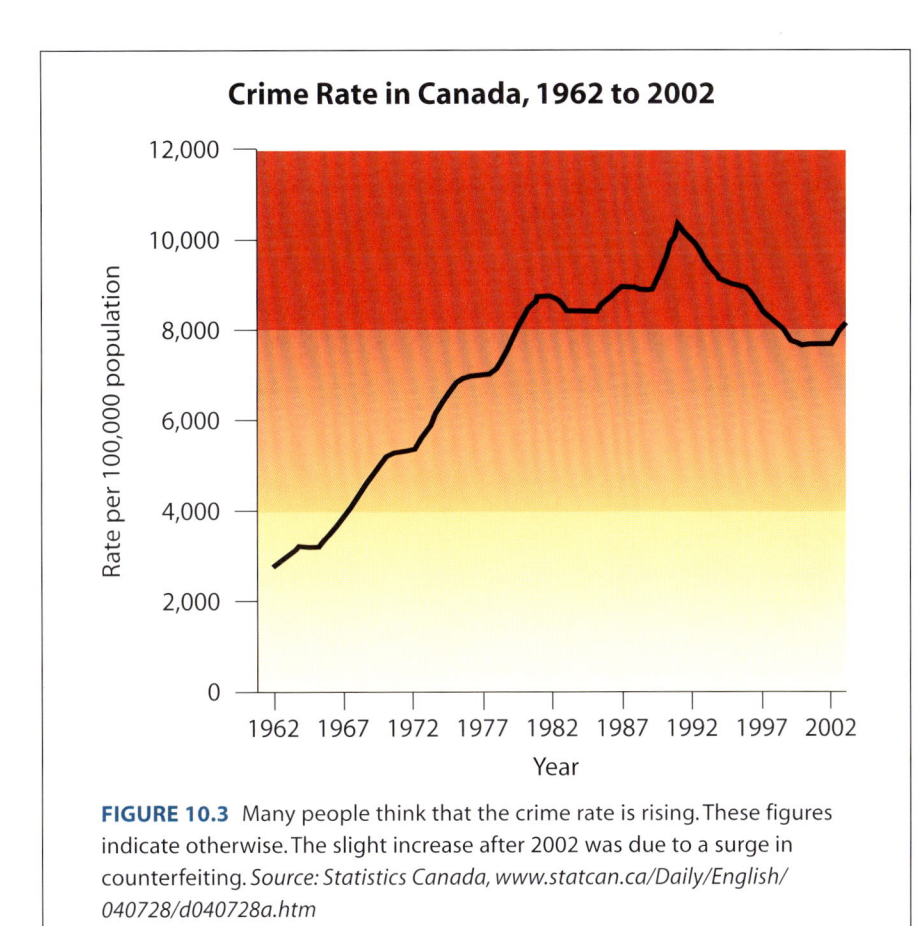

Crime Rate in Canada, 1962 to 2002

FIGURE 10.3 Many people think that the crime rate is rising. These figures indicate otherwise. The slight increase after 2002 was due to a surge in counterfeiting. *Source: Statistics Canada, www.statcan.ca/Daily/English/040728/d040728a.htm*

> **DID YOU KNOW**
> For several years, the highest provincial crime rates have been in the West. In 2005, for example, Saskatchewan had the highest provincial crime rate, followed by British Columbia and Manitoba. The lowest rates were in Quebec and Ontario. Why might this be so?

- People do not know much about the criminal justice system. They are often exposed to unique stories of failed prosecutions, lenient sentences, and wrongful convictions, and think these are the norm.

Trust in the justice system is important for Canadians. If the public loses confidence, then citizens are more reluctant to report crimes, act as witnesses, or serve on juries. These are all responsibilities that citizens in a democracy must be willing to perform if the justice system is to work properly.

WRONGFUL CONVICTIONS

The Canadian justice system is based on the principle that a person is innocent until proven guilty. However, sometimes this principle is overlooked when the system is busy pursuing someone it believes to be guilty.

David Milgaard, James Driskell, and Thomas Sophonow are three Canadians who were convicted of serious crimes they did not commit. Milgaard was convicted of the rape and murder of nursing assistant Gail Miller in Saskatoon, Saskatchewan. He spent 20 years in prison. Driskell was found guilty in 1991 of the murder of Perry Harder in Winnipeg. He received a life sentence and spent 12 behind bars. Sophonow, also of Winnipeg, was tried three times for the 1981 murder of doughnut shop clerk Barbara Stoppel. He spent four years in prison.

The new science of DNA testing exonerated both Milgaard and Sophonow. In Driskell's case, it was later revealed that hair samples found in his van did not belong to the victim, as had been originally claimed by the Royal Canadian Mounted Police. In all three cases, police and the prosecution appeared to have a single theory about the crime that prevented them from considering alternative theories and suspects.

CivicStar

DIANNE MARTIN

Dianne Lee Martin was born in Regina in 1945, the youngest of three daughters. She attended law school in Toronto, formed her own law firm with two partners, and later became a law professor.

Those details merely scratch the surface. What drove Dianne Martin was a passionate belief in advocacy—standing up for people who have no voice. During her career, she defended women's rights, helped reform Canada's rape laws, and brought national attention to the plight of the wrongfully convicted.

Martin helped found the Innocence Project at Osgoode Law School. She was also one of the founding directors of the Association in Defence of the Wrongfully Convicted (ADWC).

She was fascinated by the "psychology" of wrongful convictions and the circumstances that led to them. She once said that when police see cracks in their own case, they sometimes persevere in the belief that they are right by maintaining tunnel vision: "Once they have reached a conclusion they stick to it and ignore or rationalize evidence pushed their way."

Martin died of a heart attack, suddenly, in 2004. She was remembered by colleagues as "a passionate defender of social justice." Osgoode Hall Law School established the Dianne Martin Medal for Social Justice through Law, awarded annually to "a member of the Canadian legal community who has exemplified Dianne's commitment to law as an instrument for achieving social justice and fairness."

Your Play

Dianne Martin once described three classic features of wrongful conviction cases: (1) a tragic event, (2) a suspect who lacks power or authority, and (3) suspicious evidence. Explain how you think these three factors might combine and lead to a wrongful conviction.

YOUTH CRIMINAL JUSTICE

Canadians between the ages of 12 and 17 who commit an offence are sometimes called **young offenders** and fall under the *Youth Criminal Justice Act*. This Act recognizes that a youth must be held accountable for criminal activity, but not to the same extent as an adult. The Act emphasizes rehabilitation so that the youth can become a productive member of society.

Young offenders are not always arrested if they commit an offence. Police have options. A young shoplifter may be persuaded to return goods. Police might contact parents when a young person disturbs the peace. If the offence is serious, however, the police must arrest the youth suspected of the crime.

All the rights of adults upon arrest (see pages 198–199) apply to young offenders. Some special provisions apply. A youth must be told in clear language that he or she has the right

- to have a parent, guardian, or other adult present during questioning
- to have a lawyer, with one supplied by legal aid if necessary
- not to make statements that could be used against him or her.

One reason that a youth's rights must be spelled out so clearly is that young people are often unaware of their rights. A young person who is frightened and confused during an arrest may make statements that he or she does not really mean.

> **THE WEB**
> Learn more about youth justice in Canada at www.emp.ca/ccw

PAUSE, REFLECT, APPLY

1. a) What are the two goals that the Canadian judicial system tries to achieve?
   b) Which of the two is more important, in your opinion?
   c) How do these two intentions sometimes conflict with each other?
2. Define the term "rule of law." Why is it essential for a democracy to work on a basis of equality?
3. Why do people have less confidence in the courts than in the police? In what sense is lack of knowledge about the judicial system as a whole a problem?
4. How would you rate your confidence in the judicial system?
5. Refer to Figure 10.3 on page 201. Offer some reasons why people perceive the crime rate to be going up when in fact it is going down.
6. Do you think that a particularly disturbing crime sometimes places too much pressure on the police to solve it, possibly leading to a wrongful conviction? Explain.
7. a) What differences are there between the arrest procedures for teenagers and for adults?
   b) Are teenagers given more rights than they deserve upon arrest, or are they given enough? Explain your answer.

> **KEY QUESTION**
> Why are there procedures for investigating crimes and trying defendants?

The Criminal Justice Process

Carl, 18, and his friend Matt, 16, are suspected of being part of a gang that severely beat up two youths. Each will be tried in a different justice system—one as a youth and one as an adult. Let us follow both.

THE CRIMINAL INVESTIGATION

Acting on information from witnesses, police obtain **warrants** (legal documents) for arrest from a judge. This empowers them to arrest Carl and Matt. The police are also allowed to take each suspect into custody, search his home and person, ask him questions, and seize evidence. As we have seen, Carl and Matt have legal rights. No matter what the police believe about their guilt or innocence, Carl and Matt are innocent until proven guilty in a court trial.

FIGURE 10.4 Carl, age 18

FIGURE 10.5 Matt, age 16

Both suspects are charged with committing an **indictable offence**. This is a serious offence, one that involves, for example, violence or theft over a certain amount. Minor offences are called **summary offences**. Carl, as an adult, is informed of the charge, told that he may consult a lawyer, and brought before a judge. The judge decides whether there is enough evidence to proceed with the case, and whether bail can be granted. Carl is then released to await trial.

As a youth, Matt is handled differently. The charge is carefully explained to him in language he can understand. He is told that he can contact a parent or other adult to assist him at the police station. He does not have to make a statement that might be used against him in court. The police fingerprint and photograph him and release him into the custody of his parents.

THE COURTS

Carl's trial takes place in a provincial superior court. He can be tried before a judge alone, or before a judge and jury. On his lawyer's advice, Carl chooses a jury trial. The jury is selected from a large number of citizens who have received notices requiring them to appear for jury duty.

Each of the 12 jurors in a criminal case must be approved by the defence lawyer and the **Crown** (prosecution).

Matt's case will be decided in a different court—a Youth Justice Court. This court was created by the *Youth Criminal Justice Act* to deal with youth aged 12 to 17.

In the Youth Justice Court, a judge normally conducts a trial alone, although an accused may request a trial by judge and jury if the offence is very serious. The rules are the same as in adult court, and the trial is public. Because the offence is serious, Matt's name could possibly be made public. Usually, however, young offenders' names are not publicized. While sentences in the Youth Justice Court are lighter than those in adult court, a youth court judge may, in certain circumstances, impose a stiffer, "adult sentence."

THE TRIAL

Whether Carl or Matt is found guilty will be decided in a clash between two adversaries: the prosecution and the defence. This system is called the **adversarial system**. It is based on the idea that when two opponents argue their case to the best of their ability, one will be stronger than the other and the truth will emerge.

As stated earlier, the burden of proof rests upon the prosecution. This means that the prosecution must prove the defendant's guilt. The prosecution must be able to show that the defendant is guilty beyond a reasonable doubt.

The quality of the evidence against Carl and Matt is a major concern. **Hearsay** evidence is not allowed. "Hearsay" applies to things witnesses have heard other people say, not what they have personally observed. Witnesses are not allowed to comment on Carl and Matt's character or any past problems that either may have had with the law. The judge can also rule evidence **inadmissible** (unable to be considered). This is likely to happen with any evidence that was gained through violation of the defendant's rights, such as unreasonable search and seizure. Finally, Carl and Matt cannot be forced to give evidence. It is up to each to decide whether to take the stand and testify.

VERDICT AND SENTENCING

Carl's trial involves a jury. The jury hears evidence and retires to make its decision after lawyers for the defence and the prosecution make their final arguments. The jury must also hear the judge's **charge to the jury**. This is the judge's review of the facts of Carl's case, and an explanation of the law that applies to it.

Once the jury has decided whether Carl is guilty or not guilty, the judge either allows him to leave immediately (if he is found not guilty) or sentences him (if he is found guilty).

Sentencing is based on several ideas:

- **punishment** of the offender to a degree that the public understands that the offence is serious
- **deterrence**, or discouraging the offender and others from repeating or committing the offence
- **protection** of the public from dangerous people
- **rehabilitation** of the offender so that he or she can rejoin society as a law-abiding, productive citizen.

The sentence can range from a fine to jail time. Recently, the Canadian justice system has also been experimenting with **alternative sentencing**, programs that release offenders back into the community. While supervised, offenders may be confined at home, allowed to work, or sentenced to perform some community service. Counselling is usually part of the package. Young people who have committed a **misdemeanour** (a minor crime punishable by less than one year in prison) are most likely to receive alternative sentencing.

Probation is a suspended prison sentence. Probation allows the offender to live free in his or her community, but remain supervised by a probation officer. Offenders on probation must also abide by certain conditions—for example, restrictions on travel, people they can associate with, and alcohol consumption.

Matt's case proceeds in the same way as Carl's, but without a jury. If the judge decides that Matt is guilty, he or she will pass an appropriate sentence. As a young person, Matt is considered to have a better chance of being rehabilitated than an adult. The judge may consult with youth workers and probation officers. Often, the judge will draw upon school records and interviews with parents and others before deciding on a sentence. The sentence may range from a reprimand to community service, **open custody** in a group home, or **secure custody** in a prison separate from adults.

Both Carl and Matt have the right to appeal their verdicts if they and their lawyers believe them to be unfair.

☐ DISCUSSION POINT

In 2006, the Supreme Court of Canada rejected an appeal to increase the one-day sentence of a 15-year-old from Winnipeg convicted of beating a man to death with a billiard ball wrapped in a sock. The Crown wanted a 10-month sentence to send a warning. The Supreme Court said: "General deterrence is not a principle of youth sentencing under the present regime." What would you consider an appropriate sentence?

SOURCES

This is what the Manitoba justice ministry has to say about jury duty:

> Trial by jury is the foundation of our judicial system. Now, and for centuries past, trial by jury has been the process through which facts of cases are uncovered and determined. Through jury duty, members of the community actively share in the delivering of justice. To serve on a jury is your democratic right, your civic responsibility, and a great honour.
>
> Source: www.gov.mb.ca/justice/court/jury.html

Which of the three reasons for serving would prompt you to serve on a jury?

Number of People in Prison (per 100,000 population), 2006

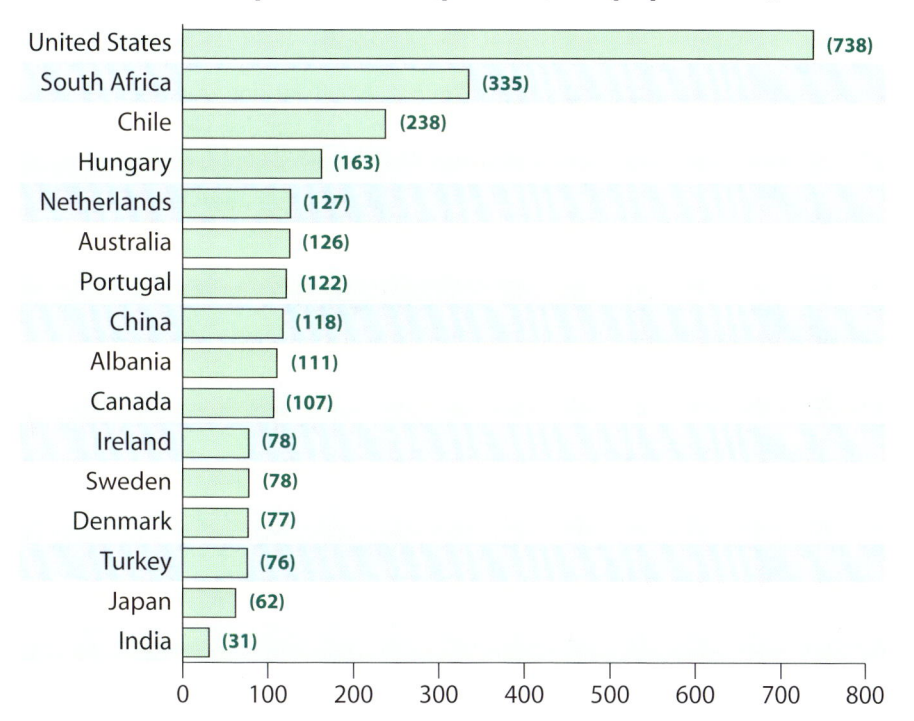

United States	738
South Africa	335
Chile	238
Hungary	163
Netherlands	127
Australia	126
Portugal	122
China	118
Albania	111
Canada	107
Ireland	78
Sweden	78
Denmark	77
Turkey	76
Japan	62
India	31

FIGURE 10.6 The number of people sent to prison varies a great deal around the world, as this graph shows. What else would you want to know about the countries with high or low rates of **incarceration** (imprisonment)? *Source: Data from www.prisonstudies.org*

FACE OFF: Young Offender or Young Adult?

In 1997, Canadians were shocked after 14-year-old Reena Virk was beaten and left to drown by a group of teenagers under a bridge in Victoria, BC. The case focused national media attention on teen violence and the youth justice system.

The brutal killing raised a serious question: Should teenagers be treated as adults when they commit crimes of violence?

Some people think that teens should be treated as adults by the justice system. They say that violent crimes show a shocking disregard for human life. Anyone who commits such a crime should be punished severely. Victims of violent crime feel diminished when a young offender gets a light sentence. Shorter sentences also give society the message that young people will be excused for their behaviour. Some people point out that teenagers often want to be treated as adults.

> Teens ask to be treated like adults by their parents, but not the courts. ... it doesn't make sense, they want the responsibility at home, but nowhere else. ... HELLO—treat them like the adults they want to be!!!
>
> — Internet debater, www.lawyers.ca

Other people say that youths need special rights and consideration. Teenagers are not adults and may not understand their rights upon arrest. They may waive (give up) their rights without understanding what they are doing. Moreover, the lighter sentences often given to youths reflect the idea that they are more likely to be rehabilitated than adults. Teenagers should not be sent to adult prisons, where they may be surrounded by hardened criminals.

FIGURE 10.7 Reena Virk's mother talks to reporters following the trial of one of the defendants in her daughter's case.

> Sending a kid to an adult prison is not a disciplinary measure intended to reform and teach—it's about revenge. If you want to cut back on youth criminal activity then you should focus on prevention and intervention (like counselling, not jail) for at-risk youth ... .
>
> — Internet debater, www.lawyers.ca

What Do You Think?

1. In the discussion above, list the arguments from strongest to weakest in favour of
   a) treating young offenders as youth with special rights
   b) treating them as adults.
2. Which do you think is the better approach to the problem of teenage violence—harsher penalties or prevention and rehabilitation programs?

PAUSE, REFLECT, APPLY

1. Why does the law insist that police use search and seizure procedures carefully?
2. Why is Matt fortunate that his case is tried in a youth court?
3. Can you think of any reasons why a jury is not normally used in youth court?
4. Why do you think each juror has to be approved by the defence and the prosecution?
5. What is meant by the "adversarial system"? Do you think that it is the best way to "get at the truth" of innocence or guilt?
6. Explain how the rules regarding types of evidence in a trial serve to protect the rights of Carl and Matt.
7. Which of the four sentencing principles do you believe is the most important for a judge? Do you agree with the emphasis on rehabilitation for Matt if he is found guilty?
8. Why is the right of appeal an important right?

Civil Law

> **KEY QUESTION**
> How does civil law differ from criminal law?

Civil law is different from criminal law in an important way. Criminal activity is a public offence against society. The police must arrest and charge anyone who has broken the *Criminal Code*, and a court must hear the case.

Civil law is concerned with private disputes between individuals. An individual who feels wronged by another in some way may **sue** (take legal action against) that person. Police are not involved, and there is no arrest. Civil law deals with claims resulting from accidents, all kinds of contracts, property ownership, and family matters.

PROCEDURE IN CIVIL CASES

Suppose you are hurt because you fall into a small ditch while crossing a company lot. You believe that the owner has been negligent (careless) in not posting a warning about the ditch, which is almost impossible to see. If you decide to sue, you are known as the **plaintiff** in the civil case. The owner, or the party you are suing, is the **defendant**.

Plaintiffs file a plea with the court outlining their complaint and the **remedy** (what they expect to receive in compensation). The court considers the information, issues a document with the court's seal on it, and delivers it to the defendant.

Defendants must reply by providing the court with a statement of defence. If they do not do this, the court will assume that the facts

FIGURE 10.8 Warning signs need to be visible. This one is clear and visible from a distance.

presented by the plaintiff are true. In this case, the defendant will be liable (responsible) for damages (a fixed amount of money).

Defendants may call upon a lawyer for help, and the case can be settled out of court. If there is no out-of-court settlement, the two sides participate in an "examination for discovery." This allows both sides to examine the evidence that each will bring to the trial.

At the trial, the plaintiff must prove that it is more probable than not that the defendant is liable. This is less of a burden of proof than is required at a criminal trial. (At a criminal trial, the prosecutor must prove that the defendant is guilty beyond a reasonable doubt.)

Civil cases can be decided before a judge alone or before a judge and jury. Civil juries usually have only six jurors.

DECISIONS IN CIVIL CASES

Decisions in civil cases can take several forms. If the plaintiff is successful, the judge will order the defendant to pay damages. Another type of decision is called a **declaratory order**. In this situation, the court outlines or declares the rights of the two parties who are having the dispute. For example, the court might say who can do what according to a contract, or who will get what according to the terms of a will. A third type of decision is an **injunction**. This requires the defendant to stop doing something, such as making noise, or to do something, such as remove an offensive sign from a property.

PAUSE, REFLECT, APPLY

1. Identify the following terms as part of either criminal law procedures, civil law procedures, or both:
   - plaintiff
   - accused
   - defendant
   - statement of defence
   - prosecution
   - damages
   - sentence
   - injunction.
2. Why do police not become involved in civil cases?
3. Why do you think most civil cases are decided out of court?

Aboriginal Justice

Just over 1.3 million people in Canada claim some Aboriginal heritage (2001 census figures). In many parts of Canada, Aboriginal groups operate separate justice systems and their own police forces.

One reason supporting an Aboriginal justice system is the high number of Aboriginal men and women in the prison population. Aboriginal leaders and governments in Canada are concerned about this situation. About 18 percent of male inmates and 29 percent of female inmates in federal prisons, for example, are Aboriginal. The percentage is even higher in the prairie provinces. In Manitoba, for example, more than 50 percent of inmates are Aboriginal. Social and economic inequalities are a contributing factor, but the criminal justice system itself must bear some of the blame.

> **KEY QUESTION**
> What can be learned from Aboriginal justice?

THE MANITOBA EXPERIENCE

In Manitoba, as in other parts of Canada, Aboriginal justice developed because of inequities in the mainstream system. Thirty years ago, for example, crimes committed against Aboriginal victims typically received less attention than other crimes because of **systemic racism** (racism directed against a group of people through an institution's rules and policies). As well, when it came to Aboriginal offenders, the justice system ignored Aboriginal customs around crime and punishment.

The Manitoba Aboriginal Justice Inquiry

In Chapter 6, you read that the murders of Helen Betty Osborne in 1971 and J.J. Harper in 1988 prompted the Manitoba government to launch an inquiry into its own justice system. How had it been dealing with Aboriginal victims? Though Aboriginal leaders knew that police often ignored crimes committed against their people, this was the first time the government faced its own record of "selective" justice.

The details of both cases were shocking. Nineteen-year-old Osborne was a Cree student preparing to enter teacher's college when she was kidnapped near The Pas by four white men. They stabbed her repeatedly with a screwdriver and beat her to death. Harper, 37, was executive director of the Island Lake Tribal Council when he was shot dead by a Winnipeg police officer.

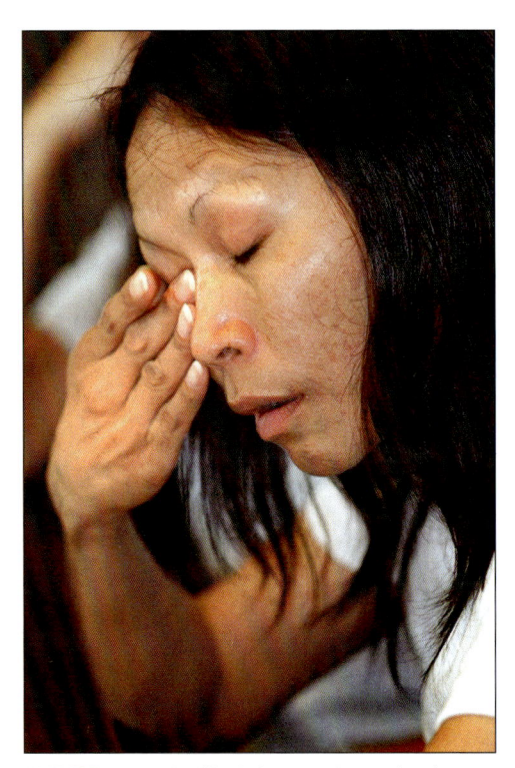

FIGURE 10.9 Cecilia Osborne, sister of Helen Betty Osborne, wipes tears from her eyes in 2000 after Manitoba's justice minister formally apologized for the death of her sister and announced a scholarship in her name. Cecilia continued to seek justice for Helen long after her death in 1971.

In both cases, justice was slow and incomplete. It took 16 years for three of Osborne's killers to come to trial, though all four suspects became known to the Royal Canadian Mounted Police within months of the event. One suspect was never charged; one was acquitted; and one was protected from prosecution by his agreement to reveal the details of the crime. Only one suspect, Dwayne Archie Johnston, was ever convicted, and he was sentenced to life in prison. The Manitoba Aboriginal Justice Inquiry didn't mince words. It said that because Osborne was Aboriginal, both the justice system and The Pas community considered the case "unimportant."

Harper's case unfolded in a different way. Robert Cross, the police officer who shot Harper, was exonerated (cleared) by a police panel—six hours after the shooting. Two days later, a judicial inquest into the shooting also cleared Cross.

Yet the record shows that Harper was not even a suspect in any investigation; he had simply been walking home when Cross detained him for questioning. When Harper said he didn't have to answer the officer's questions, Cross grabbed him by the arm. A scuffle ensued, and Harper was shot dead.

The 1991 report of the Manitoba Aboriginal Justice Inquiry concluded that during the Harper investigation

> evidence was mishandled and facts were obscured by police attempts to construct a version of events which would, in effect, blame J.J. Harper for his own death. Our review of the taking of Cross's statement leads us to conclude that he was assisted in its compilation rather than being questioned. We have found that at least one officer rewrote his record of events.

THE WEB
You can access the full report of the Manitoba Aboriginal Justice Inquiry by going to www.emp.ca/ccw

In 1999, the Aboriginal Justice Implementation Commission (AJIC) was created to make changes to the justice system recommended in the 1991 report. It reports four times a year to the Manitoba government. One of its goals is to encourage greater Aboriginal participation in the justice system at all levels—policing, the court system, and so on. The goal is for the justice system to become better equipped to deal with Aboriginal perspectives and traditions and to ensure justice for everyone.

Restorative Justice: An Aboriginal Model

Canada's criminal justice system is European in origin. It relies on the state (government), not the community, to punish offenders. As you read on page 206, when sentencing offenders, it has four main goals in mind:

- punishment
- deterrence
- rehabilitation
- protection of the public.

Do you notice anything about this approach? Under the European model, offenders are treated in isolation from their communities and their victim.

A **restorative justice** model does just the opposite. Restorative justice brings together the offender, the victim, and the community when a crime has been committed. This system of justice has been practised for generations by indigenous peoples around the world, including Manitoba First Nations and Métis. A principle of restorative justice is that a crime cannot be addressed unless the community understands why it occurred.

Restorative justice can help victims, offenders, and communities because

- victims can talk about their needs
- offenders must take responsibility for their actions in front of the victim and the community
- communities can address crime because they understand it better.

Restorative justice systems use both sentencing circles and healing circles.

In a **sentencing circle**, the offender is brought before the victim and other members of the community, or band. The victim confronts the offender and conveys the hurt he or she has suffered. The circle of band members decides on an appropriate sentence. This could range from banishment for a specified time to community service.

In a **healing circle**, the offender admits guilt and seeks forgiveness from the victim. The offender works toward reconciliation with the rest of the community.

SOURCES

Most healing circles use the "Seven Sacred Teachings" as the basis of their activities. The Seven Sacred Teachings of Aboriginal spirituality are love, courage, wisdom, truth, respect, honesty, and humility.

Below, Dave Courchene Jr., an Anishnaabe elder at Turtle Lodge, Sageeng First Nation, Manitoba, describes the Seven Sacred Teachings:

Love

To feel true love is to know the Creator. One's first love is to be the Great Spirit. You express love for the Great Spirit by loving yourself and how the Great Spirit made you. Only then can you truly love others.

Courage

To have courage is to have the mental and moral strength to listen to the heart. It takes courage to do what is morally right.

Wisdom

To live in wisdom is to know that the Great Spirit gave everyone special gifts. Showing wisdom is using your gifts to build a peaceful and healthy family and community.

Truth

Always seek the truth. The truth lies in spirit. Prayer is to be done every day at sunrise to give thanks to the Great Spirit for the gift of life. Each of the gifts and ceremonies is given by the Great Spirit to the Original human beings to help them find the truth and the true meaning of their life on Earth.

Respect

First Nations people are always to respect all life on Mother Earth. To show real respect is to share and give of yourself for the benefit of all life. Respect the Elders from all races of people who uphold the sacred teachings of the Great Spirit.

Honesty

To be honest with yourself is to live in the spirit of how you were created. Never lie or gossip about each other. The more honest you are the bigger you become as a person.

Humility

Always carry out actions in humility. Think of your family, your fellow human beings, and your community before you think of yourself. To know humility is to understand that you are not more or less important than anyone else.

Source: Abbreviated and adapted from http://www.theturtlelodge.com/teachings.htm

Restorative Justice in the Mainstream

Recently, Canada's mainstream justice system has been experimenting with restorative justice in dealing with young offenders and adults who commit non-violent crimes. There is some evidence that restorative justice does a better job of preventing criminals from re-offending than traditional approaches. However, it is not suitable for everyone. Some victims never want to meet the offender, and some offenders are only interested in "doing their time" and returning to a normal life.

DID YOU KNOW

Onashowewin is an Ojibwe term that is roughly translated as "the process by which we see justice."

FIGURE 10.10 In 2005, Onashowewin won a Manitoba Attorney General's Safer Communities Award. Onashowewin is Winnipeg's Aboriginal Restorative Justice Program. Volunteer-based, the organization works with victims, communities, and elders to deal with offenders and prevent crime. Why do you think "process" and "community" are such important concepts in Aboriginal justice systems?

The government of Manitoba funds a number of restorative justice programs, mostly geared to Aboriginal peoples. Some of these are the Manitoba Keewatinowi Okimakanak (MKO) First Nations Justice Strategy, the St. Theresa Point Aboriginal Youth Court, and the Hollow Water Community Holistic Circle Healing Project. These agencies work with offenders and victims and help to establish new Aboriginal courts (with procedures in Aboriginal languages) and healing circles.

THE WEB

Learn more about Onashowewin at www.emp.ca/ccw

PAUSE, REFLECT, APPLY

1. How does the Aboriginal concept of justice differ from the European idea? In what way does it reflect the traditional way of life of Aboriginal peoples?
2. Why do Aboriginal peoples in Canada have the right to manage their own justice? In your view, is this system fair? Explain your opinion.
3. What is the value of restorative justice for the offender? For the victim? Can you think of situations in which restorative justice would not be appropriate? Outline these situations as you see them, and state why this method would not be an option.

LITERACY COACH

When doctors and scientists read journal articles, they often begin with the summary. You can use the Replay feature in this book in the same way—to help identify key concepts in the chapter and to fill any gaps in your understanding. Next time, try reading the Replay feature first, before you read the chapter. Then assess how this strategy helped you.

REPLAY

In this chapter, you have explored these concepts:

1. Justice systems try to balance the need for social order with the need to guard individual rights.

2. The rights of a person when arrested and tried flow from the basic idea that a person is innocent until proven guilty.

3. Young offenders have the same rights as adults along with special provisions. They can be transferred to adult courts for very serious offences.

4. Civil law concerns the settlement of differences between individuals.

5. Aboriginal justice brings offenders, victims, and the community together in sentencing circles and healing circles. This approach, called restorative justice, is being adapted to Canada's judicial system.

SKILLS TOOLKIT

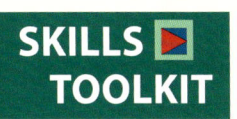

How to Organize Information

Organizing the information that you have gathered is an important step before writing a paper or delivering an oral report. This step will show you

- how much information you have gathered on each aspect of your topic
- whether your information is useful or relevant
- areas where you need more information.

There are several ways to organize information so that it is clear and usable. Suppose the topic for investigation is: Should marijuana possession be decriminalized? You could cluster your information in a fairly straightforward outline that uses categories and subcategories:

1. Marijuana in general
   - past and present laws
   - penalties
     - for possession and use
     - for growing, smuggling, selling
   - medical, scientific evidence regarding effects
2. Attitudes
   - past attitudes
   - changing attitudes
3. Law enforcement
   - difficulties in enforcing law
   - problems with growing operations
   - role of organized crime
4. Options
   - legalize growing and using?
   - legalize using, regulate growers?
   - don't change the law?

Another way to organize information is to use a sequence chart. This is particularly effective when looking for the connections among a series of ideas or events. For example:

past attitudes about marijuana ▶ known as harmful substance ▶ harsh laws ▶ changing attitudes ▶ seen as less harmful ▶ widespread flouting of law ▶ difficulties for courts, police

As you can see, a sequence chart can go on indefinitely.

A third information organizer is the mind map. This can reveal how one part of a topic fits in with another. (See Figure 10.11 as an example.)

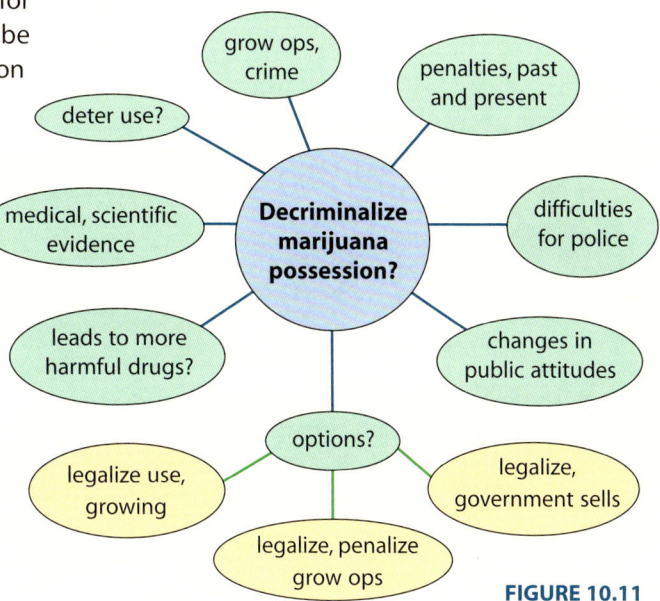

FIGURE 10.11

Skill Practice

Identify the method above that you think would be best for organizing information for writing or giving an oral report on

1. the development of laws dealing with youths from past to present
2. Aboriginal justice methods and their potential impact on the Canadian judicial system
3. actual crime rates and public perceptions.

STUDY HALL

Be Informed

1. a) What rights must the police have in order to perform their duties efficiently?
   b) The police can obtain court approval to tap a suspect's telephone line, yet wiretap evidence cannot usually be admitted as evidence in court against the accused. Why do you think this contradiction exists? Should wiretaps be allowed as evidence, or should they be forbidden entirely?

2. Why are each of the following rights important for a citizen charged with an offence?
   - right to hear the charge immediately
   - right to a lawyer
   - right to bail

3. Which of the following acts would result in a) a summary offence or b) an indictable offence?
   - theft over $5,000
   - bank robbery
   - disturbing the peace
   - gang fight
   - speeding 60 km/h over the speed limit
   - carrying a concealed weapon

4. a) Distinguish among punishment, deterrence, protection, and rehabilitation as goals of sentencing.
   b) What are the goals of restorative justice?

Be Purposeful

5. How can the need for social order conflict with the need to protect individual rights? Give three examples.

6. Which result do you think is more likely to occur because of the rights extended to a person accused of a crime: an innocent person would be wrongfully convicted, or a guilty person would be set free? Be specific in referring to the rights of an accused person.

7. What factors should lead a youth court judge to sentence a convicted youth as an adult?

Be Active

8. "Violent crimes deserve longer sentences than are currently given out." Do you agree with this statement? Make a list of arguments either for or against, and share it with the rest of the class.

9. The United States has one of the highest incarceration rates in the world. What do you think are the reasons for this? Consider:
   - social or economic factors
   - gun control laws
   - length of sentences.

10. The use of cameras in schools, stores, and streets to record illegal behaviour has become commonplace in many communities. Some people believe that cameras are an invasion of citizens' privacy; others see them as an effective means of law enforcement. What do you think about this issue?

11. Research the reasons that the *Young Offenders Act* of 1984 was changed to the *Youth Criminal Justice Act* in 2002, and highlight the major changes.

12. The Sources feature on page 214 summarizes the Seven Sacred Teachings. Create a presentation—written, multimedia, oral, or graphic—that compares this approach to justice with that of Canada's mainstream justice system. Keep in mind the importance of one's relationship to the land.

13. How might Aboriginal concepts of justice create opportunities and challenges for Canada's evolving sense of citizenship and identity?

14. The death penalty was abolished in Canada in 1976. However, recent polls indicate that a majority of Canadians support it as a punishment for violent crime. Hold a class debate on whether or not Canada should reinstate the death penalty. Possible sources of information include Amnesty International and the CBC Archives.

CHAPTER 11
Citizenship in Action

George Orwell wrote *1984* long before satellites, the Internet, and camera cell phones. Today, is Big Brother watching you? Or are you watching Big Brother?

"At one end of [the hallway] a coloured poster ... had been tacked to the wall. ... BIG BROTHER IS WATCHING YOU, the caption beneath it ran."

—From *1984*, by George Orwell

The famous novel *1984* was written in 1948. In it, Orwell imagined a bleak future world. In Oceania, "Big Brother" monitors everything citizens say, read, and think. Big Brother is the central government. It knows and sees everything.

1984 raised troubling questions about democracy and governance: How much privacy do citizens really have, and how much personal decision-making power? Do citizens care about government, as long as they get what they think they need?

"For the ordinary man is passive," wrote Orwell. "So far from endeavouring to influence the future, he simply lies down and lets things happen to him." Do you agree?

As you explore this chapter, look for evidence to support the argument, "George Orwell is wrong. Ordinary people are not passive consumers. They take action and do not simply let things happen to them."

- What forms of negotiation are used in Canada to deal with social issues and conflicts?
- How do Canadians resolve problems and issues outside the judicial system?
- Besides government, what individuals, agencies, and organizations take action on social issues and needs?
- How do democratic ideals such as diversity, rule of law, and equality shape social values and legislation in Canada today?
- What limits are placed on the right to dissent?
- How influential are lobbying, organizing, civil disobedience, and citizen participation?
- How can you make an effective speech?

Key Terms

compromise	secular
sovereignty	dissent
secession	ombudsman
civil disobedience	trade unions
conscience	strike
pluralistic society	collective bargaining

Key Question

Is decision making as open and democratic as it should be in Canada, in your province, and in your school?

219

Canadian Issues and Conflicts

As citizens and members of society, we interact with many people. We often run into differences and negotiate agreements on a personal level. On a government level, negotiation would not be necessary if everyone always agreed. But this is impossible. Negotiation would also be unnecessary if one person or central authority made all decisions. This, however, would be undemocratic.

NEGOTIATION AND COMPROMISE: THE CANADIAN WAY

Canada did not become a country through violent civil war. It became a country through negotiation and **compromise**. During the Charlottetown, Quebec City, and London conferences (1864–1866) leading up to Confederation, all sides gave up some things to get other things. Confederation thus created a federation (alliance) of provinces from formerly independent colonies.

Compromises led to two levels of government. As you saw in Chapter 6, the federal government deals with national and international areas, such as defence, trade, and so on. Provincial governments deal with local social, political, cultural, and economic matters. To this day, both levels disagree over who has more power in overlapping areas such as health care and the economy.

Constitutional Complexities

Negotiation and compromise also shaped the conferences leading up to the *Constitution Act, 1982*. Satisfying all governments was not simple or easy. Federal and provincial negotiators had to work out several formulas for amending the constitution:

- *The basic 7/50 amending formula:* the federal government plus seven provinces (representing at least 50 percent of the population) must agree
- *Unanimity:* the federal and all provincial governments must agree to a change—for example, a change in the amending formula or the use of English or French as official national languages

---

LITERACY COACH

Different people can have very different positions on the same issue. One way to understand different sides of an argument (not just the side you support) is to take a position you personally disagree with. Now try to argue that position by bringing forward the very best evidence to support that claim. Difficult, isn't it? By going through this exercise, you can understand opposing viewpoints better and also find flaws in your own reasoning.

▶ **DID YOU KNOW** ◀

The United States became a country through armed revolution, not evolution, as in Canada's case.

- *The federal government and provincial government(s) that are involved in a change:* for example, to change provincial borders or official language(s)
- *The federal government alone:* changes to the Senate or House of Commons.

Canada's Aboriginal peoples were not consulted or included in these constitutional negotiations, an issue that continues today.

Quebec: Compromise and Clarity, or the End of Canada?

Quebec did not sign the constitution in 1982. It has held two referenda (in 1980 and 1995) asking Quebeckers for the power to negotiate separation from "the rest of Canada." In both cases, a majority of Quebec voters chose to remain within Canada (59.56 percent in 1980 and 50.58 percent in 1995).

Even though a Yes vote would have ended Canada as we know it, the Quebec referenda were peaceful events. Quebec **sovereignty** (complete independence from outside control) and **sovereignty-association** (independence with close economic ties to Canada) remain key issues in Canada.

▶ **DID YOU KNOW** ◀

Only three national referenda have ever been held in Canada: in 1898, on prohibition; in 1942, on conscription; and in 1992, on the Charlottetown Accord. Why have national referenda been held so rarely?

Canada: Nations within Nations

The 11 Aboriginal nations in Quebec did not support sovereignty or separation. Then Grand Chief of the Northern Quebec Cree, Matthew Coon Come, told *Maclean's* magazine in 1995:

> If Quebeckers want to paddle away, that's their business. But it's our business to decide whether we want to jump in the canoe with them—or remain behind on dry land.

Two federal–provincial efforts have tried to get Quebec to sign the constitution. In 1987, federal and provincial leaders negotiated the Meech Lake constitutional amendments with the goal of getting Quebec to sign. However, the Meech Lake Accord failed to achieve the required unanimous agreement. (See the CivicStar feature on Elijah Harper, page 109.)

In 1992, provincial and federal leaders negotiated new amendments to have Quebec sign the constitution. This was the Charlottetown Accord.

FIGURE 11.1 Just say no? People board a bus to take part in the Canadian unity rally in Montreal during the 1995 Quebec referendum. Businesses across Canada gave discounts for people to travel to Quebec. How might different groups in Quebec view these actions?

In a national referendum, citizens in a majority of provinces, including Quebec, rejected the accord.

The federal government promoted Canadian unity, but it did not dispute Quebec's right to hold the referenda. It did, however, criticize the 1995 Quebec referendum's wording and passed the *Clarity Act* (2000).

The *Clarity Act* lays out rules to govern the **secession** (formal withdrawal) of any province. Any referendum on separation must be based on a clear question and win a "clear majority." The Act states that "it would be for elected representatives to determine what constitutes a clear question and what constitutes a clear majority."

> **THE WEB**
> Read the preamble to the *Clarity Act* at www.emp.ca/ccw

SUBJUGATION, CONFRONTATION, NEGOTIATION: ABORIGINAL PERSEVERANCE

Debate, negotiation, court cases, constitutional conferences, land agreements, **civil disobedience** (non-violent resistance and peaceful breaking of laws), and confrontations: these are just some of the processes that have been used to deal with issues between the Aboriginal peoples and governments of Canada (see also Chapter 9).

The *Constitution Act, 1982* recognized basic rights of Aboriginal peoples as Canada's first inhabitants. These rights pertain to land and to Aboriginal cultural traditions. For the first time, the Act also recognized the right of Aboriginal peoples to participate in the constitutional process. The Act promised action. A First Ministers' Conference on Aboriginal Rights followed (1983–1987).

Later, in 1996, the Royal Commission on Aboriginal Peoples affirmed the right to forms of Aboriginal self-government (see also Chapter 2). Aboriginal leaders lobbied for this. They believed it would help them negotiate to solve many social and economic problems.

> **THE WEB**
>
> Learn about stand-offs between First Nations activists (who were demanding recognition of land claims and social reforms) and police at Oka, Quebec; Ipperwash, Ontario; and Gustafsen Lake, BC, at www.emp.ca/ccw. What led to the violence?

SOURCES

I found the Indians suffering, deprived of responsible government and public liberties. We have made petitions to the Canadian government; we have taken time. I have done my duty. — Louis Riel, Métis politician and leader, on trial in July 31, 1885 (Riel was found guilty of treason and hanged)	Recognition of Aboriginal nationhood poses no threat to Canada or its political and territorial integrity. Aboriginal nations have generally sought coexistence, co-operation, and harmony in their relations with other peoples. What they seek from Canada now is their rightful place as partners in the Canadian federation. — From the *Report of the Royal Commission on Aboriginal Peoples*, 1996	We are denied a voice in our own land. Our peoples have the right to live in a world where our Nations are recognized as nations. For seven generations our Nations have been under attack. … I believe in using the courts, the media, the judicial system. I know when to fight and when to negotiate. — Matthew Coon Come, former National Chief of the Assembly of First Nations, 2002

PAUSE, REFLECT, APPLY

1. What significant constitutional compromise was negotiated in a) 1867? b) 1982?
2. What is the meaning of the "7/50 amending formula"?
3. Describe the federal government's position during the Quebec referenda.
4. What rights for Aboriginal peoples were recognized in 1982?
5. What was the major recommendation of the Royal Commission on Aboriginal Peoples?
6. The *Clarity Act* says a successful referendum on secession would require a "clear majority." In your opinion, what would that be?
7. Compare the quotations in Sources, above.
    a) How many years separate Riel and Coon Come? What does this span of time indicate to you?
    b) What is the main point of the quotation from the royal commission? How do you view that position?

What Beliefs Should Guide Elected Representatives?

> **KEY QUESTION**
> On what basis should the people we elect to represent us in government make decisions that involve questions of conscience?

In Orwell's *1984*, citizens do not make decisions. They have no choices, no power. They are passive victims. In Canada today, citizens and politicians have to make choices and decisions every day.

MORAL ISSUES AND CONTROVERSIES

Like all of us, legislators have personal values. Sometimes their personal values may conflict with their public roles. Capital punishment (the execution of people convicted of certain crimes), euthanasia ("mercy killing"), assisted suicide (the "right to die"), abortion, the age of consent—the list of controversial issues is long.

All legislators and voters will face this riddle at times: Which is more important—not to impose your personal beliefs on others, or to stand up for what you believe in, even when that stance is unpopular?

During elections, voters can ask candidates about issues of **conscience** (personal sense of right and wrong). If elected, would the candidate vote on legislation according to

- personal beliefs?
- religious teachings?
- the party's position?
- the will of the majority?

Or, would the candidate look at each case individually?

The choices MPs make have political consequences. Bev Desjarlais was the NDP member of Parliament for the Manitoba riding of Churchill when Bill C-38 was introduced in the House of Commons in 2005 (see

FIGURE 11.2 Marcel Tremblay was suffering from a painful terminal illness that would cripple him before he died. At a press conference in 2005 he announced he would end his own life while he still could. Reporters waited outside his home. Inside, Tremblay placed a helium-filled bag over his head and died of suffocation. He was surrounded by family. No one helped or tried to stop him. Tremblay believed that terminally ill people need access to assisted suicide. How might his public action change social values?

Face Off, below). The NDP supported the same-sex marriage bill as party policy, but Desjarlais voted against it. She said she was personally "not accepting of changing the traditional definition of marriage." She also said that she was respecting the wishes of her constituents. Desjarlais was relieved of her parliamentary duties by the party and lost the NDP nomination in Churchill before the 2006 election. She ran as an independent, but lost.

Canada is a **pluralistic society**. The ideal is for diverse groups—religious, **secular** (not affiliated with any religion), ethnic, cultural, and so on—to coexist peacefully. Obviously, this requires tolerance and respect. To answer the above questions, then, can be a real challenge for candidates and elected representatives.

Would you vote for someone who acts only according to personal conscience? Would it matter whether or not his or her view is different from your own? Would you vote for someone whom you consider to be honest and intelligent, and trust that person's choices?

Personal and Social Values

We each have personal beliefs and values. We also have social values. In a democracy, these interact. For example, some people believe that schools and parents should have the right to use corporal (physical) punishment to discipline children. Canadian social values say this is no longer appropriate. One may personally believe that it is wrong to work on a holy day, but socially believe that the choice is an individual one.

Changes in social and personal beliefs about human sexuality also create controversy. Same-sex marriage is one example.

FACE OFF: Church? Conscience? Constitution? The Same-Sex Marriage Debate

After courts in many provinces had ruled that the traditional and exclusively heterosexual definition of marriage was unconstitutional, the federal government studied the issue. In 2005, then Prime Minister Paul Martin introduced Bill C-38 to redefine marriage to include same-sex partners. It was a question of equality and minority rights, he said.

Many MPs believed this was the correct thing to do, legally and morally. Others believed that it was "gravely" and morally wrong.

Some churches and religious authorities in Canada supported the bill; many churches organized to oppose it. The Roman Catholic Church, for example, officially instructed Catholic legislators to vote against Bill C-38. The Congregation for the Doctrine of the Faith, the source of the Church's legal and moral teaching, stated on June 3, 2003:

It is one thing to maintain that individual citizens are free to behave in a certain manner [homosexual behaviour]; this falls within the civil right to freedom. It is quite different to give these activities legal recognition. ... Where legislation in favour of the recognition of homosexual unions is proposed for the first time in a legislative assembly, the Catholic law-maker has a moral duty to express his opposition clearly and publicly vote against it. To vote in favour of a law so harmful to the public good is gravely immoral.

In Vatican II's *Document of Religious Liberty*, the Catholic Church also advised that a person knows the will of God through his or her own conscience:

> He is bound to follow his conscience faithfully. ... He must not be forced to act contrary to his conscience.

Paul Martin, a devout Catholic, struggled with the issue. When he introduced Bill C-38 to the House of Commons in February 2005, he said this:

> [M]any of us in this House, myself included, have a strong faith, and we value that faith and its influence on the decisions we make. But all of us have been elected to serve here as Parliamentarians. ... [W]e are responsible for serving all Canadians and protecting the rights of all Canadians. ... [W]e must not shrink from the need to reaffirm the rights and responsibilities of Canadians in an evolving society.

Religious alliances formed both for and against Bill C-38. The Religious Coalition for Equal Marriage represented a spectrum of Jewish, Muslim, Sikh, and Christian churches. In its "Affirmation of Diversity" it made this public statement in June 2005:

> Members of many of our communities are from racial and religious minority groups that themselves experience discrimination, and we understand that human rights as guaranteed in the Charter of Rights and Freedoms must extend to everyone, including gay men and lesbians. Same-sex marriage is a human right.

In June 2006, Prime Minister Stephen Harper announced he would hold a fall vote in the House of Commons on whether to re-open the same-sex marriage debate. By that time, 10,000 same-sex weddings had been held in Canada.

What Do You Think?

1. In your own words, define a) a moral decision, b) civil law, c) faith, d) evolving society, and e) diversity.
2. a) On what grounds does the Congregation for the Doctrine of the Faith oppose laws intended to recognize homosexual unions?
   b) What kind of language does it use to describe the same-sex marriage bill?
3. How did Prime Minister Martin justify introducing the same-sex marriage bill? What kind of language does he use to describe the bill?
4. Using the Internet, research churches and religious leaders that supported those that want to overturn legal recognition of same-sex marriage. Summarize their positions.
5. The Religious Coalition describes same-sex marriage as a minority human rights issue. Assess the advantages and disadvantages of the democratic processes in Canada on a) same-sex couples; b) the Roman Catholic Church; c) legislators.

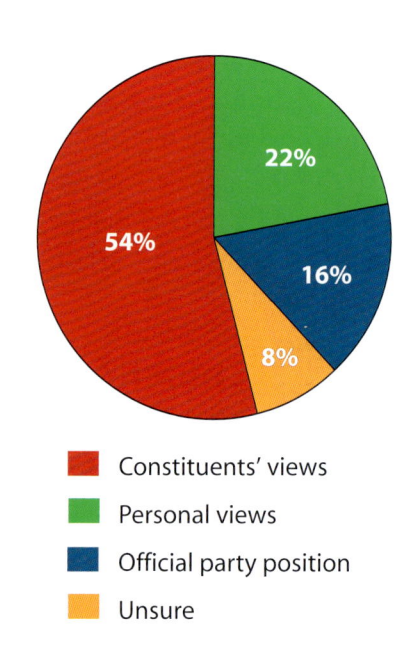

Constituents' views 54%
Personal views 22%
Official party position 16%
Unsure 8%

FIGURE 11.3 Canadian opinion on how MPs should base their vote on same-sex marriage (based on a 2005 poll). *Source: SES Research, "Same-Sex Marriage: A Nation Divided," February 6, 2005*

PAUSE, REFLECT, APPLY

1. What does "pluralistic society" mean?
2. How does pluralism complicate legislators' decisions?
3. What is the difference between "personal beliefs" and "social values"?
4. Clearly explain why elected representatives should vote on issues based primarily on
   a) conscience
   b) the wishes of constituents
   c) party policy.
   Is there a way in which all three concerns can be addressed?

How Can Citizens Act on Their Beliefs and Values?

> **KEY QUESTION**
> What limits, if any, should be placed on citizens' ability to respond to issues?

The very first clause of the *Canadian Charter of Rights and Freedoms* guarantees freedom of thought, belief, opinion, and expression "subject only to such reasonable limits prescribed by law as can be demonstrably justified in a free and democratic society." Citizens discover what those "reasonable limits" are when they **dissent**, or disagree, with government.

CIVIL LIBERTIES ORGANIZATIONS

Thousands of ordinary Canadians volunteer for and support non-profit, non-governmental organizations.

The Canadian Civil Liberties Association (CCLA) has been active for more than 40 years. It supports the democratic right to dissent, even when views may be offensive to many. That means it works to keep "reasonable limits" (see Chapter 3) as broad as possible. For the CCLA, the right to dissent is the foundation of all freedoms. The best protection against unjust government is an atmosphere of free and open debate.

The CCLA uses public forums—such as trials, government committees and rallies, and the media—to identify and oppose attempts by governments and courts to infringe upon citizens'

FIGURE 11.4 Canadian Heritage invites Canadian youth to work against racism. Its annual National Video Competition for youth has been running since 1996. Find entry rules and view past winners at www.emp.ca/ccw.

rights. The belief is that it is better to **censure** (criticize) offensive people through the media than to **censor** (gag or repress) them by law. It is a belief that is easy to put into words, but often controversial in practice.

Other organizations also work to protect civil liberties and promote human rights. The Manitoba Association for Rights and Liberties, for example, has been active in both areas since 1978. The association works to eliminate discrimination through such means as anti-racism programs for high schools.

PEACE, ORDER, GOOD GOVERNMENT— AND PROTEST?

How far does the right to dissent go?

When FLQ terrorists in Quebec resorted to mail bombs and kidnappings in October 1970, Prime Minister Pierre Trudeau declared a state of "armed insurrection." He invoked the *War Measures Act*. This gave the government far-reaching emergency powers and suspended the *Canadian Bill of Rights*. Hundreds of people were arrested for belonging to or supporting—or even simply being suspected of supporting— the FLQ. Most people who were arrested were never charged.

The day after the Act was invoked, the FLQ killed a Quebec cabinet minister. The majority of Canadians outside Quebec supported Trudeau's action, but Quebeckers did not. (You will further explore terrorism and related issues in Chapter 14.)

Many years later, in April 2001, 25,000 people protested the Quebec Summit of the Americas. They believed that international trade policies were being made secretly that would hurt poorer nations. Riots erupted, and police and demonstrators accused each other of using unnecessary force. The two sides disagreed on "reasonable limits."

A police spokesperson explained: "We have full intentions of allowing the democratic right of people to demonstrate, but if personal behaviour becomes violent, the police will respond."

In September 2002, Jewish organizers invited former Israeli Prime Minister Benjamin Netanyahu to speak at Montreal's Concordia University. Concordia has many Jewish, Palestinian, and Arab students. Ongoing conflict in the Middle East had created tensions between the pro-Israeli and pro-Palestinian factions on campus.

Many students objected to Netanyahu's policies and organized a protest. Police were called in when protestors turned violent. Netanyahu's speech was cancelled. Later, a speech by an anti-Israel critic was cancelled for fear of further violence. The university banned any future events related to the political climate of the Middle East.

Intimidation and Freedom of Expression

Groups such as the CCLA say public demonstrations are one of the few ways that disadvantaged people can be politically active. Protests, however, should be used to criticize, not intimidate. How democratic is it when scare tactics stop a person from speaking?

In contrast to the CCLA, some groups endorse **direct action** (the use of disruptive behaviour in marches and protests). They also advocate civil disobedience (passive resistance to government and peaceful breaking of laws). These are seen as necessary tools of dissent against unjust governments and social inequalities.

Direct action and civil disobedience are often justified on the grounds that large banks, corporations, and businesses run the economy and influence government policy yet are not democratic institutions.

> **THE WEB**
> In "Big Mountie Is Watching You," the CCLA warns against police "targeting democratic radicals" in the fight against terrorism. Read that warning at www.emp.ca/ccw

OTHER WAYS TO STAND UP FOR YOUR RIGHTS

In an attempt to reduce court time and costs, federal and provincial governments set up agencies, boards, and tribunals to deal with disputes that concern citizens. Some of the areas covered include

- human rights
- accommodation
- conservation
- environmental assessment
- liquor control
- immigration and refugees
- parole
- labour relations.

> **THE WEB**
> Find out more about youth rights on the job, at school, and in the justice system at Ombudsman Manitoba at www.emp.ca/ccw

Most provinces have an **ombudsman**, a public official who investigates complaints about government departments and agencies. Manitoba's *Ombudsman Act* was proclaimed in 1970. Since then the Ombudsman Division has investigated and resolved thousands of complaints. It also directs complainants to appropriate agencies or boards. The Ombudsman Division acts independently from government.

FIGURE 11.5 A farmer flags motorists on Main Street in Winnipeg in 2001. Hundreds of farmers drove farm vehicles and pickup trucks to the Manitoba legislature. It was part of a national day of protest demanding government aid for farmers. How is this an example of civil disobedience?

PAUSE, REFLECT, APPLY

1. Explain the difference between a) "censure" and "censor," and b) "criticize" and "intimidate."
2. What is the CCLA, and why do citizens support it?
3. a) Why does the CCLA not support the use of direct action?
   b) How would an organization or group justify the use of direct action?
   c) Which position(s) do you agree with? Explain.
4. Why did student protestors at the Quebec Summit and Concordia feel justified in their actions?
5. Describe whether you have the right to dissent in your school, home, and any organizations to which you belong.
   a) If not, why is dissent not allowed?
   b) If dissent is allowed, how can it be expressed effectively and respectfully?

Finding Positive Ways to Effect Change

> **KEY QUESTION**
> Aside from participating in government and protests, how can you express your beliefs and values and make a difference?

☐ **DISCUSSION POINT**
How does the message of the starfish story differ from Orwell's message in *1984*?

This story is a favourite with volunteer groups:

A man walking along a beach sees a local woman picking up starfish, one at a time, and then throwing them into the water. Washed up on shore, the starfish are dying from lack of oxygen. The man points out that there are thousands of starfish on the beach and that this is happening at thousands of beaches. "You can't possibly make a difference," he says. "Made a difference to that one," replies the local as she throws another starfish out to sea.

PEOPLE TAKING ACTION TOGETHER

There are thousands of not-for-profit, non-governmental groups in Canada. Their goal? To save the world, one person, one project, at a time. Their causes cover the political spectrum.

1. Leaders Today

Canadians Marc and Craig Kielburger (who founded the organization Free the Children) run workshops that train students in organizational and leadership skills. They also provide opportunities to volunteer globally—while participants are still in high school!

2. Centre for Social Justice

This Canadian organization is more politically activist (more aggressive) than Leaders Today. It educates the public about social and economic inequities. At summer camps, university students work with people from various backgrounds to learn how to lead and dissent more effectively.

CivicStar

JOE OPATOWSKI

In his brief life, Joe Opatowski influenced many, many people:

Joe Opatowski ... walked away from a troubled home life to inspire tens of thousands of schoolchildren to help change the world. ... [He] criss-crossed North America for Leaders Today, a group associated with Free the Children, an organization founded by Toronto-area activists Craig and Marc Kielburger. ... He had just given a speech [in October 2004] to schoolchildren in Buffalo, New York when, driving home ... , he died in a car accident. ... In one year alone, Opatowski is estimated to have spoken before 100,000 children ... .

His message was repeated again and again: The young people of today have an obligation to care for one another and to care for the less fortunate.

—Excerpted from Phinjo Gombu, "He Changed Himself: Then He Started Changing the World" (obituary), *The Toronto Star*, November 4, 2004

But perhaps Joe Opatowski's story is best told in his own words:

Riverton, Jamaica. I'm bouncing down a country road in a bus with a group of volunteers, ready to "get involved"... . On either side of the bus were piles and piles of garbage. Suddenly one of the piles moved. A flap opened and out climbed a young boy and an old man. The flap of garbage was the front door to their home. ...

Out of breath and seriously thirsty, I wandered over to a street vendor and bought a carton of juice. As I raised it to my mouth, I noticed a small boy ... staring up at me. ... Guilt quickly kept me from drinking the juice. I handed him the carton. ...

I expected a look of gratitude, but instead I watched ... him walk toward the other children, carton in hand. I couldn't believe my own eyes as I saw this ... boy making sure that each of his friends had an equal sip. ... To this day, I am left with the fact that I, a kid from North America, took a sip of that juice before a 6-year-old kid who lived in a garbage dump.

I quickly realized that it wasn't all about me, after all. I wasn't the only victim. ... [I]n this case, ... a poverty-stricken little boy—wasn't just surviving. He was aliving. This was a lesson I would never forget.

—From "My Story: Joe Opatowski," in *Me to We: Turning Self-Help on Its Head*, compiled by Craig and Marc Kielburger (Toronto: Wiley, 2004, pp. 187–189)

Your Play

1. How did meeting a Jamaican child affect Joe Opatowski's identity and his commitment to activism? Do you think Opatowski's difficult background played any part in turning him into an activist (someone who actively campaigns for or against a policy or social reform)?
2. What contribution do people like Joe Opatowski make in dealing with large problems such as child poverty around the world?
3. Can people such as Joe Opatowski help the situation of the world's poor children? What other steps must be taken?
4. Suggest other inspirational individuals or groups who help mobilize opinion on social injustices.
5. So far in this book, you have explored many of your rights as a Canadian and citizen of the world. What does Opatowski's life say to you about your responsibilities? Describe these in a chart, poster, or public service announcement for radio or TV. If you belong to a minority group in Canada (e.g., francophone or Aboriginal), be sure to describe how this perspective affects your sense of responsibility.

3. Habitat for Humanity (H4H)

H4H International is ideal for the non-political person who wants a hands-on way to make a difference. H4H acquires land and materials; then a band of volunteers works with families to build affordable homes. H4H does not eradicate homelessness—it reduces it, one house at a time.

SERVICE CLUBS, YOUTH GROUPS, AND COMMUNITY ORGANIZATIONS

Service clubs, youth groups, and community organizations allow citizens to socialize and, at the same time, contribute to society. Goals can vary, from providing scholarships to funding shelters for street youth.

This year, about 6.5 million volunteers will be active in 180,000 charity organizations across Canada. And it is membership fees and fund-raising—not government funding—that keep these groups running.

Most communities in Canada have service clubs. The Kinsmen, Shriners, Lions, Kiwanis, YMCA/YWCA, Civitans, Elks, B'nai Brith, and Zonta are just a few. Each group aims to create community spirit by working on local and global projects.

The United Way of Canada–Centraide Canada has 1,400 member organizations in communities across Canada. In each community, the organization is independent and serves as an umbrella group to support and strengthen different local community and charity organizations.

> **THE WEB**
> Find links to hundreds of volunteer sites and service groups in your Manitoba community at www.emp.ca/ccw

FIGURE 11.6 Organizations use logos to get their missions and messages across. Can you match these logos to the club or organization mentioned in this chapter? Check them out at www.emp.ca/ccw.

1. **Rotary International**

This network has 31,000 clubs in 166 countries with a total of 1.2 million members. Its global PolioPlus Campaign set 2005 as a target to eradicate polio. Starting in 1988, Rotarians raised $500 million and contributed more than 1 billion volunteer hours for global immunization. By 2006, it had helped achieve a 99 percent reduction in polio.

2. **4-H Clubs**

For almost 100 years, 4-H clubs have offered Canadian youth (aged 8–21) opportunities to take part in and create projects to develop their technical, interpersonal, and leadership skills. Often, the focus is agricultural. But projects can include everything from photography to developing a Web site to attending international conferences and taking part in international exchanges. Nationally, 4-H Canada awards about $100,000 in scholarships each year.

COMMUNICATING, CELEBRATING, AND COMMEMORATING

Canadians communicate their beliefs, values, and opinions in countless ways. This is not true in countries with authoritarian governments. Below are some of the ways that you, as a Canadian, can express your beliefs, values, and opinions:

- Send letters, articles, and opinions to local and national media, including newspapers, magazines, radio and television phone-in shows, Web logs (blogs), and so on.
- Participate in walk-a-thons, marathons, bike-a-thons, wheelchair marathons, hunger strikes, and sit-ins.
- Attend meetings, join school councils, join in rallies and marches, and distribute pamphlets.
- Wear signs, labels, buttons, poppies, and hats.
- Wear ribbons, cause bracelets, and other symbols to express sympathy, remembrance, solidarity, and support. There are white ribbons (men against male violence against women), red ribbons (AIDS, MADD), green ribbons (environmental action), blue ribbons (campaign against second-hand smoke), and purple ribbons (remembrance of victims of the 1989 Montreal massacre).

CivicStar

JEAN VANIER AND L'ARCHE

Attitudes toward people with mental disabilities reveal society's values. At one point, people with mental disabilities were confined in institutions in Canada.

Eugenics (the study and use of controlled procreation to "improve society") was embraced by many people and authorities around the world, starting in the 1920s. Eugenics became a core Nazi belief in Germany, and it led to murderous policies. The Nazi government systematically eliminated people it classified as "inferior" in order to create a superior race.

In Alberta, under the *Sexual Sterilization Act*, 1928, doctors sterilized mentally ill or "retarded" people without their knowledge or consent. The law was in effect until the 1970s.

Jean Vanier, son of former Canadian Governor General Georges Vanier, stands for a different choice. In 1964, he purchased an old house in France, which he shared with two mentally disabled men. From there he began "L'Arche," a community for people with learning and developmental disabilities. Today there are L'Arche communities in 30 countries, including Canada.

L'Arche is a community, not an institution. It is composed of core members and assistants—not patients, clients, and staff. Each community member has a role and makes contributions, all according to his or her skills. Hundreds of volunteers also assist in teaching life and vocational skills, sharing household chores, and creating a world where everyone is treated with respect.

Vanier believes that social order is often based on fear—even of the poor, weak, and disabled. If citizens are not watchful, society will create an order where "the rich and powerful are at the top, and at the bottom are the weak, the fragile, and the crushed."

"The aim of L'Arche is not to change the world, but to create little places where love is possible," says Vanier.

Your Play

1. Describe how Jean Vanier put his values into practice in the world.
2. Research the organization and the meaning of the word "L'Arche." Vanier had a strong religious background. Why might he have chosen that name?
3. How do Vanier's values and beliefs contrast with social beliefs and policies based on eugenics? (You may want to research eugenics and Nazism; see chapters 1, 8, and 13.)

FIGURE 11.7 L'Arche Winnipeg volunteers participate in the annual fundraiser, Walk With L'Arche, in 2006.

Canadian beliefs and values are also expressed in days chosen to celebrate people, causes, and events. Some examples: National Day of Action and Remembrance on Violence Against Women (December 6), International Day for the Elimination of Racism (March 21), Raoul Wallenberg Day (January 17), Sovereign's Birthday (Victoria Day, third Monday in May), A Day of Commemoration of the Great Upheaval (Acadian Exile, July 28), Canadian Multiculturalism Day (June 27), Louis Riel Day (November 16), and Heritage Day (third Monday in February).

PAUSE, REFLECT, APPLY

1. a) Create a comparison chart of the organizations described in this section of the chapter. Show what all have in common and how each is different.
   b) Who are the "starfish" that each organization is helping?
2. More people in Canada volunteer than take part in protests. Why might that be?
3. What criteria would you use in a) identifying a social injustice and b) deciding how best to take a stand on a social injustice?
4. Research volunteer organizations using the Web feature on page 232.
   a) With which organization(s) would you volunteer?
   b) What criteria would you use to make that decision?
5. Identify groups in your school that deal with community problems (e.g., bullying, gossiping, drinking and driving, drug abuse) and that also work on issues through such means as food drives, environmental protection, and social outreach. Do you belong to any of them? Explain your reasons.
6. Create a table, poster, or display of federal, provincial, and civic flags, symbols, flowers, animals, and logos.
7. Which of these communications options (table, poster, display) do you feel would be most effective in the following situations?
   a) fundraising
   b) changing a school rule
   c) getting a candidate elected
   d) getting a traffic light installed on your street
   e) raising student awareness of drug abuse

Labour Negotiations, Strikes, and Lockouts

Most of us will spend a huge part of our adult lives as workers. Today, workers in Canada have a legal right to negotiate with employers for better wages and working conditions. Working conditions include work hours, workplace environment, provisions for sickness and injury, job expectations, protection against being laid off or fired, health and pension benefits, and so on.

> **KEY QUESTION**
>
> What options are available to workers and employers, other than the courts and legislatures, to resolve conflicts?

▶ DID YOU KNOW ◀

Labour Day is celebrated around the world at different times and under different names, but it started in Canada. In 1872, 10,000 people held a peaceful demonstration for workers' rights in Toronto. Trade unions were illegal at the time.

THE WEB ▶▶▶

The Canadian Union of Public Employees and the Canadian Auto Workers are two of Canada's largest unions. Link to them and many other unions at www.emp.ca/ccw

☐ DISCUSSION POINT

Labour strikes make headlines, but peaceful negotiations between workers and employers do not. Why do you think this is so?

Some groups of workers form organizations known as **trade unions**. As union members, workers elect representatives to negotiate with employers collectively on their behalf. Government regulates how workplaces unionize. Approximately 30 percent of all workers in Canada belong to unions.

Generally, unionized workers have the right to **strike** (refuse to work) if the employer does not bargain seriously during contract negotiations. An employer can use a **lockout** to force a union to bargain seriously. Employers have often resisted union activity because it may interfere with how they run their businesses, increase labour costs, and affect profits.

METHODS OF LABOUR NEGOTIATION

Provincial and federal laws set out rights and protections for all workers regarding working conditions, minimum wages, and conditions under which a worker can be fired or laid off. Manitoba Labour and Immigration is charged with this responsibility. Employers and employees can take disputes to the Manitoba Labour Board for a hearing to settle grievances. The board is independent of government. Manitoba's *Labour Relations Act* also sets out the rules and procedures for negotiating and settling labour disputes.

Methods of reaching agreement include:

1. **Collective bargaining**: Employer and employee representatives meet to negotiate between what the workers want or need and what the employer is willing or able to afford.
2. **Mediation**: If collective bargaining fails, an impartial person is brought in to re-examine the issues and suggest solutions. Mediators cannot impose a solution.
3. **Arbitration**: A mutually agreed upon or government-appointed impartial person (or panel) studies the dispute and draws up a solution. Arbitration may be binding (must be accepted) or non-binding.

Essential Services

Not all unionized workers can strike. Some services are considered "essential" and cannot be legally shut down. Many people would include police, firefighters, and doctors as essential workers; other jobs are open to debate. What about garbage collectors, transit workers, snow removers, airport workers, or ambulance drivers?

What about teachers? Are they so essential that they should not be allowed to strike? In some provinces, teachers can legally strike. In Manitoba, teachers have not had that right for more than 40 years.

According to Manitoba's *Essential Services Act*,

> "essential services" means services that are necessary to enable the employer to prevent
> (a) danger to life, health or safety,
> (b) the destruction or serious deterioration of machinery, equipment or premises,
> (c) serious environmental damage, or
> (d) disruption of the administration of the courts or of legislative drafting.

This Act applies only to collective agreements that cover people employed by the government of Manitoba, hospitals, personal care homes, child and family services agencies, and regional health authorities.

☐ **DISCUSSION POINT**
Which services and jobs do you consider essential?

THE WEB ▶▶▶
Compare your responses with the *Essential Services Act* by linking to www.emp.ca/ccw

FIGURE 11.8 US-based Wal-Mart is the world's largest retailer and prefers to deal with individual workers, not unions. In Jonquière, Quebec, workers voted to make their store the first unionized Wal-Mart in North America in 2004–2005. In April 2005, Wal-Mart closed the store, saying it was no longer profitable. In this ad, Wal-Mart explained its decision. How might the closing affect attitudes toward Wal-Mart? Toward unions?

PAUSE, REFLECT, APPLY

1. Describe collective bargaining, mediation, and arbitration in your own words.
2. What areas are included in "working conditions"?
3. a) What is the role of the Manitoba Labour Board?
   b) Why do you think the board is independent of government?
4. a) Why would workers feel it necessary to form unions?
   b) Why would many businesses oppose unions?
5. Research the situation of Wal-Mart in Jonquière, Quebec, and produce a list of arguments for both sides.
6. Statistics Canada reports that the rate of unionization is rapidly declining among young men but rapidly increasingly among women. How might this affect wages? (Check StatsCan's *The Daily*, Friday, April 22, 2005 at www.emp.ca/ccw.)

REPLAY

In this chapter, you have explored these concepts:

1. Canada's constitution has been developed through conflict, negotiation, and compromise.
2. Personal values and beliefs can influence social values and political policies.
3. Canadians use many different agencies and processes in politics, the community, and the workplace to address social injustices and conflicts.
4. Canadians can express their values and beliefs in a variety of democratic ways through words and actions.
5. One of our greatest freedoms is the right to dissent.
6. Canadian society and identity evolve through the practice of peaceful negotiation.

SKILLS TOOLKIT

How to Be Heard: Preparing an Effective Speech

Speaking in public terrifies most of us. But anyone who wants to express his or her point of view will probably need to speak publicly. Oral communication is a fundamental skill. Like most skills, it can be learned.

There are three basic types of speeches:

- an impromptu talk (1–2 minutes, little or no preparation)
- a prepared speech (2–5 minutes, lots of preparation)
- a major address, such as a valedictory speech (even more preparation).

Here are some speech-making tips:

- *Know your purpose.* Is it to present information, or to persuade? Do you want to make a specific point, or to amuse? If you are not clear on what you want your speech to do, chances are you will lose your audience.
- *Know your audience.* Are they peers, friends, family? What are their ages? How much do they know about this subject? This will help you decide on the amount of information and the level of vocabulary to use.
- *Research.* Know your subject; know your facts. Research will improve your speech and your self-confidence. Locate and include compelling data, examples, illustrations, quotations, and sources.
- *Don't drown them in data.* If it doesn't relate to your main point, drop it. Otherwise, you will bore your audience.
- *Make a "speech burger":*

    Tell them what you are going to tell them

    Tell them what you want them to know

    Tell them what you told them

- *Make an outline.* Prepare a summary of your main points and crisp, clear, concluding remarks. What do you most want your audience to remember? How do you want them to respond?
- *Hook your listeners.* Start with a catchy introduction, and clearly describe what your speech is for and about. Avoid clichés.
- *Be brief.* Limit yourself to three or four main points. Speakers often use the words "First," "Second," "Third" to keep their thoughts in order. Speeches need unity and coherence.
- *Lighten up.* If appropriate, include humour or a personal anecdote (story).
- *Practise and assess.* Ideally, videotape yourself giving the speech. Review the tape with a partner or someone with public speaking experience. During playback, look for
    - vocal clarity and projection
    - vocal variation in tone and emphasis
    - pronunciation and enunciation
    - eye contact with the audience
    - stiffness, fidgeting, over-reading of notes
    - appropriate hand, body, and facial gestures
    - sincerity.

Skill Practice

1. Prepare a three- to four-minute persuasive speech.
2. Your topic is either a) "teachers provide an essential service and should not be entitled to go on strike" or b) "teachers are workers and students should support their right to strike."
3. Videotape your speech away from the classroom and submit it on tape.
4. Have your presentation assessed by peers or the teacher in preparation for your end-of-chapter assignment.

STUDY HALL

Be Informed

1. a) Explain how the federal system and the amending formulas are examples of negotiated compromises in Canada's constitutional development.
   b) Why were these deals necessary?
2. a) What types of powers and recognition are Aboriginal peoples negotiating with Ottawa and the provinces?
   b) Why do Aboriginal leaders insist on achieving these goals?
3. a) What rights do Canadians have under the Charter to hold public protests?
   b) What is meant by the right to dissent?
   c) What restriction is put on the freedom of expression?
4. What is the role and purpose of the provincial ombudsman?
5. Define the following terms and concepts: dissent, civil disobedience, activist, eugenics, binding arbitration, and essential services.

Be Purposeful

6. Select a volunteer organization from this or another chapter and research its structure and work. Create a newsletter, brochure, pamphlet, or computer presentation to promote the group and raise funds to support its work.
7. Referenda have been suggested as a way to settle such issues as Quebec sovereignty, Aboriginal land claims, and same-sex marriage. Referenda have also been strongly opposed. For each issue, give reasons why a referendum is a) acceptable and b) unacceptable. Consider these criteria: minority rights and majority rule; public participation; level of public understanding; clarity of the question.
8. Employees and employers can negotiate using collective bargaining, mediation, arbitration, and strikes.
   a) Use a table or other graphic organizer to show benefits and drawbacks of each method.
   b) Which method would be the ideal way to negotiate and settle issues? Why?

Be Active

9. In groups of four, work as an imaginary team of assistants to a member of Parliament. A vote is to be held on whether to allow assisted suicide. You are to compile three lists: a) all groups and viewpoints to be considered; b) all arguments for assisted suicide; and c) all arguments against assisted suicide. Don't forget public opinion polls. Finally, you must advise the MP on how to vote. Research the issue. (Go to www.emp.ca/ccw for some good links.) As a bonus, submit your material to a class vote.
10. Select any issue from this chapter and prepare and deliver a three-minute speech on it. Consult with your teacher. Referring to the appropriate Skills Toolkits, conduct research and prepare your speech. Record your speech visually for evaluation, using the guidelines.
11. Set up a class or school calendar highlighting commemoration dates in Canada from this chapter and elsewhere. Each class member should
    a) select one date and research its history
    b) simply and accurately explain the history of the date
    c) prepare a series of 30-second infomercials for your school's morning announcements to celebrate Canada's democratic achievement.
12. Create a two-column list of examples from this chapter that support and oppose George Orwell's view of the ordinary person as a victim of events. Research evidence to support your point of view. Alternative: You and a partner each prepare a speech, pro and con.
13. Is Big Brother watching you? Through observation and discussion in class, at home, and at work, brainstorm and list the ways in which governments or other authorities track what you do. Do you find this surveillance threatening or comforting or both? Explain your view.

UNIT 3

Canada in the Global Context

Chapter 12
Canada and the Global Economy

Chapter 13
Canada in the Global Community

Chapter 14
Global Conflicts and Global Interdependence

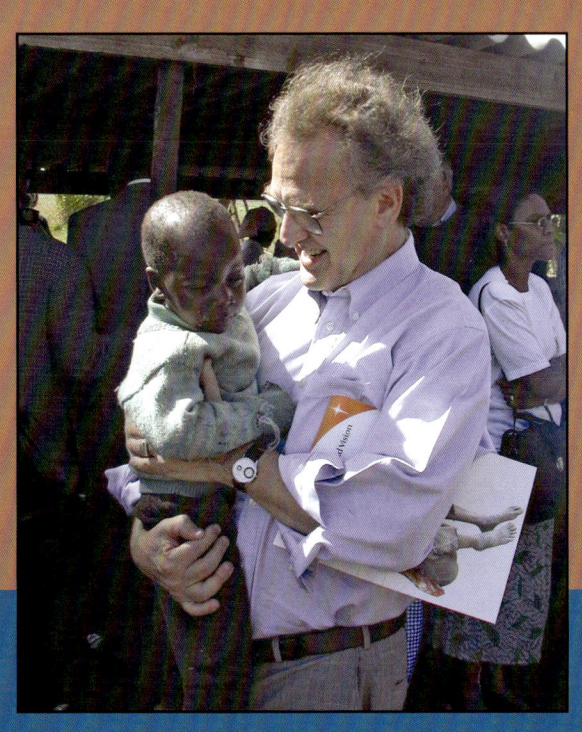

CHAPTER 12
Canada and the Global Economy

What does this image say to you about how the economy works? On which side would you place yourself in the cartoon?

What You Need to Know
- What characteristics describe Canada as an industrialized country?
- What are the benefits and problems of living in a consumer-based economy?
- How do Canada's global connections affect our economy, culture, and politics?
- What impact do our consumer choices have locally, nationally, and globally?
- How can you select, use, and interpret different kinds of graphs?

Key Terms
economy
pre-industrial stage
industrial stage
post-industrial stage
globalization
transnational corporations
capitalism
demand economy
command economy
mixed economy
gross domestic product
free trade
protectionism

Key Question
As citizens, how much control do we have over the economy of our society, country, and world?

"Greed ... is good. Greed is right. Greed works. Greed clarifies, cuts through and captures the essence of the evolutionary spirit. ... Greed for life, for money, for love, knowledge—has marked the upward surge of mankind."

—Gordon Gekko, fictional investment guru, in the US movie *Wall Street*, 1987

"[T]he next generation will have to think in global terms. Will have to think in terms of sharing the abundance we have with those who have not. ... That's the task we have: those of us who are shaping the lives of the citizens of tomorrow."

—Tommy Douglas, addressing a teachers' conference in the 1960s (see CivicStar, page 251)

One of these quotations is fictional and American; the other is factual and Canadian. They represent starkly different ideas of the **economy**: the system of production, distribution, and consumption in a society.

Imagine that you can bring the two speakers together in your classroom. What would you have them debate about Canada's economy today? Whom might you ask to join the discussion?

Canada: An Industrialized Nation

Canada might be described as one country, but many places. In how many different ways can you describe it?

You might call Canada an economy, the topic that concerns us here. To get the "big picture," you would have to consider Canada's place within the world economy. You would also need to take into account place-to-place differences within Canada. Another complication: economies are always changing. Any account is only a snapshot in time. This chapter looks to the past for context and toward the future for possible changes.

CANADA WITHIN THE WORLD ECONOMY

Dividing countries into categories is a simplification, but it can help us understand the world. Several systems do this. This book uses one widely accepted classification: **more developed country** (one that is technologically advanced and wealthy) and **less developed country** (one that is at a relatively early stage in the process of economic development). Canada is a more developed country. For statistical purposes, most major organizations define the more developed world as all of North America and Europe (including Russia), Japan, Australia, and New Zealand. All other countries are classified as less developed, including all countries in Central and South America, Africa, and most countries in Asia.

STAGES OF ECONOMIC DEVELOPMENT

Canada's economy grew through three stages: pre-industrial, industrial, and post-industrial (see Figure 12.1). These stages are simplifications. However, they reflect how the economies of all more developed countries have changed.

Using the flow chart in Figure 12.1, you can trace how different types of economic activities become more important at different stages.

In the **pre-industrial stage**, most workers are involved in **primary activities**. These include collecting and using natural resources and agriculture. After European contact, Canada's economy was initially in the pre-industrial stage. Many products, known as staples, were sent to Europe using natural waterways.

> **LITERACY COACH**
>
> If you come across an unfamiliar word in the text, don't give up! Check to see if the word appears in bold type somewhere else on that page or earlier in the chapter. For example, the labels in Figure 12.1 (page 244) include some technical vocabulary. Those words appear in bold type on this page and the next, indicating that you can look them up in the Glossary.

Pre-Industrial
(primary activities)

Industrial
(secondary and tertiary activities)

Post-Industrial
(tertiary and quaternary activities)

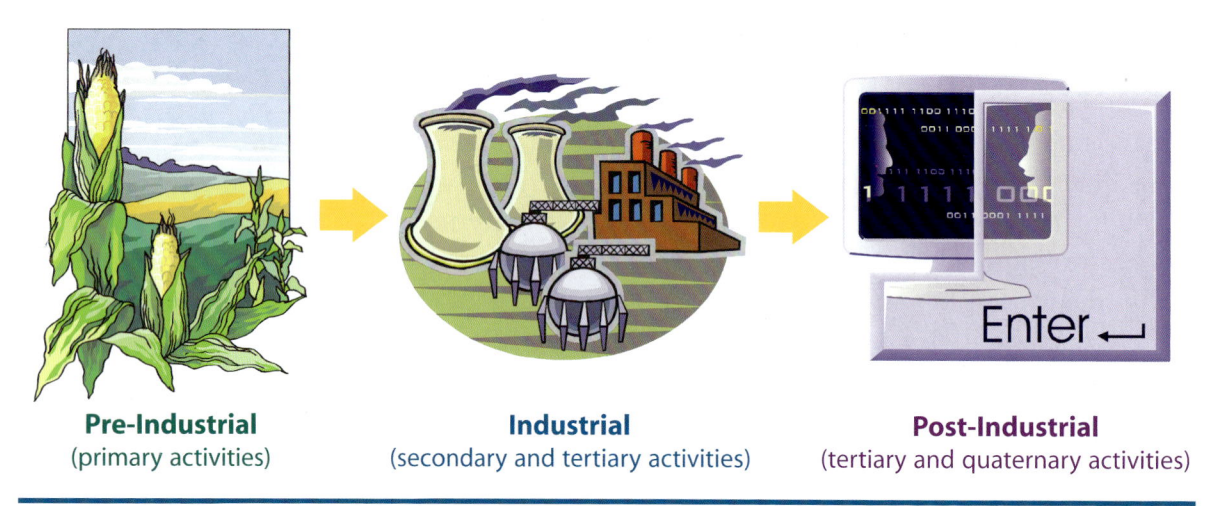

FIGURE 12.1 Stages of economic development. What kind of work opportunities do the four different activities offer? Which jobs would probably pay the most? Which would interest you the most?

A **staple** is a primary product that becomes very important to an economy. The sequence of staples during Canada's pre-industrial stage went from fish ➡ to fur ➡ to lumber ➡ to wheat ➡ to mining products.

In the **industrial stage**, **secondary activities** dominate the economy: processing raw materials (for example, from mining and agriculture) and manufacturing (for example, pulp and paper mills and assembly plants). Also during the industrial stage, **tertiary activities** start to become more important. Tertiary activities provide services (for example, insurance, banking, and retailing) that keep the economy running.

Some parts of Canada entered the industrial stage in the late 19th century. Communication systems and railways were built to connect the regions of Canada. Government safeguarded industries with **protective tariffs**: it charged duties and taxes on imported goods to make them more expensive than domestic goods.

In the **post-industrial stage**, most people work in tertiary and **quaternary activities**. Quaternary activities are based on knowledge and information. They include research and development. This stage is part of any trend toward **globalization** (activity that is worldwide in scope). The post-industrial stage and globalization require easy interaction among economies and highly efficient transportation and communication systems. Protective tariffs are reduced or eliminated. Some parts of Canada entered this stage in the 1970s.

▶ **DID YOU KNOW** ◀

Canada joined the G6, or Group of Six, in 1976, when the group became the G7. The other members were the major industrial democracies: the United Kingdom, Germany, France, Italy, the United States, and Japan. Russia became a member in 1998, when the group became the G8.

How Is Canada's Economy Post-Industrial?

Several factors show how and why Canada's economy is becoming post-industrial:

- About three-quarters of all jobs are in the services (tertiary and quaternary) sector. Primary and secondary activities are still important, but less so.
- The Canadian and US economies are becoming more integrated. The 1989 Canada–US *Free Trade Agreement* and the 1994 *North American Free Trade Agreement* (including Mexico) removed tariffs. Today, a Canadian-based business can more easily sell its products to the United States and Mexico, and vice versa. (See the timeline in Figure 12.9 on page 258.)
- Increased integration places Canadian businesses in competition with US and other businesses.
- Research and development (quaternary activities) are becoming so important that Canada's future prosperity is tied to "knowledge industries."
- Canada is part of a larger global economy, which is made up of more than national economies. It includes international institutions—such as the World Trade Organization (WTO) and the World Bank—that can overrule or challenge national policies.
- **Transnational corporations** drive trends toward globalization. These powerful businesses operate in two or more countries and can influence a country's economic policies.
- More women are in the workforce, and more jobs are part-time.
- The world economy is very dynamic. Today, more than ever, it is being driven by one feature of **capitalism**: private businesses and individuals seeking to produce and sell goods and services at a profit.

▶ **DID YOU KNOW** ◀
Between 1990 and 2005, world trade increased as much as it had in the entire 20th century. Canada was a front-runner in that growth. Canada's per capita (per person) trade amount is $5,000—one of the highest in the world.

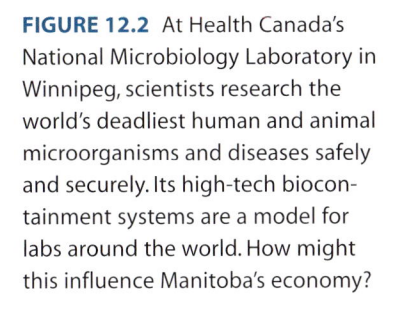

FIGURE 12.2 At Health Canada's National Microbiology Laboratory in Winnipeg, scientists research the world's deadliest human and animal microorganisms and diseases safely and securely. Its high-tech biocontainment systems are a model for labs around the world. How might this influence Manitoba's economy?

PAUSE, REFLECT, APPLY

1. List the more developed countries of the world.
2. In what ways is Canada a part of a larger global economy?
3. Create a web diagram to show how Canada's economy has become post-industrial.
4. The G8 focuses on economic issues. At annual summits, G8 leaders discuss such topics as health, law enforcement, labour, development, energy, the environment, terrorism, and trade. How are these issues important to Canada's economy?
5. In a post-industrial economy, more people become self-employed. People may work part-time, full-time, or on contract rather than remaining in the same job for years. This situation presents students like you with challenges and opportunities. Go to the Web site of several of Manitoba's four universities and/or community colleges. What types of programs are being offered? Choose five that you might be interested in and determine whether they would lead to a career in the primary, secondary, tertiary, or quaternary workforce. What does this exercise tell you about the types of workers needed in a post-industrial economy?

> **KEY QUESTION**
>
> Why are some places in Canada richer than others—and will this situation get better or worse in the future?

Economic Divisions within Canada

In Canada, economic development has been uneven. Different regions are at different stages of development. This **regional disparity** results in different levels of wealth in different regions.

One way to look at these divisions is to describe Canada as having a **heartland** region (a centre of dense population and economic power) and a **hinterland** region (one that is distant from the heartland and has less economic activity).

Chapter 1 described the Great Lakes–St. Lawrence Lowlands as both a physiographic and a climate region. It is also home to the economic heartland in southern Quebec and Ontario (see the maps in Figures 1.6, 1.8, and 1.9). The Lower Mainland of British Columbia, centred on Vancouver, also has heartland characteristics. All other regions of Canada belong to the hinterland. Why are these facts important?

THE GROWING SIGNIFICANCE OF CITIES

The transition from the pre-industrial to the industrial stage happened first in Canada's heartland, mainly in the cities. In the rest of Canada, the pre-industrial phase often continued for many years. Basic physical geography helps explain the differences.

The St. Lawrence Lowlands region has many advantages: good soils, temperate climate, opportunities for generating hydroelectricity, early attraction of European settlers, closeness to the major US industrial region and market, and direct access to the Atlantic Ocean. Together, these advantages allowed the St. Lawrence Lowlands to enter the industrial phase before other regions in Canada.

The transition from the industrial to the post-industrial stage has also been geographically uneven and closely related to urbanization (the growth of cities). The cities of the heartland were the first to become post-industrial. Then the transition began to occur in other important cities, notably, Vancouver, Calgary, and—to a lesser extent—Edmonton, Winnipeg, and Halifax.

WHY HEARTLAND AND HINTERLAND?

The heartland–hinterland distinction is also a simplification, but it can help us understand changes in Canada's economy. Canada has a basic economic division that relates directly to a basic geographic division: hinterland regions have fewer advantages than heartland regions. This fact helps explain why primary and secondary activities continue to dominate hinterland economies.

Hinterland regions depend, to some extent, on the heartland for growth and change. Economic decisions involving capital (money), services, federal transfer payments (see Chapter 6), and so on move from the heartland to the hinterland. Usually, the same is also true of cultural and social changes.

☐ **DISCUSSION POINT**
What kind of push and pull factors to Canada's heartland regions do you feel in your community?

FIGURE 12.3 Hundreds of Aboriginal citizens protested outside Manitoba's legislative building recently. What might "heartland" and "hinterland" mean to these people? One picket demands government to stop "violating our social and economic human rights." Why is the right to economic development considered a human right?

THE WEB ▶▶▶

Statistics Canada is a great source for economic and business data. It also suggests ways to graph that data. Check it out at www.emp.ca/ccw

In short, the hinterland has less economic, political, and cultural status or power than the heartland. People are generally not as wealthy and have fewer services. The hinterland contributes natural resource **commodities** (products of agriculture, lumbering, fishing, and mining) to Canada's economy. These are important, of course, but have lower economic status than the products of tertiary or quaternary activity.

How do tertiary and quaternary activities contribute to the economy? This can be hard to measure. It is easy to calculate the output of primary activities (tonnes of wheat, for example) and secondary activities (numbers of steel girders, for example). But how do you identify and measure the output of service activities such as banking, retailing, and research and development?

PAUSE, REFLECT, APPLY

1. Why is Canada's heartland located where it is?
2. Create a table showing the advantages and disadvantages of heartland and hinterland regions.
3. What do you think is meant by the suggestion that Canada's hinterland is dependent on its heartland?
4. a) Where is Manitoba's heartland? Where is its hinterland?
   b) What factors would you look at to determine this?
   c) Is your community in Manitoba's heartland or hinterland? How can you tell?
5. Canada's economic heartland is located in southern Ontario and Quebec, which geographically is southeastern Canada. The area, however, is commonly referred to as "central Canada."
   a) What does this expression say to you about the political and economic position of this region within Canada as a whole?
   b) How might people in Manitoba, which contains the geographic centre of Canada, feel about this expression?

▶ **KEY QUESTION**

Who decides what products and services are produced in Canada?

How Does Canada's Economy Work?

Canada's economy is huge and complex. The following concepts will help you explore the different forces at work in it.

Canada is sometimes called a **consumer-based economy** or **demand economy**. That means goods and services are produced based on **demand**: what we consumers are willing to buy and the prices we are willing to pay. A demand economy is a capitalist system in which government does not intervene.

Consumer demand is felt in the **market**: the region or population in which goods and services are sold. Demand often determines **supply**: the amount of goods and services businesses are willing and able to produce.

Supply can also determine demand. For example, if there is too much of a product or service, the price will probably go down. If there is too little supply, the price will probably go up.

Producers use the "laws of supply and demand" to make a profit. Consumers use them to get the best buy. These laws affect us all. If there's a bumper crop of soybeans or canola around the world, the Manitoba farmer will not be able to get top dollar: there's too much supply. The farmer must then lower the price to compete. If gasoline supplies are very low, the price of gas at the pump will go up. Consumers will pay more.

In a pure demand economy, there would be no need for government control or regulations. This is sometimes also called a free-market economy. But no economy is that pure or simple.

At the other end of the scale is another kind of system: the **command economy** (sometimes called a planned economy). In a pure command economy, a central government decides what is produced. The government owns everything and controls everything, from land and production facilities, to prices and wages. The central government must ensure that everyone's needs are met; wants are less important. **Socialist** and **communist** economies are command economies, to a degree. No country is 100 percent communist, socialist, or capitalist.

FIGURE 12.4 Death of Canadian hockey? In 2004–2005, team owners locked out players and eventually cancelled the NHL season. Players' salary demands, said the owners, would have pushed ticket prices out of reach for most fans. These shoppers at the West Edmonton mall pay their respects. How does this situation show supply and demand at work? Does anyone remember the Winnipeg Jets?

DEMAND ECONOMY VERSUS MIXED ECONOMY

Look closer at Canada's economy and you will see that it falls somewhere between a demand and a command economy. This is called a **mixed economy**. Think of an economic version of the political spectrum (see Figure 7.9, page 152). The "command" end of the spectrum is the "left," the "demand" is the right, and the "mixed" is in the centre.

In a mixed economy, the government encourages private enterprise. At the same time, it also tries to ensure that everyone's basic needs are met.

Some people believe that humans can reach their full potential and enjoy their greatest freedom only in a demand economy (capitalism). They say that competition within free (open) markets forces businesses and individuals to be inventive and creative and to work hard. That's because the only way to profit is to respond to consumer needs by producing new and better products at lower prices—or creating new needs. (See the opening cartoon on page 242.)

Others believe that the command economy (communism/socialism) creates a stronger society based on a fair distribution of wealth. This inspires people and businesses to do their best to contribute, because it contributes to the community—to the common good.

As you can see, economics is not just about numbers. It draws on our deepest values and beliefs as individuals and as a country (see the CivicStar feature, page 251).

> ☐ **DISCUSSION POINT**
> Mixed economies are sometimes called "capitalism with a heart." Why would they be described this way?

MEASURING STANDARD OF LIVING AND THE QUALITY OF LIFE

A country's economic success may be judged by how well it produces and distributes goods, services, and wealth to its people. Sometimes this is called the **standard of living**.

One method calculates the standard of living mathematically. It takes the **gross domestic product** (the value of all goods and services produced in a country in a given year) and divides it by the total population. The GDP per capita average is the result. But how much can GDP per capita really tell you about the quality of life in a country?

In Chapter 2, you read about the United Nations Human Development Index (HDI). Each year, the HDI measures not just economic status, but literacy, education, life expectancy, and other indicators of human well-being. Over the past two decades, Canada has always ranked in the top five, and has often been number one.

> ▶ **DID YOU KNOW** ◀
> By any measure, Canada is one of the wealthiest countries in the world. In 2005, the *World Fact Book* ranked Canada 14th in GDP per capita, at $34,000. At the bottom was Somalia, in Africa, at $600.

CivicStar

TOMMY DOUGLAS

Tommy Douglas (1904–1986) was born to Scottish working-class parents who immigrated to Winnipeg. Times were hard, but home life hummed with talk of politics, religion, and philosophy: mom and dad were proud and vocal socialists. This background, and Winnipeg's often turbulent politics, formed Douglas at an early age.

In 1919, Douglas witnessed the Winnipeg General Strike. From a rooftop, he saw two protestors shot and killed by troops. Their crime: demanding the right to collective bargaining. Douglas was 15. His early commitment to working people would never desert him.

Douglas became a Baptist preacher and turned to politics. He moved to Saskatchewan, where he was elected an MP in 1935. In 1944, he ran provincially on a socialist platform as leader of the Co-operative Commonwealth Federation (see Chapter 9). He won a huge majority and became premier of Saskatchewan. North America's first socialist government made international headlines. Douglas was re-elected and re-elected. He remained premier until 1961. From 1961 to 1971, he was the first leader of the federal New Democratic Party.

Why and how did Douglas achieve so much?

Tommy Douglas was small in stature, but he was a great orator. He believed that citizens should shape the economy to reflect their own values and needs. He inspired people to believe this was possible. He led his largely agricultural province with its small population down unknown roads.

Douglas and his ideas and policies were attacked as dangerously radical by national and international businesses and organizations (Canadian railways, insurance companies, the medical establishment, and others).

But Douglas persisted and introduced many programs and policies. Among them were provincial utilities (electrical and telephone service), provincial car insurance, trade union protection, and a minimum wage. The most famous innovation, of course, was public health care. Today these are part of life for most Canadians.

Tommy Douglas never became prime minister, but he changed Canada. In the 2004 CBC TV series of the same name, he was voted The Greatest Canadian.

Your Play

1. In describing Canada's economic and political system, Douglas once said: "Canada is like an old cow. The west feeds it. Ontario and Quebec milk it. And you can well imagine what it's doing in the Maritimes." Discuss and interpret this remark within the class. Which part of Canada was Douglas most critical of?

2. How would the following quotation explain Douglas's policies? "Man can now fly in the air like a bird, swim under the ocean like a fish, he can burrow into the ground like a mole. Now if he could only walk like a man, this would be paradise."

3. Douglas's most famous parable was his "mouseland story." Find it at www.emp.ca/ccw or through library research. Explain his message to the voters in your own words, or in a comic book or animated or computer presentation.

INFLUENCES IN A CONSUMER-BASED SOCIETY

Our basic needs seem pretty simple: clothing, shelter, food, education, protection, and medical care. In Chapter 4, you explored how mass media, advertising, popular culture, and consumerism can influence our wants and needs. How much do they influence what you think you need? Do you need—or want—a computer and Internet access? What about the latest fashions, sound systems, video games, and so on?

Economic forces heavily influence society. To compete, businesses try to produce goods and services at lower prices. Consumers benefit because Ford and Toyota, for example, must find ways to make better cars for less money in order to keep us buying their products.

One way to lower costs is to improve efficiency. Robots may assemble cars more cheaply and quickly than humans. Or, machines may increase the number of cars that workers can assemble. As you can see, the "profit motive" has social side effects. In the case of car assembly, this means reducing the need for workers, if possible.

Also, what if businesses limit production to keep the supply of cars (or doughnuts or computer games or gas) low? What if professional associations limit the number of people in a profession? High demand and low supply result in scarcity. As a result, the consumer will be willing to pay more, and the price will go up.

Social concerns—about the environment, child labour, and so on—may also affect demand. For example, trade unions may promote a campaign to "buy Canadian" when businesses move production to less developed countries where wages are lower.

HOW WELL DO PRIVATE PROFIT AND THE PUBLIC GOOD WORK TOGETHER?

Canada has a highly developed **infrastructure** that supports its economic activity. The infrastructure includes systems of highways, electricity, transportation, communication, and so on. Canada also has many public services and programs, including education, transportation, housing, and health care. Locally, water supply, garbage collection, and other services keep public and business life running. But who should run them: government or private businesses? (See Face Off, page 253.)

> **DID YOU KNOW**
> Statistics Canada reported that in 2004 the average Canadian household spent $1,495 on tobacco and liquor products and $294 on reading materials.

> **THE WEB**
> Check out where the federal tax dollar goes—and the pie graphs—at www.emp.ca/ccw

FACE OFF: Do Taxes Benefit or Harm the Economy?

Government collects taxes to pay for itself and the public services it provides. There are three types of taxes:

- *Income tax* is a proportional tax: the more you earn, the more you pay.
- *Consumption taxes* are direct taxes based on the amount the consumer spends. GST and sales taxes are visible. Tariffs charged on goods and services are indirect and invisible.
- *Business tax* is a proportional tax charged on business earnings and profits.

There are also different positions on the impact that taxes have on the economy.

Position A: High Taxes Harm the Economy

High taxes take money from the businesses and people who earn it. If taxes are low, people and businesses can decide how to use the money they have earned. Businesses can invest more in growth and research and development. They will then create better products at lower prices. The result: consumers buy more, which leads to more jobs and even lower prices. Lower taxes also attract more people and businesses to Canada. High taxes discourage the efforts of citizens and businesses and take away individual incentive to work hard to build a better society.

Position C: Taxes Benefit the Economy

Taxes allow government to provide services that benefit society. Good and accessible schools, public health care, public transit, community facilities, affordable housing—these are essential to a caring society. Public services cannot be operated just to make a profit, but to fulfill the needs of all, rich and poor alike. All taxpayers, businesses included, benefit from such programs. Workers are better educated and healthier, people and goods are transported more efficiently, and proper housing and facilities create safer, more diverse

FIGURE 12.5 What is the cartoonist saying about the public's relationship with taxes?

communities. Studies on business costs (such as the 2006 KPMG Competitive Alternatives Survey) repeatedly show that even with high corporate taxes, international businesses still locate in Canada. One reason: they do not have to pay basic health benefits for their workers.

Where Do Canadians Stand?

A 2000 Queen's University poll indicated that a majority of Canadians believe social welfare programs are very important, but

- make people less self-reliant
- make people more dependent on government.

It also showed that most Canadians believe that government

- should reduce taxes
- must ensure a decent quality of life, or standard of living
- provides for the basic needs of all citizens
- wastes a lot of money.

What Do You Think?

1. a) What services do you expect the government to provide to you?
   b) How should we best pay for those services?
2. Canada's economy is not based entirely on Position A or Position C. We have a middle ground: Position B, a mixed economy. Conduct a survey of your local community and identify five examples each of
   a) tax-supported services
   b) privately owned businesses.
3. a) On what basis did you decide which examples belonged in 2a) and 2b)?
   b) Based on your observations, define what is meant by a "mixed economy."
4. If you had to support either Position A or Position C, which would you choose? What criteria did you use to decide which was better? Which position would benefit you personally?
5. Based on the opinion polls, do you believe most Canadians support Position A, B, or C? Justify your answer.
6. The term "brain drain" refers to highly educated people leaving Canada to find better-paying work in other countries, particularly the United States.
   a) Is brain drain a factor in your area?
   b) Because education is heavily subsidized by taxes, explain why you think people should or should not be free to leave Canada immediately upon graduation.

PAUSE, REFLECT, APPLY

1. What is a consumer-based economy?
2. Who decides what is produced and provided in a) a demand economy, b) a command economy, and c) a mixed economy?
3. If Canada were a pure demand economy, what services might your family not be able to afford?
4. List the last five items you bought based more on want than need. What factors influenced you to make each purchase?
5. What causes prices to be kept low in a demand economy?
6. a) Describe how GDP per capita and the Human Development Index are calculated.
   b) Which is the better indicator of quality of life? Why?
   c) What indicators of human well-being would you add as criteria for the Human Development Index?

Globalization

In how many ways are Canadians connected to the world? How are these connections changing, and how are they changing us? Are these connections increasing or decreasing?

Figure 12.6 indicates a few of the global connections that affect us daily. Once you are conscious of globalization trends, you may also become more aware of concerns about globalization.

POSITIVE AND NEGATIVE EFFECTS OF GLOBALIZATION FOR CANADIANS

When an economy is becoming more global, products, services, and capital move across borders more easily and in greater volumes. For Canada, a trading country, international trade becomes even more important.

Globalization brings increased **foreign investment**. Transnational corporations may set up more facilities (such as stores, factories, and service centres). They may also buy up more Canadian businesses. Canadian transnationals may expand around the world.

> **KEY QUESTION**
> How does being a part of a global economy help and harm Canadian society and its economy?

> **DID YOU KNOW**
> Tribal Councils Investment Group of Manitoba was formed by 55 First Nations in Manitoba in 1990. It aims to generate enough wealth to contribute toward First Nations economic self-sufficiency. To quote its chief executive officer: "TCIG is witnessing our integration into the global economy, as we grow from a strong regional presence with a national scope to an international investment company."

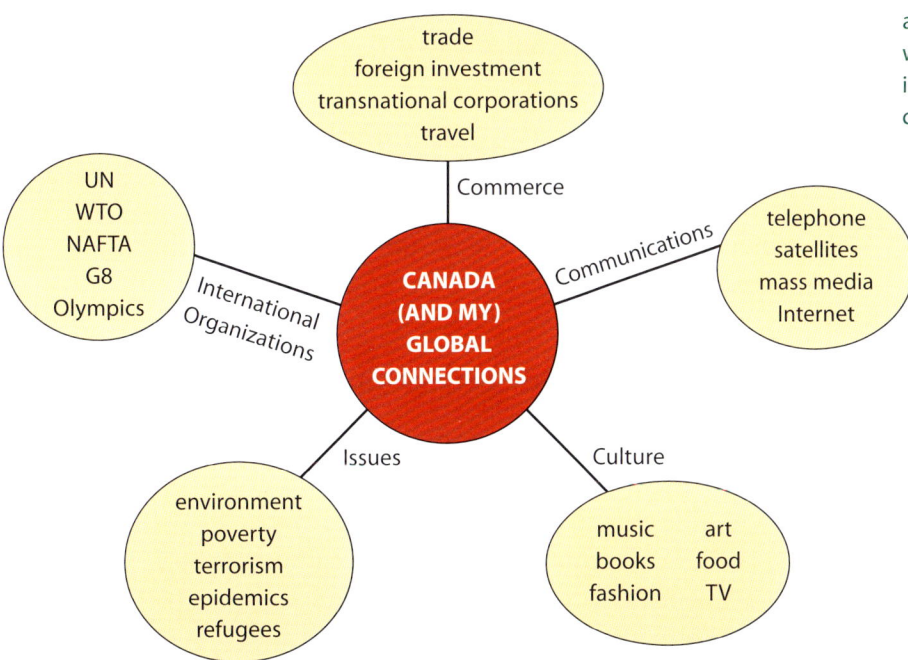

FIGURE 12.6 This mind map shows some of the many ways that Canadians are connected to the world. Each item could be the centre of another mind map or web. Try it with "trade," for example, or "music," or "food."

FIGURE 12.7 These "golden arches" are located in Shanghai, China. Where else might you find them? Some people have called globalization the "McColonization" of the world. Based on this photograph, what do you think that term might mean?

The next two sections look first at the benefits of globalization and then at its hazards.

Pros of Globalization: Benefits and Promise

1. Statistics Canada research indicates that manufacturing plants in Canada owned by transnational (or "multinational") corporations are more productive than plants owned by domestic businesses that operate only in Canada. Transnational plants, whether Canadian or foreign,
   - were more innovative
   - used more advanced technology
   - employed more skilled workers
   - conducted more research and development
   - paid better wages.

   "Transnational" benefits tended to spread to domestic businesses.

2. Transnationals keep prices lower by a) producing large quantities and b) contracting competing businesses in many different countries: for example, tires in one country, engines in another, and assembly in a third.

3. By buying products from less developed countries, transnationals help them develop economically.

4. UN studies have found that transnationals promote positive social policies, democracy, social peace, and environmental standards in countries where they operate.

5. Greater interaction and integration can promote global harmony and peace.

Cons of Globalization: Harms and Threats

1. So much power in the hands of fewer and bigger transnational corporations can weaken any country's unique culture, values, and identity. Because of their power, transnationals can influence national governments. As a result, many governments have less sovereignty, especially small, less developed countries.

2. By their sheer size, transnationals make it harder for a diversity of small businesses to grow and thrive. For example, what happens to small local retail businesses when transnationals such as Wal-Mart and Home Depot open giant "big box" stores?

3. Transnationals exist to make a profit. The competition they inspire often leads to poor treatment of workers, low wages, child labour, and weak environmental policies.
4. Because they belong to no one country, transnationals have no great stake in society. Their commitment to the environment, workers, and social needs is limited. If a host government makes too many demands, the transnational may simply close down its plant or operation in that country.
5. If transnational corporations are not accountable to citizens and governments, globalization could lead to greater international inequality, instability, and conflict.

FOREIGN INVESTMENT IN CANADA

Foreign investment in Canada is significant, and can lead to foreign control. This possibility concerns many Canadians.

Industry Canada reports that from 1985 to 2005 almost 4,000 foreign-owned companies set up facilities in Canada. In 2005 alone, there were 554 foreign takeovers or new businesses set up in Canada.

Figure 12.8 is based on recent Statistics Canada research. It reflects foreign control of Canada's economy over a period of 35 years.

▶ **DID YOU KNOW** ◀
Companies such as The Hudson's Bay Company, Tim Hortons, Petro-Canada, and Molson are all seen as distinctly Canadian—yet now are actually foreign-owned or controlled.

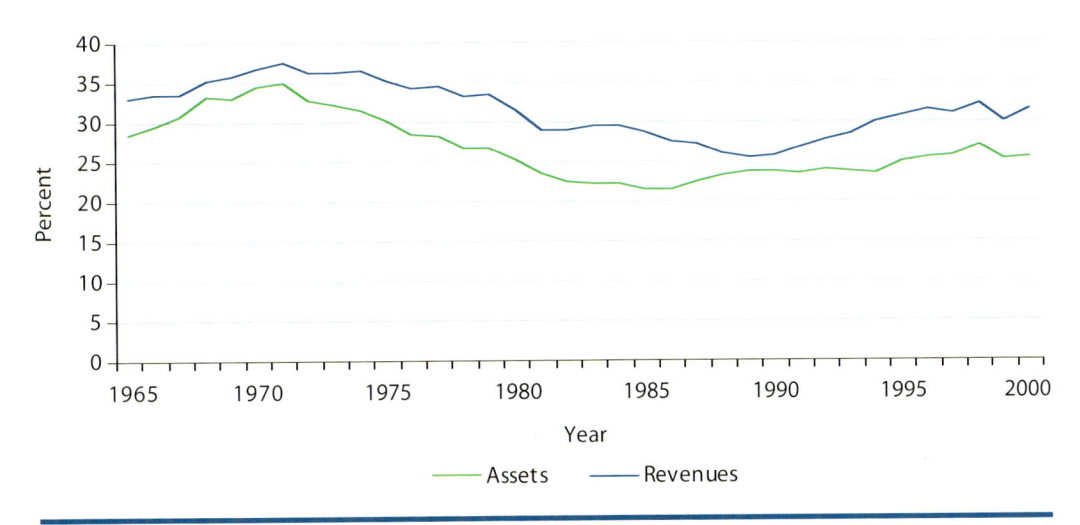

FIGURE 12.8 Foreign control of non-financial corporations in Canada. What does this graph say to you about Canadian concerns over foreign control of the economy? (Note: "Assets" refers to inputs into production; "revenue" refers to outputs, or earnings.) *Source: John R. Baldwin and Guy Gellatly,* Global Links: Long-Term Trends in Foreign Investment and Foreign Control in Canada, 1960 to 2000 *(Ottawa: Statistics Canada, Catalogue no. 11-622-MIE — No. 008, 2005), Figure 2, p. 17*

FREE TRADE BETWEEN CANADA AND THE UNITED STATES

Free trade (removal of tariffs) and open markets support globalization, but governments sometimes impose tariffs to protect their own industries. They may also impose tariffs if they feel a country is trading unfairly. Then, that country may retaliate with its own tariffs. A trade war may result. Figure 12.9 traces some of the turning points of free trade and **protectionism** (imposition of high tariffs) that have marked Canada–US trade relations and the world economy.

FIGURE 12.9 Important developments affecting Canada–US trade

■ 1854: *Reciprocity Treaty*
tariffs between the United States and British North America are reduced

■ 1866: *Reciprocity Treaty* rescinded
United States cancels the *Reciprocity Treaty*

■ 1879: National Policy
Canada imposes tariffs on US imports to protect Canadian industries

■ 1911: Liberals propose reciprocity
Prime Minister Wilfrid Laurier campaigns for free trade with the United States and loses election

■ 1929–1939: The Great Depression
protective tariffs are raised around the world and international trade shrinks; poverty becomes widespread. Eventually, tariffs are lowered; many governments introduce public welfare programs

■ 1947: General Agreement on Tariffs and Trade (GATT)
world leaders form this organization to promote international trade and prevent another depression

■ 1965: Canada–US automotive agreements
The Auto Pact creates free trade between Canada and the United States in the auto industry

■ 1989: Canada–US *Free Trade Agreement* (FTA)
Canada and the United States agree to eventual elimination of all tariffs; a tribunal is established to resolve trade disputes

■ 1994: *North American Free Trade Agreement* (NAFTA)
the FTA is opened up to include Mexico

■ 1995: World Trade Organization (WTO)
a new organization replaces the GATT to open up global markets to trade. Canada and the United States are founding members and refer trade disputes to it

FIGURE 12.10 Young Canadian and American activists stopped traffic on the Peace Bridge between Fort Erie, Ontario and Buffalo, New York in 2001. They were protesting NAFTA and negotiations to establish the Free Trade Area of the Americas (a free trade zone among 34 countries in North, Central, and South America). The FTAA is still being negotiated and is still controversial. Why would activists choose such a bridge? How do you respond to what their signs say about free trade?

NUMBERS TELL A STORY

Consider this information on Canada's international trade:

In an average month, Canadian merchandise exports to the United States exceed $30 billion; imports from the United States are approximately $20 billion. Canada's total monthly exports, worldwide, are about $38 billion, and imports about $32 billion. Energy products, such as oil, are the largest export item to the United States; machinery is our leading US import. Canada's next biggest trading partner is Japan, with exports of about $800 million and imports of about $1 billion (2006 figures, Statistics Canada). (See also the international trade map in Figure 12.11.)

Is This a Trade War? The Softwood Lumber Dispute

The United States has been slapping tariffs on Canadian softwood lumber (pine, fir, and spruce, used in construction) for decades. Its claim: Canada's lumber industry trades unfairly.

▶ **DID YOU KNOW** ◀

Canada is the world's sixth largest importer and exporter of merchandise following the United States, Germany, Japan, the United Kingdom, and France.

THE WEB ▶▶▶

Two Canadian boys organized a "McBoycott" to protest US tariffs on Canadian softwood lumber. They called their Web site We Want Our Money Back. Read about them at www.emp.ca/ccw

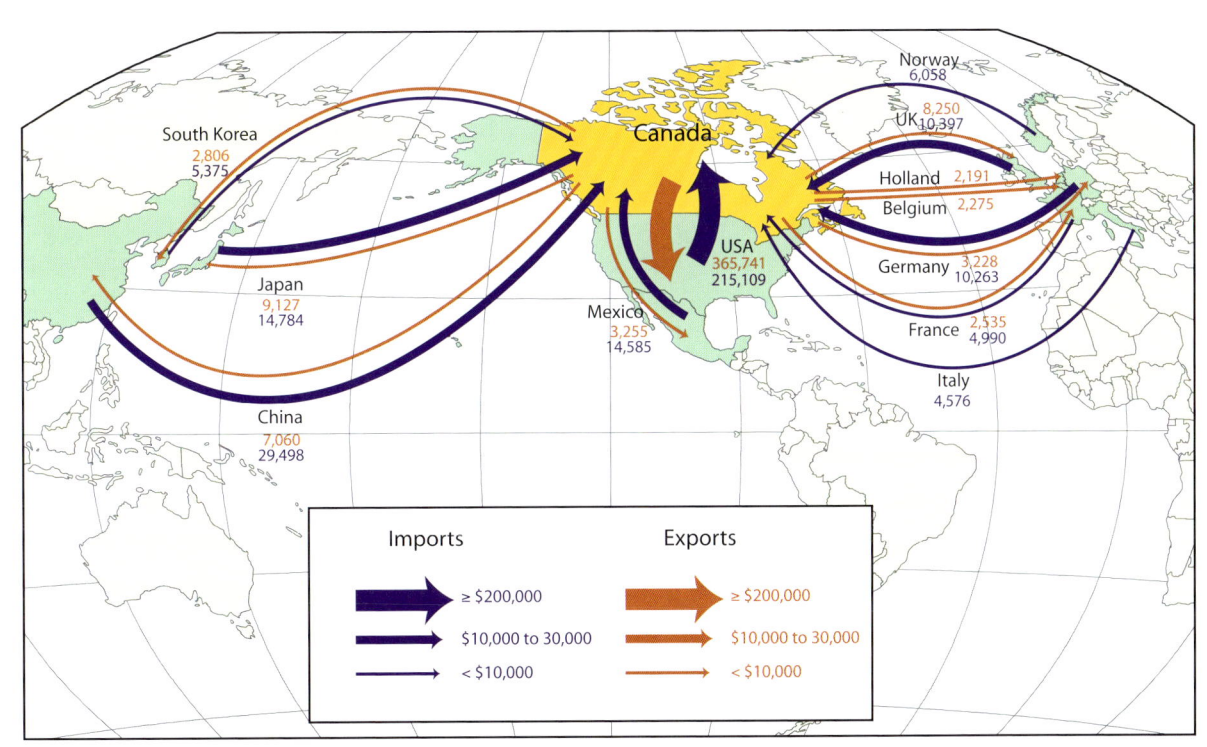

FIGURE 12.11 Canada's top 12 trading partners, in both imports and exports, in 2005 (millions of Canadian dollars).
Source: Data from Strategis Canada, http://strategis.gc.ca/sc_mrkti/tdst/tdo/tdo.php#tag

In 2002, the United States accused Canada of subsidizing the industry (supporting it through government grants). This, they said, puts US producers at a disadvantage. The United States imposed a 27 percent duty (tax) on imports of Canadian softwood.

Canada disputed the US tariffs. The case went to the NAFTA tribunal, and later to the WTO. Both bodies found the US tariffs to be excessive and unfair. The United States refused to return any money or lower the tariff. By 2006, it had collected $5 billion in taxes on Canadian lumber imports. Lumber exports to the United States collapsed. More than 15,000 forestry workers in Canada became unemployed.

On July 1, 2006, the two countries negotiated an agreement to end the softwood lumber dispute. The United States promised to return about $4 billion. But several provinces and major Canadian lumber producers opposed the agreement. They said it imposed unfair conditions on Canada.

FIGURE 12.12 In July 2006, five months after being sworn in as Canada's 22nd prime minister, Stephen Harper officially visited US President George W. Bush in Washington. What does this photo say to you about their relationship? Why do you think the softwood lumber agreement was not the focus of their joint press conference?

PAUSE, REFLECT, APPLY

1. Globalization is often described in terms of the world "shrinking." What is meant by this expression?
2. Look at the interconnections described in this section and then identify specific ways in which you are connected to the world beyond Canada.
3. Would you support or oppose a foreign transnational corporation's purchase of a local Canadian business? Explain your criteria.
4. Use the following items to create a table or diagram of your personal consumption of Canadian and US culture: TV shows, radio, publications, Web sites, sports events, and movies. For each item, list which products or services you use that are Canadian and which are American. Summarize your findings.
5. Referring to the map in Figure 12.11, list the top 10 countries for Canada's exports and imports. Note any differences that you think are important. Go to www.emp.ca/ccw to find more recent data.
6. When you watch US TV and movies, read US books and magazines, and listen to US music stations, do you detect cultural differences between Americans your age and Canadians? Create a Venn diagram to show differences and shared traits between the two cultures.
7. "Mad cow" disease stopped Manitoba cattle farmers from exporting to their biggest global customers: the United States and Japan. Both countries closed their borders to beef imports from Canada. Research the impact on Manitoba's cattle producers and the federal and provincial governments' response.

How Can Consumers Influence the Economy?

Throughout this book, you have looked at how citizens can positively influence Canada. You may be too young to vote, but you can question party policies and political and business leaders. What are their positions on the economy, transnationals, global trade, human rights, and foreign ownership? You can work alone or with others; individuals and groups can make a big difference in how the economy works.

NON-PROFIT ORGANIZATIONS AND CHARITIES

One sector (subdivision) of Canada's economy works differently from government and for-profit business. **Non-profit organizations** (NPOs) and charities exist to promote social well-being and civic improvement. Hundreds of thousands of Canadians work and volunteer in this sector.

NPOs and charities raise billions of dollars annually. Some produce goods and services—for example, Winnipeg-based Aboriginal Peoples Television Network, the first national broadcaster of programming by and for Aboriginal people in the world. All NPOs rely on fundraising and government grants to generate revenue.

NPOs and charities support everything from human rights, public health, heritage preservation, and environmental protection, to professional cooperation, arts, sports, and culture. You are probably familiar with such NPOs as the Humane Society, the David Suzuki Foundation, and the Terry Fox Foundation.

Consumer Action and Awareness

Some NPOs publish 'zines and Web sites on being responsible consumers. Information is available on sweatshops, child labour, "green" shopping, fair trade, investing in your community, which businesses to patronize and which to avoid, and more.

At the school level, a number of student groups in Canada have convinced school boards to adopt "sweatshop" policies. Such boards do not purchase merchandise that has been made in sweatshops, that is, through child labour or forced labour, unfair wages, discrimination, denial of reproductive rights, and so on. Policies like these prove that socially responsible consumers can make demands—and make a difference.

> **KEY QUESTION**
> What limits, if any, should be placed on the way business is conducted in Canada?

> **DISCUSSION POINT**
> Manitoba often leads Canada in the percentage of income that citizens and businesses donate to charities and NPOs. What might account for this?

> **DID YOU KNOW**
> Studies consistently show that, on average, Americans donate almost twice as much to charities as Canadians.

> **THE WEB**
> Many Manitoba NPOs and charities involve youth. Explore them and others at www.emp.ca/ccw

SOCIAL AWARENESS AND CORPORATE SOCIAL RESPONSIBILITY

As a consumer, you can also get businesses, even transnationals, to listen. They may change their practices and products as a result.

Consumer pressure has led many businesses to adopt voluntary standards of corporate social responsibility (CSR). These guidelines are meant to ensure that businesses don't shortchange social responsibilities in order to make a profit.

To achieve a high CSR rating, a business may use a variety of strategies:

- pay employees to do charity and community work during work hours
- sponsor NPOs and charities
- provide safe working conditions and pay fair wages
- respect the rights of workers
- maintain affirmative action programs
- promote environmental respect and protection
- practise sustainable development and environmental stewardship
- protect the consumer through fair prices and reliable quality.

What will motivate businesses to respect CSR standards? Altruism (doing something selflessly, because it is right) and philanthropy (giving for the good of the community or humanity) might motivate some.

By being socially responsible, businesses may

- become more appealing to consumers
- attract and keep more skilled employees
- reduce costs by reducing waste
- pay lower taxes because of donations, and employment and environmental policies
- raise their profile by sponsoring community and arts events.

THE WEB
Find more information about socially responsible corporations at www.emp.ca/ccw

BACK TO THE FUTURE: SOME BASIC QUESTIONS

Figure 12.13 shows what an average Canadian household will spend for eight basic items in a typical year (2004). It lists broad, provincial costs for Manitoba, Newfoundland and Labrador, and Ontario. Which items are wants, and which are needs?

Consider how the dollar amounts in Figure 12.13 would change if we did not have publicly funded education. Private schools cost $10,000 to

| | Average Household | | | |
Expenditures	Canada	Manitoba	Newfoundland and Labrador	Ontario
Total expenditures	$63,636	$56,317	$49,867	$71,583
Food	6,910	6,414	6,180	7,106
Shelter	12,200	9,582	8,259	14,679
Clothing	2,506	2,260	2,296	2,830
Health care	1,690	1,467	1,448	1,471
Transportation	8,626	7,726	7,333	9,851
Education	1,078	722	719	1,383
Recreation	3,678	3,392	3,274	3,883
Charitable giving	1,652	2,007	1,193	1,996

FIGURE 12.13 Average household expenditures in Canada, 2004. *Source: Statistics Canada, www40.statcan.ca/l01/cst01/famil16a.htm and www40.statcan.ca/l01/cst01/famil16d.htm*

$20,000 a year. What if we did not have public health care? How much would it cost to visit a doctor, have blood tests, get shots, stay in the hospital? What if there were no public transportation? What if we had to pay tolls on every highway?

Canada is a consumer-based economy. The consumer-driven (demand) part of it relies on profit. We count on private businesses to produce goods and services that the public needs and wants to buy. Canada's prosperity rests on businesses creating new, better, more inventive, more fashionable, faster, and more advanced goods and services.

Combining the "command" side of the economy with the "demand" side raises some basic questions:

1. How do we make sure that what is produced is best for Canada and meets the needs of all citizens?
2. How can we stay connected to the wonders, riches, and knowledge of the world if we try to "protect" ourselves—our cultures, languages, industries—and not be part of the global economy?
3. How do we make sure that all peoples of the world, including all our citizens, have the opportunity to benefit from a global economy?
4. If, as consumers, we always look to buy at the lowest price, can we be sure that we are not
    a) exploiting workers in other countries
    b) damaging the global environment
    c) sacrificing jobs here at home

d) using up resources that future generations might need?
How can we make the best choices?
5. Does the "shrinking world" make it less or more difficult to preserve our cultures and identities, and control our society? What evidence can we bring forward to support our view? What can we do to resolve problems?

PAUSE, REFLECT, APPLY

1. a) Describe how non-profit organizations operate in the economy.
   b) On what basis do NPOs distribute wealth and resources?
2. Looking at Figure 12.13, in which province would it cost the most to live? Why might that province have such high costs?
3. What is meant by the phrase "average household expenditure"?
4. What is the single biggest advantage to living in a consumer-demand economy?
5. What is the single biggest advantage to a global economy?
6. Select two of the basic questions from the list above. Using this chapter, your own thoughts, and peer and class discussion, provide some possible answers to these questions.
7. Conduct a poll among your parents, relatives, and neighbours. How many of these people work in private business, government, and non-profit jobs? Ask: "Do you think you work for a socially responsible employer?" Use the criteria listed above. Make a class list of the different jobs and the CSR companies.

REPLAY

In this chapter, you have explored these concepts:

1. Being aware of Canada as a more developed country helps us understand our economy and our links with the world.
2. Canada has developed through economic stages.
3. Because economic development has been uneven across Canada, we must be aware of the different "economies" of the country's regions.
4. As a mixed economy, Canada combines features of a demand economy (private enterprise, consumer-based) and a command economy (government controlled).
5. In a "globalizing" world, countries become interdependent through international trade, communications, culture, migration, and travel.
6. Transnational corporations drive globalization; tariffs and protectionism work against it.
7. Consumer activism can influence businesses to practise corporate social responsibility.

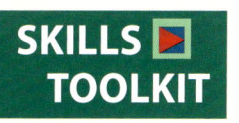

SKILLS TOOLKIT: How to Select, Use, and Interpret Graphs

Good graphs can often communicate economic information more quickly, visually, and meaningfully than words or numbers alone. Here we explore three types of graphs: pie, bar, and line. These are often used in the media and social sciences. Knowing how and when to use and interpret them is an important literacy skill.

Pie Graph

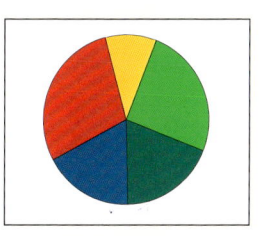

The pie graph is an ideal way to show percentages or fractions. For example, Figure 6.2 on page 116 breaks down a provincial budget. A pie graph could also show how various brands share a market. For example, companies A, B, and C sell "widgets." Company A sells 20 percent of all widgets. To calculate its "slice" of the market is simple: 20% × 360 degrees (the whole circle) = 72 degrees. You would then do the same calculation for the other companies.

Bar Graph

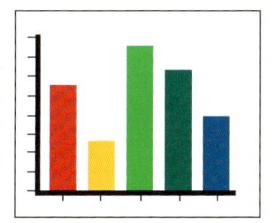

The bar graph compares different numbers or amounts very effectively. It is created using a horizontal X axis and vertical Y axis. Either axis can be the constant. (See Figure 13.11 on page 284 and Figure 14.1 on page 294 for two examples.) Let's say you want to compare the number of widgets sold in each of the western provinces. For vertical bars, you would mark off a scale along the vertical Y axis showing, perhaps, thousands of widgets. On the X axis you would mark off the constant: the provinces. Using your data, you would then plot a bar for each province.

Line Graph

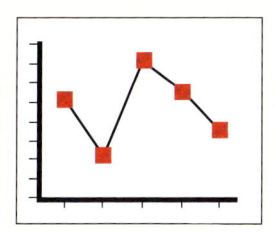

The line graph is often used to show something changing over time. Figure 12.8, on page 257, for example, looks at foreign ownership in Canada over a period of 35 years. Line graphs also use the X–Y axis model. Let's say you want to chart annual sales of Company B's widgets from 2000 to 2010. You use the Y axis to provide the scale for numbers of widgets sold and the X axis to show the constant, in this case the years. Above each year you would measure up and place a dot at the correct spot. Once dots are drawn for each year, you would draw a line joining the dots.

Skill Practice

(Because graphing involves mathematical skills, your math teacher may be a helpful resource.)

1. Using the following numbers, make a pie graph, a bar graph, or a line graph. First, show the percentage of sales among companies A, B, and C in 2005. Second, show Company B's sales in each western province. Third, show Company C's sales from 2000 to 2007. Your major decision is to select the most appropriate graph.
   a) Industry Widget Sales (in thousands), 2005: Company A, 300; Company B, 200; Company C, 500; Total Market, 1,000
   b) Company B Widget Sales (in thousands), 2005: British Columbia, 50; Alberta, 200; Saskatchewan, 100; Manitoba, 150
   c) Company C Widget Sales (in thousands), 2000–2007: 2000 = 200; 2001 = 500; 2002 = 600; 2003 = 300; 2004 = 400; 2005 = 200; 2006 = 250; 2007 = 600
2. Why is "pie" used to name one of the graphs?
3. How and why would a line graph be an effective way for businesses to examine sales records?
4. Why is it helpful to use graphs together with written text to provide statistical information?
5. Industry Canada provides extensive trade information online. Check out the data at www.emp.ca/ccw. Then, run a detailed report on Manitoba's international trade over the past five years with the top 10 countries. Create a pie, bar, or line graph to show what you think is important information about Manitoba's trade connections.

STUDY HALL

Be Informed

1. Provide two examples of the ways in which the world is interconnected. Select ways that directly affect your life on a daily or regular basis and explain how.

2. You teach it: Select two Key Terms from this chapter. Explain them in such a way that a new student could easily understand them, using your own examples. Some terms to choose from include economy, demand economy, command economy, mixed economy, globalization, free trade, and so on. (Your teacher may want to divide terms among the class as a class project.)

Be Purposeful

3. Israel, South Korea, and Singapore are all classified by the United Nations as less developed countries. Identify them on a map and state whether you think each would be better described as a more developed country. Conduct economic research to justify your responses.

4. Dividing Canada into heartland and hinterland may affect regional and national identity. Create a mind map showing the usefulness of these terms, and the implications of their use.

5. Fish, fur, lumber, wheat, and mining products were all once staple products. Create a presentation based on the suggestion that the history of Canada is a history of staple production.

6. Use the following data on Canadians' spending on culture (in 2003) to construct a pie graph, bar graph, or line graph.
   - By category: 52% on home entertainment, 9% on works of art, 20% on reading materials, 9% on photography, 6% on movie theatres, 4% on musical instruments and art supplies
   - Per capita: British Columbia $787, Manitoba $739, Ontario $802, Quebec $677, Newfoundland and Labrador $607
   - Movie admissions ($ billions): 1997, 0.8; 1998, 0.9; 1999, 1; 2000, 1.1; 2001, 1.15; 2002, 1.3; 2003, 1.25
   - Museum and heritage site admissions ($ billions): 1997, 0.35; 1998, 0.35; 1999, 0.35; 2000, 0.35; 2001, 0.35; 2002, 0.4; 2003, 0.4

7. Referring to the data in activity 6, explain whether it is worthwhile in a demand economy for government and businesses to build and run museums and historical sites. Should we simply build more movie theatres? What, besides profit, should influence these decisions?

8. Your family owns a small cattle business. A transnational corporation offers to buy it. Before making your decision, brainstorm. Create criteria (e.g., price, effect on family, effect on Canadian workers, impact on less developed countries, etc.) on which to base your decision. Explain why the criteria are important, and rank them. Write out your decision based on your criteria.

9. It's election time. The Globcan Party supports free trade and globalization, while the Autarky Party is against them. Select one party, and write the script/storyboard for a clear one- or two-minute advertisement for radio, TV, or the Internet. Describe your images and audio and other effects.

Be Active

10. Referring to the pre-industrial, industrial, and post-industrial stages of development, think about Canada's history and identify some of the activities in your community that belong to each stage.

11. Create a map showing the regions of Canada and whether each region has entered the post-industrial stage. Under the map, list reasons why regions pass through these stages at different times. Finally, consider whether the word "development" is culturally appropriate for you

STUDY HALL (cont.)

and your community when describing transitions through these stages.

12. Read the business section of a newspaper for a week. Clip stories that have implications for your family's jobs, purchasing decisions, savings, or lives in some way—or the life of your community. Select three stories and explain the implications. Discuss and compare with your classmates, but write your own analysis of your own stories. Be sure to show connections between each item or issue and your life. (Example: A story about Sirius Satellite Radio describes it as a financial success; many people, like you, listen to it, but Sirius is making it harder for Canadian broadcasters to stay in business.)

13. Conduct a household survey: List 20 to 30 goods or services that you have recently consumed. Now, create a map of the world showing where they were produced. Use your map to demonstrate what you have observed about the cultural, political, economic, and social impact of globalization on you, your family, and your community.

14. If you had to decide between buying Canadian and non-Canadian products, which of the following criteria would most influence your decision? Place them in priority order and state your reasons. Also keep in mind local and Manitoba businesses and Manitoba's economic needs.

- price
- brand
- Canadian jobs
- quality (how durable)
- advertising
- personal taste
- child labour
- needs of less developed countries
- patriotism

CHAPTER 13
Canada in the Global Community

Employees make shoes at a factory in Zhongshan, China.

What You Need to Know
- What are the responsibilities of global citizenship?
- How can you combat racism?
- How did international law change to recognize human rights?
- How has Canada contributed to universal human rights?
- How has Canada contributed to international aid and development?
- How is Canada connected to other nations through culture and sports?
- How can using multimedia tools enhance your presentations?

Key Terms
global citizenship
Geneva Conventions
genocide
Nuremberg trials
International Criminal Court (ICC)
non-governmental organizations (NGOs)
foreign aid

Key Question
How and why did Canada and the world come to recognize the importance of universal human rights?

"We have a factory in China where we have 250 people. We own them; it's our factory. We pay them $40 per month and they work 28 days a month. They work from 7 a.m. to 11 p.m. [that's nine cents per hour]. They all eat together, 16 people to a room, stacked on four bunks to a corner. Generally, they're young girls from the hills."

—President of Ava-Line (a company that makes lapel pins), *Business News*, August 21, 1996, p. 98

How could this company and others like it be held accountable for their treatment of workers? How might you feel if one of your family members worked in that factory?

268

What Is Global Citizenship?

There is no official certificate or ceremony to make one a global citizen. **Global citizenship** is a state of mind, an attitude. People who call themselves global citizens usually have certain attitudes and interests. They

- appreciate that the peoples and countries of the world are all interconnected
- understand that poverty, pollution, epidemics, natural disasters, and terrorism require international cooperation
- respect diversity and the human rights and perspectives of all peoples
- realize that Canada is not the centre of the universe
- take action to make the world a more just place.

In this chapter, you will have the opportunity to explore how Canada—through its people and governments—has responded to the call to think and act globally.

PROTECTING HUMAN RIGHTS INTERNATIONALLY

At the start of this course, you learned that the United Nations passed the *Universal Declaration of Human Rights* in 1948. The time was right for many reasons:

- World War II (1939–1945) had shown what can happen to people when human rights are violated.
- In Europe, some governments became authoritarian. They violated the rights of citizens and invaded other nations.
- A few brave people resisted and inspired others by showing the power of the individual to effect change.

Before 1948, nations had agreed to many human rights principles, although the term "human rights" was not used. In the early 19th century, for example, Britain led other countries in abolishing the slave trade. Some prominent British abolitionists included William Wilberforce, Olaudah Equiano (who came to London via Nigeria), and Harriet Martineau. These people were activists. They were global citizens because they spoke out about global injustice. Martineau, for example,

> **KEY QUESTION**
> What does it mean to be a global citizen?

> **DID YOU KNOW**
> A Canadian Museum for Human Rights—destined to be the largest museum of its kind—is planned for Winnipeg, Manitoba. Manitoba was chosen as the location because it is the "crossroads of Canada." The idea for the museum came from the late businessman Israel Asper and the Asper Foundation.

wrote that American slavery made a "mockery" of America's ideals of justice and freedom.

Henri Dunant, a Swiss, was another global citizen. Around 1860, he travelled to Italy to visit a battlefield. He was stunned when he saw thousands of wounded soldiers left to die. Dunant wrote a book, and his graphic portrayal of the problem prompted his government to establish the Red Cross. The Swiss government also held the first of a series of international conferences to establish rules for war. The first of the four **Geneva Conventions** was signed in 1864. It protected the sick and wounded in wartime.

Slowly, a body of international law began to come together to protect the rights of all citizens, no matter what their situation or the activities of their governments.

FIGURE 13.1 Harriet Martineau, an anti-slavery activist and global citizen of the 19th century. How might Martineau's perspective as a woman have influenced her sense of social justice?

TYRANNICAL REGIMES IN EUROPE

During the early 1900s, several European nations experienced upheavals. In the fall of 1917, a communist revolution overthrew the Russian monarchy. **Communism** promised to free the people from the tyranny of the monarchy and improve life for all Russians. What happened instead was that Vladimir Lenin and, later, Joseph Stalin led the Communist Party as dictators.

To increase production and industrialize the Soviet Union rapidly, Stalin eliminated all private ownership. The state would own and run all factories. It would also own and run all farms as "collectives." The peasant farmers, however, resisted. Stalin sent the army to crush them. Millions of peasants were deported to Siberia to die of cold and hunger. Food production collapsed, and famine swept over Russia.

In 1935, Stalin decided to eliminate all possible political opposition. He set up a system of informers, secret police, and torture. Thousands of Russians were charged with treason and either shot or sent to labour camps in Siberia.

FASCISM IN GERMANY AND ITALY

At the same time, and as the Great Depression (see Figure 12.9, page 258) was spreading hardship throughout Europe, dictators gained power in

Italy and Germany. They established governments based on **fascism**, a political system that played on people's fears and appealed to extreme nationalism and patriotism as the solution to all problems. Fascist governments are anti-democratic, anti-communist, and authoritarian. They encourage citizens to believe that the nation and its government can do no wrong, and that any kind of measure to protect and promote national greatness can be justified. Fascist governments ruthlessly suppress all opposition.

Germany's fascist dictator (from 1933 to 1945) was Adolf Hitler. Hitler preached **anti-Semitism** (hatred of Jews) and blamed all of Germany's economic problems on "the Jews." His Nazi Party passed laws that stripped German Jews of all property and all rights—legal, civil, and economic. Eventually, Hitler moved from persecuting Jews to imposing an official Nazi policy, the "final solution"—the extermination of all Jews.

Nazi Germany pursued its policy with ruthless efficiency and a huge commitment of human and material resources. Millions of Jews from across Nazi-occupied Europe—men, women, and children—were rounded up. Often, they were shipped in boxcars, like cattle, to camps where they were worked to death or subjected to mass extermination.

Decades later, the question of what ordinary Germans could have or should have done is still being debated.

FIGURE 13.2 Nazis burn books in Berlin in this famous 1933 photograph. The books were looted from the Institute for Sexual Science. The Institute conducted research into human sexuality. It advocated social reform, including decriminalizing homosexual acts. Why would the Nazis condemn the books as "un-German"? What do you think happened to the Institute?

OTHER NATIONS RESPOND

DISCUSSION POINT
Is "no action" sometimes an action? Explain your point of view.

THE WEB
Link to The Righteous Among the Nations, an Israeli program that honours individuals who risked their lives to save Jewish people from the camps, at www.emp.ca/ccw

How did Western democracies respond to these mass murders numbering in the millions? The world was not well informed about the crimes committed by Stalin against the Russian people; the communist government hid its secrets well. However, the conditions that Jews faced in Germany were gradually being publicized.

In 1938, after Germany seized Austria, Austrian Jews tried to flee to the United States, Britain, Canada, and other countries. That year, US President Franklin Delano Roosevelt held an international conference in Evian, France, to address the problem. Thirty-two countries attended; Germany was not invited.

During the nine-day Evian Conference, delegate after delegate expressed sympathy for Jewish refugees. But only one country—the Dominican Republic—offered to accept more Jewish refugees desperate to escape the Nazis.

SOURCES

Canadian Complicity

... Tim Reid's link to the Holocaust—although he has no recollection of it—dates back to 1939. He was just three years old.

His father, a newly minted Foreign Service officer, was second secretary at the Canadian Embassy in Washington. One of Escott Reid's jobs was to turn away Jews who wanted to bring their relatives into the United States through Canada.

The U.S. had a quota for accepting Jews but it was filled. Desperate to get their loved ones out of Germany as Adolf Hitler herded them into urban ghettoes, American Jews begged for Canada's help.

It tore Reid apart to say no. "Every time one of them comes in it leaves me shaken and ashamed of Canada," the young diplomat wrote. "It's like being a bystander at an especially cruel and long drawn-out murder. If I could find a loophole, I'd feel I'd justified my existence."

Reid did everything in his power to convince his superiors in Ottawa to relax their opposition to Jewish immigration. He made the case on humanitarian grounds, arguing that Canada could at least let in children. He tried economics, arguing that Canada needed the dollars that European Jews would bring to finance the war effort. ...

During the 12-year Nazi regime, Canada let in just 5,000 Jews, as Irving Abella and Harold Troper recount in their heart-rending book, *None Is Too Many*. (The U.S. admitted 200,000; Britain accepted 70,000; and Argentina took 50,000). ...

It doesn't seem possible to say "never again" without understanding the forces that allowed a nation such as Canada to slam the gates on refugees facing almost certain death.

And it doesn't seem fair to overlook the fact that a few principled public servants dared to speak out against their own government. ...

Source: Carol Goar, "The Man Who Said No to Evil," *The Toronto Star*, Friday, February 4, 2005, p. A20

PUTTING WAR CRIMINALS ON TRIAL

After World War II ended in 1945, the world saw pictures of the dead and dying in the concentration camps scattered all over Eastern and Central Europe and Germany. The countries that had defeated Germany charged those who directed the "final solution" with **genocide**.

Twenty-two German leaders were tried during the **Nuremberg trials**, including Hermann Göring, second in command to Hitler. They were charged as individuals for planning an aggressive war, and with the murder of millions of people. It was the first time that individual leaders and military officers were held personally responsible for war crimes.

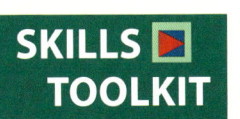

SKILLS TOOLKIT

How to Respond to a Racist Remark

Your best friend utters a racist remark about a classmate. What do you do? You know what is at stake—justice itself. But that can feel rather abstract when you are in the middle of the situation. What can you do to make a difference?

Something you could do is tell your friend a story:

About 195,000 years ago, a new species of humans, Homo sapiens sapiens, evolved in Africa and migrated around the world, replacing all earlier human species. All humans today are members of this one species. As this species migrated around the world, its members settled in different places. Each group developed different cultural characteristics, including different languages.

Some minor biological evolution also occurred over those 195,000 years, as groups adapted to their natural environment. The most visible of these adaptations is skin colour, with warm environments favouring darker skin colours and cool environments favouring lighter skin colours. However, these minor biological variations do not alter the fact that all humans belong to a single species, Homo sapiens sapiens.

Your friend may ask, "Does that mean there is no such thing as race?"

Yes, that is exactly what it means.

Race is a biological concept that refers to a genetically distinct subgroup of a species. There is no such thing as "race" within the human species. There are genetic differences between individuals because of the long period of isolation of groups in different environments. But these differences do not add up to separate races.

The idea that the human species can be divided into several distinct races—what might be called the fallacy of race—was thought to be true by most people until quite recently. This fallacy was often accompanied by **racism**, which is the assumption that so-called races possess different levels of intelligence and ability. Today, race is a category of discrimination in human rights codes around the world. However, these codes are based solely on currently accepted political beliefs. Maybe one day, these human rights codes will recognize that race is more "social invention" than science.

Don't let your friends make the race mistake. You can make a difference by speaking up.

Skill Practice

1. Paraphrase (rewrite in your own words) the information on race that appears above. Then use the Web site below to check your understanding and for additional information.
2. Imagine that someone makes a racist remark in your presence. Practise how you can counteract that remark by referring to the fallacy of race in your own words. Be sure to refer to your answer to question 1. You can practise in front of a mirror or with a partner.
3. Look for evidence of racist content in media sources, and bring these to the attention of your class. Analyze what is racist about the writing or visuals (refer to the Skills Toolkit in Chapter 3, page 68), and discuss why such content is inappropriate.

THE WEB ▶▶▶
Visit www.emp.ca/ccw for more information on the evolution of humans and a clear statement on the myth of race and its relationship to human intelligence.

PAUSE, REFLECT, APPLY

1. Why do you think countries could more easily agree on human rights violations during wartime than in peacetime?
2. How can individuals make a difference by protesting the mistreatment of people?
3. Why can't universal human rights be enforced?
4. How did the Evian Conference expose the prejudices of Western democracies? How could it have encouraged the Nazis to go even further in their persecution of Jews and other minorities?
5. Defence lawyers for the German leaders being tried at Nuremberg for genocide argued that the victors (the Allies) were looking for revenge, not justice. They argued that the individual officers could not be held responsible for the actions of a country because they were simply following orders. What do you think of this defence?

Human Rights Since the Universal Declaration

▶ **KEY QUESTION**
What impact has the *Universal Declaration of Human Rights* had on human rights?

The *Universal Declaration of Human Rights* (UDHR) has never had the force of law (see Chapter 1). Instead, it is a guideline that nations can follow or an ideal to which they can aspire. The *Canadian Charter of Rights and Freedoms*, for example, echoes the UDHR's ideals.

The UDHR has inspired other UN human rights agreements (see Figure 13.3, page 275).

These conventions have addressed emerging violations of human rights. For example, the use of child soldiers in combat prompted protocols (additions) to the original *Convention on the Rights of the Child*. Pledging governments agreed not to force children to bear arms.

Some UN Conventions

Agreement	Purpose
Convention on Genocide (1948)	Defined genocide as the attempt to destroy a national or racial group, and forced governments to recognize genocide as a crime against humanity
Convention on the Elimination of All Forms of Discrimination Against Women (1979)	Urged nations to abolish all laws and customs that discriminated against women
Convention Against Torture (1984)	Defined torture by the state against a citizen and outlawed it
Convention on the Rights of the Child (1989)	Outlined the rights of children, including the right to protection from harmful influences, abuse, and exploitation, and to participate fully in family, cultural, and social life

FIGURE 13.3 Why do you think it took so long for children's rights to be recognized?

FIGURE 13.4 An Amnesty International march marking International Human Rights Day, December 10, 2002, in Belleville, Ontario. Such events raise public awareness of human rights violations by governments. How effective are they in getting governments to take action?

RWANDA: A UN FAILURE

The United Nations' ideal of peacekeeping failed in Rwanda. The small central African country is composed primarily of two peoples, the majority Hutu and the minority Tutsi. As a colony of Belgium (1919–1945), Rwanda and its people were brutally exploited. The Belgians favoured the Tutsi and gave them more power than the Hutu. This created tension between the two groups.

In the 1950s, power shifted as administrators began replacing Tutsi authorities with Hutu. Many displaced Tutsi resettled elsewhere in Rwanda; another 10,000 fled as refugees. In 1961, some of these refugees began to attack Rwanda. Hutu officials later retaliated by attacking Tutsi inside Rwanda. During these years, some 20,000 Tutsi were killed; more than 300,000 fled abroad.

Open conflict between the groups erupted in the 1990s. In response, a UN peacekeeping force, under the command of Canadian General Roméo Dallaire, was sent to restore order in 1994 (see Chapter 2, page 47, and Chapter 14, page 304). Dallaire and various humanitarian groups warned of a possible disaster. He asked the UN to send more troops and for permission to use force to protect civilians.

When a plane carrying the Hutu president was shot down in April 1994, Tutsi were blamed. Almost immediately, some Hutu began to slaughter Tutsi and moderate Hutu with machetes. Moving from the towns into the countryside, they hacked to death hundreds of thousands of men, women, and children.

Dallaire's plea for help to UN headquarters in New York went unanswered. No major power would get involved. Dallaire's small forces could not use their weapons—not even to save lives. Then, Belgium pulled its peacekeepers out of Rwanda when 11 of its soldiers were killed. In July 1994, after the extremist Hutu government lost power, many Tutsi sought revenge. By the time the slaughter ended, close to 1 million people, most of them Tutsi, had been killed.

> **LITERACY COACH**
>
> After you read a profile or a description of someone featured in this textbook, write down any questions you have about that person's life and work. Then, type the person's name into a search engine. Click on the top three articles the search returns and try to find the answers to your questions. If you can't, refine your search by typing in more key words, such as "Roméo Dallaire" or "Belgian soldiers."

> ▶ **DID YOU KNOW** ◀
>
> "In the 20th century, genocides and state mass murder have killed more people than have all wars."
>
> —Web homepage banner for the Institute for the Study of Genocide (www.isg-iags.org)

Year	Region	Number of Deaths
2003–2006	Darfur	400,000
1992–1999	Sierra Leone	*
1992–1995	Bosnia–Herzegovina	*
1994	Rwanda	1,000,000
1988	Iran (Kurds)	5,000
1975–1979	Cambodia (Pol Pot)	2,000,000
1975–1979	East Timor	*
1972	Burundi	*
1965–1966	Indonesia	*
1938–1945	Germany (the Holocaust)	6,000,000
1937–1938	Nanking	300,000
1932–1933	Ukraine (forced famine)	5,000,000
1915–1919	Turkey (Armenians)	1,500,000

* Statistics in dispute

FIGURE 13.5 Genocides in the 20th and 21st centuries

The UN had failed to prevent another genocide, one of the very reasons it had been founded.

Following the Rwandan genocide, the UN set up an international tribunal (special court) to try individuals accused of the killings. Similar tribunals tried those associated with conflicts in the former Yugoslavia (now Serbia, Croatia, Bosnia–Herzegovina, Kosovo, and Montenegro).

THE INTERNATIONAL CRIMINAL COURT

For many years, human rights advocates tried to set up a permanent international court to prosecute individuals responsible for genocide, crimes against humanity, and war crimes. In July 2002, that goal was achieved with the establishment of the **International Criminal Court (ICC)** at The Hague in the Netherlands. The ICC works with national courts, acting only when countries are unable or unwilling to investigate or prosecute suspected war criminals.

THE WEB
Learn more about the ICC at www.emp.ca/ccw

The court was ratified (formally approved and recognized) by 120 countries. Seven voted against it, including the United States, China, and Israel. These governments were reluctant to give power to an outside body that might, for political reasons, try to punish their soldiers and citizens.

A Canadian chaired the first group that met in Rome to work out how an international court could be organized. Canada also helped finance poorer countries to send delegates to the Rome Conference. In 2003, in recognition of Canada's contribution, Canadian Philippe Kirsch was elected the first president of the ICC. Kirsch has also served as one of 18 judges from around the world elected to the court.

FIGURE 13.6 Canadian Louise Arbour received international attention when she was named chief prosecutor for the International Criminal Court. Today she is the human rights chief for the United Nations. Here, she is shown at a Cambodian jail that is now a genocide museum. Under a regime that lasted from 1975 to 1979, millions of Cambodians were tortured and killed in their own country for being too "western" or "urban." Why would Arbour take on this work, even if it includes death threats?

FACE OFF

The International Criminal Court: Giant Step or Stumble?

> In the promise of a universal criminal court lies the promise of universal justice.
>
> —UN Secretary General Kofi Annan, "War Crimes After Nuremberg"; www.law.umkc.edu/faculty/projects/ftrials/nuremberg/NurembergEpilogue.html

Supporters say that the International Criminal Court (ICC) is a great improvement over the tribunals set up to try war crimes. Tribunals set up to deal with Germany after World War II, and Rwanda and Yugoslavia in the 1990s, risked looking like victors trying the losers. But attempting to try individuals charged with crimes against humanity in the countries where those crimes were committed might mean no justice at all. A permanent international court with recognized laws and procedures was seen as a better alternative.

The ICC tries individuals only if their country of origin refuses or is unable to prosecute. The prosecutor and the 18 judges are chosen by a majority of the countries supporting the ICC. Countries can still try their own citizens under their own laws. The ICC is intended to complement, not compete with, national laws and procedures.

FIGURE 13.7 Judge Sylvia Steiner of Brazil (far left) is sworn in with other judges (seated) during the first session of the International Criminal Court in The Hague on March 11, 2003. Judges were sworn in by Prince Zaid of Jordan (far right).

> [The ICC] has the same flaw as all international institutions. In a world ruled by force, the rich and powerful [countries] do pretty much what they like. It is next to inconceivable that the ICC could try, even investigate, Western criminals.
>
> —Noam Chomsky, The ZNet Forum System, June 30, 2002; www.globalissues.org/Geopolitics/icc/intro.asp

Critics say that an international court to promote human rights can be effective only if it is recognized by the United States and China. The US government, however, believes that its citizens have the right to be tried only by US law. In fact, the United States has tried its own citizens for war crimes (for example, those committed in Vietnam and Iraq). Is there any reason to believe that an American guilty of crimes against humanity would be more lightly treated in a US court than at the ICC?

> [I]t appears that many of the legal safeguards American citizens enjoy under the U.S. Constitution would be suspended if they were brought before the court. Endangered constitutional protections include the prohibition against double jeopardy [being tried twice for the same crime], the right to trial by an impartial jury, and the right of the accused to confront the witnesses against him.
>
> —"Reasonable Doubt: The Case Against the Proposed International Criminal Court," Cato Institute; www.cato.org/pubs/pas/pa-311es.html

What Do You Think?

1. Do you think countries can handle their own human rights abuses without international institutions such as the ICC? Explain.
2. Who do you think should be tried by the ICC? Why?

> **PAUSE, REFLECT, APPLY**
>
> 1. Why were conventions and protocols needed to support the rights listed in the UDHR?
> 2. Does signing a convention or protocol solve or prevent human rights abuses?
> 3. What factors explain (but do not excuse) the Rwandan genocide?
> 4. What is the purpose of the ICC?

Canada: Facing the Human Rights Challenge

Canada's record in human rights has evolved. Over time, and pressured by individuals and groups, government respect for human rights at home improved dramatically.

Today, respect for human rights also influences relations with other countries. Canada not only helped found the UN, it has signed every UN human rights convention since 1948 (see Chapter 1, pages 9–10). Canada also accepts refugees from countries with poor human rights records. These refugees and many others want Canada to pressure those countries to reform.

Promoting human rights internationally makes sense in many ways. Governments that respect the rights of citizens are less likely to erupt into civil conflicts, creating a flood of refugees requiring humanitarian assistance.

> **KEY QUESTION**
> Has Canada been a poor, fair, good, or excellent global citizen when it comes to human rights?

> **DISCUSSION POINT**
> What does the record actually show about Canada and human rights since the *Universal Declaration of Human Rights* was signed in 1948?

NOT A PERFECT RECORD

Canada's human rights record is not perfect. In the past, Canada's immigration policy was called discriminatory and racist. Canada's treatment of Aboriginal persons has also been criticized, as has its treatment of certain ethnic groups during wartime (see Chapter 2, pages 28–30 and 38–41).

For example, during World War I (1914–1918), approximately 5,000 Ukrainian Canadians were interned (held) in camps in Alberta and Manitoba. Their newspapers and schools were closed. Why? Most Ukrainian Canadians had emigrated from an area administered by the Austro-Hungarian empire. During World War I, as a part of the British Empire, Canada was at war with Austro-Hungary.

> **DID YOU KNOW**
>
> Through the Aboriginal Holocaust and Hope program sponsored by B'nai Brith Canada, Aboriginal educators tour Israel to gain an understanding of Jewish culture. What are the advantages of this kind of cultural cooperation?

During World War II, Japanese Canadians were uprooted from their homes, separated from their families, and interned in camps. The government viewed Japanese Canadians on the West Coast as a security risk because Canada was at war with Germany, Italy, and Japan.

Although no Japanese Canadian was ever charged or convicted of being a spy, Japanese Canadians lost their homes, businesses, automobiles, and fishing boats (which were sold at a fraction of their worth). The camps were lonely, isolated places, where many families spent up to four years. Released at the end of the war, Japanese Canadians had to rebuild their lives and businesses. Some were deported to Japan, and many others left British Columbia to settle in Ontario. Many of those deported had been born and raised in British Columbia.

Canadian Reparations to the Japanese Community

For years, Japanese Canadian and human rights interest groups lobbied the Canadian government to apologize to all Japanese Canadians. In 1988, it did. Prime Minister Brian Mulroney said, "We cannot change the past. But we must, as a nation, have the courage to face up to these historical facts."

A $300 million compensation package included $21,000 for each of the 13,000 survivors, $12 million for a Japanese community fund, and

FIGURE 13.8 As a child, Canadian scientist David Suzuki was interned with his family in the British Columbia interior from 1942 until 1945. The Canadian government sold the Suzukis' dry-cleaning business and kept the money. The family was forced to move after the war, eventually settling in London, Ontario.

FIGURE 13.9 (Above:) An internment camp for Japanese Canadians, 1942. (Right:) This notice was distributed throughout British Columbia. Any Japanese Canadian found in a prohibited area would be jailed. How does the notice use race?

NOTICE TO ALL JAPANESE PERSONS AND PERSONS OF JAPANESE RACIAL ORIGIN

TAKE NOTICE that under Orders Nos. 21, 22, 23 and 24 of the British Columbia Security Commission, the following areas were made prohibited areas to all persons of the Japanese race:—

LULU ISLAND (including Steveston)	SAPPERTON
SEA ISLAND	BURQUITLAM
EBURNE	PORT MOODY
MARPOLE	IOCO
DISTRICT OF QUEENSBOROUGH	PORT COQUITLAM
CITY OF NEW WESTMINSTER	MAILLARDVILLE
	FRASER MILLS

AND FURTHER TAKE NOTICE that any person of the Japanese race found within any of the said prohibited areas without a written permit from the British Columbia Security Commission or the Royal Canadian Mounted Police shall be liable to the penalties provided under Order in Council P.C. 1665.

AUSTIN C. TAYLOR,
Chairman,
British Columbia Security Commission

$24 million to create a Canadian Race Relations Foundation, to ensure that such discrimination never happens again.

THE INTERNATIONAL CENTRE FOR HUMAN RIGHTS AND DEMOCRATIC DEVELOPMENT

In 1988, the Canadian government established the International Centre for Human Rights and Democratic Development. Its purpose is to educate Canadians about human rights issues and to work with other countries to promote human rights. In 1993, it warned of a looming human rights catastrophe in Rwanda (see page 276).

> **THE WEB** ▶▶▶
> Learn more about the Canadian Race Relations Foundation by linking to its Web site at www.emp.ca/ccw

PAUSE, REFLECT, APPLY

1. Why does Canada have an interest in promoting human rights in other countries?
2. a) Why did Canada take actions against Ukrainian Canadians during World War I and against Japanese Canadians during World War II?
   b) How did those actions violate the people affected?
3. How did the Canadian government compensate Japanese Canadians? In your opinion, was the compensation adequate? Explain.

> **KEY QUESTION**
> Has Canada been a poor, fair, good, or excellent global citizen in dealing with global humanitarian crises?

Canada's Foreign Policy

The federal government is in charge of Canada's international relations. Foreign Affairs Canada, International Trade Canada, and the Department of National Defence are three major departments that deal with international responsibilities.

As you have seen, Canada belongs to many international organizations and agencies, such as the World Trade Organization, the Organization of American States, and the United Nations. **Non-governmental organizations (NGOs)** also play a vital role in Canada's global relations (see Chapter 11).

FOREIGN AFFAIRS AND INTERNATIONAL TRADE

> **THE WEB**
> Visit the main page of Foreign Affairs and International Trade Canada for late-breaking updates on trade, travel, and international trouble spots at www.emp.ca/ccw

Foreign Affairs Canada manages Canada's international relations and maintains embassies and consulates in 180 countries. Ambassadors (top diplomats who officially represent a country) and their aides act as Canada's eyes, ears, and voice. These people listen carefully and bring insights to Canada's international relations. Foreign Affairs issues passports and assists Canadians who travel or live outside Canada.

> **THE WEB**
> For more on Zahra Kazemi, go to www.emp.ca/ccw

FIGURE 13.10 Stephan Hachemi sits outside Iran's embassy in Ottawa, July 2004, beside a portrait of his mother, Iranian-born Canadian photographer Zahra Kazemi. Kazemi died from a blow to the head while jailed in Iran for taking pictures of a student protest in June 2003. Hachemi wanted Canada to take the case to the International Court of Justice and criticized Foreign Affairs Canada for doing too little.

Through trade, countries interact and develop economically. International Trade Canada sends representatives around the world to locate potential buyers for Canadian goods and services. It also negotiates trade agreements with other governments and with businesses.

> **LITERACY COACH**
>
> When you read a statement or claim that intrigues or puzzles you, or that you agree or disagree with strongly, don't just skim over it. Write it down in your journal and continue to think about it. Or discuss it with a friend, as in, "Hey, do you think it's true that...?" Statements or claims that capture your attention can often turn into great essay topics.

THE CANADIAN INTERNATIONAL DEVELOPMENT AGENCY

The Canadian International Development Agency (CIDA) distributes approximately $3 billion a year in aid and loans. Funds are distributed through grants to projects in developing countries in Africa, Asia, the Middle East, and South and Central America. Funds for projects are granted either directly or through NGOs.

Since 1968, CIDA has funded projects in over 150 countries. Key development areas include

- basic human needs
- gender equality
- infrastructure (for example, water supply, electricity, communication networks)
- business
- the environment.

> **THE WEB** ▶▶▶
>
> Check out an application form for CIDA's Global Classroom Initiative at www.emp.ca/ccw

WORLD POVERTY AND FOREIGN POLICY

Recent Canadian and UN studies report that more than 1 billion people live in extreme poverty; 104 million children lack any kind of schooling; 1 billion people have no access to safe drinking water; and 2.4 billion people lack proper sanitation (see also Chapter 14).

Global poverty does not just happen. Neither do the foreign and trade policies of wealthy, more developed countries. The policies of more developed countries could be changed—and many critics say they must.

For instance, the more developed countries could invest in education and new industries in less developed countries. We could also reduce government subsidies (grants) that support our industries; our governments could adopt fairer trade policies with less developed countries. We could forgive debts owed to us by less developed countries.

Such policy changes, of course, would incur costs—perhaps higher prices for imported clothing and foodstuffs. Competition for jobs and business with the less developed world might also increase.

The 0.7 Percent Solution

Canada has a history of caring and of proposing solutions through **foreign aid** (assistance provided by one country to another).

In 1969, Prime Minister Lester Pearson led a panel of the world's wealthiest countries to set a goal for foreign aid to less developed countries: 0.7 percent of gross domestic product (GDP). The UN adopted the "0.7 percent solution," which has recently been reaffirmed by such celebrities as Bono of the rock band U2. How are we doing?

Annually, Canada pledges about $3 billion to foreign aid and development (2005), approximately 0.3 percent of our GDP. In the same year, the United States gave 0.13 percent. Of the world's wealthiest countries, only Norway (0.87 percent), Denmark (0.84 percent), Luxembourg (0.85 percent), Sweden (0.77 percent), and the Netherlands (0.74 percent) gave 0.7 percent or more of their GDP to foreign aid.

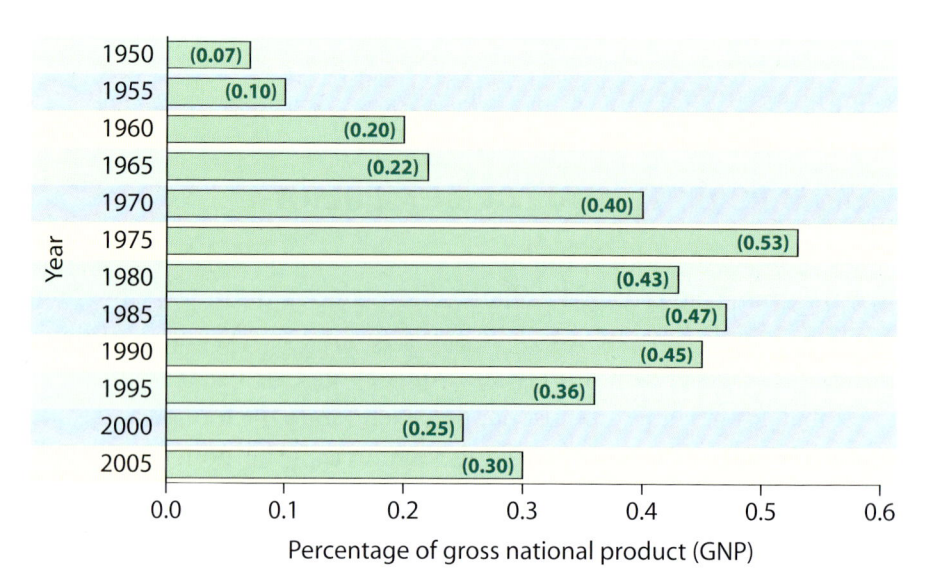

Year	Percentage of GNP
1950	0.07
1955	0.10
1960	0.20
1965	0.22
1970	0.40
1975	0.53
1980	0.43
1985	0.47
1990	0.45
1995	0.36
2000	0.25
2005	0.30

FIGURE 13.11 Canada's foreign aid contributions as a percentage of GNP (gross national product; similar to GDP) since 1950. When was the level highest? What has been the trend in the last decade? *Source: Data from Canadian International Development Agency, Statistical Report on Official Development Assistance, Fiscal Year 2003–2004, Table A, p. 1*

PAUSE, REFLECT, APPLY

1. Identify the three federal departments or agencies that deal with international relations, and describe the role of each.
2. What do the following abbreviations stand for? Explain the meaning or function of each: UN, CIDA, NGO, and GDP.
3. What kinds of projects does CIDA fund?
4. What policies of more developed countries can hurt less developed ones?
5. Describe the concept of the "0.7 percent solution."
6. When a celebrity embraces a cause, what do you think is achieved?

NGOs and International Relations

Non-governmental organizations work to improve the world. They are not associated with any government or political party and they don't work for profit. NGOs focus on longstanding global issues, such as poverty, hunger, disease, and educational needs. They also respond to sudden disasters, such as earthquakes, droughts, and political crises.

In Canada, CIDA fully or partially funds many NGOs. Each NGO must apply for sponsorship assistance, usually for a specific project. NGOs are also expected to raise funds through individual or business donations. CIDA inspects the work of the NGOs it funds, but it does not control staff or operations. Like service organizations, NGOs rely on volunteers.

NGOs operate on the belief that privately run projects administered by volunteers work better than government-run projects. Why? For one thing, NGOs can criticize government. And volunteers who work for NGOs do so out of a deep sense of commitment, not because it is their job.

Thousands of NGOs operate in Canada in a wide variety of areas (see Figure 13.12).

▶ KEY QUESTION
How can ordinary people improve the world without relying on governments?

▶ DID YOU KNOW ◀
Greenpeace founder Bob Hunter was born in Winnipeg. After his death in May 2005, his ashes were spread along a 300-km stretch of the Seal River in Northern Manitoba.

DOCTORS WITHOUT BORDERS

Médecins Sans Frontières (MSF), or Doctors Without Borders, is a well-known and widely respected NGO. Founded in France in 1971, MSF started in Canada in 1991. In 1999, MSF International won the Nobel Peace Prize.

When international crises occur, MSF sends staff to evaluate the local population's medical needs. It then recruits both medical and non-medical volunteers. Its resources and services include sanitation equipment; food,

Development	Environment	Humanitarian/Health	Human Rights
Canadian Council for International Cooperation	Greenpeace Canada	Canadian Red Cross	Amnesty International
CUSO	Pollution Probe	Care Canada	Free the Children
Development and Peace	Sierra Club of Canada	Doctors Without Borders	Human Rights Watch
Oxfam Canada	David Suzuki Foundation	Foster Parents Plan	Physicians for Human Rights

FIGURE 13.12 A few well-known NGOs operating in Canada

> **THE WEB**
> Link to the Canadian Council for International Cooperation (CCIC), a coalition to end global poverty, which lists hundreds of NGOs and campaigns on global issues, at www.emp.ca/ccw. Many organizations—such as Canadian Feed the Children, Operation Beaver, and Canada World Youth—have a youth focus.

water, supplements, and nutritional advice; and vaccinations and other medical services.

Like many NGOs, MSF trains local people to run its projects. Since 1991, the Canadian MSF has operated in more than 40 countries. Doctors and nurses who could be establishing well-paid careers sometimes volunteer years of their lives to this work.

DIFFERENT CRISES, DIFFERENT RESPONSES

On December 26, 2004, a massive earthquake under the Indian Ocean sent tsunamis (giant tidal waves) ripping through coastal areas in Asia. In Indonesia, Malaysia, Thailand, Sri Lanka, India, and Somalia, entire villages were swept away. More than 200,000 people were killed. Almost immediately, the news media broadcasted images of the devastation around the globe.

After the tsunami disaster, some NGOs, such as MSF, received more funds than they needed for tsunami relief. MSF asked the public to donate to other crises that desperately needed action—such as HIV/AIDS in Africa and Asia. (HIV stands for human immunodeficiency virus, which attacks the body's immune system and is believed to lead to acquired immune deficiency syndrome, or AIDS.)

The spread of HIV/AIDS in the less developed world is a terrible crisis. It is often overlooked by the wealthy countries of the developed world. A Canadian was appointed by the UN to advocate for change (see the CivicStar feature on page 287).

CivicStar

STEPHEN LEWIS

Even as a toddler, Stephen Lewis had a social conscience. It's something that has shaped his life. Lewis was elected to the Ontario legislature in the 1960s at 25 years of age. By the mid-1970s, he was leader of the Ontario NDP. In 1984, he was appointed Canadian ambassador to the UN. From 1995 to 1999, Lewis served as deputy executive director of the United Nations Children's Fund (UNICEF).

In 2001, Lewis was appointed UN Special Envoy for HIV/AIDS in Africa. The posting consumed him. No wonder. In 2005, the UN predicted that more than 80 million people in Africa would die of AIDS by 2025. If the international community does not do more, and soon, another 90 million Africans will become HIV positive in the same period.

In speeches around the world, Lewis describes a "litany of lunacy," from genocide and war crimes to epidemics and inhuman indifference. He condemns the growing gap between rich countries and poor.

Nowhere is the "lunacy" more heartbreaking than with HIV/AIDS in Africa. In sub-Saharan Africa alone, more than 25 million people are living with HIV/AIDS.

"Every day, there are more than 11,000 new infections in sub-Saharan Africa alone, half of them contracted by young people between the ages of 15 and 24," says Lewis.

"Country after country faces monumental dilemmas: what to do about mother-to-child transmission; how to establish a network of testing and counselling; where to find the money to pay for treatment; how to fashion a campaign of prevention for adolescents; above all, how to absorb 10 million orphans into extended families when there are no extended families left?"

Lewis's passionate speeches have raised public and political awareness of the catastrophe in Africa. Governments have increased aid. Pharmaceutical companies have made HIV/AIDS drugs more accessible. But for Lewis, the pace is cruelly slow. In 2005, he was invited to give the annual Massey Lecture at the University of Toronto. He opened his lecture by saying, "I have spent the last four years watching people die."

Lewis works seven days a week, 17 to 19 hours a day. He has admitted that his commitment may have "an element of the irrational to it." But knowing what he knows, seeing what he has seen, what else can he do?

Your Play

1. How does Stephen Lewis demonstrate global citizenship in action?
2. Create a table or graph comparing the populations of Canada and Ontario with the numbers of people living, dying, and being infected with HIV/AIDS in Africa from 2004 to the present day. Include AIDS orphans.
3. Locate the Web site of the Stephen Lewis Foundation, and report on three ideas for actions that you can take.

CANADA ON THE WORLD STAGE

Canada participates in many international cultural and sporting events. As a member of the Commonwealth, a voluntary organization of 53 countries, Canada also helps to promote democracy, fair government, and human rights. Some of the Commonwealth's specific goals include

- protecting citizens' personal freedoms
- recognizing racial equality and the need to combat racism
- working to minimize the disparities between poor and rich countries of the world.

> **DID YOU KNOW**
> Canada hosted the Francophonie summits in Quebec City in 1987 and in Moncton, New Brunswick in 1999.

In the 1990s, Canada took a lead role in the Commonwealth in demanding the end of apartheid in South Africa. As you learned in Chapter 4, Canada also belongs to La Francophonie, an international organization of French-speaking countries that promotes culture, human rights, and democracy among member states.

Canada has a long and proud record of participating in the Olympic Games, and has been awarded both the summer games (Montreal, Quebec, 1976) and the winter games (Calgary, Alberta, 1988; Vancouver/Whistler, British Columbia, 2010).

Canadian Dick Pound became one of the most powerful members of the International Olympic Committee (IOC). He was the first person to convince the IOC to brand and market the "Olympic rings" logo. Pound also negotiated profitable television rights for the Olympics. Today, Pound heads the World Anti-Doping Agency. He speaks out regularly about drug use and corruption in sports.

FIGURE 13.13 A drummer drums a prayer song in Whistler, BC, to celebrate the announcement by Olympics officials and local chiefs that a First Nations cultural centre will be built near the 2010 Olympics site. The Squamish Lil'Wat Cultural Centre will include a First Nations village, a ceremonial gathering area, a high-tech theatre, a conference centre, a display of Aboriginal art, a crafts market, a restaurant, and a tour-guide expedition.

PAUSE, REFLECT, APPLY

1. How does CIDA work with NGOs?
2. Why do some people believe NGOs run projects more effectively than governments?
3. a) Why do you think Canadians reacted so generously to the 2004 tsunami disaster?
   b) Why do you think there was not a similar response to the HIV/AIDS crisis in Africa?
4. List three reasons why the AIDS epidemic is worse in less developed countries than it is in more developed ones.
5. How does Canada's participation in cultural organizations and the Olympics reflect its position in the global community?

REPLAY

In this chapter, you have explored these concepts:

1. Global citizenship involves an appreciation that all the peoples of the world are interconnected.
2. The Nuremberg Trials marked the first time individual leaders and officers were held accountable for war crimes.
3. The United Nations *Universal Declaration of Human Rights* has inspired many human rights agreements.
4. Canada's attitude toward human rights has evolved over time; some old injustices have been addressed.
5. There are ways to improve the world outside government, including volunteering or becoming a member of a non-governmental organization.

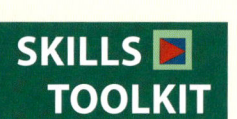

SKILLS TOOLKIT: How to Use Multimedia Technology

Multimedia presentations are more effective than simple oral presentations for three reasons:

1. Multimedia technology offers a better way to communicate any topic. Visuals, sound, and music stimulate the right side of the brain, the seat of our intuitive and emotional nature. Speech stimulates the left side, the seat of our logical and deductive nature.
2. Multimedia presentations appeal to audiences. An appreciative audience is more likely to ask questions and participate in discussions.
3. Audience participation improves a speaker's confidence. An average speaker can look better with a good multimedia presentation than a good speaker relying on notes alone. For example, bulleted point-form notes on a screen provide both visual interest for the audience and cues to the presenter, who no longer needs to refer to paper notes.

The most common presentation software today includes three major functions:

1. a slide show system to display multimedia content
2. an editing function to manipulate text and shapes
3. a graphics system for creating graphs and tables.

Visual material can be downloaded to the program from the Internet, a digital camera, or a scanner. Music and auditory effects can also be downloaded.

Preparing an effective multimedia presentation requires planning. Suppose your topic is "A Day in the Life of a Politician."

1. Decide what you are trying to communicate about your subject (a politician has many duties and busy days) just as you would in preparing an oral presentation. You could create a typical schedule on the computer (in point form) to serve as cues for both you and the audience as you explain the politician's working day.
2. Prepare a storyboard outlining the content of each slide you plan to use. Consider the kinds of visuals that you wish to include as slides. Be sure to gather materials that are relevant to the subject and are not too distracting.
3. Gather visual materials (e.g., photos, graphics, video footage). Use the editing function to modify and enhance visuals. Try using different fonts, colour schemes, and transitions.
4. Consider adding special slides with discussion topics and questions for the audience. Give these slides a common appearance to set them off from the rest of the slide show and encourage audience participation.
5. Use the program's clip art and design features to dress up your slides.
6. Consider printing a handout (including questions for discussion) for your audience.

Remember, the multimedia format is meant to liven up your ideas, not take over the presentation.

Get ready for presentation day by doing three things:

1. Rehearse your presentation.
2. Check the space where you will be presenting beforehand to locate air conditioning controls and electrical connections.
3. Make your speaking voice the most important sound in your presentation.

Skill Practice

1. What techniques do television news programs use to hold viewers' interest? Are any transferable to an individual multimedia presentation?
2. Prepare a storyboard for a social studies topic that you think is important. Consider visuals, sound, and music, and any other element that you can use to support your topic dramatically and effectively.

STUDY HALL

Be Informed

1. What are the characteristics of a global citizen?
2. What was the importance of the *Universal Declaration of Human Rights* (UDHR) to the recognition of human rights?
3. Explain why wars are likely to produce human rights abuses.
4. What essential principle or precedent important to universal human rights was established at the Nuremberg trials?
5. List three ways in which humanitarianism is practised through CIDA and NGOs.

Be Purposeful

6. State the major arguments that support the International Criminal Court. Why does the United States not support it? State your opinion on the US position.
7. Research a specific recipient of the "Righteous Among the Nations" honour (see page 272), and assume the role of that person. Explain how you assisted Jewish citizens, reflecting on your actions and the reasons you took action.
8. Other genocides have occurred since World War II and the events in Rwanda. Do some research to discover details—key events, why they occurred, world reaction.
9. Can human rights principles alone bring about good behaviour without an enforcement agency? Explain your answer.
10. Imagine an international human rights enforcement agency. Who would be involved? What would the agency do?
11. Analyze the types of humanitarian assistance that Canada has contributed globally. What sacrifices might Canadians have to make to help less developed countries?
12. Identify a person who exemplifies good global citizenship. Justify your choice using the criteria in this chapter. A starting list: Aung San Suu Kyi; Nelson Mandela; Wangari Maathai; Mother Teresa; David Suzuki; Ken Saro-Wiwa.

Be Active

13. Do some research into the International Court of Justice (ICJ). How does it differ from the International Criminal Court (ICC)?
14. Research the reasons behind the US and Chinese decisions not to participate in the ICC. What is your opinion of these countries' dissent?
15. Amnesty International is an organization dedicated to protecting human rights. Locate the group's Web site and report on its methods and results.
16. Prepare a piece of artwork or a presentation that illustrates your perspective on global interconnectedness. Focus on one area, or several. You may wish to search the Internet for examples. CIDA and the UN Cyberschoolbus, for example, run contests on global cooperation and youth involvement. Your goal: to convince yourself and others to take action.
17. Write a one-minute radio or television advertisement urging people to donate to an NGO that inspires you. Be sure to connect your NGO's work to the gap between more developed and less developed countries. Use an NGO from this book, or check out the CCIC Web site for a list of suggested organizations.
18. Research ways in which your class or school could become active in assisting people in need. Check out Project Love at www.emp.ca/ccw to learn about one student initiative focusing on literacy and school supplies.

CHAPTER 14
Global Conflicts and Global Interdependence

This puzzle, "Only the Educated Are Free," won second prize in the Canadian International Development Agency's Butterfly 208 contest (Group Visual Art and Multimedia category). The butterfly represents the spirit of global cooperation. What do the other symbols and words say to you about global citizenship and responsibilities? (Learn more about the art at www.emp.ca/ccw.)

What You Need to Know
- How can we measure, understand, and do something about inequalities in Canada and globally?
- How does Canada's demography influence its perspectives nationally and globally?
- What impacts do human activities have on the physical environment?
- What are the implications of Canada's military and peacekeeping roles?
- What current events show that we are connected with the rest of humanity?
- What actions can you take to be a responsible global citizen?
- How can you use self-assessment to become a better global citizen?

Key Terms
tropical rainforest
desertification
biodiversity
Industrial Revolution
population aging
net migration
sanctions
multilateralism
terrorism
weapons of mass destruction
sustainability
stewardship

Key Question
What makes a "global citizen"?

Imagine a school where only Class A has books and a teacher. Any adults in other classes are there only to keep order. At lunch, Class A goes to the cafeteria. Once Class A is finished and leaves, small bowls of soup are set up for sale to the other students. Only a few can afford them, but there isn't enough soup to go around, anyway. Fights erupt in the non-A classrooms and no one breaks them up. Bigger kids beat up smaller kids. After lunch, Class A uses two new washrooms. The other classes share two dirty washrooms that have neither flush toilets nor running water. One day, a few angry kids break into Class A. They are caught and forcibly expelled as troublemakers. The violence only gets worse.

How does this fictional scenario parallel world events today?

A World of Inequalities and Interconnections

Canada belongs to the exclusive "more developed country" club, while most other countries belong to the "less developed country" club. The gap between the two categories reflects a disturbing fact: we have been unable to work collectively for the benefit of all people, both within Canada and around the world. As you have learned in other chapters, not all parts of Canada share equally in Canada's wealth.

Doing something about inequality is a challenge. Identifying it can be a start. Inequality can be measured using specific variables, such as these three: clean drinking water, education, and life expectancy.

1. Clean Drinking Water

Human beings need clean drinking water to survive. Unfortunately, many people in less developed countries have little or no access to safe drinking water. This is especially true throughout much of Africa.

A lack of clean drinking water not only means we may become thirsty; it means we may become vulnerable to sickness, disease, and death. The less access people in a country or region have to clean drinking water, the weaker that country or region's economy.

Lack of clean drinking water is a crisis affecting First Nations across Canada and the Inuit. In 2006, for example, the drinking water in almost half of all First Nations reserves in Manitoba was unsafe or at risk.

2. Education

Any individual's success depends to a large extent on education, but not everybody in the world has equal access to education. Figure 14.1 shows the **literacy rate** (the percentage of people who can read and write) for the world's major regions. Countries with low literacy rates lack the human resources to flourish economically, politically, and culturally.

3. Life Expectancy

Life expectancy indicates the number of years that people are expected to live. What more telling indicator of inequality could there be than a low life expectancy? (See Figure 14.2.)

> **KEY QUESTION**
> How is the world a collection of unequal places?

> **THE WEB**
> Learn about the UN Water for Life Decade (2005–2015) and the Inuit and First Nations water crisis at www.emp.ca/ccw

> **DID YOU KNOW**
> Canadians with the lowest level of literacy skills have an unemployment rate of 26% compared with 4% for Canadians with the highest literacy levels.

CivicStar

RYAN HRELJAC

In 1998, six-year-old Ryan Hreljac learned that thousands of children die each year because they lack safe drinking water. Disturbed by this information, he began doing extra chores to raise $70 for a village well in Africa. Ryan's determination attracted media attention, and soon donations were coming in from across Canada. Then, CIDA gave a matching grant to the well project.

Within two and a half years, Ryan travelled to Angolo Public School in Uganda, where the well was located. Five thousand local children lined up to cheer the Canadian boy who had done chores to help them have safe water.

Today, Ryan's Well Foundation works with CIDA and has raised over a million dollars. It has projects in 10 African countries, and counting. Ryan Hreljac travels internationally to promote the cause of the 1.1 billion people worldwide who need safe water. "I want all of Africa to have clean drinking water," says Hreljac. "I think I'll get there when I'm 50."

Your Play

1. a) Describe the impact of the news media on Ryan Hreljac's work.
   b) Why do you think the media paid so much attention?
2. How is Ryan's Well Foundation an example of a personal decision that reflects the responsibilities of a global citizen?

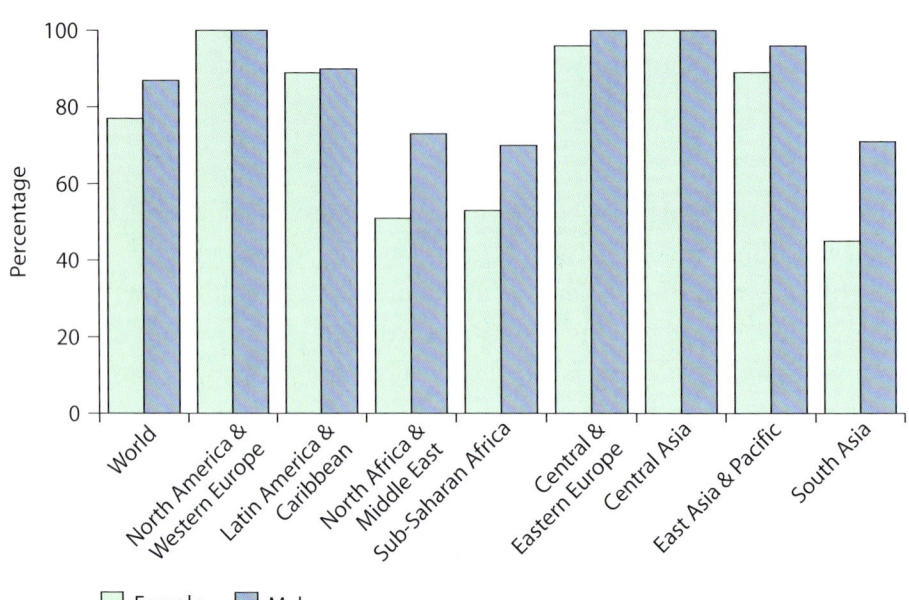

FIGURE 14.1 World literacy rates, age 15 and over. *Source: Data from CIDA, Canadian Geographic; www.canadiangeographic.ca*

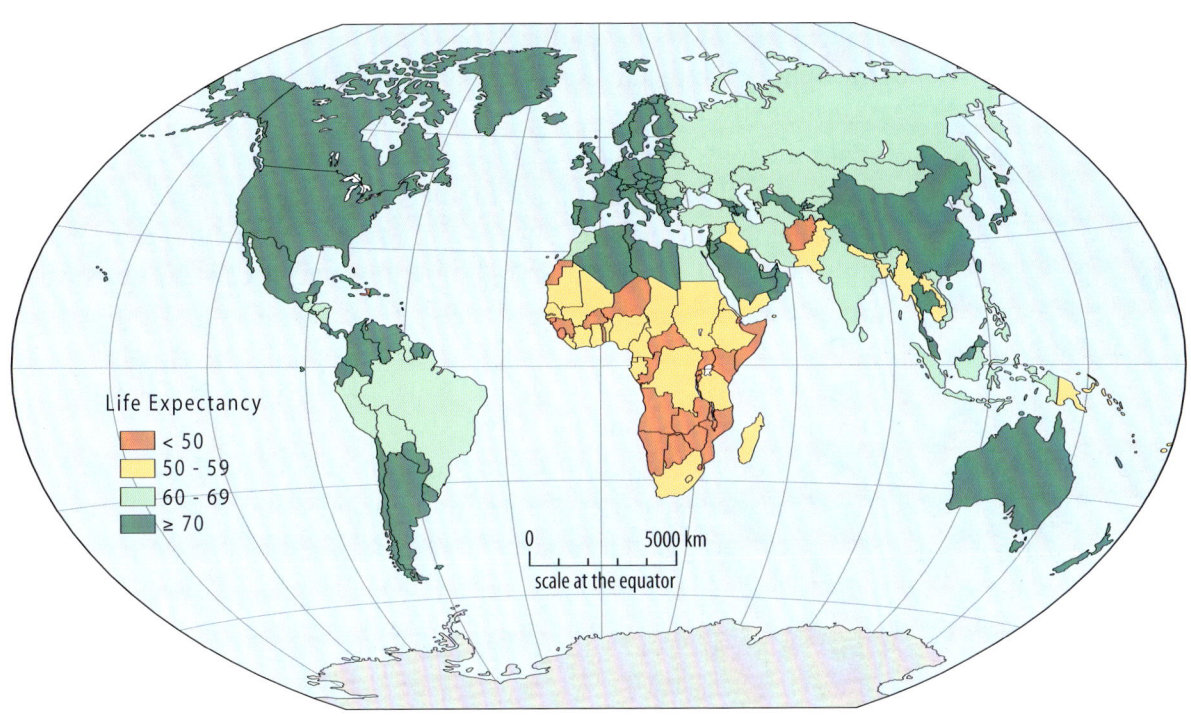

CHAPTER 14 GLOBAL CONFLICTS AND GLOBAL INTERDEPENDENCE   295

FIGURE 14.2 World life expectancy rates. *Source: World Population Data Sheet (Washington, DC: Population Reference Bureau, 2005)*

GLOBAL POVERTY AND HUMAN DEVELOPMENT

Wealth and poverty can also be measured using economic indicators. In earlier chapters, you used GDP per capita to measure quality of life. You also referred to the Human Development Index (HDI). Because of the values and beliefs behind it, the HDI is worth investigating more closely (see Sources, below).

THE WEB
Find HDI data and the *Annual Human Development Report* at www.emp.ca/ccw

SOURCES

Human development is about much more than the rise or fall of national incomes. It is about creating an environment in which people can develop their full potential and lead productive, creative lives in accord with their needs and interests. People are the real wealth of nations. Development is thus about expanding the choices people have to lead lives that they value. And it is thus about much more than economic growth, which is only a means—if a very important one—of enlarging people's choices.

—United Nations, Human Development Report; http://hdr.undp.org/hd/

> **DID YOU KNOW**
> The 10 countries with the lowest HDI ranking are all in Africa.

The HDI ranks all countries, ranging from a value of 0.000 to 1.000. Each statistic indicates a shortfall in human development. For example, Canada's HDI of 0.95 shows a shortfall of 5 percent (HDI data from 2005). Niger, in West Africa, has an HDI of 0.28, for a shortfall of 72 percent.

Identifying low levels of development is helpful in analyzing the problem of global inequalities, but explaining those inequalities can do more to bring about change. Although opinions on the causes of inequality differ, two facts emerge:

- Less developed countries are usually former colonies (colonialism created economic dependence).
- Many of these countries have corrupt, authoritarian governments. (See the discussion of authoritarian and democratic governments in Chapter 5, pages 96–98, and Figure 5.9, page 108.)

HUMAN ACTIVITIES AND GLOBAL ENVIRONMENTS

> **DID YOU KNOW**
> According to chaos theory, in complex systems such as the global ecosystem, a small change in one place can have big effects elsewhere. For example, a butterfly flapping its wings in Rio de Janeiro might change the weather in Brandon. This is known as "the butterfly effect."

We live in a global ecosystem. That means changing one aspect of nature will affect other aspects. Burning **tropical rainforests** in Brazil to clear land, for example, affects the climate in Africa—and Manitoba. Only recently have we recognized that environmental impacts from human activities may threaten our survival. Activities and development that ignore this fact will work against us.

Everything humans do has an impact on physical environments, even breathing! We hunt, fish, cut down trees, remove oil, gas, and minerals, raise livestock, and plant crops (primary activities). We process raw materials into finished products (secondary activities), and we perform varied services and research activities (tertiary and quaternary activities).

Human activities affect the physical environment often in small, but cumulatively significant, ways. Four well-known examples include tropical rainforest removal, **desertification**, loss of **biodiversity**, and global warming. Human environmental impacts are of special concern and are most damaging in less developed regions, where people have few resources to cope with them.

FACE OFF Famine and Misery? Or Future Abundance?

Discussions about the state of the world often refer to an Englishman, the Reverend Thomas Malthus. Back in 1798, Malthus published a work in which he argued that population will always grow faster than food supply, by necessity. Population grows by one mathematical progression: 1, 2, 4, 8, 16, and so forth. Food production, over the same time, increases by 1, 2, 3, 4, 5, and so on. Based on this theory, Malthus predicted that the world's population would always exceed the food supply. The result: famine, vice, and misery.

Was Malthus Right?

The answer to this question depends on how we choose to look at the world and our assumptions about the four driving forces of human impact (see page 298).

Some thinkers today agree with Malthus. They're sometimes called pessimists, or *catastrophists*. They assume that population growth will continue and that food production will not keep pace. When they gaze into the future, they see poverty, increasing conflicts over resources, and environmental damage. We will always be divided into rich and poor.

Other thinkers reject that gloom. They see technology offering a future of unlimited abundance. These thinkers are called *cornucopians*, from "cornucopia," the ancient symbol of a horn of plenty. Cornucopians say humans always find new ways to cope with problems: things are steadily improving. The food supply is increasing—so is life expectancy. There are fewer conflicts, democracy is spreading, more developed countries are starting to help less developed countries, and the poor can improve their lives.

Looking at the world as a whole, it seems clear that Malthus has not been proven correct. However, there are regions where famine, vice, and misery prevail. There are also positive signs—widespread improvements in health, education, and nutrition. There are also international efforts to promote human well-being. Later in this chapter, you will analyze the UN Millennium Development Goals. These targets require specific national commitments and offer promises that may, or may not, be achieved.

Regardless of how we view the state of the world—or our future—it is clear that global inequalities have tragic consequences and must be addressed.

FIGURE 14.3 On July 2, 2005, 1,250 musicians performed in live concerts in nine countries, including Canada, that were broadcasted to a global audience of 3 billion people. Their goal was to "Make Poverty History." A few days later, Live 8 representatives met political leaders at the G8 Summit with specific demands for action. How effective do you think Live 8's "Global Call to Action Against Poverty" can be?

What Do You Think?

1. What are the basic features of Malthus's theory?
2. Are you a "catastrophist" or a "cornucopian" about the state of the world? Or do you not know enough to say? Explain how you arrived at your position.

Four Driving Forces of Human Impact

Four forces drive human impact on the physical environment:

> **THE WEB** ▶▶▶
> For updates on world population data, go to the population clock at www.emp.ca/ccw

- *Increasing population:* Generally speaking, more people use more resources and produce more waste. Consider this: from 1900 to 2000, world population increased from 1.6 billion to 6.1 billion. It is expected to reach 9 billion by 2050.
- *Changing technologies:* Technological advances, especially since the onset of the **Industrial Revolution** (which started in England in the mid-1700s), have affected physical environments on a global scale. Many impacts are related to the burning of fossil fuels (see Figure 14.11, page 309). Technological advances, of course, also have positive consequences. Technology, in other words, is a double-edged sword.
- *Improving living standards:* The wealthier we are, the more we want and the more we consume.
- *Increasing interconnections:* Different regions of the world are connected through trade, travel, and communication. For example, transnational companies now conduct business in many countries, and the resulting human activities often have global consequences.

PAUSE, REFLECT, APPLY

1. List four ways of measuring health and development.
2. The map in Figure 14.2 (page 295) has been called "the most important map in the world." Why do you think this is so? Do you agree?
3. List two or more reasons why poor areas of the world are poor.
4. Describe four driving forces that help explain human impacts on physical environments.
5. Choose one less developed country and compare its access to safe drinking water and rates of life expectancy and literacy with Canada's overall rates.
6. Many youth groups in Canada work to promote education and literacy in the less developed world. Find out more about Project Love and also about literacy in Manitoba at www.emp.ca/ccw. Create a report—written or multimedia—based on what you find.

The Globe within Our Borders: Canadian Demographics

> ▶ **KEY QUESTION**
> Has Canada been a poor, fair, good, or excellent global citizen in dealing with its demographic needs?

As you learned in Chapter 1, Canada's population is growing slowly (see Figure 14.4). Two demographic factors explain that growth: **natural increase** and immigration.

	2001	2002	2003	2004	2005
Population	31,021.3	31,372.6	31,669.2	31,974.4	32,270.5
Increase (%)	1.1	1.1	0.9	1.0	0.9

FIGURE 14.4 Growth of the Canadian population and percentage of increase, 2001–2005 (population in thousands). *Source: Statistics Canada, CANSIM Table 051-0001; www40.statcan.ca/l01/cst01/demo02.htm?sdi=population*

1. Since the "baby boom" (1951–1971), Canada's annual birth rate has been declining for decades. It is now approximately 10.5 births per thousand. Women are choosing to have fewer babies. This trend will likely continue. At the same time, Canada's annual death rate (7.3 per thousand) is likely to continue increasing. This is explained by **population aging** (an increasing percentage of elderly people in the population). Elderly people are more likely to die than younger people. As a result, Canada's **rate of natural increase** is only 0.3 percent: birth rate 10.5 − death rate 7.3 = 3.2 per 1,000 = 0.3 percent (rounded decimal).
2. Each year, more people immigrate to Canada than emigrate from Canada. The numerical difference between immigration and emigration is called **net migration**. Figure 14.5 shows how, in a typical one-year period, net migration is the main contributor to Canada's population growth, not natural increase.

Component	Number
Births	337,856
Deaths	234,645
Immigration	244,579
Emigration	35,866

FIGURE 14.5 Components of population growth, Canada, 2004–2005. *Source: Statistics Canada, CANSIM Table 051-0004; www40.statcan.ca/l01/cst01/demo33a.htm*

CANADA'S POPULATION CHALLENGES

Demographers also study the **age–sex ratio** (how many young and old people there are, and how many males and females there are, in a population). The **population pyramid** is most often used to display this ratio as a graph (see figures 14.6 and 14.7). It shows how many people of each sex there are in each age group, usually comprising a five-year range.

Analyzing the age–sex ratio reveals a great deal. Figure 14.6 shows Canada's age–sex ratio in 2006. The base bars (ages 0 to 14) are narrower

▶ **DID YOU KNOW** ◀
A population pyramid is just two bar graphs turned on their sides and sharing a common baseline.

LITERACY COACH

Graphs will make more sense to you if you follow these simple steps:

- Make sure you understand what is being represented.
- Check the graph's labels and legend for place names and dates.
- Determine what the sets of numbers stand for. In the graph opposite, one set of numbers represents age in five-year increments, and another set of numbers represents population in millions.

Canada 2006

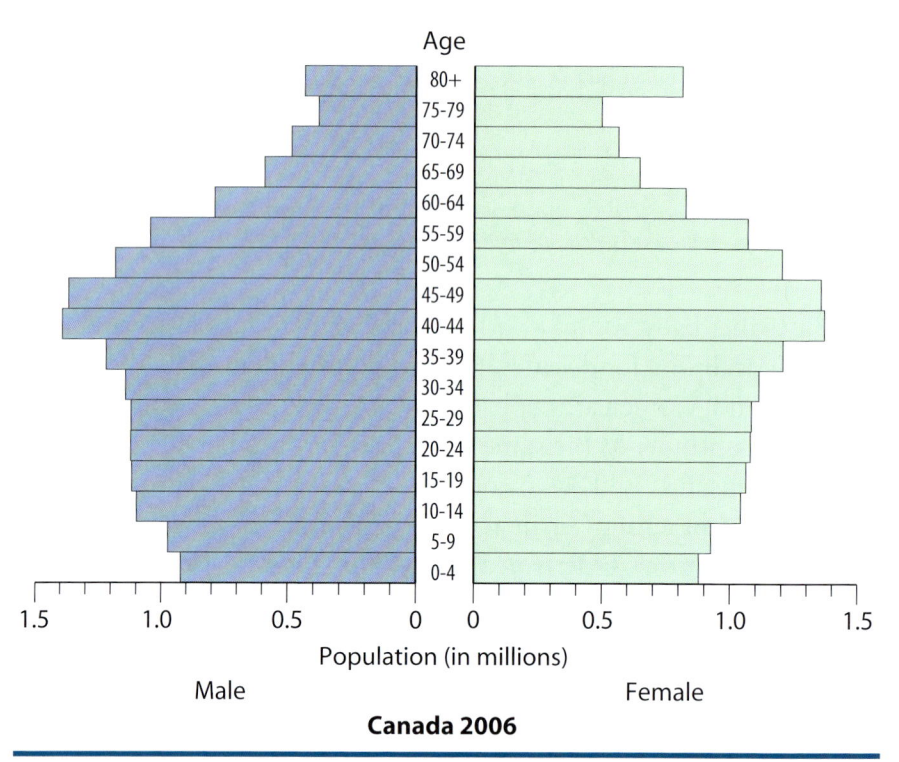

FIGURE 14.6 Population pyramid, Canada, 2006. *Source: US Census Bureau, International Data Base, Population Pyramids; www.census.gov/ipc/www/idbpyr.html*

than the bars above. This indicates a falling birth rate. The group with the most people is the 40–44 group; this tells you that the birth rate was quite high 40–44 years ago. Figure 14.7 projects Canada's age–sex ratio for 2050. Notice how many people are in the 80-plus group. What does that say about population aging? Demographers will likely have to add new groups to future pyramids; say, 80–84 and 85–89.

Population aging is a challenge for governments, communities, and families. How will we deal with a population in which many more people are not active in the labour force and are becoming more dependent on social programs (for example, health care and pensions)?

CANADA'S POPULATION GROWTH IN HISTORICAL PERSPECTIVE

It is important to place population growth in historical perspective:

- Canada's current rates of natural increase and net migration are very low historically.

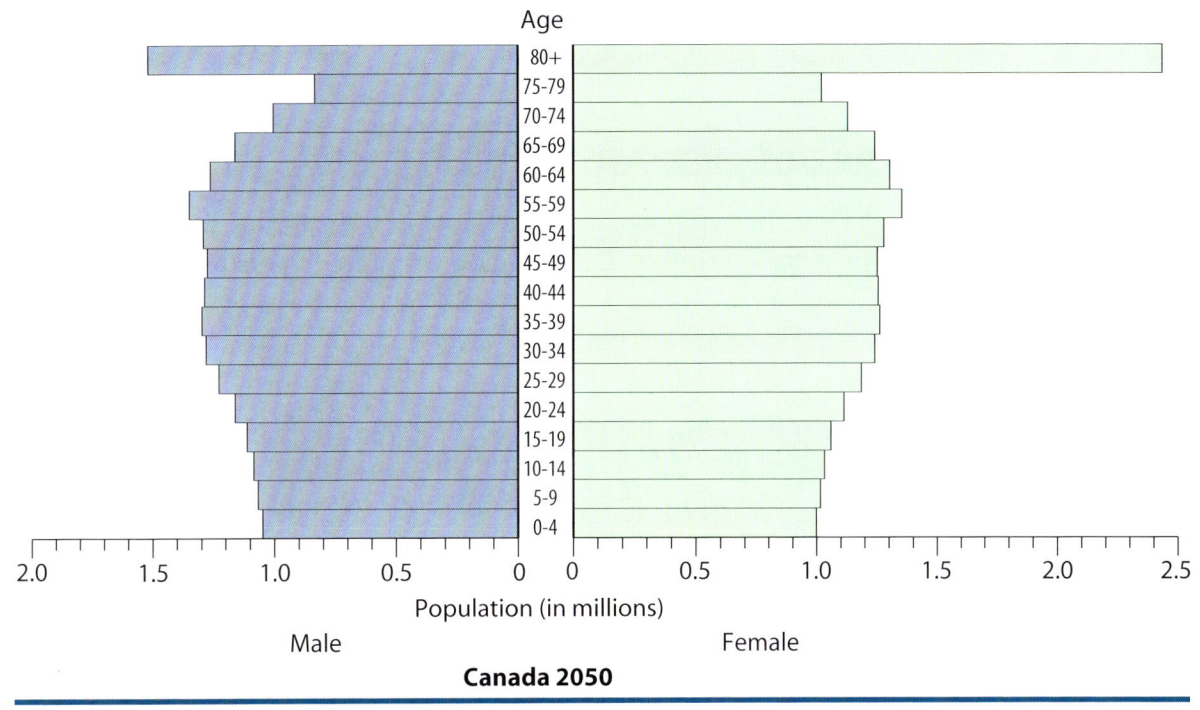

FIGURE 14.7 Population pyramid, Canada, 2050 (projected). *Source: US Census Bureau, International Data Base, Population Pyramids; www.census.gov/ipc/www/idbpyr.html*

- Until about 1971, Canada's population growth resulted mainly from natural increase.
- After 1971, most of Canada's growth has resulted from net migration.
- Net migration will likely be even more important in Canada's future population growth.

The Stories Behind the Numbers

Demographic data can be dry or fascinating—it depends on how well you can you read them. Figure 14.5 (page 299), for example, says a great deal about Canada, now and in the future. It tells us that in 2004–2005, net migration accounted for population growth at twice the rate of natural increase. Within a few years, immigration will likely comprise about 80 percent of Canada's population growth (and natural increase the remaining 20 percent).

There are other stories behind these numbers. Canada's population growth continues, but not all regions share in it equally. Since the end of World War II (1939–1945), Ontario and British Columbia have grown most rapidly. While the populations of Atlantic Canada and Quebec have increased, each has declined as a percentage of Canada's total population.

SOURCE AREAS OF IMMIGRATION

☐ **DISCUSSION POINT**
Most immigrants and refugees move into large Canadian cities, such as Toronto and Vancouver. As a result, social geography in these cities is changing much more than the social geography of rural areas. How will these changes affect life outside Canada's "heartland" cities?

Perhaps the most dramatic demographic change in Canada relates to immigration. Today, immigrants and refugees come from all regions of the globe. This influx is changing Canada's social geography. It will have profound political implications, both within Canada and in Canada's connections to the world.

Chapter 2 described how Canada's "colour-blind" policies removed barriers in the 1960s and 1970s. Immigration increased from Asia, especially, and from Latin America, the Caribbean, the Middle East, and Africa (see Figure 14.8). About 80 percent of immigrants now come from non-European areas. Canada continues to become much more pluralistic, with increasing diversity.

THE WEB ▶▶▶
Statistics Canada is the best source for Canadian demographic data. Find information from the most recent census at www.emp.ca/ccw

Source Region	Number of Immigrants
Europe	2,287,555
Asia	1,989,180
Central and South America	304,650
Caribbean	294,050
Africa	282,600
United States	237,920
Oceania and other countries	52,525

FIGURE 14.8 Place of birth of immigrant population, Canada, 2001. *Source: Statistics Canada, Census of Population, 2001*; www40.statcan.ca/l01/cst01/demo34b.htm

PAUSE, REFLECT, APPLY

1. State what is meant by the term "population aging."
2. What is meant by the term "net migration"?
3. Referring to Figure 14.5, what is Canada's net migration and natural increase?
4. What is a population pyramid, and why is it a useful tool in demography?
5. Why are increasing numbers of immigrants to Canada coming from non-traditional source regions?
6. How might immigration patterns affect Canada's global connections? Consider trade, communication, entertainment, sports, travel, cultural exchanges, global conflict areas, and so on.

When and How Does a Good Citizen Intervene?

Canada has not only been a destination for immigrants and refugees. Canada's interventions in world conflicts have often earned it respect. Sometimes those actions have been non-military, such as **sanctions** (actions to show disapproval). For example, the Canadian government may stop trade with countries that deny citizens their rights or that attack other countries. In 1977, Canada imposed trade sanctions against South Africa to protest apartheid (racial segregation).

In some cases, the military enforces sanctions. Canada has also stopped aid as a form of intervention. Such measures are intended to pressure governments into respecting human rights and international law.

Canada has also intervened militarily through peacekeeping.

> **KEY QUESTION**
> Has Canada been a poor, fair, good, or excellent global citizen in dealing with world conflicts?

PEACEKEEPING: 50 YEARS AND CHANGING

A Canadian, Lester Pearson, proposed the creation of UN peacekeeping in 1956 in the midst of a world crisis. The next year, he was awarded the Nobel Peace Prize. Since then, Canadian forces have often been peacekeepers. This reflects Canada's commitment to **multilateralism**: an approach to peace and security based on cooperation among countries.

Traditionally, peacekeepers literally came between combatants to ease tensions. In the 1990s, however, peacekeeping evolved. Actions now include

- supervising elections
- delivering humanitarian supplies
- setting up local police forces
- mediating or arbitrating differences.

Canadian peacekeeping activities have created an image of Canada as a good global citizen. At times, Canadian soldiers have paid for this image with their lives.

> **THE WEB**
> Learn more about why Pearson was awarded the Nobel Peace Prize and read his acceptance speech at www.emp.ca/ccw

PEACEKEEPING: AT THE BREAKING POINT?

In recent years, a cluster of conflicts has strained multilateral peacekeeping. From 1991 to 1999, ethnic civil wars broke out in the Balkans,

FIGURE 14.9 (Left:) The UN's blue helmet and blue beret identify soldiers as peacekeepers. They have become international symbols of Canadian pride. (Right:) An eagle feather adorns the beret of a Mi'kmaq peacekeeping veteran at Remembrance Day ceremonies in Halifax. What does this image say to you about how we commemorate those who risk their lives to honour our commitments to global citizenship and peace? Where else in this book have you seen the eagle feather? What does it represent?

in south-central Europe. UN missions struggled to establish peace in Bosnia and Serbia, where bitter historic rivalries between Serbs (Orthodox Christians), Croatians (Catholics), and Muslims led to fighting that was punctuated with major atrocities. In Kosovo, Albanian rebels fought the Serb government. Hundreds of thousands of people were slaughtered, including civilians and soldiers.

As you saw in chapters 2 and 13, genocide engulfed Rwanda in 1994 while UN forces under Canadian General Roméo Dallaire looked on. In his book, *Shake Hands with the Devil* (2003), Dallaire described his horror after the international community could not agree to take action: "We watched as the devil took control of paradise on earth and fed on the blood of the people we were supposed to protect."

Death in Darfur: Another Genocide, Another Failure?

In 2003, catastrophe gripped Darfur, in western Sudan, the largest country in Africa. After decades of civil war, Sudan's Arab-dominated government and militias fought local rebels. They killed tens of thousands of Darfur's black population. Homes and farms were burned and destroyed. More than 1 million people became refugees.

The UN called Darfur the "worst humanitarian crisis facing the world." The UN and NGOs found evidence of genocide, with Sudanese government involvement. Hundreds of thousands were at risk, but again the UN could not impose sanctions. It could not get international agreement that genocide was involved. Critics said the UN had learned nothing from Rwanda.

Is There a Better Way?

The UN can intervene in a country's business (or territory), without its consent, on two conditions:

- the country threatens the peace and security of other countries
- there is proof of genocide.

As Rwanda and Darfur showed, tragically, getting international agreement that either condition exists can be impossible.

Addressing the General Assembly in 2004, Canadian Prime Minister Paul Martin reminded the UN of its responsibility to protect civilians: "We should have the legal right to intervene in a country on the grounds of humanitarian emergency alone when the government of that country is unwilling or unable to protect their people from extreme harm as a result of internal war or repression."

Later, at the 2004 World Economic Forum in Switzerland, Martin warned that "the concept of intervention could be misused." One controversial example he cited was the US-led invasion of Iraq, which did not have UN support. "What is required," said Martin, "is an open discussion about the need for intervention in situations that offend the most basic precepts of our common humanity."

PAUSE, REFLECT, APPLY

1. What is multilateralism?
2. What actions can UN peacekeeping troops take in a conflict?
3. Locate Bosnia–Herzegovina, Serbia, Rwanda, and Sudan on a world map. What similarities were there in the conflicts in all three areas?
4. Under what circumstances did Prime Minister Martin want the UN to be able to intervene in a country?
5. Should any other country, or the UN, have the right to tell Canada how to treat its own citizens? Discuss, and write a supported-opinion paragraph.

The Changing Face of Global Conflict: Terrorism After 9/11

> **KEY QUESTION**
> How have Canada and the United States differed in their responses to terrorism? Why?

Terrorism is not new. Unlawful and extreme violence has been used for centuries to achieve political or ideological goals. The 20th century was full of bloody instances of terrorism—for example, by the Irish Republican Army (United Kingdom), the Tamil Tigers (Sri Lanka), and the FLQ (Quebec).

In the 21st century, terrorism has redefined international relations. The term "nine-eleven" is part of everyday speech. It refers to the terrorist attacks on the United States on September 11, 2001. Three thousand civilians died in those attacks. Their deaths have changed how the United States—and the world—approaches global peace and security.

Terrorists see themselves as patriots, freedom fighters, and idealists. Victims see them as fanatics who use kidnappings, assassinations, suicide bombings, beheadings, hijackings, missile attacks, and even killings of schoolchildren to achieve their goals. Usually, terrorists operate outside government, but they may be secretly sponsored by states—sometimes their own governments or outside governments.

Terrorist goals may include

- overthrowing a government
- achieving political independence
- expelling oppressive businesses
- pursuing religious goals.

FIGURE 14.10 A relative floats anniversary remembrance candles for victims of Air India Flight 182 on June 23, 2005. Twenty years before, the airplane was shattered by a terrorist bomb and plunged into the sea near Ireland. All 329 people on board, mostly Canadians, perished. In 2005, two men were finally tried for the worst mass killing in Canadian history. They were found not guilty. After years of demands, a public inquiry into the bombing of Air India Flight 182 was announced. It began hearings in July 2006. Why do you think it took so long? What do you think it will find?

MODERN RESPONSES TO TERRORISM

Modern terrorists can use technology to coordinate their activities—and attacks—across borders. Governments have responded by cooperating to identify and combat terrorist groups.

Months after 9/11, Canada passed the *Anti-terrorism Act* and the United States passed the *USA PATRIOT Act*. Both acts increased police and security powers to collect and keep information on anyone suspected of being a terrorist. People can be stopped, searched, and questioned at borders and held for questioning for long periods of time. Phones can be tapped, banking and purchasing records followed, e-mail exchanges hacked into. People can be detained without being told of the evidence that led to their arrest.

Critics—and courts—have found that these new anti-terrorism laws infringe on the democratic rights and freedoms guaranteed in the *Canadian Charter of Rights and Freedoms* and the US constitution. Police and security forces have also been accused of targeting members of visible minority groups, such as Muslims. Both governments, however, defend the changes as necessary to fight terrorism.

CANADA'S DILEMMA: GOOD GLOBAL CITIZEN OR GOOD NEIGHBOUR?

The 9/11 attacks were carried out by al-Qaida, an Islamist terrorist organization led by Osama bin Laden. Based in Afghanistan, al-Qaida was sheltered by the extremist Taliban government. After 9/11, the Taliban rejected UN and US requests to hand over al-Qaida's leaders for trial.

In October 2001, the United States led a UN-endorsed multilateral invasion of Afghanistan. Canada sent troops, as did Britain, Australia, Germany, and other countries. The Taliban government was quickly overthrown. Many members of al-Qaida were killed or captured; many others, including leaders such as bin Laden, escaped.

Canada worked with the UN-mandated international forces to help rebuild Afghanistan's economy and establish democratic institutions until late in 2005. In February 2006, Canadian troops joined a multinational battle brigade of 2,000 based in southern Afghanistan, near Kandahar, under Canadian command. This military operation is more aggressive, as troops seek to capture or kill Taliban rebels. Taliban rebel attacks have been frequent and deadly (see the cartoon that opens Chapter 8, on page 156).

► **DID YOU KNOW** ◄

The UN has recently ranked Afghanistan's education system as the worst in the world. Nearly three-quarters of adults are illiterate, and in many areas girls do not go to school. How do you think this widespread illiteracy will affect the conflict in Afghanistan?

THE WEB ►►►

See the faces and names of Canadian soldiers who have been wounded or killed in Afghanistan, and read Prime Minister Stephen Harper's speech to Canadian troops in March 2006, at www.emp.ca/ccw

US-Led Invasion of Iraq

After the invasion of Afghanistan, the United States accused Iraqi dictator Saddam Hussein of supporting terrorists. It also accused Iraq of hiding **weapons of mass destruction** (WMDs)—nuclear, biological, and chemical weapons designed to kill large numbers of people. The United States and its ally, Britain, lobbied the UN to support an invasion of Iraq. Instead, the UN sent in weapons inspectors. After months of inspections, no WMDs were found.

The UN opposed an invasion of Iraq. Prime Minister Jean Chrétien was equally clear: Canada would not take part. In March 2003, the United States led an invasion into Iraq, with Britain as its chief ally. Hussein was quickly overthrown.

Canada–US relations became strained. Canada had made a decision that did not support its neighbour to the south (see Sources, below).

No WMDs were ever found in Iraq. Later, the reports on which the US and Britain based their claims to the UN about Iraq's potential WMDs were found to be unreliable and misleading.

SOURCES

"The Canadian position is that on matters of peace and security, the international community must speak and act through the UN Security Council. ... We believe in multilateralism very strongly."

— Prime Minister Jean Chrétien, January 15, 2003, on not joining the US invasion of Iraq

"The Canadian Alliance—the official Opposition in Parliament—supports the American and British position because we share their concerns, their worries about the future if Iraq is left unattended to, and their fundamental vision of civilization and human values."

— Stephen Harper, as leader of the Canadian Alliance (which merged with the Progressive Conservative Party in 2003), supporting the US invasion of Iraq in a March 28, 2003 letter to the *Wall Street Journal*

PAUSE, REFLECT, APPLY

1. In what ways is a terrorist similar to and different from a traditional soldier?
2. Why would a terrorist feel justified in killing?
3. What laws were passed in Canada and the United States to deal with the threat of terrorism?
4. What are the benefits and sacrifices for Canadians under the *Anti-terrorism Act*?
5. What were the main reasons that Canada and the UN a) supported the United States in Afghanistan and b) did not support the United States in Iraq?
6. Refer to the Sources feature, above. Compare Jean Chrétien's and Stephen Harper's positions on the US invasion of Iraq, and multilateralism in particular. Research and compare Harper's position on Iraq as Canada's prime minister.

Environmental Interdependence

Environmental damage respects no borders. One of today's most urgent and controversial issues is global warming. As with terrorism and global conflicts, the UN is involved in leading and coordinating international efforts.

The UN predicts that the Earth's temperature will rise 5°C over the next 100 years. The result will be floods, storms, heat waves, droughts, and melting polar icecaps. Entire ecosystems will be upset.

Most scientists believe that global warming is caused by greenhouse gas (GHG) emissions, which trap the sun's heat in the atmosphere. Carbon dioxide (CO_2) is considered one of the most damaging GHGs. It is produced when fossil fuels—such as gas, coal, and oil—are burned.

In 1997, 160 countries signed the *Kyoto Protocol* to combat global warming. The goal is to cut GHG emissions overall by 5 percent by 2012. Canada promised a 6 percent reduction.

> **KEY QUESTION**
> How can our purchasing decisions, and the way we separate our garbage or get to work, make us responsible global citizens?

> **DID YOU KNOW**
> Canadians generate 4.42 t of CO_2 per capita each year. Only Americans produce more, at 5.48 t. The figure for India is 0.29 t. What might account for these differences?

> **THE WEB**
> Check out Environment Canada's Youth & the Environment Web page for ideas on how to make a difference at www.emp.ca/ccw

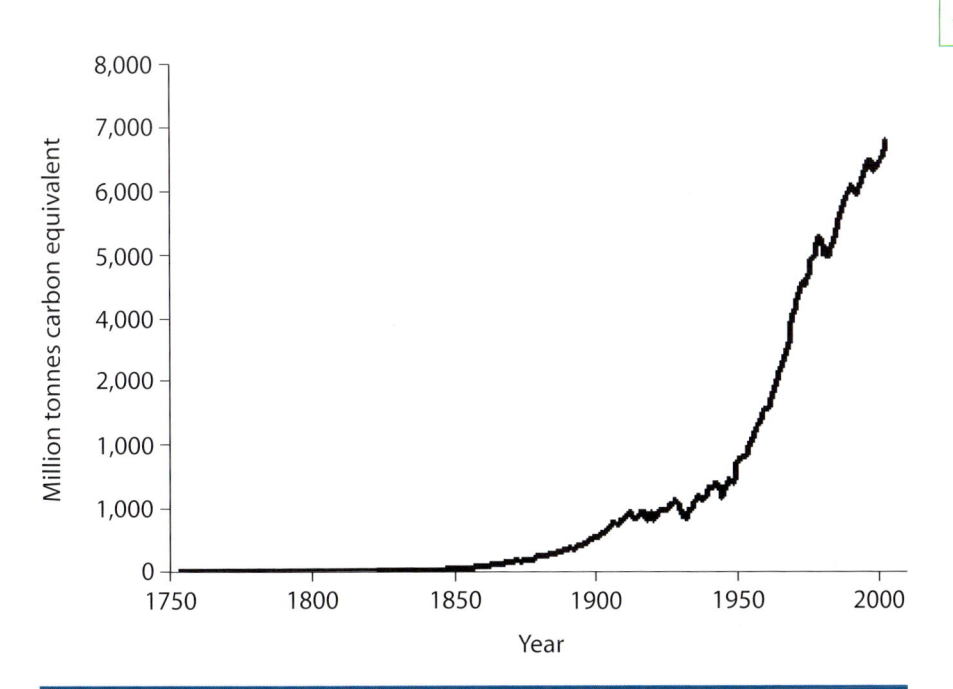

FIGURE 14.11 Carbon emissions from fossil fuel burning, 1751–2003. *Source: Earth Policy Institute; www.earth-policy.org/Indicators/CO2/index.htm*

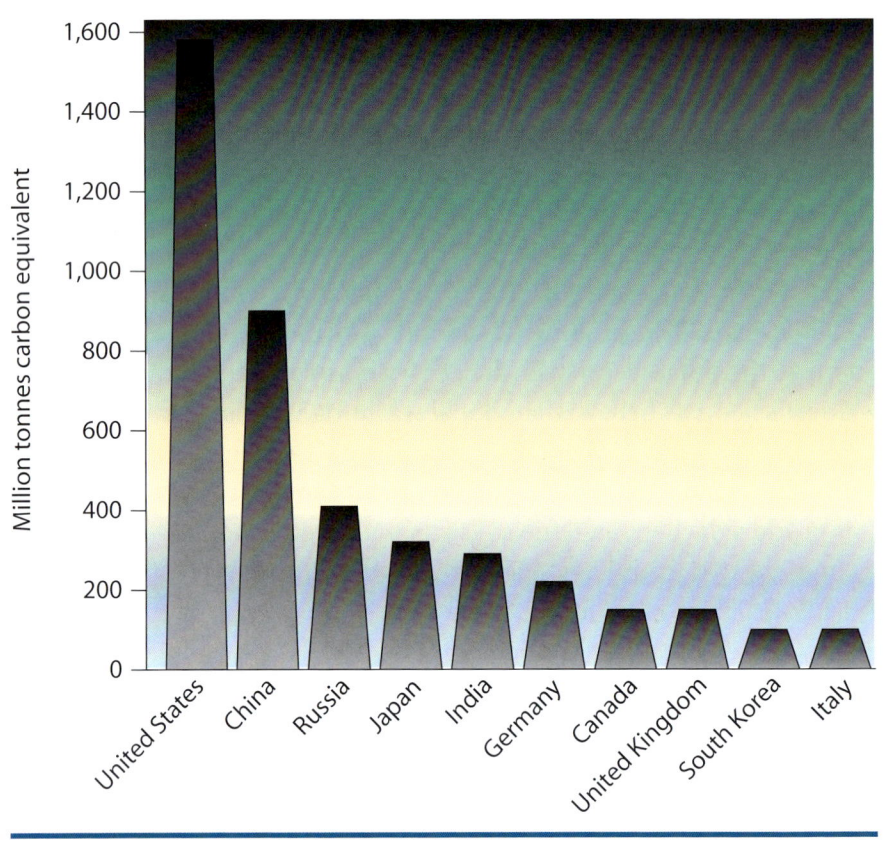

FIGURE 14.12 Carbon dioxide emissions by the top 10 emitting countries, 2002. *Source: Earth Policy Institute; www.earth-policy.org/Indicators/CO2/CO2_data.htm*

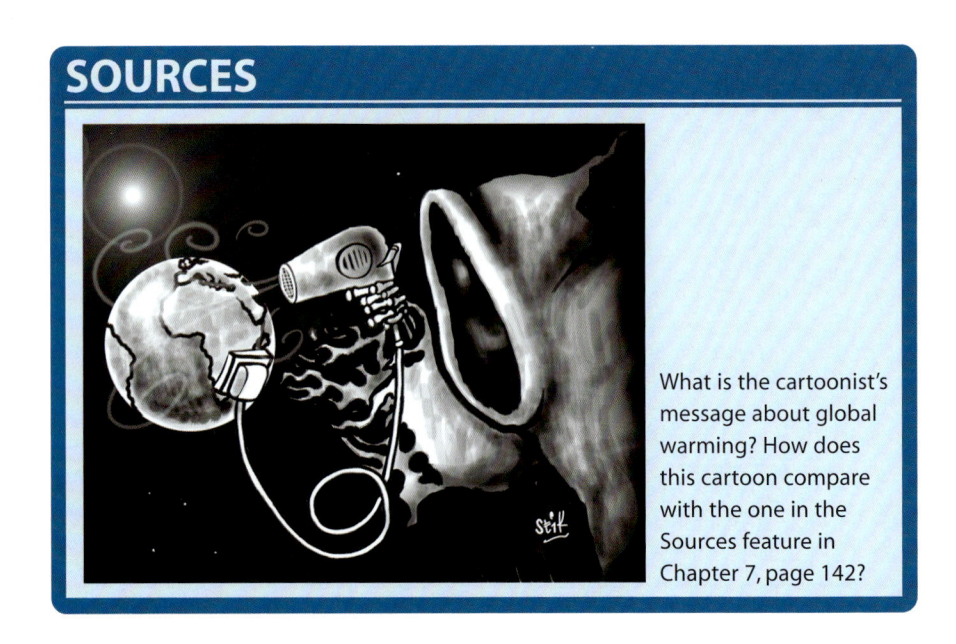

SOURCES

What is the cartoonist's message about global warming? How does this cartoon compare with the one in the Sources feature in Chapter 7, page 142?

> **FACE OFF** The *Kyoto Protocol*: Is It Worth the Price?

Supporters say the *Kyoto Protocol* is an essential example of international cooperation, a critical first step. Others have called it a colossal waste. Canada ratified the agreement in 2002. Kyoto still stirs debate about economics and science and often about political and social beliefs and values. Main arguments go something like this:

No

Kyoto's goals are costly and unreachable. To reduce emissions, industries will have to cut energy use and production. In 2002, Lorne Taylor, Alberta's environment minister, warned that doing so would eliminate 450,000 jobs. It would also wipe out $8 billion a year from Alberta's oil-producing economy. Alberta spent $1.5 million for advertisements opposing Canada's ratification of Kyoto. Taylor questioned Kyoto's science:

> I think that's a bunch of what I would call hokey science. The South Saskatchewan River was dry in 1862. Are you going to tell me that that was caused by global warming?
> —Source: www.cbc.ca/fifth/kyoto/debate.html

The Canadian Manufacturers and Exporters organization said consumers would have to "drive less, drive smaller cars, take public transit, and pay up to 100 percent more for electricity." Pierre Alvarez, president of the Canadian Association of Petroleum Producers, questioned public will:

> What are those folks in Toronto prepared to do? Are they prepared to use less electricity? Drive less? Change their work patterns and their commuting patterns? I've not seen evidence of that.
> —Source: www.cbc.ca/fifth/kyoto/debate.html

The biggest "no" came from US President George W. Bush, who rejected Kyoto in 2001, saying it would harm both US sovereignty and businesses. Canadian manufacturers warned that they would now have to compete with US businesses, which did not face the burden of Kyoto.

Yes

Kyoto supporters argue that the science behind Kyoto is rock solid. If ignored, they say, global warming will be as destructive as a nuclear war. In 1999, then federal Environment Minister David Anderson issued a warning:

> Even if countries meet their Kyoto targets, we may only succeed in slowing the rate of climate change. In other words, ... [Kyoto targets] clearly are only the beginning of what is necessary to combat climate change. It's time we woke up to that reality.
> —Source: www.ec.gc.ca/minister/ speeches/kyoto_s_e.htm

In 2002, Manitoba Premier Gary Doer, a strong Kyoto supporter, placed Alberta's objections in an interesting light:

> We're going to have David versus Goliath in this debate. We're going to have the people of Canada who want this accord, who want to take action on climate change, being David, and Goliath is obviously Alberta, with its money and its resources.

Doer and other Kyoto supporters see many benefits to Kyoto, both environmental and economic. Ralph Torrie, of the David Suzuki Foundation, agrees that Canadians will pay to reach Kyoto goals. People will have to retrofit homes and buy energy-saving appliances. But long-term benefits will outweigh those costs. Businesses and consumers will save on energy, not to mention reducing costs associated with environmental disasters.

Wind, solar, and hydro power are sustainable. And they are more environmentally friendly and more efficient than oil, coal, and gas. Besides, supplies of oil, coal, and gas are not renewable—they will eventually run out.

A 2005 survey of senior Canadian businesspeople showed that 57 percent believed emission levels could be cut with little economic damage. Other polls show that 60 percent of Canadians are willing to combat global warming, even if it costs them money.

What Do You Think?

1. In an election, one party promises to meet Kyoto goals. Another promises to pull out of the agreement. Make a list of points for each side. Add a third list of questions that you want answered to improve your understanding of the issue of climate change. Consider Canada's global interconnections.
2. In 2006, Canada's newly appointed Conservative environment minister, Rona Ambrose, announced, "it is impossible, impossible for Canada to reach its Kyoto targets." She said Canada would set new targets. Research newspaper archives or go to the Web sites of Environment Canada and the government of Manitoba and report on both governments' most recent actions on Kyoto and climate change. Look for answers to your list of questions from question 1.

PAUSE, REFLECT, APPLY

1. What is global warming?
2. What are greenhouse gases?
3. How do US policies regarding the *Kyoto Protocol* influence Canada's decisions?
4. List six international environmental issues other than global warming that global citizens are addressing. Greenpeace and the United Nations Environment Programme (Tunza) have helpful Web sites; see the links at www.emp.ca/ccw.

> **KEY QUESTION**
> How can we identify major global problems and begin to address them as global citizens?

Hope through Global Citizenship

At the turn of the century, all UN members formally authorized the Millennium Declaration. In a commitment to global renewal, all countries agreed to work to achieve the Millennium Development Goals by the year 2015:

1. Eradicate extreme poverty and hunger.
2. Achieve universal primary education.
3. Promote gender equality and empower women.
4. Reduce child mortality.
5. Improve maternal health.
6. Combat HIV/AIDS, malaria, and other diseases.
7. Ensure environmental **sustainability** (meeting the needs of the present without compromising the ability of future generations to meet their own needs).
8. Develop global partnerships so that countries can trade fairly and develop.

MEASURING PROGRESS

United Nations Secretary General Kofi Annan presented a report on the Millennium Declaration to the General Assembly on its fifth anniversary. He called for major UN reforms and action:

> I am profoundly convinced that the threats which face us are of equal concern to all. I believe that development, security and human rights go hand in hand. In a world of interconnected threats and opportunities, it is in each country's self-interest that all of these challenges are addressed effectively.
>
> We all know what the problems are, and we all know what we have promised to achieve. What is needed now is not more declarations or promises, but action to fulfill the promises already made.

THE WEB
Learn more about the Millennium Development Goals at www.emp.ca/ccw

THE GLOBAL CITIZEN TAKES TIME TO THINK

> "Knowledge is power. Information is liberating. Education is the premise of progress, in every society, in every family."
> —UN Secretary General Kofi Annan, June 22, 1997, Toronto, addressing the GlobalKnowledge 97 Conference

This has been called the Information Age. The Internet links citizens around the globe, offering a bombardment of information. No single source can provide all that you can and should know about world events. However, there are good starting places, and you have acquired many thinking tools. You will find Web sites for the following at www.emp.ca/ccw:

- Foreign Affairs Canada and CIDA offer good resources. See also the UN's Cyberschoolbus, designed for students and teachers.
- Background information and breaking news on national and global issues are available at the Canadian Broadcasting Corporation. The CBC News Indepth main page lists hundreds of topics alphabetically, as does CBC Archives.
- Different countries have different perspectives. The Internet Public Library lists hundreds of the world's newspapers and magazines.

CivicStar

LLOYD AXWORTHY

As Canada's foreign affairs minister from 1996 to 2000, Lloyd Axworthy took a leading role in the movement to ban landmines.

Millions of landmines are buried in former war zones. In Afghanistan alone, 10 to 15 million mines continue to maim and kill civilians, especially children. Adults caught in the blast of an anti-personnel mine often survive with treatment, though they usually lose limbs. Children are smaller and thus less likely to survive a blast.

Axworthy cooperated with other people, particularly US activist Jody Williams, in building a global network dedicated to banning landmines. In just over a year, Axworthy helped persuade 121 countries to sign the *Mine Ban Treaty* in Ottawa in 1997. It became known as the Ottawa Convention. For his efforts, Axworthy was nominated for the Nobel Peace Prize.

In 2000, after a 30-year career as a powerful Manitoba Liberal, Axworthy left politics. He became director of the Liu Institute for Global Issues, a foreign policy think tank at the University of British Columbia. In 2004, he was appointed president of the University of Winnipeg. In 2005, Axworthy helped establish the university's Global College. The college offers a setting for international scholars and students to explore global issues—from human security to global citizenship and climate change.

Axworthy remains deeply committed to human rights and to working with thinking students, two things he sees as the hope of the future.

FIGURE 14.13
Lloyd Axworthy addresses the United Nations as Canada's foreign affairs minister in 1999. What does the UN logo on the podium say to you about the UN's mission?

▶ **DID YOU KNOW** ◀
It costs less than $3 to manufacture a mine, but about $1,000 to remove it.

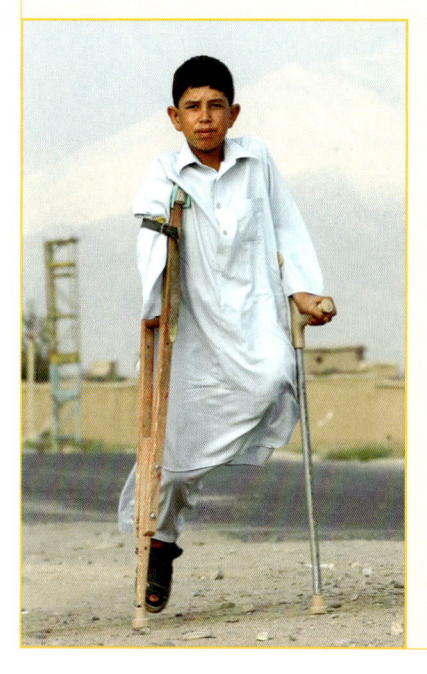

Your Play

1. Suggest reasons why some countries (such as the United States, Cuba, and Russia) did not sign the *Mine Ban Treaty*. Consider a) financial and b) military reasons. Go to www.emp.ca/ccw for helpful links.
2. Lloyd Axworthy lost the Nobel Prize to Jody Williams of the International Campaign to Ban Landmines (ICBL). Which do you think is a more powerful force in human rights campaigns: statesmen like Axworthy, or a network of 1,400 NGOs, like the ICBL? Explain.
3. Lloyd Axworthy's insights can be both sharp and blunt, and you can often find them in articles that appear in newspapers. Research and compare some of Axworthy's thoughts with your own and those of other leaders in Canada and around the world.

FIGURE 14.14 Jamshaid, 10, starts school in Bagram, north of Kabul, Afghanistan. Months earlier, he lost an arm and leg when he stepped on a landmine. Afghanistan is one of the most heavily mined countries in the world.

PAUSE, REFLECT, APPLY

1. Why are the UN's development goals called "millennium" goals?
2. Explain the meaning of "gender equality" in education.
3. Explain why the UN sees universal education as a critical need.
4. At what ages is a child most vulnerable? Why?
5. What types of information can be found at the Cyberschoolbus Web site? (Hint: Take a look.)
6. What two goals would you add to the Millennium Development Goals? Justify your choices.
7. a) What Millennium Development Goal(s) could you address? Explain how you would address them, based on the criteria of the goal's importance and your ability.
   b) Which goals will be the most difficult to meet? Why?

REPLAY

In this chapter, you have explored these concepts:

1. Demographic trends reveal a great deal about a country, domestically and globally.
2. All countries are interconnected; Canada cannot isolate itself.
3. The world is made up of unequal places.
4. We are all part of a global ecosystem that connects us physically in nature.
5. Multilateralism has shaped Canada's foreign policy and sometimes strained our relations with the United States.
6. Canada is committed to the UN's Millennium Development Goals to reduce global poverty and inequality.

SKILLS TOOLKIT ▶ How to Assess Yourself and Your Work

Self-assessment is not an easy thing to do. It can be very uncomfortable, maybe even intimidating. Many, maybe most, people avoid it if at all possible. But self-assessment can force you to look at yourself and your work in a methodical way. It can lead to self-knowledge, and that can lead to self-improvement and better, more interesting, choices.

How can you be objective about yourself or your work? Certain steps can be followed in any self-assessment. This is true whether the task is academic, such as writing a report, or behavioural, such as becoming a global citizen.

1. Examine where you are now.
   - How successful has your work been to date; what area(s) need improvement?
2. Understand terms and concepts related to the task.
   - For writing a report, what is the best structure or format? Ensure the accuracy of your information.
   - For becoming a global citizen, examine information and concepts in this chapter and other resources.
3. Identify your assessment criteria. Be specific.
   - On what basis will you assess your report? (Examples: accuracy, clarity, grammar, bibliography, unity, coherence.)
   - What are the characteristics of a global citizen? Review the information and definitions in this chapter and Chapter 13.
4. Find models or standards for comparison.
   - Your teacher will have a variety of models (exemplars) of good report writing.
   - Consider the actions and attitudes of people profiled in this chapter. Research other people whom you admire.
5. Set goals. Plan the steps you will undertake. Be realistic.
   - You cannot research and write about everything. Decide in advance what points you want to make, what examples you are going to use, and how long the report will be.
   - Do not set up unrealistic expectations. Identify what you actually can do.
   - Define your "levels of achievement." What is the difference between excellent, good, fair, and poor?
   - Apply these levels to your criteria (e.g., rate the grammar in your report as excellent, good, etc.).
   - Know how your results can be proven and measured. How will you know how well you have achieved each goal?
6. Review and revise. Do you have:
   - correct information?
   - clear criteria?
   - reasonable standards?
   - examples or models?
   - a way to measure your success?

Skill Practice

1. a) Write a 150-word report on the topic "Am I a Global Citizen?" Assess yourself using the steps above. Alternatively, write a report or create a presentation recognizing someone whom you consider to be a model global citizen.

   b) Assess the quality of your report. Edit and re-edit.
2. Share your report with a peer or peers. How do your assessments compare?
3. Have your teacher look at your assessment. Compare his or her comments with your own.

STUDY HALL

Be Informed

1. What are some of the specific implications of population aging in Canada? On balance, is this a good, bad, or neutral phenomenon?
2. Immigration patterns are increasing Canada's cultural diversity. What are some of the specific implications of this immigration? On balance, is this a good, bad, or a neutral phenomenon?
3. Identify some of the environmental problems resulting from human activities.
4. How did multilateralism affect Canada's actions in conflicts in the Balkans, Rwanda, Afghanistan, and Iraq?
5. What makes terrorism more difficult to fight than traditional warfare?
6. How does the *Kyoto Protocol* attempt to reduce global warming?
7. What objectives are the Millennium Development Goals meant to achieve?

Be Purposeful

8. Using the UN Cyberschoolbus Web site or another reliable source, find Canada's per capita GDP. Compare it to the per capita GDPs of the United States, Japan, four western European and four African countries, and two countries from each of Central America and East Asia. (Alternatively, or additionally, conduct research to find the GDP per capita in a) an immigrant community, b) a First Nations reserve, and c) an Inuit community in Manitoba.) Create a graphic poster or chart that shows the disparities. Why is it important for global citizens to know these statistics?
9. There is much debate about whether, in the long term, aid money helps countries that receive it. Some countries have received much foreign aid with few apparent benefits—Malawi, Zimbabwe, and Zambia are examples. On the other hand, Botswana has benefited from aid significantly. The difference? It is hard to be specific, but Botswana is well governed. A 2005 report by two major NGOs, Oxfam and ActionAid, suggests that only about one-fifth of aid money goes to the countries that most need it. Find out more about this very complex issue, and suggest ways that aid money might be made more effective.

Be Active

10. Create a work of art, song, short documentary, or presentation expressing your perspective on global interconnectedness. Focus on one area or several. You may wish to search the Internet for examples. CIDA and the UN Cyberschoolbus, for example, run contests on global cooperation and youth involvement. Your goal: to convince yourself and others to take action.
11. Conduct research and then prepare a report to describe how Environment Canada is approaching the *Kyoto Protocol* and dealing with climate change. Compare and contrast statements from both Liberal and Conservative environment ministers and prime ministers. Be sure to look past partisan (politically biased) statements to get at the core ideas of their positions.
12. In earlier chapters, you explored traditional relationships that Aboriginal peoples have with the land in Canada and customs around the distribution of wealth (e.g., the potlatch). These relationships are often based on **stewardship**. Do more research into the concept of stewardship and the traditions of Aboriginal peoples in Canada and indigenous peoples around the world. Create a comparison chart, mind map, or Venn diagram that places these traditions and perspectives alongside perspectives described in this chapter, particularly the Face Off (page 311 [*Kyoto Protocol*]).
13. Write a one-minute radio or television advertisement to increase public awareness of the Millennium Development Goals.
14. The issue identified in activity 9, above, could be misinterpreted. Some people might conclude it suggests that many countries do not require development money, humanitarian aid, disaster relief, AIDS education, or drugs to combat disease. Nothing could be farther from the truth. Select one country in sub-Saharan Africa and learn more about its people's needs.

UNIT 4
Canada: Opportunities and Challenges

Chapter 15
Challenge 1: Identity and Citizenship

Chapter 16
Challenge 2: Technology, Society, and Change

Chapter 17
Challenge 3: Pioneers of Tomorrow

Throughout *Canada in the Contemporary World*, you have explored ideas, values, structures, people, and events that have shaped Canada's culture and identity. As citizens, you share in and contribute to both.

No single book can stay up to date on political, social, and economic issues. And no one book can include all relevant information and developments. Constant technological, demographic, and scientific developments make that impossible. These developments, however, affect how you see yourself in society and the role you choose to play.

How can you, the student-citizen, decide which developments will be the most significant? What significant decisions will you have to make? What people, or types of people, do you see becoming future leaders? How will you decide what has lasting value, is worth preserving, is worth fighting for?

Introduction to the Activities

Ripples of Significance

If you've ever thrown a pebble or rock into a body of water, you know what you get: ripples. The size and shape of the object determines the size and speed of the splash—and how far the ripples will spread. Maybe the ripples dissipate quickly. Maybe they touch other objects and set them in motion, creating further effects that set more objects in motion, which... You get the idea: the extent and effects of the ripple determine its significance.

We can look at people, issues, and events in this way.

Criteria of Significance

The significant criteria are those that

- touch the most lives
- change the way we live
- have long-lasting impacts.

In the Chapter Challenges that follow, you will be invited to use these three Criteria of Significance to assess people, issues, and events. They may be individuals or groups; technological, scientific, or economic developments or ideas; natural forces (for example, environmental, biological, climatic) or political forces; popular movements; or global conflicts.

Guiding Questions

Throughout this unit, you may also use four Guiding Questions as tools to help you judge what might or might not be significant:

1. How long-lasting an effect might there be? Has it (the person, issue, or event) influenced other people, events, or issues so far? If so, then to what extent? (You may want to use a mind map to plot the answer to this question.)
2. How far has the ripple spread: locally, nationally, internationally, globally?
3. How does the event, person, or issue affect you (or those around you) or the way in which you perceive key concepts such as citizenship, equity, justice, global responsibilities, rights and responsibilities, or the needs and concerns of your community?
4. How does the event, person, or issue affect any decision you would make or have already made?

To look into the future, you must first speculate. You may be right; you may be wrong—predictions are, by their very nature, uncertain. Eventually, though, you will reach a point where you must gather hard evidence and information.

A Practice Run

This exercise should be done as a class or a group along with your teacher. You will select a person in your life, local community, province, or nation whom you consider to be significant, now and in the future. This is a brief exercise only, but it will give you some practice in applying the Criteria of Significance and the Guiding Questions.

STEP 1 Your teacher will write the words "Significant people in our local community" on a flipchart. As a class, suggest some names. (You don't have to know the individual personally.) Try to suggest names that the other students would easily recognize. You can suggest people other than politicians—for example, a local religious leader or community leader.

STEP 2 Beside each name, make a brief note indicating what this person has achieved that makes you feel he or she is significant.

STEP 3 In each instance, make a simple mind map to list the specific effects the person has had in the local and wider communities. Is this person significant because he or she

- has had an effect on many other people? If so, who are those people? What is that effect?
- has a national or global impact? What is that impact?
- has affected your views (or classmates' views) on the ideas listed in Guiding Questions, particularly Guiding Question 3?
- has affected decision making in a way that would lead you to vote for a particular party or person, or vote a certain way on an issue? What effect would that be?

STEP 4 How did you do? Debrief your trial run.

Your teacher will share more information with you before you begin the Unit 4 Chapter Challenges. Each activity is accompanied by line masters to support your work, provide additional information on the skills of researching and presenting information, and allow peer- and self-assessment during the process.

CHAPTER 15
Challenge 1: Identity and Citizenship

Throughout your Social Studies course, you have been asked to think, to state your point of view and defend it, and to make choices. Now, you will go a little further. You will be asked to judge the significance of some key issues, and their related issues. How do these issues already touch your life? How might you influence the outcome of these issues?

Premise

In this activity, you will identify an issue that you believe is significant and will continue to be significant. Remember: you are not looking into a crystal ball! You can, however, make reasonable assumptions.

Process

STEP 1 Form a team of five students and assign each member a specific role from the table below. Try to choose roles that best suit each student's strengths. When you are finished, show your roster to your teacher. (Note: If you have a small in-school library, you can omit the library researcher role.)

STEP 2 As a team, review the Criteria of Significance on page 319.

STEP 3 As a team, examine the numbered issues that follow. Select three that you either find interesting, know something about, or care about.

(Steps continue on page 322.)

Roles	Responsibilities
Online researcher	■ identifies credible Web sites and collects information (see Skills Toolkit, Chapter 6, page 136)
Library researcher	■ searches for books and journal articles
Outreach coordinator	■ contacts individuals or groups willing to share their perspectives
Editor	■ assists team members in pulling the research together (see Skills Toolkit, Chapter 10, page 217) ■ records inquiry questions
Coordinator	■ chairs the organization meetings ■ monitors progress on tasks ■ provides feedback on ideas and research assistance ■ meets with teacher to report progress ■ pulls the combined report together and submits it

1. Aboriginal Peoples: Treaties and Aboriginal Rights

LAND CLAIMS Have Aboriginal land claims been settled fairly? How is the settlement of land claims connected to the issue of Aboriginal identity within Canada?

POVERTY How serious is the problem of poverty among Canada's Aboriginal peoples? What are the statistics? How has this issue affected the way other Canadians see Aboriginal peoples? How has it affected the identity of Aboriginal peoples?

EDUCATION Why are Aboriginal peoples so interested in pursuing their own education initiatives? What are the statistics?

DISCRIMINATION Are there clear examples of discrimination against Aboriginal peoples in Canada? Are there examples in your own community? What are they?

2. Canada: An Officially Bilingual Country

SEPARATISM How possible is the break-up of Canada? Is this a real issue or threat? How strong are the separatists and separatist parties in Quebec? What do the electoral numbers and polls show? How would the loss of Quebec affect Canadian identity?

FRANCOPHONES IN CANADA Who are the francophones outside Quebec? How do they identify themselves? What language rights do francophones have in Manitoba? Is the number of francophones in Manitoba rising or falling in numbers and percentages? Do francophones have a distinct identity in Manitoba or in your community?

3. Rights and Freedoms

SOCIAL RIGHTS Should the Charter include social rights such as the right to education, health care, social benefits, and a guaranteed income? If social rights were included, what would that say about the values of Canadians? How might the inclusion of social rights affect Canadian identity in the eyes of the world?

RIGHTS VS. LIBERTY Should public safety be more important than rights? Should those who are suspected terrorists be denied legal rights that are accorded to the public? What is the current law? Are you prepared to give up rights to ensure your protection? How would that affect Canadian identity?

4. Multiculturalism

IMMIGRATION What should be the basis on which Canada decides who can immigrate to Canada? What are the current rules? How does immigration policy affect our national identity?

CANADA'S CURRENT IDENTITY What is the current cultural makeup of Canada, Manitoba, or your community? What are the statistics? How have these numbers changed over the past two to three decades? What effect has this change had on the identity of Canada, of Manitoba, or of your community?

ASSIMILATION VS. MULTICULTURALISM What are the arguments for and against multiculturalism and assimilation? How does each option affect the identity of people living in Canada? How does each option affect Canada's image in the world?

5. Americanization

ECONOMY How is Canada tied to the US economy? What are the statistics? What effect does Canada's interdependence with the United States have on our political decisions and policies? What effect does it have on our identity as a distinct nation? Is the situation changing? If so, how? What does the future hold?

CULTURE Are Canadian culture and values different from those of the United States? Should we have laws to control the amount of American TV, radio, movies, or music we import to protect our distinct identity? What are the trends? What does the future hold?

6. The Environment

SUSTAINABILITY What is involved in the concept of "sustainability"? Identify four or five aspects of sustainability. Is it your role to ensure that the environment is sustainable outside your immediate community? Why or why not? Trace one of your actions (for example, buying or using a certain product) and determine its potential impact on the sustainability of the environment.

STEWARDSHIP Do governments always try to protect the environment? If not, why not? Identify examples of governments acting or not acting in a stewardship role. Give at least one example of each. What could happen in the future if governments ignore the call to stewardship?

STEP 4 Narrow your team focus to one area. Then, develop inquiry questions to guide your investigation into the issue. (Use Skills Toolkits, Chapter 2, pages 48–49, as a guide.) As you develop your inquiry questions, ask:

- What is the issue about?
- What examples illustrate the importance of this issue?
- What is being debated?
- If there is a problem, what are the possible causes of that problem?
- What are the ripples of significance within the local or national community?

Have the editor record the questions.

STEP 5 Set up a research plan. Begin by reviewing the information in the textbook that is pertinent to your issue focus. As a team, discuss where to look for more information and possible people to contact. (Remember that the outreach coordinator makes the initial contact.)

STEP 6 You will have one week to collect the information, including facts, examples, statistics, and viewpoints, that you need to address your inquiry questions. When you have finished collecting the information, check with your teacher to determine whether

- you have the correct information on which to base your analysis
- you have the right balance of facts, statistics, examples, and viewpoints
- you have used credible sources.

During this step, you can access some helpful line masters about using statistics and credible sources at www.emp.ca/ccw.

STEP 7 Prepare your own analysis of the issue in your journal. This individual analysis should be developed until the product stage.

- Is the issue or problem significant? (Use the Criteria of Significance on page 319.)
- How does this issue or problem affect you?
- Why should you care about this issue?
- What could you do about this issue?

STEP 8 Participate in a 15-minute panel discussion with two or three other students drawn from other teams. Spend five minutes reviewing your findings and discussing the ripples of significance of your issue—locally, nationally, or globally. Make brief notes on the discussion, especially when someone from outside the team gives you an idea. Add any new ideas to your own ideas.

STEP 9 The coordinator should check in with the teacher to make sure everyone is on track before the final presentation.

Product

STEP 10 As a group, submit a report on the issue that includes your findings and conclusions. The coordinator and the editor are responsible for submitting this section, with information, findings, and conclusions from others. Note: Your findings remain your own, although they are submitted together with those of your teammates.

STEP 11 Submit your journal to your teacher.

Assessment

Throughout this activity, your teacher will be assessing your ability to follow a research process, assemble information, and present your ideas about the significance of your issue. At the end of the assignment, the teacher will be looking for the following:

> **Did you...**
> - form good inquiry questions and record them?
> - choose an issue area and a focus?
> - set up a research plan?
> - collect information, including examples, diagrams, statistics, and viewpoints?
> - analyze the issue individually and as a group?
> - submit your findings and conclusions?
> - show why the issue is significant, how it affects you, why you should care about it, and what you could do about it?
> - cooperate as a team?

CHAPTER 16
Challenge 2: Technology, Society, and Change

Today, we have access to more information, from a wider variety of sources, than at any other time in history. But not all the information we hear or read about is accurate. When you decide what you think about an issue, you have to filter that information through your own thinking. That's what this challenge is about.

Premise

In this activity, you will be presented with a series of hypotheses—ideas and opinions that are commonly presented as fact, even though some of them contradict each other. You must choose one hypothesis and then gather facts and data

- to support or refute the hypothesis, or
- to illustrate different perspectives on the issue.

Process

STEP 1 Form a team of five students and assign each member a specific role from the table below. Try to choose roles that best suit each student's strengths. When you are finished, show your roster to your teacher.

You will also do some tasks as a team—determining whether the information is relevant to the hypothesis and framing inquiry questions, for example, for the interviews (see Skills Toolkit, Chapter 2, pages 48–49).

STEP 2 As a team, examine the following hypotheses, and pick one:

1. There is no clear definition of poverty in Canada, and therefore no proof that poverty in

Roles	Responsibilities
Online researcher	■ identifies credible Web sites and collects information (see Skills Toolkit, Chapter 6, page 136)
Library researcher	■ searches for books and journal articles
Reporter	■ contacts individuals or groups willing to be quoted in an interview about the issue ■ conducts person-on-the-street interviews/surveys to determine how the public sees the issue
Editor	■ reviews information provided by the researchers ■ contacts teacher to ensure that the information is correct and the sources are credible ■ keeps the teacher up to date on members' work ■ coordinates the preparation of the group's presentation
Coordinator	■ chairs the organization meetings ■ sets up the plan of action and responsibilities. This would include starting points for research, timelines, possible contacts ■ maintains all records, contacts, and references

> **TIP**
> Before you select an issue, consider your research options. Where would you go to find credible information, opinions, and data? Also, can you keep your issue focused enough to be able to draw a conclusion rather than just draft an overview or general description?

any true sense exists in this country. No one is starving or incapable of finding food; no one is denied medical attention; no one is unable to obtain shelter if they wish it.

2. The school system in Manitoba is unsuccessful in accomplishing its task: turning out citizens who have acceptable literacy and numeracy skills. We do not have enough graduates with needed technological skills.

3. Canada is an unjust, inequitable society. The differences between the very wealthy and the very poor are huge. There is too much wealth in the hands of too few people, while others lack the basic necessities of decent food and shelter.

4. Aboriginal peoples in Canada (First Nations, Inuit, and Métis) are victims of an inequitable society. Levels of education, health care, and employment are far below those of the non-Aboriginal majority in Canada.

5. Global warming is a proven fact. It is a fact that if our present level of emissions continues we will suffer the consequences of drought, flood, climate change, and weather disasters within our lifetime. (See the Face Off feature on the *Kyoto Protocol*, Chapter 14, pages 311–312, as a starting point.)

6. Canada is guilty of allowing the worst destruction of humankind in history to go untreated—AIDS. It is failing its duty as a global citizen.

7. Canada's health care system and social welfare programs are raising life expectancies in Canada. At the same time, people are choosing to have smaller families or no children at all. As a result, we will not be able to sustain our current lifestyles and social programs; there will not be enough people to pay for them. We must change our lifestyles, learn to accept less, or increase immigration rapidly.

8. We do not have free and open media (press, radio, television). The media are owned and controlled by a few corporations and people. They care more about their own interests and profits than the common good.

9. Child poverty is a national disgrace. It is endangering the health and growth of the next generation, and it is not being addressed.

10. Canada's justice system is failing our Aboriginal population. It does not protect them; it does not resolve their problems. They are more frequent victims of crime and are more frequently incarcerated.

11. Option: There may be another issue of local, provincial, national, or global concern that you wish to pursue. (A group may wish to extend its study of one of the issues or Face Off features tackled in previous chapters of the text.)

STEP 3 Gather your information based on your assigned roles and chosen hypothesis.

STEP 4 About a week later, hold a planning and synthesizing meeting chaired by your coordinator. Use the Skills Toolkits from Chapter 3 (page 68), Chapter 6 (page 136), Chapter 8 (page 175), and Chapter 10 (page 217). As a team, examine the information and agree upon

- the information that is relevant
- the statistics, sources, and quotations that will be used
- the sources that require further validation
- the conclusions based on the hypothesis
- whether the information is adequate. It is preferable to have limited but strong evidence and sources than to have a great deal of information that is not relevant to the hypothesis, not credible or verifiable, or inconclusive.

Product

STEP 5 Organize your information into a 10-minute news report combining a topic focus and hypothesis, person-on-the-street interviews (to be taped), in-depth expert interviews, research data, graphics, opinions, and conclusions. Your report must include

- statistical information to prove, support, or clarify a point. Your statistics should be presented in a statistical table, chart, or graph (see Chapter 12, page 265).
- two articles or news reports to provide background research or analysis of the issue.
- a conclusion that explains your team's position on the hypothesis and why this information is important to your classmates.

You will find some helpful line masters about using statistics and credible sources at www.emp.ca/ccw.

Assessment

STEP 6 All reports will be juried by a group of peers from another team. At the end of the presentation, jury members will provide feedback to the presentation team:

> **Did you ...**
> - provide clear information?
> - use credible sources?
> - draw a clear conclusion based on the hypothesis?
> - make a clear and logical connection to students' lives?
> - provide an engaging presentation?

Your teacher will also meet with the team and review the peer jury findings.

Alternative Challenge 2: Technology, Society, and Change

Throughout history, people have developed different technologies to improve their lives. These developments might involve new and better means of transportation or communication or, on the other hand, destructive weaponry. Advances have included medical techniques and devices to cure or manage illness, and appliances and gadgets to make life more comfortable, interesting, or enjoyable.

Premise

In this activity, you will envision new inventions and technologies to be developed during the next decade. You will base your ideas on four factors:

- existing technology that could be developed further
- the most pressing needs of society that must be addressed
- the types of products people now buy to make their lives more comfortable
- proposals and predictions based on current literature and research.

Process

STEP 1 Form a team of four students, and assign each member a specific role from the table below.

STEP 2 Set up a research plan. Review the Skills Toolkits on locating information (Chapter 6, page 136) and identifying the main idea (Chapter 7, page 155). What area do you wish to pursue: communication, transportation, medicine, general science, computer science, other? Decide where researchers will look for information and which people reporters will contact for interviews.

Roles	Responsibilities
Library researcher	■ conducts a search for credible articles or books that propose or predict technological or scientific developments of the near future. Scientific journals, rather than an Internet search engine scan, are a recommended starting point
Outreach coordinator	■ identifies and interviews a scientist or researcher in your area. The local university or college or scientific institute, medical research centre, or, if possible, local company (e.g., Bell Canada) are recommended starting points
Assistant	■ assists and accompanies the researcher and the outreach coordinator
Producer/Editor	■ reviews information provided by the researchers ■ chairs the planning meetings ■ keeps the teacher up to date on members' work ■ coordinates the preparation of the group presentation

> **TIP**
>
> Look for ideas that you can build on through your imagination and creativity. For example, if there is a development in alternative fuels for cars, could you advance that idea to eliminate the use of carbon fuels completely?

STEP 3 Conduct your research.

STEP 4 Meet as a team to review findings. Decide which advance or advances will be developed and presented. Prepare to show

- the area to be advanced
- the innovations or background that led up to this proposed advancement
- the credibility of your sources. Who are they? What are their credentials? Accept no anonymous sources.
- possible developments that could result from this technology. Be logical, be clear, but also be creative and take risks.
- how that innovation will affect the lives and future of members of your class, that is, why it is significant.

STEP 5 Develop a presentation format.

Product

STEP 6 Deliver your 10- to 15-minute presentation to the class.

Assessment

STEP 7 All presentations will be juried by a group of peers from another team. At the end of the presentation, jury members will provide feedback to the presentation team.

> **Did you ...**
>
> - provide clear information?
> - use credible sources?
> - make a clear and logical connection between what has been done to date and what is being proposed by researchers?
> - make a clear and logical connection between what is being proposed by researchers and what the team envisions?
> - make a clear and logical connection to students' lives?
> - provide an engaging presentation?

Your teacher will also meet with the team and review the peer jury findings.

CHAPTER 17
Challenge 3: Pioneers of Tomorrow

In 2004, when the CBC launched its popular series, *The Greatest Canadian*, it gave Canadians the chance to honour someone with that title.

The results of the survey were interesting. Of the top 100 nominees:

- 40 percent were entertainers or sports figures
- 20 percent were politicians
- 6 percent were scientists or physicians
- 3 percent were from industry
- 17 percent were women
- 4 percent were Aboriginal
- 2 percent were from another visible minority.

The winner? Tommy Douglas (see CivicStar, Chapter 12, page 251).

What if "The Greatest Canadian" had been changed to "The Most Significant Canadian"? How might that have changed the outcome? Remember that significance means various things (see Criteria of Significance, page 319). How would these criteria apply to these individuals? Is fame the same as significance?

Premise

You will identify a Canadian you believe is significant (or has been seen by others as such) and will continue to be significant. Remember: You cannot be sure your choice is the "right" one; you can only make a reasonable judgment.

Process

STEP 1 Form a team of five students and assign each member a specific role from the table below. Try to choose roles that best suit each student's strengths. When you are finished, show your roster to your teacher.

STEP 2 As a team, review the CivicStar features from chapters 1 through 14 to provide some examples of the significant contributions of these Canadians.

Review the Skills Toolkits for Chapter 2 (pages 48–49), Chapter 6 (page 136), and Chapter 10 (page 217).

Roles	Responsibilities
Online researcher	- identifies credible Web sites and collects information (see Skills Toolkit, Chapter 6, page 136). Two excellent starting points are the CBC Archives and Statistics Canada, available through www.emp.ca/ccw
Library researcher	- searches for books and journal articles
Outreach coordinator	- searches for groups and individuals who can provide input into the discussion or who might have strong views on significant people
Editor	- assists the researchers in collecting information (see Skills Toolkit, Chapter 10, page 217) - coordinates design if a presentation is made
Coordinator	- monitors tasks, organizes and chairs meetings, provides feedback, ideas, and research assistance, meets with teacher

STEP 3 As a team, identify a significant individual in a particular field from your community. Some possible fields follow. You can locate people who were underrepresented in *The Greatest Canadian* by considering ethnic background and gender in your search.

STEP 4 As a team, conduct a search of the Internet, newspapers and magazines, and telephone books. (Ideas for search words are listed in the table below.) Your goal is to locate a group or organization to which a significant individual might belong or where he or she might be known. Put together a shortlist of nominees (three or four), and then select one person.

> **TIP**
> Service organizations such as the Rotary Club are always on the lookout for significant individuals. (See Chapter 11 for ideas.)

> **TIP**
> Do not select a subject without carefully examining other possibilities. (You cannot use the individual you selected in the Unit 4 practice run.)

STEP 5 Once you have identified your significant person, set up a research plan as a team. Give your online researcher, library researcher, and outreach coordinator some directions to follow. The coordinator should assist in these efforts and in keeping tabs on the work in progress.

You will have one week for this part of this assignment. Stay in contact with your group members (face-to-face, by phone, or through e-mail).

STEP 6 Submit your findings, sources, and information to your editor to pull together. Have the coordinator check in with the teacher to examine your progress. The teacher will

- decide whether you have located credible sources of information
- confirm that you have the correct information on which to base your analysis
- suggest alternatives if required.

STEP 7 Ask the outreach coordinator to set up an interview with the individual or a close associate.

STEP 8 As a team, weigh the accomplishments of the individual against the Criteria of Significance on page 319. (Note: Each team member is responsible for maintaining his or her own set of notes in addition to the editor's notes.) As you apply the criteria, think about the following:

Community	Field	Search Words
Examples of communities include - geographic - cultural - linguistic - ethnic - religious Note: The individual should be close enough to be contacted readily.	This refers to an occupation or area of activity, such as - business - social action - cultural leadership (e.g., ethnic community centres) - law and justice - arts and communications - education - economic development - science and medicine - public policy	- chamber of commerce - university faculties (input specific names) - trade unions - political parties - law societies - medical societies - awards programs

- Has the person done something that will affect a large number of people, directly or indirectly, or continue over a long period of time? You must justify this answer.
- Can you determine future significance from what has happened already?
- Whom will the person affect? Is there evidence of this already?
- What parts of the province, country, or world will be affected by this person's actions? Is there evidence of this already?
- Is there evidence that this person will reach out to many people or many places for an extended period of time?
- Is there evidence that the activity or its effects would not exist without this person?

Product

STEP 9 Each team member must write a formal report (250 to 500 words) answering these questions:

- How might this individual affect or alter your life, directly and indirectly?
- How might your life or community be different if this person had not acted?
- In what way could this person be a model?

STEP 10 Optional: As a team, create a product to make your chosen individual's significance known to others:

- Create a TV or radio news feature. You may include a real or simulated interview. Use the Skills Toolkit, Chapter 13, page 290, as a guide.
- Create a Web site or blog about this individual.
- Write a magazine article with pictures, quotations, and interviews.
- Other (with teacher approval).

STEP 11 Prepare your product by first submitting a pre-production plan to your teacher and then sharing it with the class at a designated time. When all the presentations have been given, you could create a "Pioneers of the Future from (community name)" for your school archives.

Assessment

Peer Assessment

One of the most effective methods of establishing whether you are on track and doing a good job is to have immediate feedback from your peers. Several times throughout this activity, your team will be paired with another team to review one another's work and determine how well everyone has followed the process. This is not a competition. The more you help one another, the more you trust one another, the more the whole class will achieve. The meetings should be short (about 10 minutes of class time at the end of a period). To guide your feedback, use the line master for peer assessment at www.emp.ca/ccw.

Teacher Assessment

Your teacher will assess your research process by asking the following questions. (Optional presentations may also be assessed as products.)

At the end of the assignment, your teacher will be looking for the following:

> **Did you...**
> - follow the steps as prescribed?
> - keep a journal recording and detailing the steps?
> - use a wide variety of sources to identify your individual? (Alternatively, did you contact only one or two very knowledgeable and credible sources?)
> - select an individual and match that person to the criteria?
> - show a clear connection to that person and his or her significance to your life?
> - come up with an information dissemination plan?

CULMINATING ACTIVITY
Active Citizenship: A Critical Thinking Approach

Go back to Chapter 5 and Rousseau's belief in the "social contract" and the common good (page 99). A culminating activity is a way for you to review and use what you have already learned. In this activity, you will apply your new knowledge and thinking skills by taking action for the common good: you will fulfill your democratic responsibility. You will contribute to or participate in a civic action project.

For your assessment, keep a portfolio of all of the lists, charts, and notes you make throughout this activity. Be sure to update your portfolio regularly.

STAGE 1: Review what you have learned.

STEP 1-1 Make a list of the skills you have learned in the Skills Toolkit features in each chapter of this book, and record the page numbers for each feature. Know when to use the Toolkit skills.

STEP 1-2 Draft a short list of "ordinary citizens" from the individuals profiled in the CivicStar features in each chapter. Identify one person who stands out as an example for you. Why do you think this particular individual is special?

STEP 1-3 Review the Pause, Reflect, Apply and Study Hall questions you answered during the course. As a class and working from your notes, make a list of ways in which citizens can take action to influence government policy or effect change in their community or in the world. (See Chapters 4, 8, 12, and 13.)

STAGE 2: Prepare to select a project.

STEP 2-1 Identify an issue that is important to you. Consider the following resources to help you identify an issue:

- Publications (e.g., *Take More Action* by Mark and Craig Kielburger, Toronto: Gage Learning, 2004; available in most schools)
- The Internet (e.g., check out volunteer activities at www.emp.ca/ccw and link to a Seven-Step Guide to getting organized for action)
- Your community (e.g., invite representatives from service clubs [see Chapter 11], social agencies, the police, or political parties to speak at your school)
- Your school (e.g., brainstorm local or school issues in class or with your principal)

Consider the following issues:

- School issues (e.g., smoking, bullying, littering, organizing a charity event, organizing forums on important social issues)
- Community issues (e.g., street safety/jaywalking, assisting youth or seniors, informing students about gang activity)
- National or international issues (e.g., disaster relief, collecting library materials for isolated communities, raising funds for or distributing information about HIV/AIDS, digging a well)

STEP 2-2 Identify a civic activity that you will contribute to or participate in. Look for activities that you (or your group) can accomplish in a few weeks.
Consider the following activities:

- Fundraising for a local, national, or international group (e.g., Red Cross, food banks)
- Fundraising for a specific project (e.g., Ryan's Well, building a school in the developing world)
- Raising awareness (e.g., letter-writing or poster campaigns, speaker forums)
- Social service (e.g., helping out at a seniors' home, targeting an area for litter or graffiti cleanup)
- Participation (e.g., in cultural or political activities or celebrations; see Chapters 2, 4, 7, 8, 9, and 11 for examples)

STAGE 3: Prepare a project proposal.*

STEP 3-1 Research your project. To learn more about it (the issue and the action you will take), answer the following questions:

- What is the issue or problem that you are addressing?
- How did this issue or problem come about?
- Who are the stakeholders, and what are their interests?
- Where is your focus (e.g., school, community, international site)?
- When is this project to be done? Is this a long-term project or something you can complete?
- Why does this issue or problem need to be addressed?
- What actions have citizens taken so far to address the issue or problem?
- What civic activities have worked and what activities have failed? (Skills Toolkits, Chapters 2, 3, 6, 7)

Remember to take on a manageable, small-scale task.

Use the skills from the Toolkits in planning your project. Organize your project research and plan for civic action using lists, charts, and graphs. (Skills Toolkits, Chapters 3, 6, 10, 12)

STEP 3-2 Define project success. How will you know if you have succeeded? Develop a list of your own criteria with which to evaluate your work. Ask yourself:

- What are my indicators of success? Be realistic, specific, and concrete. You do not have to change the world (but you might change it for one person!).
- Have I considered different perspectives in judging my success? Review the issue of homeless people (Face Off, Chapter 8, page 164) for clues to what to look for. (Skills Toolkits, Chapters 8, 14)

Meet with your teacher to assess how your project proposal is shaping up (both your understanding of the issue and your plan for civic action).

STEP 3-3 Submit a project proposal to justify your project selection and plan of action (or a reflection to explain the reasons that your project is important). Include the actions you will take; what you will achieve; and how much time you will spend. (Skills Toolkits, Chapters 11 and 13, on multimedia)

If you are working as part of a group, identify what each group member will do, and get teacher approval for your evaluation plan. (Skills Toolkit, Chapter 14)

STAGE 4: Do it.

Approach the issue with caring. Be prepared to persevere. Keep an open mind (i.e., consider new ideas and perspectives).

Throughout your project, follow these general guidelines:

- Stay focused on the manageable task.
- Plan thoroughly.
- Keep records.
- List clear, measurable goals.
- Make the issue your own (i.e., make it personal).
- Be original.

STAGE 5: Evaluate your success.

Do not leave the evaluation stage to the last minute. Ask your teacher to assess how well you are doing throughout this activity, and review your own criteria for success (Step 3-2).

STEP 5-1 Create a written article, speech, video, or multimedia presentation to communicate your achievements. (Skills Toolkits, Chapters 11 and 13, on multimedia)

STEP 5-2 With your teacher, evaluate your civic action project based on one or more of the following criteria, depending on the time available:

- Organization and planning
- Tracking your actions through a portfolio
- Participation in or contribution to a civic action
- Achieving a goal based on selected criteria
- Communication of your findings (oral, visual, or written)
- Knowledge, perspective, understanding gained (a reflection).

---

* These considerations for analyzing an issue are adapted from Roland Case et al., *Active Citizenship: Student Action Projects* (Richmond, BC: The Critical Thinking Consortium, 2004).

GLOSSARY

Aboriginal justice: a justice system for Aboriginal people within Canada's criminal justice system that respects and employs Aboriginal traditions (also see "healing circle" and "sentencing circle")

Aboriginal peoples: in Canada, First Nations, Inuit, and Métis peoples

Aboriginal rights: rights held by Aboriginal peoples in Canada based on ancestral and longstanding use and occupancy of the land, as outlined in section 25 of the *Canadian Charter of Rights and Freedoms*

activist: one who actively campaigns for or against a policy or social reforms

adversarial system: a system in which two or more sides have opposing interests and argue different positions

advertising: the paid promotion of goods or services by the business that produces them

age–sex ratio: the composition of a population as determined by the number or proportion of males and females in each age category

alternative sentencing: programs that release offenders back into the community, allowing them to be confined at home, to work, to perform community service, and to receive counselling

amendments: changes to an existing law or to a bill in the process of being made into law

Anishnaabe: Ojibwe term meaning "the people and the land"

anti-Semitism: prejudice against or persecution of Jewish people

apartheid: the government system of South Africa that denied rights to non-white citizens from 1948 to 1990

arbitrate: to decide or settle a dispute

arbitration: the process of deciding or settling a dispute

assimilation: the process of absorbing one cultural group into another so that the characteristics of the absorbed group are suppressed

asylum: a safe place or refuge; the special protected status given to a refugee

authoritarian: a form of decision making or a government system in which one person or a small group holds all power (also see "dictatorship")

authority: the right to give orders or make decisions

backbenchers: elected members of a parliament or legislature who are not government ministers or spokespersons for an opposition party; the "front bench" is where cabinet ministers and the opposition's "shadow cabinet" sit

bail: money or other security given to the court in exchange for an arrested person's temporary release from jail and to ensure his or her later appearance in court

band councils: government bodies elected by Aboriginal peoples to look after certain local matters

basic needs and wants: things that are required for survival, such as food, shelter, and water, as well as more complex desires, such as recognition or a sense of belonging

beliefs: what one accepts as true

bias: a distorted or prejudiced view not based on fairness and accuracy

bill: a written proposal for a law that is presented to a legislature or parliament for approval

biodiversity: the variety of flora (plant life) and fauna (animal life) contained within an ecosystem; for example, a tropical rainforest ecosystem has very high biodiversity, while a boreal forest ecosystem has much lower biodiversity

birth rate: the number of live births per 1,000 population in a given year

boreal: needle-leaf forest

burden of proof: the duty to prove a disputed fact or facts

bylaws: laws passed by local governments

cabinet: advisers selected by the prime minister or premier to head ministries or departments and run the executive branch of government

cabinet solidarity: the rule that cabinet members must publicly agree with government policy or resign

***Canadian Charter of Rights and Freedoms*:** part I of the *Constitution Act, 1982*, which sets out constitutionally protected rights and freedoms

Canadian content: radio or television programming that is produced primarily by Canadians

capitalism: an economic system of producing goods and services based on private enterprise

cartographers: mapmakers

censor: to edit, ban, suppress, or prevent public display or expression; not to be confused with "censure"

censure: to criticize; to condemn formally; not to be confused with "censor"

centrist: one whose political beliefs lie between left and right on the political spectrum

charge to the jury: the judge's review of the facts of a case on trial and instructions concerning the law that applies

citizenship: membership in a political community, such as a country, including rights, duties, and responsibilities

civics: the study of the rights and duties of citizenship

civil disobedience: non-violent refusal to obey laws in order to publicize an issue or political viewpoint and force reforms

civil society: the broad web of voluntary organizations, movements, and associations outside government and business that take action on important public issues in a democracy

clan: a group connected by blood or kinship; a basic social and political organization used by some Aboriginal societies

coercion: the use of force or threats to ensure orderly behaviour; sometimes known as "government by force"

collective bargaining: a process in which representatives of employees negotiate with employers to reach an agreement on wages, hours, workplace safety, job security, and other working conditions

command economy: an economic system in which the supply and pricing of goods and services are determined entirely by government; also known as a planned or centralized economy

commissioner: the representative of Canada's monarch in each of the three territorial governments (Yukon, Northwest Territories, and Nunavut)

commodities: products of primary activities such as agriculture, lumbering, fishing, and mining

common good: that which benefits all (or most) people in a community or society

Commonwealth: an association of independent countries, including the United Kingdom and Canada and most of the former British colonies, which work together in such areas as development, democracy, debt, and trade

communism: a left-wing political system that eliminates private ownership in favour of public ownership of all property, and uses central planning to achieve economic equality among citizens. Russia was under **communist** control until 1989; by the beginning of the 21st century, communist dictatorships held power only in China, Cuba, Laos, North Korea, and Vietnam

compromise: to settle differences by finding an acceptable middle ground in which all sides give up something to get something

confidence: majority support by elected representatives for the governing party in the legislature on important legislation (also see "non-confidence")

conscience: one's inner sense of morality that distinguishes between right and wrong

consensus: a group decision reached through discussion to which all members agree

conservative: politically, a person who tends to oppose change and favours tradition and less government involvement in people's lives; contrast "liberal"

constituency: the body of voters represented by an elected legislator or official

constituents: the residents (voters and non-voters) in a riding, whose interests are looked after by the elected representative

constitution: the fundamental laws that establish the structure and processes of government and the rights of the people governed

constitutional monarchy: a government system in which the supreme law is the constitution but the formal head of state is a monarch

consumer-based economy: a capitalist economy in which goods and services are produced based on consumer demand with little or no intervention by government

consumerism: the belief that happiness can be found in buying goods and services; the theory that increased consumption of goods and services benefits the economy

councillors: elected representatives in municipal government; a councillor may be elected citywide or may represent specific geographical areas, known as wards

Crown: in Canada, the lawyer(s) representing the state in a criminal case, also known as the prosecution; "Crown" refers to the head of state, that is, the monarch of Canada

culture: the beliefs, values, behaviours, and traditions of a community, period, or people, including language, arts, and other human activities

damages: a legal term that refers to money paid to compensate for injury or loss

decentralization: distribution of power and decision making to lower levels of government (for example, in Canada, from the national to the provincial/territorial level)

declaratory order: a decision in a civil case in which the court outlines the rights of the disputing parties

defendant: the person charged in a criminal case or being sued in a civil case

demand: in economics, the ability and desire of consumers to buy goods and services; what consumers are willing to buy and the prices they are willing to pay

demand economy: a capitalist economic system in which government does not intervene

democracy: a political system based on rule of law; free, fair, and frequent elections of candidates from at least two parties; an independent judiciary; and freedom of the press and other media from government control

democratic: a form of decision making in which all group members have a vote

democratic rights: the rights to vote and hold public office as well as the requirement for periodic elections and annual sittings of legislative bodies, as outlined in sections 3, 4, and 5 of the *Canadian Charter of Rights and Freedoms*

demography: the scientific study of population with emphasis on size, births, deaths, composition (age and sex), distribution, migration, and so on

denaturalization: the act of taking away the rights of citizenship

deportation: the forced removal of a person, usually an immigrant or refugee, back to the country of origin

desertification: the spread of desert conditions into areas formerly characterized by semi-arid bush, grassland, or woodland; usually the result of overgrazing of domestic animals and overcultivation

deterrence: a means to discourage the repetition of undesirable behaviour

dictatorship: a form of government in which one person or group has absolute, unlimited power

direct action: a form of political activity that seeks to achieve a goal by the most immediate means, including civil disobedience and actions that may be violent and illegal (such as protests, strikes, sit-ins, road blockades, and so on)

direct democracy: government in which all citizens directly participate in decision making without representatives

disability rights: rights that ensure that people living with physical or mental disabilities have access to a full range of services, as outlined in section 15(1) of the *Canadian Charter of Rights and Freedoms*

discrimination: unfair treatment that is based on prejudice rather than respect for equality and individual worth

dissent: to disagree, oppose, or dispute openly

diversity: differences and variety

drainage basin: area of land that is drained by river systems

drumlin: a hill formed by glacial deposits, often oval in shape

economy: system of production, distribution, and consumption

egalitarian: based on the principle of equality among all people, especially in political, economic, and social life

environmental stewardship: the careful and responsible management of natural resources and the environment

equality rights: rights that protect people from discrimination and ensure equal access to opportunity, as outlined in section 15 of the *Canadian Charter of Rights and Freedoms*

equity: justice and fairness

esker: a narrow embankment of gravel and boulders, formed by deposits in the bed of a meltwater stream within an ice sheet

executive: the branch of a government or organization that makes decisions and enforces rules

fad: a trend that is popular for only a very short time

fascism: a right-wing political system that permits private ownership of property within an authoritarian national government. Italy under Benito Mussolini (1883–1945) and Germany under Adolf Hitler (1889–1945) had fascist governments that used a strong military to maintain control over civil society and the economy

federal: pertaining to the national level of government

federalism: a system of government in which power is constitutionally divided among levels of government: central (national), provincial/territorial, and local

fertility rate: the average number of child births per woman in a given population

figurehead: a head or chief in name only, often for ceremonial reasons; the real power is held elsewhere

First Nations: the indigenous (native, or original) nations, or peoples, of Canada, often referred to as "Indians" by Europeans; does not include the Inuit or Métis peoples

first past the post (FPTP): an electoral system in which the candidate with the most votes wins, even if he or she receives less than 50 percent of total votes; sometimes also called "simple majority"

foreign aid: aid given by one country to another in the form of money, supplies, or services

foreign investment: inputs into a country's economy by other countries, including the establishment of stores, factories, and service centres, and the purchasing of domestic businesses

franchise: the right to vote

Francophonie, La: an association of governments (including Canada) and observer states that work together to promote human rights, democracy, and cultural and linguistic diversity

free trade: the removal of tariffs and other barriers to trade to promote commerce and the exchange of technology

freedoms: rights that do not impose a duty on the government. For example, citizens can exercise freedom of religion or expression without a duty on the part of the government

***Geneva Conventions*:** internationally recognized rules of conduct during war that protect military personnel, prisoners of war, and civilians

genocide: the systematic and deliberate attempt to kill all members of an ethnic or other cultural or social group

geographic information system (GIS): a computer-based tool that enables geographic data to be stored, displayed, analyzed, and mapped

geologic: based on geology (the study of the formation of the Earth as recorded in rocks)

GLOSSARY

glaciation: landform changes caused by glaciers and ice sheets

global citizenship: a state of being aware of oneself as a citizen of the world, and of the global community, with all the related rights and responsibilities

global warming: the fact that the average global temperature is increasing as a result of human activities, especially the burning of fossil fuels. Because there is also evidence that global temperatures change for various natural reasons, the term "global warming" is best understood as shorthand for "human-induced global warming"

globalization: a trend toward greater interconnectedness of the world's economic, technological, political, and social systems

government: a system by which a group of people makes the laws that are enforced to guide the affairs of a community, such as a country, province, or municipality

governor general: the appointed representative of Canada's monarch as the official head of state in the Canadian federalist system of government

grassroots: political action taken by ordinary people and organizations at the local level

gross domestic product (GDP): the value of all goods and services produced in a country in a given year

growing season: that part of the year when temperatures are high enough to allow plants to grow (about 5°C)

harassment: unwelcome conduct (for example, of a sexual nature) repeatedly directed toward a person

healing circle: a traditional approach in Aboriginal justice in which the offender admits guilt to the victim(s) and tries to reconcile with the victim(s) and the community. The circle is a central concept in Aboriginal belief systems, representing the "circle of life" into which all things are born (also see "sentencing circle")

hearsay: information that a witness has heard at second hand rather than personally

heartland: the part of a country that is the centre of economic, political, and cultural power

hinterland: the part of a country that is dominated by the heartland and that typically supplies it with raw materials; also refers to the area surrounding and functionally related to an urban centre

Holocaust: Nazi Germany's systematic extermination of 6 million European Jews (1941–1945)

House of Commons: the building in Ottawa where the elected members of Canada's federal government meet to discuss and pass laws; sometimes called the "Lower House"

human rights: absolute rights for all people everywhere; the rights you have simply because you are human

hydrography: the study of surface waters

identity: how one sees oneself; the values and perspectives to which an individual most strongly relates; the qualities and attributes by which a thing or person is known

immigration: settling in a country that is not one's own

inadmissible: evidence that cannot be heard during a legal trial

incarceration: imprisonment or confinement in a prison or similar institution

independent: an elected representative who is not a member of a political party

indictable offence: a serious or severe offence under Canada's *Criminal Code*; contrast "summary offence"

indigenous peoples: the original inhabitants of a region

Industrial Revolution: the process of industrialization that converted a predominantly rural society into an industrial one. It began in England in about the mid-18th century and spread rapidly through Europe and North America

industrial stage: an economy that is mainly based on manufacturing and secondary activities

influence: a form of power; the ability to persuade people

infrastructure: systems such as electrical power, transportation, and communication that support economic activity

injunction: a court command to do or not do something (for example, a broadcaster may be forbidden to publish details of testimony in a trial for a period of time)

interest groups: organizations of people who share social, political, and other goals and act together to influence governments; may be local, national, or international in scope; also called "lobby groups" or "pressure groups"

International Criminal Court (ICC): the world's first permanent international criminal court, established by the United Nations in 2002 to prosecute individuals accused of war crimes and crimes against humanity

Inuit: the Aboriginal people who live in the Arctic regions of North America, once called "Eskimos"; singular, "Inuk"

Iroquois Confederacy: a political alliance of five tribes (later, six) that occupied what is now Eastern Canada before contact with Europeans

judicial: the branch of government that deals with the administration of justice and the interpretation of laws; also called "the judiciary"

laws: the principles and regulations that govern a community and that are enforced by political authority and court decisions

left-wing: the left, or liberal, side of the political spectrum (also see "liberal")

legal rights: rights that ensure fair treatment by the justice system, such as the right not to be imprisoned without just cause, the right to legal counsel, and the right not to be subjected to cruel or unusual treatment or punishment. These rights are described in sections 7 through 14 of the *Canadian Charter of Rights and Freedoms*

legislative: the branch of government that makes laws

less developed country: a country that is not technologically advanced and that has limited infrastructure for economic development; contrast "more developed country"

liberal: politically, a person who tends to favour social reform and more government involvement; contrast "conservative"

life expectancy: the average age to which a person can expect to live in a given population

literacy rate: the percentage of people in a country who can read and write

lobby groups: see "interest groups"

lockout: a refusal by an employer to allow employees to report to work; contrast "strike"

map projection: a system of representing the curved surface of the Earth on a flat surface

margin of error: an estimate of how much a poll's findings may differ from the results if all people were surveyed rather than a limited number, or "sample," of people. The smaller the sample polled, the greater the margin of error. For example, if a poll shows that 70 percent of people support an issue, with a margin of error of plus or minus 3 percent, that means the actual number of supporters could range from 67 percent to 73 percent

market: in economics, the region or population in which goods and services are sold

mass media: various means of communication used to reach very large, or mass, audiences

mayor: the head of a municipal government in a town or city

mediate: to help parties involved in a conflict negotiate a mutually agreeable solution. The mediator must be a "third party," that is, not involved in the dispute

mediation: the process of mediating a conflict or dispute

members of Parliament: the elected representatives of the people, who sit in the federal House of Commons

Métis: Aboriginal people having First Nations and European ancestry

minority government: a government that is elected with fewer than half the seats in the legislative body

minority language education rights: the right of minority anglophones and francophones to a public education in their own language, as outlined in section 23 of the *Canadian Charter of Rights and Freedoms*

misdemeanour: a minor crime punishable by less than one year in prison

mixed economy: an economy in which government encourages private enterprise but also tries to ensure that everyone's basic needs are met; it contains elements of both a demand economy and a command economy

mobility rights: the right to move around freely

more developed country: a country that is technologically advanced and wealthy (also see "less developed country")

multiculturalism: a government policy that guarantees all citizens their identity, heritage, and language

multilateralism: an approach to international relations in which nations consult and cooperate to address world problems; the opposite of "unilateralism," in which a country acts only on its own

muskeg: poorly drained bog vegetated with mosses and stunted trees

natural increase: the numerical difference between the number of births and the number of deaths in a population in a given period

naturalization: the formal process of becoming a citizen of a country

negotiate: to try to reach agreement through discussion

net migration: the net effect of immigration and emigration on an area's population in a given period; may be an increase or a decrease

non-confidence: in a parliament, a motion by an opposition party to try to force the government to resign over important legislation. If more than half the members present do not support the legislation, the government is defeated and an election will usually be called

non-governmental organizations (NGOs): non-profit organizations that work to improve social conditions around the world (e.g., Oxfam, Greenpeace, Doctors Without Borders); although they may receive some government funding, NGOs are independent of government control

non-partisan: not attached to any political party

non-profit organizations (NPOs): organizations, such as charities, that exist primarily to promote social well-being and civic improvement, largely with the help of volunteers

North American Free Trade Agreement: trade agreement that went into effect in 1994 among Canada, the United States, and Mexico

Nuremberg trials: international trials held in the German city of Nuremberg (1945–1949) to try Nazis who oversaw the Holocaust for war crimes. The trials influenced the creation of international criminal law and a movement for the establishment of an international criminal court

Official Languages Act: the federal law that made English and French Canada's two official languages and made the federal public service and judicial systems bilingual

Official Opposition: the party with the second-largest number of seats in the legislative body

ombudsman: an appointed, impartial, and independent official who investigates complaints. The ombudsman is intended to give those with less power some protection and a voice in dealing with large organizations such as government, business, and educational systems

open custody: a form of supervised detention, often in a group home, that is less restrictive than secure custody

permafrost: ground that is permanently frozen

permanent resident: a legal immigrant who is allowed to live and work in Canada but who is not a Canadian citizen

petitions: formal requests signed by members of the public and presented to legislators or other authorities in support of persons or ideas

plaintiff: the person, or party, who sues in a civil case

platform: a formal, written statement outlining the policies of a political party

pluralism: a shared belief in mutual acceptance and respect for diverse ethnic, racial, religious, and social groups within society (also see "pluralistic society")

pluralistic society: a society composed of people with different beliefs, cultures, and ethnic and racial backgrounds and in which these differences are formally recognized and respected

points system: the Canadian system that awards immigration applicants points for knowing English or French and having certain job skills. To be successful, an applicant must attain a minimum number of points. The points system was designed to be "colour-blind," that is, free of prejudice

political parties: organized groups of people with common values and goals who compete to get candidates elected and to form the government

political patronage: the granting of political favours by the governing political party in return for support

political spectrum: a line showing the range of political beliefs from liberalism (left) to conservatism (right)

politics: a human activity in which opposing individuals or groups mobilize support to obtain power to govern

poll: a survey of public opinion; the place where citizens go to vote on election day

pop culture: short for "popular" culture, the culture of ordinary people

population aging: a process in which the percentage of elderly people in a population increases. It results from falling birth rates and increases in life expectancy

population pyramid: a bar graph, arranged vertically, showing the composition of a population by age and sex

portfolios: departments that cabinet members supervise (for example, finance, justice, health, defence)

post-industrial stage: an economy in which tertiary and quaternary activities dominate

power: the ability of an individual or group to get what it wants

pre-industrial stage: an economy that is mainly based on primary activities

pressure groups: see "interest groups"

primary activities: activities that are concerned directly with collecting, harvesting, or extracting natural resources

privacy rights: rights that limit the ability of others to enter citizens' private spaces, seize property, or collect personal information

probation: a suspended prison sentence that allows the offender to live in his or her community, supervised by a probation officer. Persons on probation must abide by certain conditions (for example, restrictions on travel, people they can associate with, and alcohol consumption)

proportional representation (PR): an electoral system in which the number of seats each political party wins is in proportion to its share of the total vote

prosecution, the: the lawyer(s) working for the state, or Crown, to prove the guilt of the defendant in a criminal case

protection: shielding the public from dangerous people; one goal of sentencing. Often this is done through imprisonment, or segregation of offenders from the community

protectionism: the imposition of tariffs on foreign imports to safeguard domestic industries

protective tariffs: duties or taxes charged by a country on imports from other countries

punishment: as a goal of sentencing, the practice of imposing penalties on a convicted offender, most often through fines or imprisonment

push–pull factors: influences that compel people to migrate from one place to another

quaternary activities: activities concerned with handling or processing knowledge and information

racism: prejudice against or persecution of a person or group on the basis of perceived racial characteristics or origin

random sampling: the method by which people questioned in a poll (the "sample") are selected to ensure that everyone in the population has an equal opportunity of being interviewed

rate of natural increase: the overall rate at which a population increases

reasonable limits: limits on rights and freedoms to which a "reasonable person" would agree, as stated in section 1 of the *Canadian Charter of Rights and Freedoms*

recall election: a vote by which electors can remove (recall) an elected official before his or her term is completed

reeve: the head of a rural municipal government

referendum: a direct yes–no vote on a particular issue, policy, or law

refugee: a person who flees a country because of a well-founded fear of persecution for reasons of race, religion, nationality, political opinion, or membership in a particular political or social group

regional disparity: different levels of wealth in different regions of a country or the world

regional identity: one's sense of belonging to a place

rehabilitation: as a sentencing goal, treatment and training to help offenders acquire skills to rejoin society as healthy, law-abiding, productive members

remedy: the compensation that a plaintiff expects to receive in a civil case

representative democracy: a democracy in which citizens periodically elect others to represent them in government

republic: a form of government in which the head of state is elected rather than hereditary; often, the head of state in a republic is a president

republicanism: a political philosophy that the head of state must be elected by the people, and not be a hereditary monarch

residential schools: schools run by the Canadian government in partnership with Christian churches, starting in the late 1800s, whose aim was to assimilate Aboriginal students into mainstream Canadian society

resolution: a decision or position on an issue taken by a group

responsibilities: things for which one is accountable

restitution: compensation by one party to another for a loss or injury

restorative justice: a method of criminal justice that uses Aboriginal sentencing circles or healing circles to bring offenders and victims together to restore losses suffered by victims and the community as a whole

ridings: geographical areas, each of which elects a representative to a federal or provincial legislature; also known as "constituencies"

rights: claims to which all people are entitled by moral or ethical principles or by legal guarantees

right-wing: the right, or conservative, side of the political spectrum

royal assent: approval by the monarch or the monarch's representative (governor general or lieutenant governor) that turns a bill passed by a legislature into law

rule of law: the principle that all governments, groups, and people in society must obey the law

rural municipality: a municipality in the provinces of Manitoba and Saskatchewan with provincially conferred power that is exercised by a council consisting of an elected reeve and council members

sanctions: military or economic measures by which one or more countries try to force another country to respect international law or human rights (for example, by stopping trade or aid)

secession: official withdrawal from an association, organization, or political union

secondary activities: activities that process, transform, fabricate, or assemble raw materials derived from primary activities; activities that reassemble, refinish, or package manufactured goods

secular: not affiliated with any religion

secure custody: imprisonment for young people convicted of serious offences, with guards, usually in a youth detention centre. In contrast, "open custody" is for less serious offences

sedimentary: rock formed through the accumulation of sediments

self-determination: the right of an Aboriginal nation to choose how it will be governed (e.g., by an Aboriginal institution or by an institution that embraces both Aboriginal and non-Aboriginal people); the collective power of choice

self-government: the right of a people to exercise political autonomy; one possible outcome of the exercise of self-determination by an Aboriginal nation

Senate: in Canada, the legislative branch of the federal government that is composed of senators, who are not elected but appointed by prime ministers; sometimes called the "Upper House"

sentencing circle: a custom in Aboriginal justice in which the offender comes before a "circle" of the victim(s) and community to take responsibility for the harm he or she has caused. Through consensus, the circle decides on a sentence (punishment), which can include banishment, treatment, community service, or some combination of these

socialism: a political and economic system in which the means of production and distribution of goods are owned collectively and political power is exercised by the whole community

society: a group of interacting people who share a community

sovereignty: absolute authority and ownership; freedom from any higher or external control; independence to pass laws

sovereignty-association: in the case of Quebec, proposed independence with close economic ties to Canada

GLOSSARY

Speaker of the House: an elected representative who is selected to act as a referee to enforce the rules of parliamentary conduct and debate

stakeholder: a person who will be affected by a decision

standard of living: how well a society produces and distributes goods, services, and wealth to its people

standing committee: a small group of elected representatives from all parties that is selected to examine all bills relating to a certain area of policy (for example, finance, foreign affairs, health)

staple: a commodity of trade that plays a dominant role in the economy of a country

stateless: without citizenship or country

statute: law written and passed by a legislature

stereotype: a biased generalization about a type of person or group of persons

stewardship: the concept that we must respect environments and ecosystems and responsibly manage human use of resources to ensure healthy environments for future generations

strike: in labour issues, a cessation of work by employees to pressure the employer to bargain in good faith or to meet employees' demands (for example, compensation, work hours); contrast "lockout"

subjects: people who are under the control of a government and owe it complete obedience

subsidies: government grants or money to help support industries or social programs that are seen to benefit society

sue: to take legal action against a person, usually under civil law

suffrage: the right to vote

summary offence: a minor criminal offence; contrast "indictable offence"

supply: in economics, the amount of goods or services that businesses are willing and able to produce

sustainability: having the ability to use or harvest a resource without completely depleting or destroying it

sustainable development: development that meets the needs of the present without compromising the ability of future generations to meet their own needs

systemic racism: racism directed against a group of people through an institution's rules and policies

terrorism: the unlawful use or threatened use of extreme violence by individuals and groups to create widespread fear to achieve political goals

tertiary activities: activities involving the sale or exchange of goods and services

topography: surface landforms

trade unions: workers' organizations that seek to improve wages and working conditions through collective bargaining with employers

transnational corporation: a business that is active in multiple countries and that may have the ability to influence national economic policies

treaty: an agreement between two nations that has been formally concluded and passed into law

tree line: the zone between tundra and boreal forest

trend: a general direction or tendency

tropical rainforest: dense vegetation associated with continuously wet tropical lowlands; composed of tall, high-crowned evergreen deciduous species

tundra: vegetation system of plants such as short grasses, mosses, lichens, and dwarf shrubs

United Empire Loyalists: the approximately 40,000 English-speaking people who immigrated to what is now Canada because they were "loyal" to the British Empire during the American Revolution (1775–1783)

Universal Declaration of Human Rights **(UDHR):** the international document adopted by the United Nations in 1948 that proclaims basic human rights for all people. Even though it cannot be enforced, the UDHR firmly establishes the principle of human rights and has inspired other human rights agreements

values: qualities that one considers important

veto: the ability or right to block or reject a proposal

victims' rights: the rights of people affected by criminal acts

war crimes: crimes committed during a war that violate international agreements protecting civilian populations and prisoners of war from inhumane treatment; sometimes called "crimes against humanity"

wards: geographical areas in municipal government, each of which elects a representative or councillor

warrant: a legal document issued by a court or judge that authorizes police to perform certain acts (for example, arrest a person, search a house)

weapons of mass destruction: nuclear, biological, and chemical weapons designed to kill large numbers of people and cause widespread destruction

young offenders: in Canada, people between the ages of 12 and 17 who commit a criminal offence

Youth Criminal Justice Act: federal legislation passed in 2002 under which youths aged 12 to 17 are prosecuted in Canada's criminal justice system

youth wings: groups within political parties in which young members, including those under the voting age, can be active in forming policy and supporting party candidates

INDEX

0.7 percent solution, 284
4-H Clubs, 233
7/50 amending formula, 220
9/11, 306–8
1984, 219, 224

Abella, Irving, 272
Abella, Rosalie Silberman, 47, 60
Aboriginal Healing Foundation, 29
Aboriginal justice
    defined, 199, 333
    Manitoba experience, 211–15
Aboriginal Justice Implementation Commission, 50, 124, 212
Aboriginal Language Broadcasting in Canada, 81
Aboriginal peoples
    Charter rights of, 64
    citizenship, and, 3, 28–32
    defined, 333
    royal commission on, 223
Aboriginal Peoples Television Network, 81, 261
Aboriginal rights, 64, 333
Aboriginal self-determination, 114
Aboriginal self-government, 114
abortion, 224
absolute rights, 10
activist, 29, 333
adversarial system, 205, 333
advertising, 76, 87–88, 333
Afghanistan, 307
age–sex ratio, 299, 333
Aglukark, Susan, 80
Air India Flight 182, 306
Alexander, Lincoln, 122
Alliance of Manufacturers and Exporters, 165
al-Qaida, 307
alternative sentencing, 206, 333
Alvarez, Pierre, 311
Ambrose, Rona, 312
amending formulas, 220
amendments, 169, 333

American Civil War, 39
American Revolution, 36, 103
Amnesty International, 275, 286
Anderson, David, 311
Anishnaabe, 28
Anne of Green Gables, 82
Annan, Kofi, 278, 313
anti-Semitism, 271, 333
Anti-terrorism Act, 307
apartheid, 8, 333
Appalachian system, 13, 15
arbitrate, 102, 333
arbitration, 102, 236, 333
Arbour, Louise, 277
Arctic, 17
Arctic Lowlands, 15
Asian Heritage Month, 45, 86
Asper Foundation, 269
Asper, Israel, 269
Assembly of First Nations, 30, 124
assimilation, 29, 333
assisted suicide, 63, 224
Association in Defence of the Wrongfully Convicted, 202
asylum, 5, 333
Atlantic region, 18
authoritarian decision making, 94, 333
authoritarian governments, 96
authority, 100, 333
Axworthy, Lloyd, 314

baby boom, 299
backbenchers, 123, 333
bail, 198, 333
Bailey, Donovan, 45
band council, 132, 333
basic needs and wants, 93, 333
Battle of the Plains of Abraham, 33
Beach, Adam, 80
beliefs, 140, 224–30, 333
Bell, Alexander Graham, 37
bias, 111, 333
big box stores, 256

bilingualism, 33, 34
bill, passage into law, 167–69, 333
bin Laden, Osama, 307
biodiversity, 296, 333
birth rate
    Aboriginal peoples, 21
    defined, 21, 333
Black History Month, 44, 86
Blainey, Justine, 148
Bloc Québécois, 186
B'nai Brith, 232
Bono, 284
boreal forest, 17, 333
Bounty, The, 100
Bové, José, 78
brain drain, 254
branding, 78
British North America Act, 33, 129
buckskin curtain, 30
burden of proof, 198, 333
Bureau de l'éducation française, 143
Bush, George W., 260, 311
business tax, 253
bylaws, 141–42, 333

cabinet, 123, 124, 333
cabinet solidarity, 123, 333
Canada: A People's History, 82
Canada Assistance Plan, 173
Canada Day, 86
Canada Elections Act, 178
Canada Pension Plan, 173
Canada–US *Free Trade Agreement*, 169, 245, 258
Canada–US trade, 258–60
Canada World Youth, 286
Canadian Association of Chiefs of Police, 147
Canadian Bill of Rights, 10, 228
Canadian Broadcasting Corporation, 83, 313
Canadian Centre for Policy Alternatives, 165

INDEX

Canadian Charter of Rights and Freedoms
  Aboriginal rights, 64
  anti-terrorism laws, and, 307
  defined, 333
  democratic rights, 59
  disability rights, 61
  equality rights, 60–61, 147–48
  freedom of religion, 55–56
  freedom of thought and expression, 56, 58, 227
  judicial opinion, and, 160
  language rights, and, 34
  legal rights, 59–60, 198–99
  minority language education rights, 63
  passage of, 11, 52
  school searches, and, 147
Canadian citizenship
  Aboriginal peoples, and, 28–32
  British Canadians, and, 36–38
  creation of, 40–43
  criteria, 5
  French Canadians, and, 33–36
  human rights, and, 9
  immigration, and, 38–40
  multiculturalism, and, 43–47
Canadian Citizenship Act, 8
Canadian Civil Liberties Association, 227, 229
Canadian content, 84, 333
Canadian Council for International Cooperation, 286
Canadian Council of Chief Executives, 163
Canadian Environmental Law Association, 163
Canadian Feed the Children, 286
Canadian Human Rights Act, 52, 54
Canadian International Development Agency, 45, 283
Canadian Medical Association, 147, 188
Canadian Music Creators Coalition, 150
Canadian Pacific Railway, 39
Canadian Police Association, 147
Canadian Race Relations Foundation, 281
Canadian Radio-television and Telecommunications Commission, 84
Canadian Red Cross, 286
Canadian Shield, 13, 14
Canadian Women's Press Club, 182
candidate eligibility, 184
capital punishment, 146, 224
capitalism, 245, 333
Cardinal, Harold, 30
Care Canada, 286
Cartier, Jacques, 33
cartographer, 19, 25, 333
catastrophists, 297
censor, 228, 333
censure, 228, 333
Centre for Social Justice, 230
centrist, 151, 333
Chaplin, Charlie, 96
charge to the jury, 206, 334
charisma, 157
Chomsky, Noam, 278
Chrétien, Jean, 36, 166, 171, 308
Christiansen, Karen, 164
Churchill, Winston, 105
Citizens' Assembly (British Columbia), 191
Citizens' Committee (Quebec), 191
citizenship, 93, 269, 334
Citizenship and Immigration Canada, 4
civics, 93, 334
civil disobedience, 222, 229
civil law, 209–10
Civil Marriage Act, 61
civil society, 101
Civitans, 232
clan, 28, 334
Clarity Act, 222
Clarkson, Adrienne Poy, 46, 121
clean drinking water, 293
climate
  factors determining, 16
  regions, 17–18
coercion, 100, 334
Cold Squad, 82
collective, 270
collective bargaining, 236, 334
command economy, 249, 334
commissioner, 131, 334
commodities, 248, 334
common good, 56, 99, 334
Commonwealth, 288, 334
communism, 98, 249, 270, 334
community living, 62
compromise, 220, 334
confidence, 126, 334
Confidence in Justice: An International Review, 200
Connor, Linda, 2
conscience, issues of, 224, 334
consensus, 94, 97, 188, 334
conservative, 334
Conservative Party, 186
constituency, 125, 180, 334
constituent, 125, 334
constitution, 10, 334
Constitution Act, 1982, 11, 28, 220, 223
constitutional monarchy, 121, 334
consumer action, 261
consumer-based economy, 248, 252, 261, 263, 334
consumerism, 75, 334
consumption tax, 253
Convention Against Torture, 275
Convention on Genocide, 275
Convention on the Elimination of All Forms of Discrimination Against Women, 275
Convention on the Rights of the Child, 274, 275
Convention Relating to the Status of Refugees (United Nations), 42
Coon Come, Matthew, 221, 223
Co-operative Commonwealth Federation, 186, 251
Copernicus, Nicolaus, 48
Copyright Act, 149
Cordilleran mountain system, 13, 14, 17
Corner Gas, 82
cornucopians, 297
corporate social responsibility, 262
councillor, 132, 334
Courchene Jr., Dave, 214
crime rate, 201
Criminal Code, 209
criminal justice process
  court, 204–5
  investigation, 204
  sentence, 206
  trial, 205
  verdict, 205

INDEX

criminal law, 145–47
Cross, Robert, 212
Crown, 205, 334
culture
   defined, 71, 334
   maintenance of, 79–82
   pop culture, 76–79
   protecting and promoting, 83–86
CUSO, 286
Cyberschoolbus, 313

Dallaire, Roméo, 47, 276, 304
damages, 334
Darfur, 92, 304
David Suzuki Foundation, 261, 286, 311
death penalty, 146, 224
decentralization, 22, 334
Declaration of First Nations, 31
Declaration on the Rights of Indigenous Peoples, 10
declaratory order, 210, 334
defendant, 209, 334
Degrassi Junior High, 82
demand, 248, 334
demand economy, 248, 250, 334
democracy
   Canada, and, 109
   defined, 334
   elements of, 105–6
   important events in development of, 103–4
   obstacles to, 106–7
   spread of, 107–8
Democracy Watch, 97
democratic decision making, 94, 335
democratic governments, 97
democratic rights, 59, 335
demography, 20, 298–302, 335
denaturalization, 7, 335
deportation, 5, 335
desertification, 296, 335
Desjarlais, Bev, 224
Dessaulles, Georges-Casimir, 128
deterrence, 206, 335
Development and Peace, 286
Dianne Martin Medal for Social Justice through Law, 202
dictatorship, 96, 335
Diefenbaker, John, 10, 11

direct action, 229, 335
direct democracy, 103, 178, 335
disability rights, 61, 62, 335
discrimination, 143, 335
displaced person, 2
dissent, 227, 335
distinct society, 109
diversity, 80, 335
Doctors Without Borders, 285, 286
Document of Religious Liberty, 226
Doer, Gary, 143, 311
Dosanjh, Ujjal, 46
Douglas, Tommy, 47, 242, 251
drainage basin, 15, 335
Driskell, James, 202
drumlin, 14, 15, 335
Duceppe, Gilles, 186
Dumont, W. Yvon, 122
Dunant, Henri, 270
Dyck, Lillian Eva, 32
d'Youville, Marguerite, 33

Earley, Mary Two-Axe, 64
Earth Day, 94
economic divisions, 246–48
economic geography, 22
economy
   consumer influence on, 261–64
   defined, 242, 335
   demand versus mixed, 250
   economic development, 243
   economic divisions in Canada, 246
   economic forces, 248–49
   standard of living, and, 250
Edible Ballot Society, 193
education, 293
Edwards, Henrietta, 129
egalitarian governance, 98, 335
Elections Canada, 190
elections in Canada
   candidate eligibility, 184
   election process, 178–80
   electoral reform, 190–93
   political parties, 186–89
   recent voting record, 183
electoral reform, 190–93
Elizabeth II, 121
Elks, 232
employment equity, 47

environment
   human impact on, 296–98
   interdependence, 309–12
environmental bylaws, 142
environmental stewardship, 335
equality rights, 60–63, 335
Equiano, Olaudah, 269
equity, 9, 335
esker, 14, 15, 335
essential services, 236
Essential Services Act, 237
eugenics, 234
euthanasia, 63, 224
Every Vote Counts, 190
Evian Conference, 272
Ewatski, Jack, 124
examination for discovery, 210
executive branch of government, 120, 121–25, 335
expression, freedom of, 56, 58

fad, 77, 335
Fair Vote Canada, 190
Fairclough, Ellen, 41
Famous Five, 129
Fanning, Shawn, 149
fascism, 270–71, 335
federal, 335
federal government
   laws and regulations, 145–50
   responsibilities, 115
   revenue collection, 115
federalism, 114, 335
fertility rate, 21, 335
figurehead, 122, 335
Firearms Act, 175
First Nations, 3, 28, 335
First Nations Governance Act, 104
First Nations Justice Strategy, 215
first past the post (FPTP), 188, 190, 191, 192, 335
Fisher, Andrew, 88
Fleming, Sandford, 37
Fletcher, Steven, 62
Fontaine, Phil, 30
Foreign Affairs Canada, 282
foreign aid, 284, 335
foreign investment, 255, 257, 335
foreign policy, 282–84

Forum for Young Canadians, 189
Foster Parents Plan, 286
franchise, 104, 181–83, 335
Francophonie, La, 71, 288, 335
Free the Children, 230, 231, 286
free trade, 258–60, 335
Free Trade Agreement, 169, 245, 258
freedoms
    defined, 335
    religion, 55–56, 57
    thought and expression, 56, 58, 227
    Universal Declaration of Human Rights, and, 10
French language rights
    Bill 101, and, 36
    origins, 33
French Revolution, 104
Front de Libération du Québec, 33, 93, 306

G6/7/8, 244
gambling, 118
Geneva Conventions, 270, 335
genocide, 47, 273, 335
geologic developments, 13, 335
geographic information system (GIS), 20, 335
geography
    as destiny, 23–25
    economic geography, 22
    human geography, 18
    physical geography, 13
    political geography, 22–23
glaciation, 13, 336
global citizenship, 269, 336
global warming, 24, 336
globalization, 244, 255–59, 336
Goar, Carol, 272
Göring, Hermann, 273
government
    branches of, 119–34
    defined, 93, 336
    levels and responsibilities, 115
    types of, 96–99
governor general, 121–22, 336
Graduated Driver Licensing, 142
graphs, 265
grassroots involvement, 159, 171, 336
Great Depression, 270

Great Dictator, The, 96
Great Lakes–St. Lawrence Lowlands, 15, 18
Greenpeace, 163, 285, 286
Grieves, Billy Jack, 73
gross domestic product (GDP), 250, 295, 336
growing season, 12, 336

Habitat for Humanity, 232
Hachemi, Stephan, 282
Hall, March, 61
Handel, Buffy, 81
Hansard, 128
harassment, 143, 336
Harder, Perry, 202
Harper, Elijah, 109–10, 221
Harper, J.J., 124, 211
Harper, Lynne, 146
Harper, Stephen, 39, 62, 162, 163, 165, 166, 171, 178, 186, 260, 307, 308
head tax, 39
healing circle, 213, 336
health card, 3
hearsay evidence, 205, 336
heartland, 246, 247, 336
Henderson, Paul, 86
"Heritage Minutes," 82
Hiie, Linda, 2
hinterland, 246, 247, 336
Hitler, Adolf, 157, 271
HIV/AIDS crisis, 286–87
Hobbes, Thomas, 99, 198
Hockey Night in Canada, 83
Hollow Water Community Holistic Circle Healing Project, 215
Holocaust, 7, 39, 47, 157, 336
Holocaust and Hope, 280
House of Commons, 123, 125–28, 336
House of Commons Page Program, 172
Howlett, Jenn, 77
Hreljac, Ryan, 294
Hudson Bay Lowlands, 15
Hudson's Bay Company, 257
Human Development Index (United Nations), 30, 250, 295–96
human geography
    economic geography, 22
    political geography, 22–23

    population, 20–21
    regions, 18
human rights
    Canadian citizenship, and, 7, 9
    Canadian record, 279–81
    defined, 336
    international protection, 269–70
Human Rights Code (Manitoba), 54, 143–44, 148
Human Rights Code (Ontario), 148
Human Rights Day, 44
Human Rights Watch, 286
Humane Society, 261
Humphrey, John, 9
Hunter, Bob, 285
Hussein, Saddam, 177, 308
Hutterites, 72
hydrography, 15, 336

identity
    defined, 3, 71, 336
    factors shaping, 71
    Manitoba, 73
    mass media, and, 74–76
Igali, Daniel, 45
Iginla, Jarome, 45
immigration
    citizenship, and, 40
    colour-blind policy, 41
    defined, 336
    history of, 38–40
    points system, 41
    source areas, 302
Immigration and Refugee Board, 5
Immigration and Refugee Protection Act, 4
inadmissible evidence, 205, 336
incarceration, 207, 336
income tax, 253
independent member of Parliament, 125, 336
Indian Act, 29, 64, 104, 132
Indian Affairs, Department of, 28
Indian Claims Commission, 110
indictable offence, 204, 336
indigenous peoples, 336
Industrial Revolution, 298, 336
industrial stage, 244, 336
industrialization, 243
Infested Blanket, The, 124

influence, 100, 336
Information Age, 313
infrastructure, 252, 336
injunction, 210, 336
Innocence Project, 202
Innuitian system, 13, 15
Insurance Bureau of Canada, 165
intellectual property, 150
interest group, 66, 161, 163–66, 188, 336
Interior Plains, 15, 16
International Centre for Human Rights and Democratic Development, 281
International Criminal Court (ICC), 277–78, 336
International Day for the Elimination of Racial Discrimination, 46
International Joint Commission, 161
International Olympic Committee, 288
International Trade Canada, 283
Inuit, 3, 28, 336
Iraq, 308
Irish Canadians, 38
Irish Republican Army, 306
Iroquois Confederacy, 103, 336
Irwin, Ron, 30

Japanese internment, 280–81
Jean, Michaëlle, 45, 122
Jenkins, Ferguson, 44
Johnston, Dwayne Archie, 212
judicial system
    Aboriginal justice, 211–15
    as a branch of government, 120, 133–34
    attitudes toward, 199–201
    changes in, 199
    civil law process, 209–8
    criminal justice process, 204–7
    defined, 336
    fundamental legal rights, 198–99
    two goals, 198
    wrongful convictions, 201–2
    youth criminal justice, 203
jury duty, 207
Just Society, 30

Kariya, Paul, 40
Karklin, Riva, 189
Kazemi, Zahra, 282
Keegstra, Jim, 56
Kielburger, Craig, 230, 231
Kielburger, Marc, 230, 231
King, William Lyon Mackenzie, 40
Kinsmen, 232
Kirsch, Philippe, 277
Kiwanis, 232
Klassen, Cindy, 72
Klein, Naomi, 154
knowledge industries, 245
Kyoto Protocol, 143, 163, 165, 309, 311

Labour Act, 236
Labour Day, 236
labour negotiation, 236–37
Lac du Bonnet Senior School, 189
Ladybug Foundation, 166
Lambert Conformal Conic projection, 20
land claims, 30
landmines, 314
L'Arche, 234
Latimer, Tracy, 63
latitude, 16
Laurier, Wilfrid, 36
laws, 93, 336
lawsuit, 209
Layton, Jack, 37, 186
Leaders Today, 230, 231
left-wing, 151, 336
legal rights, 59–60, 337
Legislative Assembly, 130–31
legislative branch of government, 120, 125–32, 337
legislative process, 168
Lenin, Vladimir, 270
less developed country, 243, 337
Lévesque, René, 36
Lewis, Avi, 154
Lewis, Stephen, 287
liberal, 337
Liberal Party, 186
lieutenant governor, 122
life expectancy, 21, 293, 337
Lions, 232
literacy rate, 293, 294, 337
Liu Institute for Global Issues, 314
Live 8, 297
lobby group, 163, 337
local government council, 132
local governments
    bylaws, 141–42
    responsibilities, 117
    revenue collection, 119
lockout, 236, 337
Lord Stanley of Preston, 121

Macdonald, John A., 37
Mackenzie, Alexander, 37
Mackenzie, William Lyon, 37
MacLennan, Hugh, 38
mad cow disease, 260
Magna Carta, 103, 195
majority government, 187
Malthus, Thomas, 297
mandatory voting, 183
Mandela, Nelson, 7, 8
Manitoba Aboriginal Justice Inquiry, 211–12
Manitoba Act, 35
Manitoba Keewatinook Ininew Okimowin, 30, 215
Manitoba Labour Board, 236
Manitoba Schools Question, 65
map projection, 19, 337
MAPL system, 84
Maple Leaf flag, 173
maps
    construction of, 19–20
    projection, 19
margin of error, 171, 337
market, 249, 337
Martin, Dianne, 202
Martin, Paul, 162, 186, 225, 305
Martineau, Harriet, 269, 270
mass media, 74–76, 82, 337
Massey, Vincent, 121
mayor, 132, 337
McBoycott, 259
McClung, Nellie, 129
McKinney, Louise, 129
Médecins Sans Frontières, 285
mediate, 102, 337
mediation, 102, 236, 337
Medical Care Act, 173
Meech Lake Accord, 109
Mein Kampf, 157
members of Parliament, 123, 337
Mercer, Rick, 37

Metallica, 149
Métis, 28, 337
migration, 12
Milgaard, David, 202
Millennium Declaration, 312, 313
Millennium Development Goals, 297, 312
Miller, Gail, 202
Mine Ban Treaty, 314
minority government, 126, 187, 337
minority language education rights, 63, 337
misdemeanour, 206, 337
mixed economy, 250, 337
mobility rights, 53, 337
Molson, 257
Montesquieu, 119
more developed country, 21, 243, 337
Mother of Red Nations Women's Council of Manitoba, 66
Mothers Against Drunk Driving, 147
Mouvement pour une démocratie nouvelle, 190
Mulroney, Brian, 171, 280
multiculturalism, 41, 43–47, 303, 337
multilateralism, 337
multimedia technology, 290
municipal governments, *see* local governments
Murphy, Emily, 129
Murray, Glen, 132
muskeg, 14, 337

Napster, 149
National Aboriginal Achievement Award, 110
National Aboriginal Day, 44, 109
National Citizens Coalition, 165
National Flag Day, 86
National Indian Brotherhood, 30, 124
natural increase, population, 20, 298, 337
naturalization, 5, 337
Nature of Things, The, 82
negotiate, 102, 337
net migration, 299, 337
Netanyahu, Benjamin, 228
New Democratic Party, 186, 251
new media, 75
non-confidence, 169, 187, 337

non-governmental organizations (NGOs), 101, 282, 285–88, 337
non-partisan, 125, 337
non-profit organizations (NPOs), 261, 337
North American Free Trade Agreement, 22, 245, 258, 337
Northwest Passage, 24
Nunavut, 132
Nuremberg trials, 272, 337

Oath of citizenship, 6
October Crisis, 93
Official Languages Act, 33, 338
Official Opposition, 126, 338
Oh, Sandra, 46
Olympic Games, 288
ombudsman, 229
Ombudsman Act, 229
onashowewin, 215
Ontario Citizens' Assembly on Electoral Reform, 191
Opatowski, Joe, 231
open custody, 206, 338
Operation Beaver, 286
Organization of American States, 282
Orwell, George, 219, 224
Osborne, Cecilia, 212
Osborne, Helen Betty, 124, 211
Osgoode Hall Law School, 202
Oxfam Canada, 286

Pacific region, 17
Page, Steven, 150
Parlby, Irene, 129
Parti Québécois, 36
party whip, 123
Paterson, Barbara, 129
peace, order, and good government, 36
peacekeeping, 303–5
Pearson, Lester, 33, 46, 47, 173, 284, 303
Pericles, 103
permafrost, 18, 338
permanent resident, 3, 4, 338
permanent resident card, 3, 5, 139
Personal Information Protection and Electronic Documents Act, 52
Persons Case, 128, 129
pet bylaws, 141–42

petition, 163, 195, 338
Petro-Canada, 257
physical geography
  climate and natural vegetation, 16
  components, 13
  landforms and soils, 13
  surface waters, 15
Physicians for Human Rights, 286
physiographic regions of Canada, 14–15
plaintiff, 209, 338
planned economy, 249
platform (political party), 157, 338
pluralism, 7, 84, 225, 338
pluralistic society, 338
podcasting, 83
points system, 41, 338
policy
  areas of, 159
  consequences of, 161–62
  defined, 157
  development of, 159–61
  influences on, 159
  interest groups, and, 163–65
polis, 102
Political Equality League, 182
political geography, 22–23
political parties, 97, 184–89, 338
political patronage, 130, 338
political spectrum, 151–53, 184–85, 338
politics, 95, 338
poll, 171, 338
Pollution Probe, 286
pop culture
  defined, 76, 338
  global culture, as, 78
  other influences on, 79
  selling, 76
  US influence, 79
population
  Canadian challenges, 299–300
  growth in historical perspective, 300–1
  increase since 1867, 20
  source areas of immigration, 302
  today, 21
population aging, 299, 338
population pyramid, 299–300, 338
portfolios, 123, 338
post-industrial stage, 244, 245, 338

potlatch, 98
Pound, Dick, 288
power, 95, 338
Prairies, 18
pre-industrial stage, 243, 338
premier, 124
pressure group, 163
primary activities, 243, 338
primary sources, 32
prime minister, 123
Privacy Act, 52
privacy rights, 52, 338
probation, 206, 338
profit motive, 252
proportional representation, 188, 192, 338
prosecution, 198, 338
protection, 206, 338
protectionism, 258, 338
protective tariffs, 244, 338
provincial governments
    laws and regulations, 142–45
    responsibilities, 117
    revenue collection, 117
punishment, 206, 338
push–pull factors, 4, 338

quaternary activities, 244, 245, 338
Quebec referenda, 193, 221–22
Question Period, 95, 128

racism, 273, 338
random sampling, 171, 338
rate of natural increase, population, 20, 338
reasonable limits, 151, 339
recall election, 103, 339
Red River Settlement, 34
reeve, 132, 339
referendum, 161, 193, 221–22, 339
Referendum Act, 193
Reform Party, 186
refugee, 4, 339
regional disparity, 246, 339
regional identity, 73, 339
rehabilitation, 206, 339
Reid, Tim, 272
religion, freedom of, 55–56, 57

Religious Coalition for Equal Marriage, 226
remedy, 209, 339
Remembrance Day, 86
representative democracy, 103, 178, 339
republic, 104, 339
republicanism, 36, 339
residential schools, 29, 339
resolution, 160
responsibilities, 339
restitution, 102, 339
restorative justice, 213–15, 339
ridings, 125, 339
Riel, Louis, 34, 72, 223
right to die, 63
rights, 339
rights and responsibilities
    court protection of rights and freedoms, 54
    examples, 53
    oath of citizenship, and, 6, 53
    reasonable limits on rights, 54
    responsibilities, defined, 52, 53
    rights, defined, 52, 53
    rights in conflict, 53
right-wing, 151, 339
Robinson, Eric, 124
Roblin, Rodmond, 182
Roman Empire, 103
Roosevelt, Franklin Delano, 272
Rotary International, 233
Rousseau, Jean-Jacques, 99
royal assent, 122, 169, 339
Royal Commission on Aboriginal Peoples, 223
Royal Commission on Bilingualism and Biculturalism, 173
Royal Commission on Equality in Employment, 47
Royal Commission on the Status of Women, 173
rule of law, 101, 198, 339
rural municipality, 339
Russell, Bertrand, 178
Rwanda, 275–77, 304
Ryan's Well Foundation, 294

safety-conscious bylaws, 141
Saint-Jean-Baptiste Day, 86

same-sex marriage, 61, 225–26
sanctions, 303, 339
Sankurathri, Chandrasekhar, 50
Say Magazine, 81
Scottish Canadians, 37
secession, 222, 339
secondary activities, 244, 339
secular, 225, 339
secure custody, 206, 339
sedimentary rock, 15, 339
self-assessment, 316
self-determination, 339
Selkirk settlement, 37
Senate, 128, 339
sentence, 206
sentencing circle, 213, 339
Sergeant-at-Arms, 126
service club, 232
Seven Sacred Teachings, 214
sexual orientation, 60
Sexual Sterilization Act, 234
Shadd, Mary Ann, 44
Shake Hands with the Devil, 304
Shanawdithit, 25
Shirer, William L., 158
Shriners, 232
shrinking world, 264
Sierra Club of Canada, 286
Singh, Gurbaj, 57
Social Contract, The, 99
Social Insurance Number, 139
socialism, 339
socialist, 249
Société Radio-Canada, La, 83
society, 93, 339
softwood lumber dispute, 259–60
Sophonow, Thomas, 202
sovereignty, 24, 221, 339
sovereignty-association, 221, 339
Speaker of the House, 126, 340
Speech from the Throne, 122
St. Boniface *Riels*, 72
St. Laurent, Louis, 36
St. Theresa Point Aboriginal Youth Court, 215
stakeholder, 162, 340
Stalin, Joseph, 270
standard of living, 250, 340
standing committee, 168, 340

INDEX

Stanley Knowles Humanitarian Award, 110
staple, 244, 340
stateless, 2, 340
statute, 169, 340
Steiner, Sylvia, 278
Stephen Lewis Foundation, 287
stereotype, 22, 74, 340
stewardship, 317, 340
Stoppel, Barbara, 202
Strachan, John, 37
strike, 236, 340
Stroumboulopoulos, George, 85
subarctic, 17
subjects, 98, 340
subsidies, 26, 340
Sudan, 92
sue, 209, 340
suffrage, 182, 340
summary offence, 204, 340
Sunohara, Vicky, 46
supply, 249, 340
Supreme Court of Canada, 54, 133–34
surface water, 15
sustainability, 312, 340
sustainable development, 340
Suzuki, David, 46, 280
systemic racism, 211, 340

Tait, Chris, 56
Taliban, 307
Talon, Jean, 33
Tamil Tigers, 306
Taylor, Hannah, 165, 166
Taylor, Lorne, 311
territorial governments
    laws and regulations, 142–45
    responsibilities, 117
    revenue collection, 117

terrorism, 306–7, 340
Terry Fox Foundation, 261
tertiary activities, 244, 340
thought and expression, freedom of, 56
Tim Hortons, 257
Tootoo, Jordin, 31
topography, 14, 340
Torrie, Ralph, 311
Towers, Markie, 189
trade unions, 236, 340
transnational corporation, 245, 255, 256, 340
treaty, 28, 340
tree line, 17
Tremblay, Marcel, 224
trend, 75
Tribal Councils Investment Group, 255
triple E Senate, 130
Troper, Harold, 272
tropical rainforest, 296, 340
Trudeau, Pierre Elliott, 11, 30, 33, 36, 146, 157, 173, 228
Truman, Harry, 172
Truscott, Steven, 146
tundra, 17, 340
Turtle Island Native Network, 80

Union Jack, 173
United Empire Loyalists, 36, 340
United Nations Children's Fund, 287
United Nations High Commissioner for Human Rights, 10
United Way of Canada–Centraide Canada, 232
Universal Declaration of Human Rights (UDHR), 9, 44, 269, 274, 340
Unjust Society, The, 30
USA PATRIOT Act, 307

values, 7, 140, 340
Vanier, Jean, 234
Vatican II, 226
verdict, 205–6
veto, 128, 340
victims' rights, 199, 340
Virk, Reena, 208
voting, 178–80
voting record, 183–84

Wallenberg, Raoul, 7
Wal-Mart, 256
war crimes, 5, 273, 340
War Measures Act, 93, 228
wards, 132, 340
warrant, 204, 340
weapons of mass destruction, 308, 340
western alienation, 23
Western Cordillera, 14, 16
westernized, 78
White Bird, Dennis, 124
Wilberforce, William, 269
Williams, Jody, 314
Wilson, Cairine, 128
Windspeaker, 80
Winnipeg General Strike, 251
World Anti-Doping Agency, 288
World Fact Book, 250
World Trade Organization, 245, 258, 282
wrongful conviction, 201–2

YMCA/YWCA, 232
young offenders, 203, 340
Youth Criminal Justice Act, 145–46, 203, 205, 340
Youth Justice Committee, 146
Youth Justice Court, 205347
youth wing, 171, 340

Zundel, Ernst, 7

CREDITS

Page 1 clockwise: Tom Hanson/CP Picture Archive, Jonathan Hayward/CP Picture Archive, Perry Mah/Edmonton Sun/CP Picture Archive;

Page 2: Pier 21 Society;

Page 5: John McConnico/AP/CP Picture Archive;

Page 6: Perry Mah/Edmonton Sun/CP Picture Archive;

Page 8: Jonathan Hayward/CP Picture Archive;

Page 11: Saskatoon StarPhoenix/CP Picture Archive;

Page 21: "Population Change in Canada by 10-year Intervals, 1901–2001," adapted from the Statistics Canada Web site: www40.statcan.ca/101/cst01/demo03.htm;

Page 22: John Larter/Artizans;

Page 24: © Royal Canadian Mint — All rights reserved;

Page 25: Courtesy of Dr. Hans Rollmann;

Page 27: Steve Prezant/Corbis;

Page 31: John Russell/CP Picture Archive; Courtesy of Assembly of First Nations, www.afn.ca;

Page 32: Senate of Canada;

Page 34: Courtesy of Chris Oliveros;

Page 35: Courtesy of Société franco-manitobaine;

Page 37: Courtesy of the Rick Mercer Report;

Page 39: Zhu GeZeng & the Iron Road Chorus. Photo by Cylla von Tiedeman. Courtesy of Tapestry New Opera Works;

Page 41: "Place of Birth of Immigrants by Period of Immigration, 2001," adapted from the Statistics Canada publication "Canada's Ethnocultural Portrait: The Changing Mosaic, 2001 Census," Catalogue 96F0030XIE2001008, released January 21, 2003, URL: http://www12.statcan.ca/english/census01/products/analytic/companion/etoimm/tables/canada/period.cfm;

Page 43: Ruth Bonneville/Winnipeg Free Press/CP Picture Archive;

Page 45: Courtesy of Lalita Krishna;

Page 46: Chris Farina/Corbis;

Page 51: Images.com/Corbis;

Page 53: Reproduced with the permission of the Minister of Public Works and Government Services Canada, 2006;

Page 54: KAI/Pfaffenbach/Reuters;

Page 57: Luc Laforce/Le Journal de Montréal/CP Picture Archive;

Page 59: Royalty-Free Corbis;

Page 61: Aaron Harris/CP Picture Archive;

Page 62: Fred Chartrand/CP Picture Archive;

Page 64: Toronto Star/CP Picture Archive;

Page 66: Regina Leader-Post/Roy Antal;

Page 70: Royalty-Free Corbis;

Page 71: Tom Hanson/CP Picture Archive;

Page 72: J.P. Moczulski/Reuters/Landov;

Page 73: © Reuters/Corbis;

Page 75: Oxfam Canada;

Page 77: Frank Gunn/CP Picture Archive;

Page 78: Mel Langsdon/Reuters/Landov;

Page 80: Picture Perfect/CP Picture Archive, J. Morris/Corbis;

Page 81: Robert Dall/CP Picture Archive;

Page 83: Randy Faris/Corbis;

Page 85: Cliff Spicer/CBC;

Page 88: Image courtesy HumanAdSpace.com;

Page 91 clockwise: Johnathan Hayward/CP Picture Archive, Tom Hanson/CP Picture Archive, Wayne Glowacki/CP Picture Archive;

Page 92: Ben Curtis/CP Picture Archive;

Page 94: Reuters/Landov;

Page 95: Michael de Adder/Artizans;

Page 96: Bettmann/Corbis;

Page 100: Health Canada;

Page 104: Ken Gigliotti/CP Picture Archive;

Page 106: Jeff McIntosh/CP Picture Archive;

Page 108: Freedom House, 222.freedomhouse.org;

Page 109: Wayne Glowacki/CP Picture Archive;

Page 113: Royalty-Free Corbis;

Page 116: Provincial Revenue and Provincial Operating Expenditures. Reproduced under the permission of the Queen's Printer for Manitoba;

Page 118: Royalty-Free Corbis;

Page 122: Photo Courtesy of the Senate of Canada, Jeff DeBooy/CP Picture Archive, Tom Hanson/CP Picture Archive;

Page 124: Reprinted by permission of Eric Robinson and the Manitoba Legislative Assembly;

Pages 126, 127: With the permission of the House of Commons Collection, Ottawa;

Page 129: Paul Reynolds Photography;

Page 130: © 2006 Senate of Canada;

Page 131: Manitoba Legislative Assembly;

Page 134: Supreme Court of Canada, http://www.scc-csc.gc.ca/visitcourt/floor/main-courtroom_e.asp, 2006. Reproduced with the permission of the Minister of Public Works and Government Services Canada, Ottawa; Department of Justice, http://www.justice.gc.ca/en/dept/pub/trib/page3.html, 2005. Reproduced with the permission of the Minister of Public Works and Government Services Canada, Ottawa;

Page 138: Hulton-Deutsch/Corbis;

Page 140: Jose Luis Pelaez/Corbis;

Page 141: © J.P. Lafont/Sygma/Corbis;

Page 142: www.CartoonStock.com;

Page 143: Royalty-Free Corbis;

Page 144: © Scott Houston/Sygma/Corbis;

Page 146: CP Picture Archive;

Page 148: Courtesy of Justine Blainey-Broker;

Page 149: © Joe Heller/Heller Syndication;

349

CREDITS

Page 150: Ethan Miller/Landov;

Page 152: Ian Hodgson/Reuters/Landov;

Page 156: Michael de Adder/Artizans;

Page 61: Elections Canada;

Page 159: Adrian Wyld/CP Picture Archive;

Page 162: US Department of Defense;

Page 163: Tom Hanson/CP Picture Archive;

Page 164: Brandon Sun/Colin Corneau/CP Picture Archive;

Page 166: Ken Gigliotti/CP Picture Archive;

Page 172: With the permission of the House of Commons Collection, Ottawa;

Page 173: Bettmann/Corbis;

Page 177: Erik de Castro/Landov;

Page 180: Ryan Remiorz/CP Picture Archive;

Page 182: Provincial Archives of Manitoba Still Images Section Item No. 173/3, Negative 9905;

Page 183: Elections Canada;

Page 187: Michael de Adder/Artizans;

Page 189: Johnathan Hayward/CP Picture Archive;

Page 193: Tom Hanson/CP Picture Archive;

Page 197: Royalty-Free Corbis;

Page 200: Jeff McIntosh/CP Picture Archive;

Page 115: Statistics Canada, www.statcan.ca/Daily/English/040728/d040728a.htm;

Page 202: Reprinted by permission of Osgoode Hall Law School;

Page 204: Michael Prince/Corbis, Mauro Panci/Corbis;

Page 208: Richard Lam/CP Picture Archive;

Page 210: Roy Morsch/Corbis;

Page 212: Phil Hossack/Winnipeg Free Press/CP Picture Archive;

Page 215: Courtesy Onashowewin;

Page 219: 2 Face/Corbis;

Pages 222, 224: Fred Chartrand/CP Picture Archive;

Page 227: The Department of Canadian Heritage. Reproduced with the permission of the Minister of Public Works and Government Services Canada, 2006;

Page 229: Marc Gallant/Winnipeg Free Press/CP Picture Archive;

Page 231: Reprinted with permission — Torstar Syndication Services. From an article originally appearing in the Toronto Star, November 4, 2004, Page A3;

Page 232: Canadian Civil Liberties Association, Manitoba Association for Rights and Liberties, Leaders Today, Free the Children, The Centre for Social Justice, Habitat for Humanity, Rotary International, 4-H Canada;

Page 234: (top) Larry MacDougal/CP Picture Archive, (bottom) Photo Courtesy of Hubert Pantel;

Page 237: Paul Chiasson/CP Picture Archive;

Page 241 clockwise: Linda Vermette/CP Picture Archive, Cliff Spicer/CBC, WFP/Brenda Barton, 2003;

Page 242: James Yang/Images.com/Corbis;

Page 245: Phil Hossack/CP Picture Archive;

Page 247: Linda Vermette/CP Picture Archive;

Page 249: Tim Smith/CP Picture Archive;

Page 251: Boris Spremo/CP Picture Archive;

Page 253: Paul Fell/Artizans;

Page 256: James Leynse/Corbis;

Page 257: "Foreign Control of Non-Financial Corporations in Canada," adapted from the Statistics Canada publication "The Canadian Economy in Transition," Catalogue 11-622-MIE2005008, released November 18, 2005, Fig. 2, p. 17, URL: www.statcan.ca/english/research/11-622-MIE/11-622-MIE2005008.pdf;

Page 258: Karl Adema/Cobis;

Page 260: Dennis Cook/CP Picture Archive;

Page 263: "Average Household Expenditures, by Province and Territory, Newfoundland and Labrador, Ontario, and Manitoba," adapted from Statistics Canada, CANSIM table 203-0001; URLs: www40.statcan.ca/l01/cst01/famil16a.htm, www40.statcan.ca/l01/cst01/famil16d.htm;

Page 268: Michael S. Yamashita/Corbis;

Page 270: Bettmann/Corbis;

Page 271: Austrian Archives/Corbis;

Page 275: Darko Zeljkovic/CP Picture Archive;

Page 277: Mark Ramissa/epa/Corbis;

Page 278: Dusan Vranic/CP Picture Archive;

Page 280: Canadian Broadcasting Corporation;

Page 281: (left) Vancouver Public Library #1397, (right) Vancouver Public Library #12851;

Page 282: Jim Young/Reuters/Landov;

Page 287: Photo by WFP/Brenda Barton, 2003;

Page 288: Chuck Stoody/CP Picture Archive;

Page 292: Courtesy of the Butterfly 208 contest (www.bp208.ca) for the Canadian International Development Agency (CIDA);

Page 294: Courtesy of Ryan's Well Foundation;

Page 295: Population Referrence Bureau, 2005 World Population Data Sheet, Washington, DC: Population Reference Bureau, 2005;

Page 297: Adrian Wyld/CP Picture Archive;

Page 299: "Growth of the Canadian Population and Percentage of Increase," adapted from Statistics Canada, CANSIM table 051-0001; URL: www40.statcan.ca/l01/cst01/demo02.htm?sdi=population;

Pages 300, 301: US Census Bureau, International Data Base, Population Pyramids;

Page 304: (left) © Leif Skoogfors/Corbis, (right) Andrew Vaughan/CP Picture Archive;

Page 306: Hayden West/CP Picture Archive;

Page 309: Compiled by Earth Policy Institute from Lila Buckley, "Carbon Emissions Reach Record High," Eco-Economy Indicator (Washington, DC: Earth Policy Institute, 2004);

Page 310: (bottom) www.CartoonStock.com;

Page 314: (top) © Reuters/Corbis, (bottom) Natacha Pisarenko/CP Picture Archive;

Pages 318–320, 324, 326, 328: © Royalty-Free Corbis